Verbal Art
A Philosophy of Literature and Literary Experience

Anders Pettersson presents a comprehensive account of the foundations of literature, grounded in an original analysis of the interactions between author and reader. Drawing on post-Gricean pragmatics and Nicholas Wolterstorff's notion of presentationality, Pettersson develops the idea of the verbal text and conveys an integrated and nuanced understanding of literary experience, its conditions, and the values it affords. In the second part of *Verbal Art* he systematically examines the cognitive, affective, and formal aspects of the literary work and explores their interrelations.

Pettersson demonstrates the implications and applications of the theory through a series of detailed studies of literary works, taking care to show that his theory is compatible with a broad variety of perspectives. Combining an intimate knowledge of modern literary theory and the aesthetics of literature with innovative applications of linguistics and cognitive psychology to the literary work, he provides a thorough treatment of fundamental problems in the area, including the concept of a text or work, the concept of form, and the distinctiveness of the literary use of language.

ANDERS PETTERSSON is professor of Swedish and comparative literature at the University of Umeå in Sweden.

Verbal Art

A Philosophy of Literature and Literary Experience

ANDERS PETTERSSON

McGill-Queen's University Press
Montreal & Kingston · London · Ithaca

Legal deposit third quarter 2000
Bibliothèque nationale du Québec
Printed in Canada on acid-free paper

Publication of this book has been made possible by a
grant from the Swedish Council for Research in the
Humanities and Social Sciences.

McGill-Queen's University Press acknowledges the
financial support of the Government of Canada
through the Book Publishing Industry Development
Program (BPIDP) for its activities. It also acknowledges
the support of the Canada Council for the Arts for its
publishing program.

Canadian Cataloguing in Publication Data

Pettersson, Anders, 1946–
    Verbal art: a philosophy of literature and literary
    experience
    Includes bibliographical references and index.
    ISBN 0-7735-2068-6
    1. Literature – Philosophy. 1. Title.
    PN45.P48 2000   801   C00-900198-0

Typeset in Sabon 10/12
by Caractéra inc., Quebec City

Contents

Figures

Acknowledgments

The Swedish Council for Research in the Humanities and Social Sciences has faithfully and "resourcefully" supported both the writing and the publishing of this book, for which I am deeply grateful. Sabbaticals granted me by my faculty, the Faculty of Humanities at Umeå University, were also a great help in my work.

Paisley Livingston read a late draft of the manuscript and offered advice that has been of considerable value to me; I remember the generosity of his insights and his time with much gratitude. I should also like to extend a general thank you to the people associated with the Scandinavian Society for Aesthetics – especially, Göran Sörbom, Stein Haugom Olsen, Marianne Marcussen, and Ragni Linnet – for discussions and friendship over the years. Once more Pat Shrimpton has taken it upon herself to check my English; I admire her care and her ability always to find a way to preserve precious nuances. Thanks, too, to those closest to me – my wife and children: Kristina, Mats Petter, and Kerstin.

All translations in the book are my own unless otherwise indicated.

Ernst Jandl's "karwoche: ein turm" is reproduced from Ernst Jandl, *Poetische Werke in 10 Bänden*, ed. Klaus Siblewski, copyright © 1997 Luchterhand Literaturverlag GmbH, Munich, by permission of the copyright holders.

The excerpts from *Anniversaries: From the Life of Gesine Gresspahl* by Uwe Johnson, vols. 1 and 2, are reprinted by permission of Harcourt, Inc. Copyright © 1971 by Suhrkamp Verlag Frankfurt am Main; English translation by Leila Vennewitz (vol. 1) and by Leila Vennewitz and Walter Arndt (vol. 2) copyright © 1975 by Uwe Johnson.

"The View" from *Collected Poems* by Philip Larkin is reprinted by permission of Farrar, Straus, and Giroux LLC and of Faber and Faber Limited. Copyright © 1988, 1989 by the Estate of Philip Larkin.

"Father's Bedroom" from *Life Studies* by Robert Lowell is reprinted by permission of Farrar, Straus, and Giroux, LLC and of Faber and Faber Limited. Copyright © 1959 by Robert Lowell. Copyright renewed © 1987 by Harriet Lowell, Sheridan Lowell, and Caroline Lowell.

John Updike's "Pygmalion," from the author's collection *Trust Me*, 1987, pp. 73–5, copyright © John Updike 1987, is reproduced by permission of Alfred A. Knopf, Inc. and of Penguin Books Ltd.

The recruitment advertisement for the British Army is reproduced with the kind permission of the Recruiting Group of the British Army Training and Recruiting Agency.

Anders Pettersson
Umeå, November 1999

Verbal Art

Introduction

The Aim of the Book

Literature is a familiar phenomenon; yet it can appear mysterious. The reader is confronted with a sheet of white paper, covered with configurations of printer's ink in compliance with the author's intentions, and, potentially at least, a significant experience, "a literary experience," takes shape in her mind. What mechanisms make this possible?

The mystery is partly the same as the mystery of language, and a general theory of linguistic communication takes us part of the way to its solution. But not all the way. Literary communication differs from other kinds of linguistic communication, and it is important to understand how. What is special about literature? What are its differentia specifica, and what are the satisfactions that literature offers?

These problems underlie all literary theory, irrespective of its methodological, philosophical, or political orientation. They demarcate a field of knowledge that I call "fundamental literary theory," an area where the main questions could be: "How does literature operate?" "What constitutes the difference between literature and non-literature?" and "What is literature for?" My book is a piece of fundamental literary theory, understood in just this way.

The aim of the book, reflected in its subtitle, is to present a basic theory of literature and literary experience. The theory has, inevitably, a special prehistory and a special concentration. My point of departure is the conviction that literature is linguistic communication of a special type. (This does not mean that I regard literary communication – or any other type of communication, for that matter – as some kind of transportation of "messages.") It also appears obvious to me that the contents communicated in literature are of the same ontological kind as in other types of linguistic communication – let us call them "thoughts" or "representations." Gloria Naylor's *Mama Day* (1988), for example, tells the story of a young Afro-American woman, Ophelia Day, called Cocoa, who lives in New York and whose husband is killed during a visit to her home island on the border between Georgia and South Carolina. But these representations are not to be taken as corresponding accurately to factual realities, unlike the thoughts communicated via assertions. And they are not to be taken as delineating a state of affairs that should be brought about by the addressee, unlike the representations communicated via exhortations or instructions. Instead, the thoughts are to be taken "presentationally": the reader is supposed to make himself acquainted with them and to somehow derive pleasure from doing so.[1]

To my mind, an analysis along these lines opens up new angles of approach to many long-standing problems in literary theory. The original purpose of this book was to elaborate on some of the major implications of the perspective adopted. I categorized these implications under three main headings: implications for the understanding of the cognitive, the emotional, and the formal aspects of literature. Then, gradually, my preoccupation with individual literary-theoretical problems was eclipsed by the desire to provide a fundamental description of the nature of the cognitive, emotional, and formal components of literature and of how they interact in literary communication.

A description of that kind constitutes, in effect, an account of the basic characteristics of literature, seen as an artistic medium. In working on these problems, I began to feel the need to address more seriously the question of what it is that readers are supposed to get out of their interactions with literature – for the analyses of interrelated cognitive, emotional, and formal components seemed to lack any adequate connection with reality. I appeared to be giving a close description of a machine without specifying what the machine was actually made to produce.

It is hardly possible, however, to give a single, unified answer to the question of what literature is for. Texts from different times, and different texts from the same period, often cater to different needs. Moreover, different readers no doubt tend to seek at least partly different kinds of satisfaction in literature. Nevertheless I have allowed the functional perspective, the question of what literature gives to its readers, to play a crucial role in my work. The question is certainly too complicated and far-reaching to be considered from all angles in this work, but the problem is presented and several aspects are touched upon.

This is one of the reasons why the book has also come to deal at some length with certain psychological matters. The occupation with reader satisfaction naturally gave rise to questions concerning the mental strategies a reader might conceivably adopt in acquainting herself with, and in profiting from, the representations communicated by the presentational text. Given that context, I was forced to introduce some general observations about human motivation and about the cognitive and emotional processing of our perceptions. It is these various extensions to the original plan that have converted my work into an overall theory of literature and literary experience.

The theory has three principal constituents. One is the analysis of the distinctive character of literary communication, centred on the concept of presentationality. A second is the thorough discussion of the cognitive, emotional, and formal side of literature – their respective natures and their interrelations. A third component comprises the reflections on reading strategies and on how and why the communicated imaginings might affect the reader – what makes it possible for a purely fictional story about a young woman's relations to her husband, her older female relatives, and the place where she grew up to move a reader profoundly? In addition to these three main constituents, there is a discussion, throughout the book, of what literature is for, a necessary backdrop that I hope will add a sense of depth to the picture.

The book, in short, is a treatment of the key issues in fundamental literary theory, but a treatment with a special profile. The main emphasis is on the question "How does literature operate?" but the question of what constitutes the difference between literature and non-literature is also posed and answered, while the question of what literature is for is discussed but is not subjected to systematic analysis, although partial answers are proposed.

Students of literature have traditionally taken relatively little interest in the working out of comprehensive views on literature, literary experience, and literary communication. During recent decades there has even been a tendency to dismiss large-scale theories of all kinds as being founded on an obsolete belief in the possibility of grasping and mastering reality and thus destined to fail.

I cannot, however, see my own work as especially problematic from an ontological or epistemological point of view. We humans must orient ourselves in reality and try to survey it.[2] The task is certainly very complex, for both empirical and philosophical reasons, but that does not change matters.

For my own part, I am not willing to say that knowledge can be constructed upon absolutely safe foundations, or that there are specific, privileged conceptual frameworks for describing reality. I do believe, however, that it is possible to frame descriptions of reality that are both clarifying and, to a greater or lesser extent, suitable as bases for action. The rationality and usefulness of such descriptions can be profitably examined and discussed in several different ways.

All this also applies to the sector of reality constituted by literature and literary experience. My theory in this book is simply a careful interpretation of those realities. It is built upon, and invites, rational analysis and rational discussion, and it lays claim to being more reasonable and useful than its current competitors.[3]

The Intellectual Frames of the Book

To put it simply, fundamental literary theory deals with the question of what literature is. It appears obvious to me that fundamental literary theory should be understood as a central field of literary research, an important study in its own right. I do not see literary theory as an essentially auxiliary discipline, an adjunct to literary history or textual analysis, but as a third domain within the study of literature.

It should be stressed that there are important connections between the three areas mentioned. Literature is made up of a multitude of individual literary texts. You cannot construct a tenable theory regarding their properties and functions without understanding such texts, and this understanding requires interpretative abilities and literary-historical insight. (This is one of the reasons why questions of fundamental literary theory should not simply be relegated to philosophical aesthetics.) Conversely, the historian of literature and the textual analyst are naturally influenced in their work by conscious or unconscious suppositions about the nature of literature. A deeper understanding of literature's special characteristics and functions thus has every chance of tangibly influencing literary interpretation and literary-historical scholarship.

Descriptions of reality do not, however, automatically tell us how to act. They provide us instead with ideas about possibilities of action and about the consequences of various conceivable strategies. Likewise, fundamental literary theory does not tell us how to pursue our inquiries into literary texts. It supplies us, certainly, with a better idea of the object of study, but it is up to the interpreter or historian of literature to make this insight into the nature of literature fruitful for his or her own research interests by using it to devise new interpretative or literary-historical approaches.

In contemporary literary studies, the pronounced orientation towards interpretation has fostered a tendency to think of literary theory as a mere provider of impulses for textual analysis and to judge the value of theories of literature by how interesting the interpretative moves they may motivate are. In my view, this is to misapprehend the nature and value of literary theory, fundamental literary theory above all.

Fundamental literary theory naturally acquires an interdisciplinary character. Since literature's medium is language, general questions about the functioning of linguistic communication are inevitably brought to the fore. Since literature is created, read, and enjoyed by human beings, questions about the human mind – about our interests, our processing of perceptions, and so on – have to be raised. The study of fundamental literary theory also has close relations with philosophical work. Both demand a talent for abstract reasoning and the avoidance of intellectual traps. Some philosophical subdisciplines are also very helpful when it comes to understanding the arts (aesthetics), language (philosophy of language), or the psyche (philosophy of mind). I find it self-evident that our assumptions about how literature works have to be compatible with what we know about the mechanisms of linguistic communication and mental processing. Nor can we afford to neglect the sophisticated discussions in both older and contemporary aesthetics about the properties and the distinctiveness of the arts. Hence, philosophical, linguistic, and psychological observations will play an important part in my book.

The book should still, of course, be seen as falling within the scope of literary studies. Its purpose, its unequivocal ambition, is to clear up literary-theoretical problems, not questions of philosophy, linguistics, or psychology (a task for which I am, in any case, inadequately equipped). A small number of literary texts are used as illustrative examples, and considerable importance is attached to their analysis. In the text, there is also continuous discussion with other literary theorists, particularly post-war thinkers. However, for various reasons, little will be said explicitly about the main movements within what is generally called "theory" – movements such as structuralism, deconstruction, psychoanalysis, feminism, and Marxism.

Structuralists and deconstructionists have often treated subjects that fall within fundamental literary theory, and some ideas from those circles form part of my own standpoint. I do not, however, share the fundamental assumptions about linguistic and literary communication, about the nature of texts, and so on, that are predominant within the structuralist-poststructuralist traditions. I have criticized those assumptions at some length in other contexts;[4] considerations of space preclude reproduction and updating of that criticism here. I shall rehearse the main points briefly where relevant, but otherwise refer the reader to earlier publications.

Psychoanalytical literary research is given a somewhat more explicit treatment here. My attitude towards this tradition is a mixture of interest and scepticism. I have found many psychoanalytical contributions rewarding, especially works in the Freudian tradition, stretching from Freud's own writing to ego psychology and on to the present. Ideas from psychoanalytical literary research will turn up at several points in my argument, sometimes mentioned with assent, sometimes with criticism.

Marxist and feminist viewpoints, however, play no role at all in my book, since these two movements are essentially oriented towards the ideological and societal aspects of literature. My book deals, among other things, with how thoughts are communicated in literature and how these thoughts can be processed by the reader and integrated into his general picture of reality. Naturally, this communication and processing of thoughts give literature an ideological potential. I do not analyse, however, how that potential has been exploited, drawing in literary history and the wider social context. (Lack of space alone is enough to deter me.) Consequently, I never really get on to areas that are central to Marxism and feminism. And these movements, conversely, have had little to say about fundamental literary theory (if you disregard the elements of structuralism, deconstruction, or psychoanalysis often fused with modern literary-critical Marxism or feminism).

On the Transportation and Container Metaphors

The proper discussion of other theories of literature and literary experience comes naturally at a much later stage in my exposition. Where linguistic communication is concerned, literary communication included, there is, however, a metaphorical way of thinking that is so widespread, and so problematic in theoretically demanding contexts, that I wish to comment on it at once and to dissociate myself from it.

Our thinking about communication depends to a great extent on a quite specific system of metaphors, "the transportation metaphors" as I call them, which embodies a kind of folk theory of communication. It is not really surprising that our traditional understanding of communication is metaphorical, for communication is a complex and seemingly mysterious phenomenon. In linguistic communication, for example, it is as if the speaker's or writer's thoughts were in fact somehow externalized in speech or writing and then revived in the listener's or reader's mind. No doubt we know that thoughts cannot literally be embodied in articulated sound or written documents, or literally transmitted from one psyche to another. Still it may seem as if this is exactly what happens.

The transportation metaphors represent a kind of systematization of such ideas. The system consists of at least three interdependent metaphors. First, thoughts, those evasive phenomena in our minds, are seen as material objects. Such physicalization of abstract entities is common in our thinking but certainly metaphorical; I shall refer to this metaphor as "the materiality metaphor." Second, the materialized thoughts are seen as being transported from one psyche to the other ("the transportation metaphor"). Third, the originator is depicted, more specifically, as transporting his thoughts by stuffing them into some kind of material container which is then made available to the addressee. The addressee can take the transmitted thoughts out of the container, at which point they enter her mind. In linguistic communication the container is, of course, the text, seen as some kind of material, verbal envelope filled with the thoughts being communicated ("the container metaphor").

This picture of the mechanisms of linguistic communication is clearly absurd. Thoughts cannot be removed from their native psyche. And the physical signs used in communication – articulated sound, white paper with inscriptions, and so on – do not literally contain thoughts in some kind of inner cavity.

Certainly no one consciously believes that the transportation metaphors provide a true picture of communication. Yet Michael Reddy – who was the first to describe the system of metaphors in question (calling it "the conduit metaphor") – has demonstrated that our idiomatic way of speaking about linguistic communication is permeated with these metaphors. You can "spread" or "disseminate" your ideas; in order to do this you will no doubt have to "put" or "clothe" your thoughts "in words." (You must be careful not to "squeeze" to much "into" your text, but on the other hand your words should not be lacking in "content.") As for the reader, she must try to "get something out of" the text, "take in" the thoughts communicated, and so on. Reddy's analysis, rich in well-chosen examples, has convinced the research community that our way of speaking about linguistic communication is, in effect, guided by the transportation metaphors.[5]

One might believe that the transportation metaphors are just a system of idiomatic expressions, without any appreciable influence on our actual thinking about communication. Reddy has argued persuasively, however, that these metaphors do in fact strongly affect our understanding of communication.[6] His main example is drawn from information theory.

I shall demonstrate later that the transportation metaphors also have a firm grip on our thinking about literary communication. It is a common and important assumption in literary-theoretical contexts that meaning can be found outside originator and addressee, normally in some material envelope. For example, literary works are traditionally thought to be real, not merely nominally in existence (i.e., they do not exist merely in the sense that there are names of literary works, linguistic expressions like "*Mama Day*").[7] These literary works, in some sense, are conceived as carrying meaning.

During the last decades, it has become more and more common to speak of texts instead of works. "Text," in this modern sense, is a concept that has taken the place in the conceptual system which formerly belonged to the concept "work": the text is that which the originator creates and which exists "between" her and the addressee, it is the message in the traditional communication model. The new terminology reflects, above all, the fact that literary meaning has come to appear more and more elusive. Instead of a relatively palpable work, a verbal artefact saturated with meaning, a more diffuse entity is inserted between originator and addressee, a kind of changing, sign-sequence-carried nebula of meaning.[8] The container metaphor is still in operation, though, albeit in a vaguer version. Meaning is still referred to as if it existed, was somehow material, outside originator and addressee.

Since the work or text concept occupies such a central position within the study of literature, the transportation metaphors play an important – but mostly invisible – role in critical thought. Many (though far from all) think of meaning as ontologically independent of the meaning experiences of author and reader, as existing outside them in some material or quasi-material guise. When we talk of literary "form," the idea of the work or text as a genuine object no doubt underlies this: a real object always has one form or another.

Since the transportation metaphors leave their mark on so much critical thinking, they will play a relatively prominent role in the book. Naturally I want to get behind this system of metaphors and provide the explanation of literature and literary experience with more reasonable conceptual models. Therefore I shall have to polemicize repeatedly, from chapter 4 onwards, against different manifestations of thought that follow transportation metaphor lines. And I shall be forced to introduce other modes of thought and reject or thoroughly reconstruct several important traditional critical ideas and concepts.

On the Conventions of the Reading of Literature

In picturing *Mama Day* and other literary texts as really existing, we tend to think of the object as being a verbal container in the way explained above. In doing so, we are the victims of an illusion created by language. In reality, it is impossible to point to an entity or a complex of entities – material, mental, or abstract – that can be said to be Naylor's novel, the verbal container of meaning. It is true, for example, that a large number of copies of the novel exist. But each copy is simply a material object: a bound or unbound bunch of papers marked with printer's ink. The copies are not containers of meaning. They have no inner spaces filled with thoughts and feelings.

Literary meaning is not an immanent property of the physical copy at all, a property that the copy has in itself. But the copy is designed to be handled in a specific way: to be read in accordance with the rules of reading or, more specifically, with the rules of reading literature. Naylor no doubt expected the reader to decode the patterns of printer's ink according to the norms of linguistic communication, to construct, for instance, a text beginning "Willow Springs. Everybody knows but nobody talks about the legend of Sapphira Wade. A true conjure woman: satin black, biscuit cream, red as Georgia clay: depending on which of us takes a mind to her"[9] and meaning that everybody in Willow Springs knows, but does not talk, about the legend of the conjure woman Sapphira Wade (and so on). Furthermore, she certainly expected the reader to comprehend, among other things, that the things said are meant to be taken as fictions, and that the text still implicitly claims to have something of interest to offer him. The reader, for his part, expects the copy to be designed in a way that makes it meaningful and rewarding to read it in accordance with the rules of linguistic communication. Naylor is able to communicate the thoughts concerning Cocoa and her situation to her readers, but not because she has literally clothed these thoughts in words and then made the words available to readers so that they can literally get something out of them. Naylor can communicate the thoughts because she shares a system of knowledge and expectations, a communicative culture, with her readers. This makes it possible for her to design (and have duplicated) a complex of physical signs of such a nature that someone who processes the signs in accordance with the conventions of (literary) linguistic communication will realize that the signs are designed to give rise to precisely these thoughts. The reader can identify the thoughts that Naylor wishes to communicate to him if he reads the pages and follows the relevant rules for reading. And well he might, for he has reason to assume that the copy will prove meaningful and rewarding when read according to the rules.[10]

When analysing literature and literary experience, I will describe these phenomena as they appear when you read copies of literary works in accordance with the rules for the reading of literature. Thus, I wish to give as good an interpretation as possible of what actually happens in literary communication guided by the relevant implicit rules for reading. I do not in any way attempt to regulate or standardize the reading of literature. Understanding that fact is essential for the correct understanding of this book.

It is true that the reader may use the copy that she encounters precisely as she desires. Consequently she can, in principle, produce any reading she wishes.[11] Having said that, it would be possible to start a discussion about how we should use literature. But that is not at issue in this book. My aim is descriptive: I attempt to analyse the basic mechanisms of literary understanding and experience as they operate when you read according to normal practice. I do not maintain that a normative discussion about different ways of reading would be unimportant. But I emphatically contend that it is vital to fundamental literary theory to understand what literature is like when read in accordance with normal literary practice. That is my subject.

It appears incontestable to me that a copy of a book is, in itself, nothing more than covers, paper, and printer's ink, and that it is owing to processing conventions, systems of mutual expectations, that the copy can, in a sense, transfer thoughts from originator to addressee. Views of this kind have been put forward with great force by several leading theorists in the field.[12] What is highly controversial, however, is what conventions, what expectations, we make use of in our ordinary reading of literature. I take this up for discussion in several different contexts in later chapters. For the present, I shall only add a few remarks about reading conventions in order to preclude possible misunderstanding.

I do not subscribe to the belief that the conventions of literary communication regulate the author's and reader's activities in detail. These conventions are simply implicit expectations in both author and reader, shared assumptions which make literary communication possible. I have, for example, mentioned the expectation that the author will make her text comprehensible and worth reading, and the expectation that the reader will attempt to arrive at a verbal understanding of the text and to derive pleasure or benefit from his reading. (There are certainly more specialized expectations as well, some of which will be discussed later.) The conventions in question merely give to the author's and reader's activities their general aim and direction. You can make comparisons with the rules of language: speakers and listeners follow the rules of the language, but these rules do not determine the content of what is said or the specific formulation of the message. The scope for individuality and creativity remains extremely wide.

Furthermore, I do not deny that it is possible for both author and reader to break the rules of literary communication. Such a breach of norms may lead to the collapse of communication. But in some cases it may in fact enrich the practice of literary communication – new elements may be incorporated while the system of experiences and expectations continues to underlie the exchange. Another analogy to linguistic conventions can be used: it is possible to coin new words or use new syntactic constructions and still be understood. Such innovations may even catch on and enrich the language with new means of expression. One of many parallels of this in the literary domain is the norm-breaking introduction, early in this century, of poems devoid of linguistic meaning – poems like Christian Morgenstern's "The Big Lahloohlah" ("Das grosse Lalula," 1905), a text made up of meaningless combinations of sounds, or dadaistic sound poems by Hugo Ball like "Caravan" ("Karawane," 1916). Such poems violate the norm of linguistic intelligibility, but they have nevertheless modified our ideas about what kind of effects an author may intend to achieve. They have thereby enlarged our literary experience in a way that later authors have been able to exploit; indirectly they have provided literary communication with new means of expression.

Lastly, I admit that the conventions of the reading of literature are liable to change. (This already follows, properly speaking, from my observation that Morgenstern's and Ball's flouting of such conventions has affected our ideas about what literature may be like and thus the horizons of our literary expectations.) My opinion is that the system of literary reading conventions has remained, in its essentials, stable for centuries, while many individual elements of this system have undergone change. Again, a parallel can be drawn with language. The basic norms of linguistic communication have, in practice, proved virtually unalterable, while the particular means of expression of individual natural languages are much more variable. It is true that the morphology, vocabulary, and syntax of a language may display a remarkable continuity, but they still constantly undergo minor changes (especially concerning the lexical conventions).

The Plan of the Book

Having introduced my aim and starting points, I shall round off this introduction by saying a few words about the outline of the book.

I have chosen to explain my theory of literature and literary experience in two steps. First I provide a general presentation of the theory and its bases in psychology and the theory of language. This is done in the first part of the book, entitled "A Theory of Literature in Outline." In part two I successively fill in the details – first concerning the cognitive aspect of literature, then the emotional, and finally the formal domain. Part two, which I call "Aspects of Literary Experience," is far more like a traditional discourse on literary theory or literary aesthetics than the first part.

The book starts with the discussion, in a separate chapter entitled "Psychological Considerations," of some very general psychological subjects. Such matters are not normally treated very explicitly in literary aesthetics, and the chapter may therefore, despite its brevity, tax the patience of some readers. However, the chapter introduces concepts and perspectives that are important for my argument throughout the book, and I have found it impossible to relegate the discussion to an appendix.

Chapter 2 is called "Literature's Relevance to the Reader." There, I indicate how I conceive of the mechanisms responsible for the satisfaction that we derive from the thoughts communicated by literature; I also comment on some ideas about the human importance of literature. The first part of the book then concludes with two chapters, "Presentational Communication" and "Meaning and Text," explicating the workings of literary communication.

The second part of the book provides a more detailed analysis of the kinds of contents communicated by means of literary texts and of how these contents are processed by the reader. Chapter 5, "Communicated Thoughts in Literature," describes, primarily, various ways in which thoughts figure in connection with literary communication. Chapter 6, "The Reader's Thematization and Application," focuses on the reader's creative processing of the communicated content. From cognition I then proceed to emotions; chapter 7, "Literature and Feelings," has as its principal purpose the analysis of how emotions enter literary communication and of their importance in that context.

Chapters 5–7 contain my description of the cognitive and emotional aspects of literature. The treatment of the formal side of literature has been distributed among three less extensive chapters. Chapter 8, "A Poem: Gunnar Ekelöf's 'But Somewhere Else'" studies in depth a short literary text in order to make clear, among other things, how important textual detail may be in literature. The concept of form is an instrument used for pointing to certain kinds of textual details, and in chapter 9, "Form in Literature," I explain what traits usually figure as formal properties. The subsequent chapter, entitled "Traditional Ideas about Literary Form," is a critical examination of prevalent theories of form.

Attempts to indicate the human relevance of literature run the risk of being immediately decried as reductionistic. In a concluding remark, "On the Nature of Literature's Autonomy," I attempt to forestall that type of objection by supplying a reasoned explication of the literary-aesthetic concept of autonomy. I explain, here, the sense in which I see literature as autonomous and the sense in which I do not.

Specific literary texts are of course introduced at many points in my book. Six of these form a core group. Three are poems written by the American Robert Lowell, the Englishman Philip Larkin, and the Swede Gunnar Ekelöf respectively. Two are short stories: one by the Swedish author Sun Axelsson and one by the American John Updike. The other main literary example is a novel by the German Uwe Johnson. The six texts are introduced at different stages of my argument; on the whole, I proceed from rather easily analysed examples in part one to more intricately structured texts in part two.

The texts are used to illustrate various points in connection with literature. Some of them are treated with thoroughness, in particular the Johnson novel and the Ekelöf poem. But it should not be thought that my aim is to interpret the texts in the standard critical sense of the word. In particular, the relative banality of what I say about the texts should not be taken to prove that my theory of literature and literary experience is likewise banal. I have already warned, above, of that kind of false assumption about the relations between literary theory and textual interpretation. "Non-banal" interpretation of literature is in reality – as I shall demonstrate later – largely a creative enterprise, a making of connections and perspectives. And my purpose in this book is not to devise readings but to describe the practice of reading literature (among other things, describe the role of reader creativity within the confines of this practice).

It is also important to understand that the six texts are examples used to concretize a theory building on the whole of my literary experience – an experience of literature which is, like that of all literary scholars, quite extensive. The six textual examples should, thus, by no means be seen as the empirical material on which my description of literature and literary experience is based. If they had such a function, there would be every reason to criticize the material for lack of representativity.

Certainly you can discuss my choice of examples. The six texts all belong to Western literature, and they were all written after 1950. This is because I wish to avoid taking up here the special problems that arise in connection with the reading of texts from periods or cultures other than one's own. These are interesting problems,[13] but in my present context they are of secondary importance. When analysing how linguistic communication works, it seems well advised to use as a point of departure face-to-face oral communication between people who are native speakers of the same language. Where telephonic communication is concerned, or communication in writing, or communication where one party barely understands the language, various additional complications arise, which can in their turn be analysed. But it does not appear reasonable to take, for example, a schoolgirl's laborious attempts to decipher one of Horace's odes as the starting point for an explanation of the fundamental mechanisms of linguistic communication. In my opinion one should see, correspondingly, the reading of (or listening to) contemporary literature in the native language as the paradigm case of intercourse with literature. The reading of literature from other periods or cultures brings in its train interesting complications well worth analysing. But our study of the basic properties of literary communication should not be founded on reflections about how we read literature written for an audience in another time and culture, literature which we can understand in an anachronistic fashion only. (I do not mean to imply by this that contemporary Western literature should, in other contexts, be seen as a more significant object of research than that of other eras or civilizations.)

My collection of examples could of course still have been systematically different (other genres and other national literatures could have been represented, and so on). Some may think that I should have included more difficult or more important texts. I consider, however, that four of the texts (Updike, Lowell, Johnson, Ekelöf) are of very high quality, and that the Johnson novel and the Ekelöf poem at least are extremely complex. I also wish to point out that it was essential for me to include examples both of texts bordering on popular literature (Axelsson) and of occasional poetry (Larkin).

PART ONE

A Theory of Literature
in Outline

1 Psychological Considerations

Introduction

In this chapter, I shall comment briefly on four psychological topics: (i) human motivation, (ii) the mental processing of perceptions, (iii) experiences and mental representations, and (iv) emotions.

I have endeavoured, in speaking of these four subjects, to achieve a measure of integration through emphasizing the inner relationships between them. They do not, however, in themselves form a field with natural boundaries. My reason for thus delimiting the scope of my psychological discussion is that it is precisely these four themes that prove important again and again in later chapters.

My words about motivation and mental processing are, as I understand it, psychological commonplaces. It is my impression, however, that the corresponding facts are insufficiently known, or insufficiently taken into account, in literary-theoretical contexts.

However, while my contentions about experiences and mental representations are not in any way scientific news, my main purpose in presenting them is not simply to rehearse common knowledge. What I wish to do, first and foremost, is to introduce a simple terminology for discussing thoughts and experiences. Some of the terminology is newly coined and created specifically to answer my needs in this book.

My observations about emotions are, as far as I know, compatible with current cognitive emotion theory. Several of my ideas in this area, however, especially those about the logic of the concept of emotion, are controversial.

Human Motivation

We often find that literature is worth our while; in some way we seem to satisfy needs by reading literary texts. It is therefore appropriate to give some thought to human needs and human motivation before asking what people get out of literature.

How you describe fundamental human needs, and how you conceive of their mutual relationships, depends in part on your scientific convictions and your view of human nature. But it also depends on how concise a description you intend to give and on the point of view you choose.

If you adopt an external perspective and want to provide an extremely general account of people's interests and needs, you can say that we humans obviously strive to subsist and to propagate. For that reason, we try to procure food, drink, and rest, we try to protect ourselves from enemies, cold, and infections, and we try to find sexual partners and take care of our offspring. Since we are social animals and satisfy many of our needs by co-operating in groups or societies, we also have to belong to, and assert ourselves within, various schemes of human collaboration.

A description of that kind is interesting and instructive for its biological realism and its applicability to the general needs of animals. But it is not aimed at describing our interests and needs "from the inside," as they spontaneously appear to ourselves. Abraham H. Maslow has provided a well-known description of human needs that is undoubtedly closer to the individual's own experience. According to Maslow, the most fundamental needs – those that, broadly speaking, have to be met before the individual can take an interest in the satisfaction of more sophisticated urges – are physiological: food, water, sex, and so on. Maslow then sees the safety needs as the second most fundamental; for example, protection against the elements or against physical assault. On the next level he places the needs for belonging and love: the need to belong to a group and be accepted by it, the need to love and be loved, and so on. The various esteem needs – including the need for appreciation, from yourself and others – constitute the subsequent level in this hierarchy. Here the focus is on ambition and prestige: on knowing how, on accomplishing, on asserting oneself within the group to which one belongs. At the highest level, finally, we find the most exclusive need, the need for self-actualization. Maslow considers that we have a need to realize our inherent possibilities, to be creative, and so on, and that we endeavour to fulfil this desire unless more urgent needs intervene.[1]

Each need – in whatever terms we wish to describe it – is related to many different physiological mechanisms working together to satisfy that need. Intricate complexes of causes and effects are already in operation even where simple physiological needs like hunger and thirst are concerned.[2] This makes it even clearer that there is no self-evident way of splitting up and classifying human needs. Our inborn physiological systems have to function according to plan if discomfort (or worse) is to be avoided, and the same goes for the acquired systems of behaviour that cater for acquired needs. Human motivation ensues from individuals' attempts to make all these systems work as smoothly as possible. "That is, in fine, there is only one kind of motivation: that of establishing or maintaining proper functioning of whatever systems there happen to be ... Such general motivation is better not called motivation at all, but rather considered a basic property of animate organisms, or of the matter of which they are composed – the hardware of neurons and neuron circuits and neuroendocrine information transmission. Desire is the expression of this general property, as manifest in the activation of any given behavior system not, or not yet, having completed its proper functioning cycle."[3]

These remarks about human motivation could be amplified with many interpretations and reservations. I see no reason to go deeper into the subject, however, for my further argument will not depend on very specific assumptions about human motivation. I have therefore found it sufficient to stress that, in my context, it is relevant to ask what drives people and to outline some very general ways of viewing and answering that question.

Mental Processing

All organisms have to provide for their needs by behaving adequately, i.e., basically, by executing suitable movements of various kinds. What movements may, at any given moment, lead to the realization of the organism's actual objectives depends, as a rule, on the external situation in which the organism finds itself. Consequently, the organism should be able to receive impulses from the environment and let these affect its behaviour. In fact, the very essence of an organism's activity is to process stimuli and to execute, in the light of the information extracted, movements that are well adapted to the organism's purposes. An organism can be seen as "a perceiving and behaving system."[4]

In principle, this is true also of humans. But the connections between sense impressions received and movements executed are much more complex in homo sapiens than in any other species. Instinctual or reflex action plays a subordinate part in human behaviour. It is seldom the case that a specific configuration of incoming, neurally transmitted signals automatically causes certain movements, or a certain preprogrammed

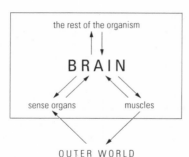

Figure 1
What the brain accomplishes:
a primitive model

series of actions, to be executed. Much of our behaviour may well *appear*
automatic – as, let us say, when you begin to cross the street at the
pedestrian crossing, see a midnight blue Ford Scorpio coming towards
you at considerable speed without any sign that the driver intends to
stop, and immediately step back onto the pavement. But what makes
you retreat is a lightning evaluation of the situation, not a reflex and not
an instinct.

There is much that we do not know about the workings of the
complicated processing mechanisms of the human brain. It is enough
for my purposes, however, to point to some aspects of the system. I
shall therefore content myself with offering a very crude and simple
description of how we process perceptions. Its essential features are
summarized in figure 1.[5]

Figure 1 illustrates that the brain (which I will regard here as a black
box) receives, interprets, and combines signals triggered by outside
sources and by the organism itself. The brain also evaluates the information thus put together, and uses it as a basis when governing the
organism's behaviour. The brain can, for example, via efferent nerve-
paths, give impulses to muscular movements, and thereby make the
organism move in a way that is adequate given the organism's needs
and the brain's picture of the environment.

I said that the brain not only has to receive the incoming signals,
but also has to interpret them and put them together. When you see
the car coming towards you at the crossing, your observation is the
result of a complicated process. The first link in this chain of events
is that light of varying wavelength and intensity strikes your retinas,
and that signals from their receptor cells are recorded and transmitted
to the brain by a system of optic nerve fibres. The last link is your
perception that a midnight blue Ford Scorpio is approaching at fairly

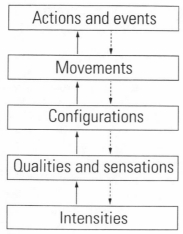

Figure 2
Possible interpretative levels in
the interpretation of perceptions

high speed and that the driver displays no intention of stopping. The distance between the first link and the last is dizzying; for several reasons, it seems plausible to think of it as filled by a series of successive interpretations on higher and higher levels.[6]

According to one theory, the excitations of the retina, passed on to the brain via the optic nerve, are first represented as a pattern of varying intensities of light. Higher-level structures then reinterpret these intensities as colours, a process which involves an element of abstraction: the same colour, blue for instance, may appear in varying intensities. From these structures the information proceeds, coded as a pattern of colours, to be later, successively, reinterpreted as a con-figuration of things (a midnight blue car), as a picture including movement (an approaching car), and as a picture of an action or event (an approaching driver with no intention of stopping). These successive interpretations are, of course, substantially influenced by the system of distinctions and concepts utilized by the interpreting individual – it requires a great deal of training and knowledge to understand that the visual signals indicate that a midnight blue Ford Scorpio, whose driver shows no sign of intending to stop, is approaching at considerable speed. In addition, feedback mechanisms must be reckoned with: higher-level interpretations no doubt have repercussions on the more elementary ones. See figure 2.[7]

This theory is not necessarily, or even probably, correct. Many different hypotheses exist about how vision and other perceptual processes work, and in any case the finer details of these processes are very incompletely understood. I have adduced the theory just to suggest the general lines on which you may reason when you try to gain some conception of the basic structure of the lightning interpretation processes underlying visual experiences.

Let us proceed. Vision is only one of many processes where signals from within or without are received, interpreted, and combined by the brain. And the brain has more to answer for: the global interpretations function as a basis when the brain decides which motor impulses to release in order to make us behave appropriately in the prevailing situation.

When you immediately retreat onto the pavement in the pedestrian crossing example, that is a simple action, but the link between what you see and what you do is exceedingly complex. It is natural to assume, for instance, that the brain, in giving its instructions, starts out from some kind of conception of states that should be realized and of possible consequences of various alternative movements. This presupposes, among other things, that the brain has access to memories – to information about previous states in the surrounding world, about your own former behaviour, and about the results of that behaviour. A complicated calculation, and a complex issuing of orders, must be presumed to underlie the action. I shall not speculate, however, about their precise nature.

Signals from the outer world and from the organism itself come in continuously; the brain receives an unceasing stream of constantly updated information, which it combines and interprets, while all the time releasing the outgoing impulses required to steer the organism and provide for its many-sided wants. The brain is involved in "a process in which information about multiple individual modalities of sensation and perception is combined into a unified multidimensional representation of the state of the system and its environment, and integrated with information about memories and the needs of the organism, generating emotional reactions and programs of behavior to adjust the organism to its environment."[8]

So far, only physiological processes have been considered. Most people, or at least most laypersons, however, would perhaps like to say that the human mind is not a wholly physiological phenomenon. They would argue that many mental processes are conscious, i.e., associated with "current awareness of external or internal stimuli."[9] Remember the scene at the pedestrian crossing. You saw a car coming towards you, you did not want to get run over, so you hastily decided to save yourself by retreating onto the pavement. It appears strange to see your visual experience, your wish, and your decision as ultimately physiological phenomena. Moreover, you can apparently observe both the car and some of your feelings and thoughts by some kind of inner looking, and it is not easy to understand how that gaze, your consciousness of the external world and of yourself, could be of a physical nature.

Others, including many philosophers and experts on the central nervous system, would, however, assert that consciousness itself is in fact a material process that occurs in the central nervous system involving the registering and monitoring of certain features of the system's activities. What we call visual experiences, decisions, intentions, wishes, and so on, they understand as being processes or states in the brain. No special, mental form of existence is ascribed to the mind; consciousness is indeed thought to be something physical.

Personally, I find this approach more convincing – it is not by accident that I have sometimes spoken above of what "the brain does." For my purposes in this book, however, no theory of the ontology of consciousness is needed; I shall simply leave the matter open. No one denies the existence of the central nervous system or of the massive information processing for which it is responsible. But it is hardly disputed, either, that desciptions and analyses of human action and interaction have to rely on the conceptual apparatus of mentalistic psychology. In common parlance you can say that you noticed, in stepping into the street at the pedestrian crossing, a midnight blue Ford Scorpio coming towards you at a rather high speed whose driver showed no sign of intending to stop, and that you consequently retreated onto the pavement immediately. This is a relatively nuanced description of how you had certain specific perceptions, evaluated them in a special way, and performed definite actions based on the information and your aims. What you refer to as your visual experience, your decision, and your action are perhaps all, in the final analysis, entirely material processes. But we cannot discern, in a sufficiently differentiated fashion, *what* materially happened in your brain. Therefore we cannot provide an equally nuanced description of the events formulated in physiological terms, a description capable of distinguishing between, for example, the sight of a midnight blue Ford Scorpio and the sight of a big black beetle. So we are obliged to draw on the mentalistic model, even if we may believe that this mode of thought is, in some important respects, illusory. Perhaps the mentalistic idiom will eventually be replaced by a workable more or less materialistic mode of expression. Our only present alternative to the use of mentalistic expressions, however, would be to stop thinking and talking about advanced human behaviour.[10] Consequently we cannot avoid referring to such things as intentions, decisions, and thoughts as if they genuinely existed, irrespective of our true convictions.

Experiences and Mental Representations

What one's consciousness registers in a given moment, I shall call one's "experience" in that moment.

It is admittedly artificial to treat the experience of a given moment as if it constituted a separable unity. The stream of consciousness is in incessant movement during all our waking hours, and our experiences form an unbroken flow. Nevertheless, if mental phenomena are to be described and analysed, differentiation of synchronic cross-sections of the flow of consciousness – "experiences" – seems unavoidable.

Even the instantaneous global experience, all that one's consciousness registers in a given moment, is an unwieldy entity. Let us consider the moment in which you step into the street at the pedestrian crossing and at the same time see that a midnight blue Ford Scorpio, whose driver manifests no intention of stopping, is approaching at a rather high speed. Breaking up your instantaneous global experience analytically, one can say that it comprises different aspects. You have a visual, but also an auditory, experience. Perhaps you have an emotional experience: you may be a little frightened when you notice the car. You certainly have some kind of general experience of your body: a consciousness of the approximate positions of your limbs, and so on. The enumeration could be extended. Moreover, the different aspects of your global experience could be subdivided. Concerning your visual experience one could speak of visual experiences of colour, of form, of perceived movement, and of objects.

It is easy to realize that accounts of experiences must always isolate parts of the experience and in addition supply a rather abstract description of them. I shall consider consciousness in a given moment as registering certain intentional states as well as certain sensations.

To be in an intentional state is to relate mentally to certain specific circumstances. In the traffic example you may conceivably be in the intentional states of *seeing a car coming towards you*, of *hearing street noises*, of *being convinced that you risk being run over if you proceed*, and of *feeling some fear of the approaching car*. You may even be consciously aware of being in these states.

As the last sentence implies, I allow for unconscious intentional states. The majority of our well-established beliefs are in fact unconscious most of the time, but are easily made conscious if required. You are, for example, undoubtedly in the intentional state of *knowing your own name*, and that was also the case a moment ago, even if you were perhaps not consciously aware of your name just then. It is, further, obvious and commonly accepted that much of the complicated mental processing of sense impressions referred to in the last section is unconscious. It is hard to see valid objections to the contention that intentional states also occur in unconscious mental processing.

I conceive of intentional states, conscious as well as unconscious, as comprising two components. They consist on the one hand of a "mental representation," i.e., a mental description or depiction[11] of a state of affairs – for example, the representation that *a Ford Scorpio is coming towards you* – while on the other including a "psychological mode," a way in which the mental representation appears to consciousness. There is a difference between *seeing* that a Ford Scorpio is coming towards you and *hearing* it, or *imagining* it, or *predicting* that it will happen. In these states, the same mental representation is in operation, but the states exhibit different psychological modes.[12] In the first two cases, the representations are in the form of perceptions; in cases three and four they are imaginings. Perceptions or imaginings may in their turn possess different more specific modes, as the example makes clear.

As I have already said, an experience is made up not only of intentional states, but also of sensations. In fact, sensations play a role even in aspects of the global experience that overtly have to do solely with the outside world, such as visual experiences. Let us imagine that you look around the room. It may appear natural to believe that one could give a full account of the content of your visual experience by describing exactly what objects you perceive in the room, exactly what properties you construe them as possessing, and exactly what spatial relations between them you apprehend. Formulated more generally: it may seem that an exact description of the states of affairs perceived would constitute an exhaustive account of the contents of a visual experience. To describe the visual experience, then, would be tantamount to describing the corresponding intentional state, i.e., the mental representation and its mode.

As Christopher Peacocke has demonstrated, however, such ideas are hardly tenable. Among other things, Peacocke calls attention to the fact that if you close one eye, your visual experience is slightly changed, but not your perception of the objects' properties and mutual relations. Another of his arguments is, basically, as follows. You see two trees, one at a distance of a hundred metres and the other two hundred metres away, and you estimate that they are about the same size (equally tall, and so on). In that case the nearer tree takes up more room in your field of vision than the more distant one, and that feature also enters into your visual experience. In describing what properties you ascribe to reality in your visual experience, however, one would note solely that you assess the two trees as being approximately equal in size. Such a description must necessarily be incomplete, since it is also part of your visual experience that the closer tree takes up more of the field of vision and in that sense looks bigger. According to Peacocke, in the same way, there are always traits of perceptual experiences – he calls those traits "sensational properties" – that are not captured by a mere description of the states of affairs perceived to obtain.[13]

In the last few paragraphs I have introduced a number of terms – giving some of them a special meaning in my context – with the intention of making it easier to reason about the workings of minds; I refer especially to "instantaneous global experience," "intentional state," "psychological mode" ("perception," "imagining," "anticipation"), "mental representation," and "sensation." One must of course have some specialized conceptual apparatus at one's disposal if one is to carry on a profitable discussion about experiences. One should not, however, because of that, forget about the concreteness of experience and begin to regard the abstract, conceptual descriptions as equivalent to the experiences themselves.

Before leaving the subject of experiences and mental representations, I should like to emphasize this last point by commenting upon a somewhat more complex visual experience. I want to stress, above all, the difficulty of describing an experience in a satisfactory fashion. I shall point out some reasons for that difficulty, starting from my visual experience on looking out of my office window.

What I see is a field covered with short grass bordered in the background by mixed forest. A small, asphalted path, edged with occasional street-lamps, leads across the field. At the extreme left of my field of vision I can glimpse a corner of a parking lot.

If you thus account for the apprehended properties of reality, you describe features of crucial importance to the experience. In a case like the one at hand, however, some fundamental prerequisites of an *exhaustive* account of that kind are missing. For a start, the experience is so nuanced that language, in part, lacks the words to make an exact reproduction of it. For example, I can see many varied shades of green in the grass, many more than I (or language) have words for. And even disregarding that limitation, an exhaustive description of the representational content of the experience is probably not feasible: there is simply too much data to be conveyed.

Furthermore, the visual experience has a complex internal structure. Those parts of the field that are in the shade I perceive as grey, but I still apprehend them as green (cf. Peacocke's remarks about the two trees). The incoming neural signals in question are perhaps interpreted as representing grey areas by a relatively low-level interpretative instance (like the instance identifying "qualities and sensations" in the model in figure 2 above). Higher-level instances (like the one identifying "configurations") may then reinterpret the area as a section of a grass-covered field, giving rise to the belief that the corresponding part of reality is in fact green. It becomes evident, here, that lower-level perceptions do not neccessarily become inaccessible to consciousness as soon as they have been utilized as bases for more complex inter-pretations. When I perceive portions of the field as grey but apprehend them as being green, several different interpretative layers are present simultaneously in my experience.

This observation brings out a third important problem for the description of experiences: no description can do full justice to the subtle relationships within and between our experiences. A thorough account of my visual experience must divide it into a multitude of separate elements, whereas these elements are, in the actual experience, indissolubly fused.[14] Besides, as I have noted earlier, the notion of a visual experience as a wholly independent, clearly delimited phenom-enon already represents an idealization. A visual experience forms part of an instantaneous global experience which has other aspects as well, and the instantaneous global experience is in its turn an idealization, extracted from the continuous flow of experience by the aid of abstract thinking. It must be remembered that a visual experience merges with other topical thoughts, sensations, and feelings, and that they all have a history and a momentum. Perhaps I am raising my eyes from my desk and looking out of the window because I am contemplating pausing in my work and taking a brief walk. If so, this assigns to the visual experience a special role in my continuous processing of reality, something that affects the very character of the experience. It also makes certain aspects of the things seen especially important – in this case, perhaps, pleasant or unpleasant features of wind and weather.

Pleasant and Unpleasant Feelings

The mention of comfort and discomfort leads me on to another dimension of the mental: affective phenomena – feelings and emotions.

The brain receives neurally transmitted signals not only from the surroundings but from its own organism as well, since it keeps itself constantly informed of the organism's states and needs. Some of these sensations are unpleasant. One example, of course, is pain (typically related to injuries to the organism), but also unpleasurable are more general sensations of imbalance between the organism's state and its physiological needs – sensations of hunger or thirst, sensations of excessive heat or cold, and so on.

Other sensations are decidedly pleasurable, above all sensations caused by the fulfilment of unsatisfied needs (think of the demand for food, drink, warmth, sex). It appears obvious that pleasure and discomfort contribute to the biologically productive steering of many organisms. Organisms are driven by the struggle to obtain pleasurable sensations or to avoid sensations of discomfort. Since, by and large, genetically functional behaviour is rewarded with comfort and dysfunctional behaviour punished with discomfort, this increases the organism's prospect of survival. This system of rewards and punishments has every chance of serving as a comparatively simple and flexible steering device. An organism where it operates does not have to *think* in the proper sense to be able to behave rationally within a certain not too narrow scope.

Especially where humans are concerned, comfort and discomfort are also generated in other ways than by the satisfaction of biological needs or automatic response to stimuli. Above all, thoughts provoked by external events, or arising within the frame of spontaneous cognitive activity, may create comfort or discomfort. If you show an audience a film describing a circumcision ritual, they are likely to feel uneasy. If you convey to them the idea that the circumcision is entirely painless, however, they will feel less discomfort.[15] Cognitive processes must be involved here. Some form of thinking has to intervene between the visual information and the affective reaction.

How is it possible for cognitive processes to affect the emergence of comfort and discomfort? Let us reflect on a simple, fictive example. Imagine a child, around one year old, who has recently had his hand stung by a wasp. Now the child is sitting at the dining-table in a highchair, and a wasp is approaching, walking on the table-cloth. The child screams; evidently he feels ill at ease. How can the mere sight of the wasp have that effect? I would like to suggest an explanation along the following lines.

The wasp sting some days ago caused pain. Pain is intensely unpleasant and something we avoid if we can, other things being equal. The memory of the event is stored in the child: the recollection of the wasp, the sting, the pain. Now the child sees a wasp coming nearer. He can foresee close contact with it, and he associates wasps with the risk of painful stings. The mental representation of possible close contact with the the wasp is therefore associated with the idea of possible pain. Consequently, the representation is unpleasurable and its association with discomfort indicates, as it were, to the mind that the realization of the corresponding situation is to be avoided. This makes the avoidance of close contact with the wasp an important aim for the child, and he chooses to scream, thus requesting adult assistance.

When speaking of comfort and discomfort as a steering device, I have so far only taken very simple objectives into account, those associated with physiological needs or safety needs in Maslow's sense.

But the aspiration towards more complex goals such as love, respect, or self-realization also brings with it agreeable and disagreeable feelings. We all know that success or failure in love life or career may give rise to sweet bliss or bitter frustration. Such pleasure and uneasiness are not in any simple and straightforward fashion connected with physiological systems, with injuries to physical organs or the satisfaction of bodily needs, and the underlying mechanisms may seem hard to understand. Nevertheless we know that these kinds of comfort and discomfort exist.

It stands to reason that an individual always pursues a multitude of aims simultaneously, that he or she normally endeavours to realize as many important aims as possible, and that the agent's behaviour is a product, among other things, of more or less intuitive weighings of the relative importance of his or her often conflicting aims. Changes in the agent's situation are liable to affect the possibility of realizing the aims (and the aims themselves may vary, as may their order of priority). Innumerable memories are undoubtedly relevant to the governing of behaviour, as are anticipations of the consequences of possible alternative actions. It is reasonable to assume that the representations in question (the perceptions, the memories, the anticipations) are often connected with more or less pronounced ideas of pleasure or discomfort.

If this is so, it explains why even our most everyday experiences are tinged with pleasure and unease. This is already true for my experience when sitting at my office desk looking out of the window. What I see is connected with memories of events that have occurred in this field, and perhaps also with fantasies or with anticipations of possible or probable situations – for example, with anticipations of what would happen if I left my job for a while and took a walk across the field into the wood. What I see – the path, the trees, and so on – may also give rise to all kinds of other associations. And these memories, anticipations, and associations are connected with pleasure and discomfort in complicated and opaque fashions. Representations with different affective charges are involved. The general emotional colouring of the experience must be assumed to depend on how powerfully representations with the respective affective charges are brought to the fore, and on the representations' current importance for me. Accordingly, the affective character of the experience comes to be most complex and individual.

A Sketch of a Theory of Emotion

The talk of sensations and feelings brings us to the threshold of a discussion about emotions (for emotion theory, unlike ordinary language, normally distinguishes between feelings and emotions).[16]

Sensations are the mind's registering of bodily changes. They may be pleasurable or unpleasant or both. (They may also be emotionally neutral.) Comfort and discomfort are things we feel, but comfort and discomfort are not themselves feelings of something. They lack intentionality; they are simply pleasure or uneasiness generated in the brain.

By a "feeling" I mean, here, a sensation of pleasure or discomfort, simple or complex, of long or short duration. What I term feelings are, accordingly, episodes of pleasure or discomfort.

An *emotion* is something different from a feeling. An emotion is, more or less, what in common parlance we refer to as a feeling: joy, sorrow, love, hatred, expectation, disappointment, and so on. Emotions do not, however, admit of a reduction to feelings in the sense just introduced. A feeling of pleasure connected with joy cannot necessarily be distinguished, solely by its affective qualities, from a feeling of pleasure connected with pride or expectation or admiration. Conversely, discomfort in connection with remorse may in itself be indistinguishable from discomfort associated with fear or shame or, for that matter, from discomfort stemming from a purely bodily cause, like a hangover.[17] The differences between emotions of various kinds are not constituted exclusively by disparities between the underlying feelings.

What, then, makes an emotion into something more than a feeling? According to the view on emotion which I shall adopt in this book, an emotion is a simple or complex feeling of comfort or discomfort, understood as motivated by certain specific circumstances. To ascribe an emotion to somebody is to attribute to him or her a type of feeling, and at the same time to provide an implicit explanation for why this person has that feeling.[18] To say that Peter feels remorse is pretty much to say that he feels a discomfort conditioned by his awareness of having performed an action he should not have performed. To say that Mary feels fear is to say, more or less, that she feels a discomfort caused by her anticipation that something very negative will happen to her – and so on. The idea behind this theory is that emotion terms do not, like sensation or feeling terms, simply denote distinguishable mental occurrences. Emotion words designate mental occurrences and simultaneously provide them with implicit causal explanations.

Comfort and discomfort are strong driving forces. It is therefore important for us to comprehend what underlies feelings of pleasure or unease in ourselves and in others. If I feel discomfort, it is important for me to understand its grounds, so that I can remove them if possible. (Is it caused by a stupid action of mine, or a risk I run, or a bodily indisposition?) For the parents of the one-year-old it is likewise important to be able to identify the reason for the child's discomfort and if possible remove it. (Is the child angry? If so, at what, or with whom?

Scared? In that case, of what or whom?) And when I meet another person, it is important for me to know what emotions eventually arise in him or her: am I inspiring sympathy or dislike? The answer to that question helps me predict and understand his or her conduct.

It is easy, therefore, to perceive the need for emotion concepts containing subtle distinctions. We require manageable ways of speaking about people's motivation – concepts indicating affective incidents and at the same time pointing to their causal backgrounds. In my opinion, the concept of emotion, and the concepts of specific emotions, should be seen in that pragmatic light.

In this section and the preceding one, I have outlined a theory of emotion. The theory stresses, in a manner quite common today, the cognitive elements of emotions: the fact that emotions possess rationality of a kind and are connected with mental representations. At the same time it emphasizes that an emotional reaction is distinct from a thought. Emotional mechanisms constitute a system for the processing and assessment of reality somewhat different from that of cognitive operations, a system driven not by logic but rather by comfort and discomfort, by pleasant and unpleasant feelings.

Where the genesis of feelings is concerned, I follow Nico H. Frijda's emotion theory in *The Emotions* (1986)[19] fairly closely. Frijda describes emotions starting from something that he calls "the emotion process." This is a process in which the individual registers a stimulus event (think of the approaching wasp), processes and evaluates the situation step by step (think of the unpleasant representation of possible close contact with the wasp), and decides upon an action in response to the situation. The process is complicated by feedback elements and conflicting forces, and it is accompanied by physiological changes of various kinds.[20]

One can hardly dispute the plausibility of Frijda's general account of the emotion process, and the general picture of the mechanisms is all that matters here. More controversial is the question of what constitutes the actual emotion. Modern emotion theorists diverge in their proposed solutions to that problem, and this disagreement cannot really be explained by differences in assumptions about the emotion process.

Frijda, for his part, wishes to define emotions in terms of changes in the individual's action readiness.[21] For the philosopher William Lyons, however, the actual emotion is the physiological reaction, seen as caused by an evaluation.[22] The philosopher Patricia S. Greenspan holds a third position. She identifies emotions with "affective states of comfort or discomfort" directed at assessments. So emotions are, for

her, "comfort or discomfort directed towards evaluative propositions."[23] In an attempt to fuse several viewpoints, the philosopher
Jerrold Levinson describes an emotion as "a bodily response with a
distinctive physiological, phenomenological, and expressive profile, one
that serves to focus attention in a given direction, and that involves
cognition to varying degrees and at various levels."[24] These definitions
are obviously divergent, and they are all different from the one I myself
suggested above. The philosopher Gregory Currie, for his part, analyses emotions as pleasant or unpleasant feelings caused by beliefs and
desires: "Our beliefs and desires, conceived of as propositional attitudes, may bear upon each other in ways that cause us to have certain
kinds of feelings. Where our beliefs and desires harmonize, they tend
to produce feelings we find pleasant, as with feelings of requited love,
or pride in the achievements of others and of ourselves. Where our
beliefs and desires are in tension, they tend to produce feelings we find
unpleasant to various degrees, as with feelings of rejection, shame, and
disappointment. *This nexus of relationships between propositional
attitudes and feelings is an emotion.*"[25] This comes much closer to my
perspective, but lacks my emphasis on the prominent interpretative
character of our ascriptions of emotions – my insistence that emotions,
unlike sensations and feelings, are interpretative constructions rather
than phenomenological realities. (It may also be the case that Currie
– like Noël Carroll, who has proposed a very similar definition,[26] but
unlike myself – wishes to include the propositional attitudes in the
emotion itself.)

I do not here want to enter into a discussion of the merits of the
definitions proposed by Frijda, Lyons, Greenspan, Levinson, and Currie,
since that would require a longer excursion than the context justifies.
I hope that the point of my analysis of the concept of emotion will
become obvious later on, especially in chapter 7, which contains my
main discussion of the relation between literature and feelings.

2 Literature's Relevance to the Reader

Introduction

In the last chapter, I emphasized that we constantly attempt to keep ourselves au fait with the world around in order to secure an adequate basis for the actions by which we strive to satisfy our needs. How can literature be integrated into such a perspective? In what way does it satisfy, or help to satisfy, our wants?

There is of course no single answer to that question. In this chapter, however, I shall introduce one partial answer which I find important.

A concise and somewhat simplified formulation of this partial explanation may start from the observation that we humans do more than just react to events which demand instant action on our part.

There are times when our mental capacity is by no means fully occupied with the satisfaction of pressing needs. These spare moments make it possible for us to improve our general view of our situation. Such understanding is exceedingly useful; it helps us get into favourable rather than unfavourable situations. If we are supplied with sensible ideas of reality at large and of our options, we will be able to plan our activities more productively.

I see literature as, essentially, associated with our framing of conceptions of reality and strategies in life. Its relation to our objectives in life is, however, in a special sense, indirect.

On reading a newspaper article dealing with the latest major international crisis, we are confronted with information or allegations – with mental representations (here: thoughts about actual realities) whose raison d'être lies in the truthful reflection of fact. Here one might speak of a *direct* connection with real life: if we judge the information to be trustworthy, we simply use it to update our beliefs about reality. (This updating may, indirectly, affect our understanding of our options, our planning, and our feeling of anxiety or assurance in face of the future.)

On reading a poem or a novel, we are also confronted with mental representations, with pictures of reality of a kind. These may be pictures of fictive, made-up realities, or they may be true to the real world. In neither case, however, do they claim to be interesting mainly as information. Instead, I should say, one of their basic functions is to give rise, *indirectly*, to thoughts about actual realities. Through the associations aroused, the implicit reflections occasioned, and so on, they compel us to form conceptions of our actual situation. Naylor's *Mama Day* deals with fictitious occurrences; the things said are not *directly* related to real events and are worthless as factual information. Yet, Naylor's story may evoke conscious or, normally, unconscious thoughts about many sorts of things – ideas about the importance and the difficulties of emancipating oneself from the dominant influences of one's childhood and adolescence, for example. *Indirectly*, reading the story may bring to the fore our conceptions regarding these matters, or even perhaps alter them. (And this in its turn may, indirectly, affect our general understanding of our options, our planning, and our feeling of anxiety or assurance in face of the future.)

The justification and specification of the explanation just outlined will be a protracted process. It might in fact be said that the explanation is substantiated, qualified, and developed throughout the book. For the time being, it should be remembered that my reflections above were meant only as a simple and preliminary presentation of a *partial* explanation of literature's relevance to the reader.

In the rest of this chapter I shall enlarge upon the functioning of the cognitive and emotional mechanisms outlined. I shall also argue that we have reason to believe that mechanisms such as these are actually in operation in the reading of literature. First I shall introduce two of my principal literary examples, two short stories: Sun Axelsson's "The Freedom of Light" and John Updike's "Pygmalion." With the aid of these I shall, then, explicate the idea that the reading of literature is, among other things, a sort of indirect thinking about reality.

Sun Axelsson's "The Freedom of Light"

The short story "The Freedom of Light" ("Ljusets frihet") was written by the Swedish author Sun Axelsson (born 1935). It forms part of an anthology of specially commissioned stories on the theme of love, *LoveStories* (*KärleksHistorier*), published in 1984. The publishing firm, on the whole, used quite well known Swedish writers; their ambition was evidently to produce something serious. At the same time, however, it appears obvious that relatively short and easily accessible texts were requested.[1]

The protagonist of "The Freedom of Light" is a Swedish woman suffering from insomnia and from disgust with her own body. She has come to conceive her body as abnormally large, and she no longer dares to look at herself naked. As her problems become successively aggravated, she withdraws from all her friends. In an attempt to recover she goes to Paris, where she has many acquaintances from earlier in her life. At first, she cannot bring herself to call on them, but gradually her shyness begins to give way. She is able to visit a café, and she can even, together with a woman friend, attend an exhibition arranged by one of her old friends. There she meets Joel, an American painter now living in South America. During the party after the showing, the attractive Joel displays an interest in her. This pleasant situation entices the woman into at least reflecting about happiness: "Was there such a thing as a happy person? A banal question. But she wondered, from the depth of her distress, whether she would ever be allowed to experience joy, unneurotic love, trust, genuine human kindness? Would she be allowed to love? Was there carnal love without fright or shame? Without excessive demands? Not alarming one? Was there a single human being who could love one's whole self?"[2]

However, when Joel finally asks for her telephone number, for her address, for permission to go home with her immediately, this gives her a shock: she flees from the party and shuts herself up in her hotel room, practically sleepless, for several days. During this crisis she realizes that she is suffering from unrealistic self-contempt caused by her own unwillingness, and that of those closest to her, to accept "her womanliness, her talent, her intelligence, her striving."[3] She also understands that her problems are a punishment for her desire to assert her real self, and

> that it was she who inflicted this penalty on herself, but that the underlying will was that of others, of some other person.
>
> Someone not wanted such as she or he is, will wish to die. And one way of dying is to let oneself be disowned and humiliated, and to disown oneself all that life may give. The light.

This insight effects a certain, though far from complete, improvement in her condition. She becomes capable of visiting an exhibition of Joel's pictures. His painting proves to be "an erotic art ... with anxiety-ridden pressures behind it." Something in these pictures arouses "recognition and tenderness" in her. Having visited the exhibition, she resumes contact with Joel. The next Sunday, he is to take her for a walk; this develops into a day with "intense, clear spring sunshine." But when Joel arrives at her hotel, he has already taken his walk. He asks her leave to use the shower, and afterwards he sunbathes, naked, on the floor, chatting with her. At last she too undresses; the story ends as follows.

> The light was intense and merciless. No blind. No draperies. He was looking at her. He was regarding all of her with joy and with tenderness. She closed her eyes. He had affirmed her! She was quite calm again and warm. Gently, very closely, entirely silent, they made love. And at last they stretched themselves out side by side and then she dared to look at her naked body. It was a strange encounter. The body she was looking at was friendly, soft, and encouraging. "I am not ugly and I am not dangerous," it whispered. "I am the house in which you live."
>
> Thus she moved out of her prison and into her house. She was free.

Sun Axelsson's short story does not present itself as autobiographical but a piece of fiction. It consequently lacks value as direct information, and for a reader who knows how to read literature this is immediately clear. According to the explanation outlined in the last section, however, there is underlying the text the implicit expectation that the reader will use it in forming, indirectly, conceptions of her actual reality. The reader is expected to take notice of certain aspects of the story, or certain aspects of the way the story is told. This is supposed to foster ideas and reactions in her involving attitudes towards actual facts.

According to the standpoint adopted here, there is no point in asking *exactly what* ideas and reactions the text should give rise to in a competent reader. Different readers may focus on different aspects, or one and the same aspect may occasion a variety of ideas in the readers. It is, by and large, up to the reader herself to connect the text with life. (Admittedly, not all conceivable readings would fall within the scope of the normal and reasonable. That complication will be discussed extensively in chapter 6 below.)

As readers, however, we have the right to expect the author to have composed the text in such a fashion that it has interesting and valuable things to offer us. Hence there is normally an expected reading of a kind, some sort of anticipated understanding, associated with a text. (That subject, too, will be enlarged upon in chapter 6.) If the author is tolerably skilful, and knows her audience, the anticipated understanding will agree relatively well with the associations and thoughts that present themselves naturally on reading the text.

One natural way of reading "The Freedom of Light," it seems to me, is to foreground the fact that this is a story about a woman who is made free and happy through an encounter with someone who loves her, body and soul, just as she really is. If you attach special importance to that aspect, it will appear natural to ask whether it is true that *it is possible for us to become free and happy through an encounter with someone who loves us, body and soul, just as we really are.* If the reader answers that question in the affirmative without reservations, this implies that *it is possible for her herself to become free and happy through an encounter with someone who loves her, body and soul, just as she really is.* That is no doubt a pleasurable notion. In a reading along these lines, "The Freedom of Light" must be expected to bring to life positive thoughts and feelings in the reader. Love will stand out as an important, gratifying, and realistic possibility. The story will point, convincingly, to an achievable satisfaction in life.

My description of this reading is consciously superficial; it merely captures the most general character of a possible reader experience. Furthermore, Axelsson's tale could be read in a wholly or partly different fashion. It is possible to focus on the theme of love but to perceive the ideas of the possibilities and powers of love arguably conveyed by the story as cheap and oversimplified. In that case, reading the story is likely to lead to displeasure. The deprecatory reader might even apprehend Axelsson's textual moves as an offensive attempt to manipulate her.

John Updike's "Pygmalion"

Let us look at yet another literary example: John Updike's "Pygmalion" from his collection of short stories, *Trust Me* (1987). "Pygmalion" is a work which I intend to discuss more thoroughly, and I shall begin by reproducing the story in its entirety.

> What he liked about his first wife was her gift of mimicry; after a party, theirs or another couple's, she would vivify for him what they had seen, the faces, the voices, twisting her pretty mouth into small contortions that brought back, for a dazzling instant, the presence of an absent acquaintance. "Well, if I reawy – how does Gwen talk? – if I *re*-awwy cared about conservation –" And he, the husband, would laugh and laugh, even though Gwen was secretly his mistress and would become his second wife. What he liked about *her* was her liveliness in bed, and what he disliked about his first wife was the way she would ask to have her back rubbed and then, under his laboring hands, night after night, fall asleep.
>
> For the first years of the new marriage, after he and Gwen had returned from a party, he would wait, unconsciously, for the imitations, the

recapitulation, to begin. He would even prompt: "What did you make of our hostess's brother?"

"Oh," Gwen would simply say, "he seemed very pleasant." Sensing with feminine intuition that he expected more, she might add, "Harmless. Maybe a little stuffy." Her eyes flashed as she heard in his expectant silence an unvoiced demand, and with that touching, childlike impediment of hers she blurted out, "What are you reawy after?"

"Oh, nothing. Nothing. It's just – Marguerite met him once a few years ago and she was struck by what a pompous nitwit he was. That way he has of sucking his pipestem and ending every statement with 'Do you follow me?'"

"I thought he was perfectly pleasant," Gwen said frostily, and turned her back to remove her silvery, snug party dress. As she wriggled it down over her hips she turned her head and defiantly added, "He had a *lot* to say about tax shelters."

"I bet he did," Pygmalion scoffed feebly, numbed by the sight of his wife frontally advancing, nude, towards him as he lay on their marital bed. "It's awfully late," he warned her.

"Oh, come on," she said, the lights out.

The first imitation Gwen did was of Marguerite's second husband, Marvin; they had all unexpectedly met at a Save the Whales benefit ball, to which invitations had been sent out indiscriminately. "Oh-ho-*ho*," she boomed in the privacy of their bedroom afterwards, "so you're my noble predecessor!" In an aside she added, "Noble, my ass. He hates you so much you turned him on."

"I did?" he said. "I thought he was perfectly pleasant, in what could have been an awkward encounter."

"Yes, in*dee*dy," she agreed, imitating hearty Marvin, and for a dazzling second she allowed the man's slightly glassy and slack expression of forced benignity to invade her own usually petite and rounded features. "Nothing awkward about *us*, ho-ho," she went on, encouraged by her husband's laughter. "And tell me, old chap, why *is* it your child-support check is never on time anymore?"

He laughed and laughed, entranced to see his bride arrive at what he conceived to be a proper womanliness – a plastic, alert sensitivity to the human environment, a susceptible responsiveness tugged this way and that by the currents of Nature herself. He could not know the world, was his fear, unless a woman translated it for him. Now, when they returned from a gathering, and he asked what she had made of so-and-so, Gwen would stand in her underwear and consider, as if onstage. "We-hell, my dear," she would announce in sudden, fluting parody, "if it weren't for Portugal there *rally* wouldn't be a *bear*able country left in Europe!"

"Oh, come on," he would protest, delighted at the way her pretty features distorted themselves into an uncanny, snobbish horsiness.

"How did she do it?" Gwen would ask, as if professionally intent. "Something with the chin, sort of rolling it from side to side without unclenching the teeth."

"You've got it!" he applauded.

"Of course you *knoaow*," she went on in the assumed voice, "there *used* to be Greece, but now all these dreadful *Arabs* ... "

"Oh, yes, yes," he said, his face smarting from laughing so hard, so proudly. She had become perfect for him.

In bed she pointed out, "It's awfully late."

"Want a back rub?"

"Mmmm. That would be reawy nice." As his left hand labored on the smooth, warm, pliable surface, his wife – that small something in her that was all her own – sank out of reach; night after night, she fell asleep.[4]

This is a humorous story, brimful of comic effects of varying subtlety. The story also has a certain satirical quality. Its unerring realism does not prevent the depiction of the male protagonist from acquiring a touch of caricature. There are, apparently, only two things he appreciates in women – sexual willingness and the ability to interpret reality for him – and the latter seems to mean the capacity to amuse him and boost his self-esteem by putting his acquaintances in an absurd light. There is no explicit criticism of the man, but the remarkable first sentence of the story – "What he liked about his first wife was her gift of mimicry," apparently giving a glimpse of Pygmalion's world of experience quite close to his own perspective and formulating a simple, morally neutral piece of factual information – already suggests that he lacks any deeper personal interest in other people, that he is, ultimately, narrowly and unconsideringly self-seeking in his approach to life.

The title "Pygmalion" provides the story with an additional dimension. The myth of Pygmalion, king of Cyprus, Venus's island, who was eminently skilled in ivory carving, has been handed down to us through Ovid's *Metamorphoses* (ca 8 AD). Ovid's Pygmalion, disappointed in real women, carves a wonderfully attractive girl in ivory and becomes deeply enamoured of her. He wishes that she were alive, and at a feast in honour of Venus he gains the impression that the goddess is prepared to make his dreams come true. He immediately hastens home to the ivory girl resting on a bed in his palace.

> And he went home, home to his heart's delight,
> And kissed her as she lay, and she seemed warm;
> Again he kissed her and with marvelling touch

> Caressed her breast; beneath his touch the flesh
> Grew soft, its ivory hardness vanishing,
> And yielded to his hands, as in the sun
> Wax of Hymettus softens and is shaped
> By practised fingers into many forms,
> And usefulness acquires by being used.
> His heart was torn with wonder and misgiving,
> Delight and terror that it was not true!
> Again and yet again he tried his hopes –
> She was alive! The pulse beat in her veins![5]

The girl awakens and returns his love; they marry and have a daughter, Paphus.

In later Western tradition, Pygmalion was often understood as one of love's heroes or fools, but he has also frequently been made to stand for the gifted artist, since he has the capacity to bring inanimate nature to life.[6] In George Bernard Shaw's play *Pygmalion* (1912), however, the myth is seen from a somewhat new angle. Professor Higgins, the brilliant phonetician who is the Pygmalion of the play, makes a bet with his friend Pickering. Higgins is convinced that his teaching can erase the vulgarity of the flower girl Eliza Doolittle, expressed not least in her Lisson Grove cockney, and endow her with a pronunciation and a manner that will make London's high society see her as a woman of quality. To Higgins, Eliza is first and foremost raw material; in working her up and reshaping her into something new, he displays his own unique insights and abilities. If Higgins is to be understood as a Pygmalion, the myth must be seen in a new light: as a tale of dominance and presumption.[7] Not surprisingly, Higgins suffers a sort of punishment for his lack of respect for Eliza as a person. He wins his bet, and despite his self-centredness and arrogance he actually seems to fall in love with Eliza; in an afterword, though, Shaw assures us that she will not marry him.

In the third act of *Pygmalion*, Higgins and Pickering visit Higgins's mother, who reproaches them with thoughtless disregard of Eliza's interests. On their way out, the two incorrigible gentlemen nevertheless instantly start planning to enjoy themselves through Eliza.

HIGGINS [*to Pickering as they go out together*] Lets take her to the Shakespear exhibition at Earls Court.
PICKERING. Yes: lets. Her remarks will be delicious.
HIGGINS. She'll mimic all the people for us when we get home.
PICKERING. Ripping. [*Both are heard laughing as they go downstairs*].

MRS HIGGINS *[rises with an impatient bounce, and returns to her work at the writing-table. She sweeps a litter of disarranged papers out of her way; snatches a sheet of paper from her stationery case; and tries resolutely to write. At the third line she gives it up; flings down her pen; grips the table angrily and exclaims]* Oh, men! men!! men!!![8]

Eliza is, thus, supposed to entertain Higgins and Pickering with imitations of people they have met ("She'll mimic all the people for us when we get home"); on this point, Updike's proximity to Shaw is manifest. And a critical view of Pygmalion has also been worked into Updike's "Pygmalion"; generally speaking, Shaw's ironic reappraisal of Pygmalion's role naturally forms an important part of the intertext of Updike's story. At the same time, associations with Ovid are not lacking, nor are relations to the art themes often associated with the Pygmalion material. Updike's Pygmalion, too, strives to actualize his ideal of a woman, though unsuccessfully. And in Updike, just as in Ovid, Pygmalion acts as a masseur of the female body; in the modern story, however, the unfortunate effects are the exact opposite of the classical, vivifying ones. Nor does one have to strain the meaning of Updike's story unduly to find problems related to art and artistry – the imitation of reality, and creativity of a kind, certainly play a palpable role in his "Pygmalion."

The mental representations communicated via Axelsson's "The Freedom of Light" make up a complex fantasy. The same is true of Updike's "Pygmalion," but in several respects the "Pygmalion" fantasy is more complex than that of "The Freedom of Light." Axelsson's short story has, no doubt deliberately, been made comparatively simple and unequivocal. It appears obvious that the reader of Axelsson's story is primarily expected to concentrate on the female protagonist's difficulties and the way she overcomes them. The positive felings likely to be created by the story are no doubt mainly due to the underlying idea of love's healing powers. Updike's "Pygmalion" is more complex: readers may focus on more varied aspects of its content, and it is difficult to determine the precise import of the humour or irony so essential to its general character.

From one point of view, "Pygmalion" describes an American upper-middle-class husband and his half-conscious attempts to remodel his new wife to correspond to his feminine ideal. The result is simply a reiteration of the pattern of his first marriage, and one senses that this pattern is determined by personal factors in the man: his egocentricity, his wish to form his wife in compliance with his own needs. This is perhaps the most immediately striking feature of the fantasy content. It may, however, also seem natural to the reader to afford the content a somewhat wider application and to understand the story as suggesting that male love, or much male love, is at bottom an egoistic thing. The introduction of the name "Pygmalion" tends to transform the man into a representative of something more general: into a Pygmalion, a specimen of a certain type of person (while the naming may at the same time involve irony, since it is obvious that by no means does the man have the stature of the mythical Pygmalion, whose own project must, moreover, in itself, appear questionable). This is the only tangible indication, though, that a wider significance can be ascribed to the story; the author avoids emphasizing, or at least overemphasizing, such possibilities.

The fantasy produced by Updike may also, however, elicit reflections about art and life. As already suggested, the traditional spectrum of associations related to the Pygmalion material makes it natural to observe the important role played by mimesis, creative imitation of reality. The man endeavours to transform reality; in his relations with Gwen, he is attempting to actualize his feminine ideal. But though he does indeed reform Gwen, the result is not likely to strike the reader as an improvement. Ovid's Pygmalion transforms art into life in awakening the ivory girl. Quite conversely, Updike's and Shaw's Pygmalions are changing, to the best of their abilities, a living person into an object of art. The original kind and uncritical Gwen with her liveliness in bed and her touching, childlike impediment is drilled, discreetly, into virtuoso acting. Her abilities to mimic are astounding. But her imitations lack generosity; they have a spiteful rather than a humorous character, and the reader is liable to perceive this sarcastic mimicry as a limited and second-rate form of art. Nor does the role give room for the real Gwen; that small something in her that is all her own eludes her director's control. Updike's modern Pygmalion lacks creative powers; he cannot reshape reality in any positive sense, and his ideas about how reality should be reshaped are without value. Nor, apparently, is he able to accept life as it is. All he can do is to fashion a human distorting mirror to reflect those around him; only such a mirror, it seems, is capable of establishing working relations between him and reality.

Thus, it appears natural for the reader of Updike's story to associate the fantasy communicated with ideas implying that *love is egoistic, art a farce, our attempts at mastering reality presumptuous and impotent*. These ideas are admittedly merely suggested by the story; nevertheless "Pygmalion" has every chance of bringing these negative thoughts to conscious life in a trained reader. "Pygmalion" would have been a pessimistic story if it had not been for the humour or irony.

In attempting to analyse the humour or irony of "Pygmalion" and define its import, one is in effect striving to capture the story's soul in a formula. This can certainly not be done in a way that is satisfactory to all, and it stands to reason that every reader will, within certain limits, be free to apprehend the tone of the story in her personal fashion. I should just like to indicate briefly three elements affecting, I believe, capable readers. One of these is the malevolent humour, the scorn, of Marguerite's and Gwen's imitations. What the imitations satirize, indirectly, is attitudes and manners: materialism, snobbery, racial prejudice, a façade of idealistic commitment. More immediately, however, the satire brings individual (fictive) persons to the fore, and a reader amused by the imitations is placed, when laughing, in a position reminiscent of Pygmalion's: she has gratefully accepted a pleasurable opportunity to look down on other people. This means – and that is element number two – that the irony directed at Pygmalion by Updike affects the reader as well, to the extent that the latter makes herself into an accomplice of Pygmalion's by laughing. Apart from the satire staged by Pygmalion, and besides Updike's irony towards Pygmalion (and to a certain degree towards the reader, and perhaps towards himself as well), it is, however, also possible to discern, as a third element, a humorous attitude, in a more usual sense, towards the world of the story, a tolerant rather than deprecating distancing on the writer's part. His attitude seems to imply that we need not feel threatened or provoked by the deficiences in the world and in ourselves illustrated by the story – it is as if the world, with all its shortcomings, were nevertheless under control.

The discussion of "Pygmalion" supplements, in two particulars, what was said of literature and positive feelings in the last section. First, and most obviously, the discussion shows that a literary work may well arouse complex positive feelings that are difficult to describe, not relatively unequivocal feelings easily characterized and explained. Second, Updike's text demonstrates that positive feelings in the reader may be aroused not only by a communicated fantasy providing a positive picture of reality, as was the case with "The Freedom of Light," but also by the depiction of a negative reality which the author makes controllable and tolerable by conveying a certain attitude towards it, by putting it into a specific perspective. This is, roughly, what Updike does in "Pygmalion." Updike's reader encounters an author transmitting a fantasy and, at the same time, supplying a very special attitude towards the imaginary individuals (and perhaps towards the reader, and towards himself), an attitude in which humour and irony are conspicuous ingredients. If the story arouses positive feelings in the reader, this is probably due to her taking over part of the humorous attitude adopted towards the imagined events. (In itself, the picture of reality would seem slightly depressing.)

If you take up this attitude towards life, at least for the moments when "Pygmalion" is having an effect upon you, you implicitly adopt it towards yourself as well. This should give rise to positive feelings: it might make a male reader look more tolerantly and dispassionately on himself and his own possible Pygmalion-like qualities, thereby helping him to see himself and his life as more acceptable.

The Reading of Literature: A Cognitive-Affective Processing Pattern

In the introduction to this chapter, I outlined a partial explanation of how literature is integrated into life. The two literary examples just discussed provide material for a few elucidations or amendments.

The gist of my explanation was that readers are doing several things simultaneously. Among other things, they are connecting communicated content with actual reality, and thus, indirectly, with themselves. It is as if, faced with the represented realities, they were constantly asking themselves, "Is reality like this?" and the attendant question, "What consequences do these facts have for me?" And it is as if, in face of the conveyed attitudes towards the represented realities, they were constantly asking themselves, "Is this an adequate attitude?" and the attendant question, "Can I learn something from this attitude?" If this explanation is correct, there is a cognitive dimension to the reading of literature. Reading literature involves, among other things, reflecting on reality.[9]

The connection between literature and reality may be variously achieved. For one thing, we readers may simply be comparing depicted and actual realities in one respect or another. Though perceiving, as we certainly do, that the persons, settings, and events in stories like "The Freedom of Light" and "Pygmalion" are essentially invented, we nevertheless sense that persons, settings, and events of more or less similar kinds do, or might, really exist. Because of this, our reading calls to mind aspects of reality, or causes us to apprehend new aspects of the world. In fact, this mechanism has every chance of functioning even where non-realistic literary characters, settings, or events are concerned. Even Frodo Baggins in J.R.R. Tolkien's trilogy of the Ring (1954–5), the world of the future in George Orwell's *1984* (1949), and Greger Samsa's transformation into a beetle in Franz Kafka's "The Transformation" ("Die Verwandlung," 1915) are reminiscent of real persons, settings, and events in somewhat more indirect and abstract fashions.

As readers we are confronted, moreover, with attitudes towards the characters, settings, and events described. This may be a matter of attitudes disclosed or expressed by the depicted characters themselves, or of attitudes in the fictive narrator (if any), or of attitudes displayed by the author, perhaps simply by the way she tells the story. It is natural for us, as readers, to evaluate such attitudes at least implicitly. We ask ourselves whether we would be prepared to adopt a corresponding approach to similar persons, situations, or events in the real world.

The relation between literature and life does not, then, consist essentially in literature's *making assertions* about reality – literature does not generally do that. (There is more about this in chapter 5.) The crux of the matter is, rather, that literature normally gets the reader to relate the things said to reality. This is apt to enlarge her cognitive register in various ways. She may acquire new knowledge (or rather, perhaps, new convictions), often concerning such trivial things as the fact that there is a place or building called "St Germain des Près" (correctly, Saint-Germain-des-Prés) in Paris.[10] She may further, and more interestingly, acquire or reinforce general factual beliefs, such as the belief that love does in fact have the capacity to disentangle our psychical knots and supply us with a new and better life. And she may, while reading, form concepts useful for assessing her own situation in life. The reading of Updike's "Pygmalion" is likely to lead to the intuitive formation of concepts such as "Updike's Pygmalion-character" and "the view of life adopted in Updike's 'Pygmalion.'" These new acquisitions will probably, to some small extent, improve the reader's ability to analyse reality. She will, in future, have all that is required to discern similarities and differences between the men she meets and Updike's Pygmalion-character. And she has been confronted with a special view of life that she can take over, or reject, or simply store as enriching her experience of possible human attitudes.

My explanation does not, however, have an exclusively cognitive character. It also describes literature as, normally, inviting reading that has positive psychological effects, strengthening us and augmenting our well-being. Literature is considered to do this by arousing comparatively positive ideas about reality, ideas that allow the reader to conceive of reality as obliging, or tractable, or at least endurable. It is true that good literature by no means avoids the tragic or alarming – it never has, and twentieth-century high-quality writing can least of all be accused of doing so. For mature readers, however, texts which also seriously address the painful aspects of life may be far more rewarding than simple success stories. Tenable views of the surrounding reality are of greater value to us than optimistic but untrustworthy notions. In enticing us into imagining negative and problematic things, and helping us to integrate these into our lives without despairing, the author is in effect reinforcing our feelings of being prepared to face life's hardships. The tragic and alarming should not, however, be allowed to get the upper hand. According to my explanation you could apply to the reading of literature what the English child psychiatrist D.W. Winnicott has said about play: "*Playing is essentially satisfying. This is true even when it leads to a high degree of anxiety. There is a degree of anxiety that is unbearable and this destroys playing.*"[11]

In short, the idea behind my explanation is that literature gets the reader to connect communicated representation with actual reality while reading, thereby making her form or bring to consciousness conceptions of the world around. The conceptions involved normally concern her general view of reality, and her general evaluation of it, rather than her immediate needs.

The explanation ascribes a cognitive dimension to literature. At the same time, however, the ideas occasioned by the reading must be thought to involve, indirectly, the reader's own situation and the conditions governing her life. Since the reader herself forms part of the reality envisaged, pleasurable or unpleasant representations of the possibility or impossibility of safeguarding her own interests are naturally brought to the fore in her reading. Consequently, my reasoning also offers an explanation for how literature acquires an emotional dimension. (I shall return to that side of the matter in chapter 7.)

The aim of this explanation is not to provide an overall analysis of the function of literature. The reading of literature may trigger aesthetically relevant effects of many kinds, not all explicable in terms of the analysis just given. I do claim, though, to have described a fundamentally important psychological mechanism that is normally in operation in our reading of literature. To my mind, the explanation supplies our understanding of the function of literature with a flexible and productive starting point. Most aesthetically important effects of the ordinary reading of literature, though not all, can be comprehended with the aid of the basic model just introduced.

But why should one believe in the existence of this cognitive-affective reading pattern? I myself can see two reasons. First and foremost, it is natural to assume the actuality of such a pattern, given what we know about human needs and human cognitive processing.

During all our waking life, we humans are occupied with receiving impressions from the surrounding world and improving upon the bases of our actions by processing these impressions. To take one example: when driving a car in dense city traffic we devote a great deal of our mental capacity to taking in the activities in and around the street.

Acting on the resulting picture of the traffic situation, we perform movements calculated to help us avoid collisions or other complications. Our processing of the constantly shifting traffic situation is normally unconscious; in any case, it does not usually necessitate thoughts formulated in language. (Cf. my earlier discussion of the Ford Scorpio example.) In Frijda's words: "Appraisal of an event's significance is neither deliberate nor a conscious process."[12] Since realities elicit feelings in us, this processing also has a more or less prominent affective dimension. If a pedestrian suddenly throws himself into the street in front of us, we experience acute alarm.

The same seemingly automatic evaluation of the relevance of a piece of information to ourselves and those for whom we care also occurs in situations where no immediate reactions are expected from us. Say that you are watching the evening news on television. There is a story about assaults on tourists in Florida, where your daughter and her boyfriend are at present spending their holiday: tourists' cars are forced to stop, whereupon the tourists are robbed or even killed. Your processing of this information is not likely to restrict itself to the assessment of these reports as trustworthy and the storing of the information as yet another factual detail relevant to your mental map of the world and its condition. You will rather automatically ask yourself, What, if anything, does this entail for me and my interests? In this case, you realize that modern highwaymen in Florida constitute a potential danger to your daughter and her boyfriend. And so you will no doubt feel some degree of uneasiness, some degree of anxiety – depending on how serious you regard the risks as being – when confronted with this news item.

For analogous reasons, true verbal stories may awaken conscious or unconscious associations in the hearer. As listeners we may enter into the situation described, asking ourselves how we ourselves would have acted in it. While we are consciously or unconsciously reflecting upon this, something in our view of the world and its risks and possibilities, or our view of ourselves, may be brought to consciousness or changed. Perhaps we experience feelings related to these new ideas, or to these ideas newly brought to life. Attention to this cognitive-affective mechanism makes it possible to see literature as exploiting and refining the general capacity of verbal compositions to arouse associations.[13] According to the explanation suggested here, literary compositions are implicitly designed to awaken somehow valuable associations.

The details of the cognitive-affective reading pattern outlined here are of course open to discussion. (They will be discussed later in my exposition.) Considering what we know about human processing mechanisms, however, it appears obvious that the path from the reader's identification of communicated representations to her aesthetic response, her reading experience in the full sense, must lie mainly via unconscious cognitive processing. As the psychologist Arthur C. Graesser and his colleagues have pointed out (apropos of narratives): "The inferencing mechanisms and world knowledge structures that are tapped during the comprehension of everyday experiences are also likely to be tapped during the comprehension of narratives; there is no justifiable reason to believe that readers would turn off these pervasive interpretive mechanisms during reading."[14]

It is also obvious from psychological experiments that our reactions as readers of fiction are not merely mechanical responses to the stimuli constituted by the fictional narratives. The American psychologist Richard J. Gerrig has recently published a comprehensive account of empirical, partly experimental, evidence that the content of fiction may affect our factual beliefs.[15] Among other things, a fictive university story was shown to have altered the convictions of Yale students in certain respects. The Yale students were more influenced when the story was placed in Princeton and not in Yale (while the opposite held true for Princeton students).[16] The results must reasonably be understood as demonstrating that the students were somehow incorporating elements of the fictional story into their current beliefs about actual reality, allowing information contained in the story to inspire revisions of those beliefs. Intimate knowledge of the setting of the story seems to have enhanced the awareness of the story's fictionality and with that the consciousness of its unreliability as a source of information.[17]

Literature's Concrete Universality

So far, I have indicated an important reason for believing in the reality of the cognitive-affective reading pattern: what we know about human cognitive processing, including the processing of reading, makes the existence of a pattern of this kind seem natural.

Assuming the pattern's existence, however, also helps us explain several interesting problems in literary theory in a simple and – as I see it – convincing manner. One such problem is how it is possible for us to be emotionally affected by fiction. In emotion theory, it is regarded as an established fact that emotions arise only when something complies with, or counteracts, our own personal interests. "*Emotions arise in response to events that are important to the individual's goals, motives, or concerns,*"[18] says Frijda, while William Lyons formulates the same idea as follows: "The angry man evaluates something as a slight *to himself*. It is this relating of events to ourselves, or to our quasi-selves, our friends and loved ones, that generates emotion.

If we didn't we would not be moved. We would be just calm and dispassionate adjudicators and evaluators of passing events."[19]

In the light of this, it may seem difficult to understand how adversities befalling entirely invented characters, like the woman in "The Freedom of Light" or Pygmalion in "Pygmalion," can give rise to feelings in the reader – *her* actual interests are not affected by the fictitious events, and she knows this very well. However, taking the cognitive-affective reading pattern into consideration helps us account for the phenomenon in a simple manner.[20] The fictional story brings to consciousness, or takes a part in changing, the reader's beliefs about the world. With that it brings to consciousness, or takes a part in changing, her ideas about her own possibilities in life. So it is not to be wondered at that her reading may have an effect on her feelings.

A still more central literary-aesthetical phenomenon is the one sometimes referred to as literature's concrete universality. In reading a literary work which really appeals to us, we perceive it as possessing an aesthetic aura of some kind, an almost magical radiation of significance. The work, and the realities described in the work, are (typically) concrete and particular. But in our reading they acquire a wider import, indefinite but unmistakably present. Assuming the existence of the cognitive-affective reading pattern helps us comprehend this phenomenon too.

I should like to approach the subject of literature's concrete universality in a roundabout way. In *The Sense of Beauty* (1896), George Santayana wishes to explain how objects may come to be experienced as being full of expression. Santayana starts from the observation that objects may arouse associations in us, and also feelings related to these associations. If we clearly realize that the object itself is a mere stimulus that releases associations in us, we will experience the object as comparatively neutral. When the causal relation is not obvious to us, however, the situation becomes different. The marginally conscious associations and feelings will then appear to be associated with the object itself, as if the object were their actual source and we were merely perceiving features already present in it. In such cases, the object itself will be experienced as charged with meaning and expressive values, as having what Santayana calls "expression."

the mementos of a lost friend do not become beautiful by virtue of the sentimental associations which may make them precious. The value is confined to the images of the memory; they are too clear to let any of that value escape and diffuse itself over the rest of our consciousness, and beautify the objects which we actually behold. We say explicitly: I value this trifle for its associations. And so long as this division continues, the worth of the thing is not for us aesthetic.

But a little dimming of our memory will often make it so. Let the images of the past fade, let them remain simply as a halo and suggestion of happiness hanging about a scene; then this scene, however empty and uninteresting in itself, will have a deep and intimate charm; we shall be pleased by its very vulgarity. We shall not confess so readily that we value the place for its associations; we shall rather say: I am fond of this landscape; it has for me an ineffable attraction. The treasures of the memory have been melted and dissolved, and are now gilding the object that supplants them; they are giving this object expression.[21]

I would not, without serious reservations, subscribe to Santayana's definitions of the concepts of beauty and (aesthetic) expression. Nevertheless, I consider that Santayana has provided a fine and suggestive description of an existing psychological phenomenon, and that his description helps to explain the occurrence of what might be termed "embodied expressivity." Santayana's analysis of embodied expressivity must be said to possess even more credibility and power today, since modern cognitive psychology provides massive support for the idea that unconscious cognitive processing is of central importance to our understanding of the world around us.

Embodied expressivity is met with in many contexts. In reading a book, we are confronted with pages that are, in themselves, physical objects: white sheets of paper with intricate patterns of printer's ink. However, the pages trigger representations of words, sentences, and meanings in us, which normally happens automatically and without reflection. Because of this, we spontaneously perceive the pages as possessing embodied expressivity. The physical pages seem to literally *contain* letters, words, meaning, and emotional tones.[22] It is not surprising, therefore, that reasoning along Santayana's lines is highly applicable to literature. When I am reading Updike's "Pygmalion," the reading releases a flow of unconscious, emotionally coloured thinking in me. I am vaguely conscious of the wealth of ideas and affective nuances in my experience, but not of the underlying processes. Phenomenologically, the richness in meaning and nuanced feeling appears to be a property of the object that releases the experience and is at the centre of my attention: Updike's "Pygmalion."[23] For that reason, Updike's "Pygmalion" stands out, during my reading, as an object which has somehow become charged with cognitive and affective import.

Throughout the history of literary aesthetics, perceptive observers have attached great weight to the fact that the literary work seems to express some more general, "universal" meaning through its descriptions of concrete particulars. Aristotle says in his *Poetics* (fourth century BC) that "poetry is more philosophical and more elevated than history, since poetry relates more of the universal, while history relates particulars."[24]

Here, Aristotle draws attention to the impression of universality that literary descriptions give rise to. According to my analysis, this universality should be understood as a projection of the wider associations that the literary composition awakens (and was designed to awaken).[25]

Concrete universality is also of great importance in the *Critique of Judgement* (*Kritik der Urteilskraft*, 1790), Kant's epoch-making contribution to aesthetics. An aesthetic idea is analysed, there, as "that representation of the imagination which induces much thought, yet without the possibility of any definite thought whatever, i.e., *concept*, being adequate to it, and which language, consequently, can never get quite on level terms with or render completely intelligible."[26] This sounds to me as if Kant places an idea, i.e., a mental representation, at the heart of the aesthetic experience, an idea whose peculiarity consists in its power to arouse associations – something which makes it impossible to find any equivalent thought to replace it with. (Just as it is impossible to replace the complex representational content communicated to us via Updike's story of Pygmalion with any other, functionally equivalent, complex of representations.) The aesthetic idea is a single representation, but it possesses a more general import in so far as it "induces much thought."

In his well-known definition of beauty as "the pure appearance of the Idea to sense,"[27] Hegel views the same phenomenon from a somewhat different angle. Hegel lays considerable stress on the sensuous character of art and on the particularity of its representational content. However, the representations of particulars, for him, allow an underlying idea to show through, and their beauty resides precisely in this. The work of art is concrete, but at the same time it makes visible something universal: "Now the form of *sensuous intuition* is that of art, so that it is art which sets truth before our minds in the mode of sensuous configuration, a sensuous configuration which in this its appearance has itself a loftier, deeper sense and meaning, yet without having the aim of making the Concept as such in its universality comprehensible by way of the sensuous medium; for it is precisely the *unity* of the Concept with the individual appearance which is the essence of the beautiful and its production by art."[28]

From the aesthetics of German idealism the idea of concrete universality is handed down, via different middlemen, to twentieth-century reflection on the arts. The conception appears within widely differing literary-theoretical schools and movements. Thus, the American New Critic W.K. Wimsatt describes this tradition of thought, and attempts an analysis of the phenomenon itself, in his essay "The Concrete Universal" (1947).²⁹ And within Soviet Marxist aesthetics the prominent literary theorist L.I. Timofeev formulates the Hegelian thought in a more materialist vein, defining the literary image, i.e., the complex representation, as "*a concrete and at the same time generalized rendering of human life.*"³⁰ Hegel's basic insight also lives on in many quarters within philosophical aesthetics. The British aesthetician Paul Crowther has recently given the idea of concrete universality an innovative formulation, connecting on to Kant, Schiller and Hegel, and Merleau-Ponty and Heidegger.³¹

Underlying these various descriptions and analyses there is – as I have already emphasized – a phenomenological reality requiring an explanation. We do in fact experience certain literary works, while reading them, as in themselves charged with a meaning far transcending the linguistic formulations and the represented events. Part of this phenomenon consists in the works' seeming to embody or physically radiate a deeper import. In that respect the phenomenon is explained, to my mind, by Santayana's analysis of the mechanisms effecting embodiment. However, we also need an explanation of how the deeper import comes into being, how literary works acquire the capacity to evoke significant thoughts and feelings in the minds of their readers. If we assume the existence of a cognitive-affective processing pattern of the kind described, we are able to supply the necessary explanation.

The Cognitive Value of Literature

In this chapter, I have described a cognitive-affective processing pattern and maintained that it must be supposed to play an important role in our reading of literature. I expect many of my readers to regard that idea with doubt and discomfort. The *occurrence* of the processing pattern can perhaps be taken for granted, but its *aesthetic relevance* may be called in question.

Superficially at least, our enjoyment of art and literature has little to do with associations. Aesthetic experience stands out, rather, as a highly differentiated perception of fine nuances in the art object with which we are confronted. An important element, even in literary experience, seems to be impressions of the object's aesthetic surface and of the object's form, structure, organization. Does not this constitute an important objection to my analysis in the foregoing?

I do not think so. Apparently, of course, the aesthetic experience is entirely directed to the object before us. In my explanation, however, this is due to the fact that ideas or feelings awakening in us while we regard or read are projected onto the physical art object, supplying it with embodied expressivity. As for the reactions to literary form, these can be seen, partly, as an additional, complementary feature of literary experience. Partly they may be understood as manifesting the very same cognitive-affective pattern already discussed. The demonstration of this will, however, have to wait until a late stage of my exposition (chapters 8–10), as it presupposes the analysis of the concept and phenomenon of literary form presented there.

I shall proceed, instead, to discuss briefly another argument against the aesthetic relevance of processing along the cognitive-affective lines in question. My analysis says, among other things, that the reader of literature normally relates the text's representations to her picture of the world, letting her reading affect her view of reality. One objection that immediately suggests itself, then, is that this cannot be an *important* function of literature, and a fortiori not an *aesthetically* important function. For as regards cognitive value, literature is necessarily inferior to common, informational discourse. It cannot, for instance, convey statements that could not have been imparted more efficiently by means of ordinary, non-literary prose.[32]

My rejoinder to that objection is that there are many ways of developing one's picture of the world. One may make use of immediate experience: gather and assess impressions *not* formulated in language. Or one may utilize informational discourse: receive and evaluate oral or written statements (from newspapers, journals, reference or special- ist books, and so on). Reading literature is a third way (and there are more). All these methods have advantages as well as drawbacks. None is superior to the others in all respects. To my mind, literature's special merits are connected with its conveying of representations that are concrete and at the same time suggest a more general, not fully determinate meaning.

By a "concrete" representation I mean here a representation of something individual, something particular. Pygmalion in Updike's "Pygmalion" is a single, unique person in the world of the fiction. Therefore, Updike's Pygmalion-representations in his "Pygmalion" are concrete in the relevant sense. Normally, literature is about particular persons, objects, places, or events – one rarely meets with literary texts representing no particulars at all.

Since literary works convey, on the whole, concrete representations, literary contents usually acquire a great deal of concreteness (in the everyday sense of "concreteness"). The bedroom scenes in "The Free- dom of Light" and "Pygmalion" are both comparatively clearly visu- alized (without being really graphic). Concrete representations confront the reader with objects and events of types that are well known to her, and are consequently apt to arouse associations. This is one important reason why many literary compositions must be supposed to be strongly conducive to the forming of associations.[33]

Reading a work like "The Freedom of Light" or "Pygmalion" is likely to elicit, among other things, ideas about future possibilities. As a reader of "The Freedom of Light" you will perhaps form ideas about how things would be if a new love affair were to intervene, revolutionarily, in your life. Such representations will undoubtedly possess affective qualities. The envisaged possibilities will perhaps make you feel that there is still a chance that life will open up before you – or perhaps you will, on the contrary, experience them as negative, as if such a love experience would have to involve a kind of madness. In these and many similar ways, literary works stimulate their readers to form emotionally charged, and hence evaluative, thoughts about their lives. Through inciting evaluative reflection about existence, and providing material for our inner dialogue about our way of life, literature may acquire powerful and incalculable effects. As I see it, literature's significance for our orientation in life lies first and foremost in its potential for creating perspectives and its capacity for influencing our ideas about what is worth striving for.

Of course I do not maintain that reading literature affords greater overall orientational values than, say, immediate experience or the reading of non-fiction. And naturally informational discourse reigns supreme where the factual description and rational analysis of reality are concerned. I am merely suggesting that we may form or sustain important ideas through our reading of literature – and that equivalent orientational support will sometimes be difficult or impossible to procure by other means.

Perhaps someone would like to inquire how the tenability of the perspectives on life induced by literature is to be assayed. My spontaneous answer would be that their crucial point is the evaluative element, and that the soundness of an evaluation cannot be proved. What we can do with evaluations is to let them help govern our lives. Like many other things, literature may affect our view of various aspects of existence, and also our way of life, for good or bad. The value of the perspectives in question will show itself in the value of the acts they inspire.

The Larger Picture

The most important feature of the chapter which I am now concluding has been the description of a cognitive-affective processing pattern which, in my opinion, plays an important part in reading, including literary reading. I see this pattern as a basic structure underlying many different types of reading of literature. I do not deny, however, that there are also other patterns involved when literature is read and experienced. More than one road leads from the reader's encounter with the literary text to the content of her reading experience.

I find it impossible, though, to conceive of the text largely as a stimulus automatically releasing a given response in the reader because of the makeup of the human mind. "It is unlikely," says the cognitive psychologist George Mandler, "that the particular configurations used by Beethoven, Rembrandt, or Rodin have innate releasing qualities. Much as some philosophers of aesthetics have argued for an immediate appreciation of the beautiful in music and art, it is unlikely from a biological or psychological point of view that such preformed structures do in fact exist in the human organism."[34] A stimulus-response model appears even less plausible in the case of literature, where the reader's sense impressions are so relatively meagre (the visual impression of the book page, the auditory impression of the orally performed text). It is certainly conceivable that some of the sensuously perceptible patterns release more or less automatic aesthetically relevant responses in the reader or listener. Nevertheless, the speech or writing undoubtedly functions for her in the first place as signs to be interpreted. In a normally unconscious process, she decodes them: by the aid of the physical signs she reconstructs a textual content, a complex literary representation.

At this point, however, a new opening for the stimulus-response thinking about literary experience paradoxically presents itself. The very activity of interpreting may be seen as a stimulus with the capacity for releasing certain responses. Many hold that the normal, successful use of our physical and mental resources in itself affords a kind of pleasure, so-called functional pleasure.[35] If this is true, successful reading should in itself be pleasurable to a certain degree. According to another relatively well known psychological idea, being confronted with material moderately compatible with our prior expectations gives rise to positive feelings (while we are bored by material wholly conforming to our expectations, and the totally unfamiliar elicits negative feelings). That idea, too, may of course be turned to account in attempts to explain positive reading experiences.[36]

I have said, further, that the reader reconstructs a textual content, a complex literary representation. It is possible to apply the stimulus-response model at that processing stage as well. One may conceive that certain elements of the representation release automatic responses: that perceiving them is, so to speak, automatically frightening, automatically sexually arousing, or the like.[37] (Think of the sexual episodes in "The Freedom of Light" and "Pygmalion.") It is a more common idea, however, that the subtler parts of literary experience arise through an *interaction* between reader and communicated representation. The reader somehow reflects on the content of the complex representation – on the woman's problems in "The Freedom of Light," or on the character of the man in "Pygmalion."

In referring to a special cognitive-affective processing pattern, I myself make use of a variant of such an idea. It occurs in many other shapes as well, however, sometimes tending towards a stimulus-response model, sometimes not. In psychoanalytical studies of art and literature the viewer or reader has often been thought to take over, wholly or in part, the artistic representation as her own fantasy, a fantasy satisfying her wishes or desires to some extent.[38] Or the literary representation may be imagined to provoke in the reader fantasies related to her own situation.[39] Within analytical aesthetics one finds the idea that the viewer or reader is using the fictional material to play a game of make-believe with various psychological effects, and also the assumption that certain cinematic or literary representations may afford positive experiences by arousing and appeasing curiosity.[40] There is also a theory of poetry, inspired by cognitive psychology, which says that poems obstruct cognitive processing in various ways, pleasurably making their readers implicitly aware of normally automatic mental processes.[41]

The cognitive-affective processing pattern foregrounded in this chapter is in my view more significant than the other postulated mechanisms. Nevertheless, I do not deny that most of the other mechanisms just described may also be in operation in the reading of literature. As already indicated, I have doubts about some of them, or about some elements in some of them.[42] By and large, however, I would be prepared to insert references to these other mechanisms into a more detailed discussion of what may be supposed to happen in the reading of literature.

Concerning literature's role in our lives I have pointed, correspondingly, to a function of literature that is in my opinion prominent in our reading practice. Literature incites us to bring to consciousness or create views of life, both more partial and more global. These views also have an affective, and hence evaluative, aspect. Reading and processing literature often, thus, becomes among other things a matter of implicitly imagining and assessing (elements of) ways of life. In describing this function I have taken cognitive, emotional, and formal aspects of our reactions to literature into account and suggested how they are functionally interrelated.[43]

Let me emphasize once again that the analysis just summarized is not normative but descriptive. It represents an attempt to describe the practice of reading literature, such as we know it from our own nineteenth- and twentieth-century Western culture. Nor, of course, is the analysis meant to be exhaustive. There is, within the practice, extensive variation not accounted for here. I pointed out earlier that the literature of different periods affords partly different types of literary value, and that the same goes for different literary genres within one and the same period. Moreover, the existing practice of reading literature is hardly precise and determinate. It is not certain that even *purely* cognitive, *purely* affective, or *purely* form-oriented reading can really be said to be beyond the scope of the accepted.

I have, further, merely discussed what might be called the primary functions of literature. However we perceive these, there are also many functions of a more secondary character to account for. For one thing, the existence and character of literature makes it possible to turn to literature for a moment's escape from reality. It also renders literary connoisseurship possible, with its attendant satisfactions, as well as the historical study of literature and reflections on bygone days starting from their literary monuments. In addition, literature exists within an economic and organizational framework of which it, in part, also constitutes the basis: printing houses, publishing firms, criticism, literary reviews and journals, libraries, bookshops, and so forth. Like another secondary formation, the academic study of literature, these all possess their own character and their own missions and functions.

In the motley picture of literature's effects and functions, I have accentuated two special configurations: on one hand the cognitive-affective processing pattern, and on the other literature's role for our orientation in life. Not rejecting or suppressing the complexity of the picture, I nevertheless find it natural to draw special attention to precisely these two patterns as being of central importance for an overall understanding of the art of literature and the practice of reading it.

3 Presentational Communication

Introduction

In the preceding chapters, I have outlined an explanation of how the fantasies created and communicated by the author may come to play a cognitive and emotional role for a reader. I have, however, still not made clear just how linguistic communication is possible, exactly how the reader connects with the author's mental creations. Describing those mechanisms is the main task of both this chapter and the next one.

What literary meaning is, how it is conveyed, and how it is understood is a big question with many ramifications. Yet a sound basic answer to this complex question is the key to understanding the conditions of literary experience and acquiring a fundamental comprehension of literary aesthetics. I shall offer, here, a reasoned though somewhat compressed account of my own view of literary meaning and literary communication.[1]

Conveying and Understanding Meaning: A Basic Example

In the section "On the Transportation and Container Metaphors" in my introductory chapter, I introduced the folk theory of language and its functioning implicit in our idiomatic way of speaking of linguistic communication. As the reader will remember, the folk theory is founded on the idea that thoughts are literally transported from originator to addressee ("the conduit metaphor" or, in my terms, "the transportation metaphor"). According to Michael Reddy, the first to describe this folk theory, it palpably influences our thinking about linguistic communication.[2]

On introducing the transportation metaphor, I stressed the essential absurdity of its picture of linguistic communication. An intentional state – a fantasy, say – cannot literally be transported from the author's mind to the reader's. Now is the time, however, for a strong warning against drawing the wrong conclusions from that fact: it does *not* imply that the author's intentional state cannot in *some* sense be conveyed to the addressee. The author may construct a sequence of linguistic signs allowing a very similar fantasy ("the same fantasy" in a loose sense) to manifest itself in a person capable of interpreting the signs according to the rules of the practice.

Assuredly, language and its conventions play a central part in this. A more thorough understanding of the processes of conveying and comprehending linguistic meaning presupposes, however, the taking into consideration of communicative mechanisms more fundamental than language.

We humans are able to draw conclusions from our impressions of the world around us. Among other things, we may draw conclusions about our fellow-beings from their appearance and behaviour. We realize that a person seen smiling spontaneously is feeling joy or satisfaction, and that a person seen wrinkling his forehead spontaneously is tense, worried, or dissatisfied. We also know that other people possess the same power of deduction, and that accordingly they may gain knowledge of us from our own appearance or behaviour.

For this reason – and since in addition we have the faculty for controlling, fairly extensively, our own appearance and behaviour – it is possible for us to convey, intentionally, an understanding of our inner states to other humans. If I want to make clear to you that I am glad to see you I may greet you with a warm smile on meeting you.[3] You are likely to conclude, from my smile, that I am pleased to meet you, since my smile strongly indicates this. I myself have, intentionally, supplied you with that piece of evidence.[4]

In this example, I find myself in the intentional state of *being glad to see you*,[5] and also in the more complex intentional state of *intending to make it natural for you to conclude that I am glad to see you*. Actually, the latter state is even more complex. There are many ways of making it natural for you to conclude that I enjoy seeing you, and in this case I intend to do so by communicating it to you.[6] I might have applied the radically different method of letting my pleasure be revealed seemingly unintentionally (meeting you with assumed indifference but, seemingly unintentionally, planting circumstantial evidence – a seemingly involuntary glance, a seemingly involuntary movement, and so on – calculated to make you presume that I am glad to see you). In the case in question, however, I want to use a transparent way, as it were, of making clear to you that I enjoy seeing you. In the example I might thus be said to be in the intentional state of *intending to make it natural for you to conclude that I intend to make it natural for you to conclude that ... I am glad to see you.*[7]

The intention of indicating to another person, with deliberate transparency, that one is in a certain intentional state, I shall call a "communicative intention." An act performed in order to carry out a communicative intention – in the example, the act of smiling warmly – I call a "communicative act." That which is intended to be revealed I shall call the "intended meaning" of the communicative act. In the example, the intended meaning of my smile is not easily defined. Its cardinal point is of course that I enjoy seeing you. But large parts of the rest of my complex communicative intention also form part of the content intentionally conveyed by my smiling warmly at you.[8]

How is it possible for me to realize my communicative intention? I have to give a sign, thereby providing you with an indication enabling you to infer my intended meaning. To be successful, I must have a good idea about the nature of your prior knowledge and experience. In the example, the situation is fairly simple. I am aware of its being common knowledge that smiles go together with satisfaction and friendliness. I also know that people have an excellent capacity for distinguishing between intentional and involuntary smiles (and, of course, between genuine and insincere smiles). Hence it should be natural for you as the addressee to believe that a genuinely warm, deliberate smile from me would be intended to communicate my satisfaction at the encounter and my friendliness towards you. So I smile, pinning my faith on your ability to draw the right conclusions.

For your part, you must know a good deal about me, and about my assumptions about yourself, to be able to interpret my smile – though the knowledge required may be of a very simple kind. It is necessary for you to know, for example, that smiles are connected with satisfaction. What else could give you a reason for believing that I counted on your using that knowledge in interpreting my smile?

The last few paragraphs demonstrate how interpersonal communication is based on the phenomenon sometimes called "mutual knowledge."[9]

In the example, you and I mutually know that smiles are connected with satisfaction. Calling this knowledge "mutual" does not merely imply that we both possess it, I knowing that smiles are connected with satisfaction and you knowing that smiles are connected with satisfaction. What is required for making this knowledge mutual is also our *both knowing that we share it*: I know that you know that smiles are connected with satisfaction, you know that I know that you know that smiles are connected with satisfaction, and so on.

In conveying an intended meaning to another person, one is building – just as in our example – on what one supposes to be mutual knowledge shared by oneself and one's addressee. One has to supply one's addressee with indications enabling him to infer what one wishes to convey. To frame a successful indication, one must have some knowledge of the addressee's beliefs. Conversely, one's addressee has to make conjectures about one's beliefs about him in order to be able to understand the indication correctly.

The reader has every reason for maintaining that my analysis of what happens in the production and comprehending of a communicative smile is excessively rationalistic. I have deliberately made the description so for pedagogical reasons and am well aware of its deficiencies. To give a correct impression of my standpoint, several reservations or qualifications must now be added.

I have no intention of suggesting that originators or addressees usually perform detailed, conscious calculations while communicating. The processes of planning and interpretation involved are certainly unconscious for the most part, and their inner structure probably differs considerably from that of logical reasoning. So my actual presupposition is, rather, that human communication depends on rational but mainly unconscious processes of forming, expressing, and reconstructing communicative intentions, processes *functionally* equivalent to those described above.

Nor do I believe that communicative intentions necessarily exist in complete form before the execution of the communicative act. On the contrary, the normal case is probably that the intention acquires its final shape while the act is being performed.

Further, I do not presuppose that it is possible to determine the originator's communicative intention exactly. It is not likely that I myself or someone else would be able to produce both a credible and highly precise description of the intended meaning of my warm smile. An approximate identification of the intention is no doubt often the best that can be achieved.[10]

I would also like to emphasize that my picture of human communication does not presuppose sincerity in the originator. I may, of course, say "How nice to see you" without meaning it, but my analysis of communication works for such examples as well. The insincere utterance would be conceived as indicating – just like the sincere smile – my being in the intentional state of *intending to make it natural for you to conclude that I intend to make it natural for you to conclude that ... I am glad to see you.*[11] Obviously, it would not follow logically from my performing a communicative act of that description that I was in fact glad to see you.

In my opinion, the simple example of the warm smile exhibits a pattern that is always present where meaning is conveyed between people and understood. The creator of meaning has a communicative intention and endeavours to follow it out by performing a communicative act. The act is calculated to supply indications sufficient to allow the addressee to identify the intended meaning.

The addressee also plays, in principle, a fairly clearly circumscribed role. If she engages in communication with the originator, she is expected to do two things. On the one hand she should endeavour to interpret the indication given by the originator, attempting to identify his intended meaning. On the other she is expected to process the communicative content conveyed. When I am smiling warmly at you, you would be acting strangely if you did not try to make out the meaning of my smile. (You could probably not avoid interpreting it even if you wished to do so.)[12] And it would be just as unnatural for your reaction to be restricted to the inner observation that I wished to demonstrate my pleasure in seeing you. The situation demands something more of you. Above all, you must decide about the invitation implicit in my smile by somehow accepting or rejecting it. In brief: *understanding* and *processing* of the content conveyed are always expected of the addressee.

Confrontation with these two tasks is implied in the very role of the addressee, hence also in the role of the reader of a story like Updike's "Pygmalion." There, the reader is expected to identify the fantasy Updike attempts to convey to her, and at the same time to forge a literary experience from her encounter with the fantasy. That is to say, she is expected to understand the communicated content and to process it, take up a stand towards it, in a special way.

Conveying and Understanding Meaning:
Some Complications

Many would say that the example of the warm smile has little relevance for an analysis of the conveyance of literary meaning. Simple mimic communication is one thing and linguistic, especially literary, discourse something entirely different, they would assert, and go on to maintain that the originator's intentions cannot be assumed to play any prominent role in literary contexts. I shall explain briefly why I take this kind of objection relatively lightly.

Each new communicative act yields new mutual knowledge once its meaning has been understood.

It is possible to perform innovative communicative acts, acts that do not entirely conform to established practices.[13] Let us imagine that you perform an innovative communicative act A, meaning m. As soon as the act is performed and has been understood by the addressee, it becomes mutual knowledge for both you and your addressee that a communicative act like A may be used to convey an intended meaning like m. If the addressee on some later occasion would like to convey to you a meaning similar to m, she would know that a communicative act similar to A would be a promising means. Thus your innovative communicative act, being understood, has given rise to new mutual knowledge at least within a minimal group. (In saying that there are semantic conventions, that signs have conventional meaning, we are referring, in the final analysis, to precisely such associations between types of communcative acts and types of intended meanings.) Thanks to the mechanism just presented – first described by P.F. Strawson[14] – the fund of more or less mutual knowledge about the use of signs, the fund of experiences and expectations available for devising and deciphering new communicative acts, has every chance of growing continuously.

There was a beginning to this process. Once language did not exist; there were no semantic conventions. They originated from human communication, and human communication was possible because individuals had mutual knowledge of each other's powers of observation and deduction. The first human communication was presumably just as simple in structure as my warm smile in the example in the last section. [15] It is true that communication is much less complex in the case of the smile than in the case of Updike's "Pygmalion." It would, however, be possible to provide a coherent and at least plausible account of the stages of the development successively enlarging our communicative repertory from comprising solely simple gestic or mimic communication to including verbal communication and, eventually, written communication in different genres, literature among others.[16] Step by step, the account would introduce new communicative complications, but at no point would it force us to revise the picture of the fundamental pattern of human communication described at the end of the last section.

The fact that language utilizes sound as a medium does not cause material problems for an intention-based account of the history of linguistic communication: sounds, calls, and cries can be made to convey communicative intentions just as easily as gestures or facial expressions. It is conceivable that a repertoire of conventionalized, communicative sounds gradually comes into existence in a group. Since it will be important to be able to keep different sound-signs apart, a conventional method of achieving this will have to be found. An efficient way, employed in human language, is to let a convention come into existence which defines the types of sounds (the phonemes) permissible, and then treat sound-signs as being different as soon as they do not consist of exactly the same sequence of sounds.

At the next stage of this development, combinations of sound-signs emerge. Two sound-signs, each carrying its own integral communicative meaning, are given in succession and made to convey, together, a more complex meaning. (It must be remembered, here, that semantic conventions are rules of thumb, not laws of nature: it is often possible to stretch or infringe them while still making oneself understood.) When such combinations of signs become conventionalized carriers of meaning, we have, in principle, reached language: we now find full-blown sentences (sequences of sound-signs) consisting of strings of phonemes (strings of sounds of defined types) constituting words (sound-signs). And there is, then, nothing radically puzzling about the possibility of rendering spoken language in writing by means of durable, physical inscriptions.

In the next two sections, I shall revert to the question of how literature may be fitted into this picture. Before that, however, I should like to say a few words about the originator's communicative intentions and about the principles of interpretation.

Few would wish to deny that human communication does in fact exhibit an intention-based pattern in simple examples like that of the smile. Many, however, maintain that this pattern fades along the road from non-verbal communication to written language, disappearing completely by the time we get to written literature.[17] Instead they see linguistic conventions, or reader creativity, as the factor which determines literary meaning. These views will be discussed in the next chapter; there is, however, one observation which I should like to make immediately.

The originator's communicative intentions play a significant role in my analysis of the conveyance and comprehension of meaning. The reader should note, though, that I in no way equate the interpretation of literature with the identification of the author's communicative intentions. It is my contention that the reader's elementary understanding of the text – what is usually called her "verbal understanding", or something similar – arises from her endeavour to identify the originator's communicative intentions. In the "Pygmalion" case, Updike obviously wishes to communicate a fantasy about certain occurrences in a man's life and, at the same time, to throw a certain ironic light on these events. In my opinion, it is through attempting to reconstruct

Updike's communicative intentions that the reader arrives at an understanding of what is happening in the fictional world and of the attitude towards the events implicitly adopted by the narrator. That, however, is only a partial description of my standpoint. For I also claim that the reader, like every addressee, is expected in addition to react to the reconstructed meaning, and that this reacting constitutes an essential part of her processing of the text.

The sort of reaction to the reconstructed meaning expected from the linguistic addressee varies depending on the type of verbal message. I shall illustrate this in the next section, and then go on to specify what the expected reaction consists in in the case of literature.

Informational and Directive Discourse

We now leave the subject of non-verbal communication. From now on, I shall almost exclusively treat of written, and published, linguistic compositions. This, however, will not lead to any fundamental change of perspective. As I have already indicated, I perceive written compositions as conforming to the same basic communicative pattern as non-verbal human communication. The written composition, too, has been designed to function as an indication of a communicative intention in its originator, an intention for the addressee to identify and react to.

Let us look at a simple written composition, a short notice from a newspaper (1990).

ELECTION CHOICE
JOHN SYKES, 33, a company director from Huddersfield, has been selected as the Conservative candidate for the safe seat of Scarborough and Whitby at the next election. Sykes, who unsuccessfully fought Sheffield Hillsborough in 1987, succeeds Sir Michael Shaw, who had a majority of 13,929 at the general election.[18]

In several ways, this example is more complicated than the smile. Language and its conventions are involved in the case of the newspaper notice. Moreover, there is neither an individual originator nor an individual addressee; and so on. I shall leave these complications aside,[19] noting instead that what I call the basic communicative pattern can be observed here too. The physical notice, the pattern of printer's ink on white paper, is meant to function as an indication making it possible for the addressee to infer a communicative intention and an intended meaning. The core of the intended meaning is the complex intentional state being conveyed to the addressee: *the conviction that the 33-year-old company director John Sykes has been selected as the*

Conservative candidate for the seat of Scarborough and Whitby (etc.).[20] The addressee is expected to reconstruct the intended meaning and to react to it.

Communicating with our fellow-beings, revealing (or pretending to reveal) some of our intentional states to them, is not an end in itself. When I endeavour to make clear to you, by smiling, that I am glad to see you, this is one element of a more comprehensive plan involving you. It is a way of greeting you, and perhaps an invitation to a talk. And when the *Sunday Times* publicly discloses its conviction that John Sykes has been selected as the Conservative candidate for the seat of Scarborough and Whitby, the newspaper does this with a view to us, its readers. The *Sunday Times* makes its conviction public in order to impart this political news to us.

To understand a communicative act, the addressee has to form a partial opinion about what the originator aims at attaining through the act. When we unequivocally apprehend the text "Election choice" as conveying a conviction, this is because we presume, depending on the context of publication, that the originator wishes to inform us by introducing it. If we had met the same text in a collection of poems, we would have ascribed other intentions to the originator, and consequently felt less certain about whether the content conveyed was to be understood as a conviction or as a fantasy. This example illustrates that an originator who wishes to be understood also has to make manifest a *purpose* in conveying the intentional state. She must make clear the spirit in which she intends the content to be taken. She has to communicate to the addressee the purpose for which she is conveying the intentional state in question.

This being so, the intended meaning of an utterance or a text is obviously more complex than earlier indicated. It does not solely comprise an intentional state. It is composed of an intentional state plus what I call a "communicated purpose": a communicated indication of the purpose of conveying this intentional state.[21] The intended meaning of the newspaper notice could be described as being, approximately, the originator's *intention to communicate – simultaneously communicating the hope that the addressee will believe her and thus acquire the same belief himself – the conviction that John Sykes, a 33-year-old company director from Huddersfield, has been selected as the Conservative candidate for the seat of Scarborough and Whitby (etc.).* In this case – given the mutual knowledge that can be counted on – the wording of the text and its publication in a newspaper constitute a sufficiently clear indication of the communicated purpose, of how the text is intended to be taken.

Each individual communicative act has its own, unique communicated purpose. But one may well speak of communicated purposes as belonging to different types, or, as I shall normally do, as instantiating different "pragmatic modes." In my context, it is useful to distinguish between three pragmatic modes: the informational, the directive, and the presentational. The fundamental division is into informational and directive communicated purposes, informational and directive pragmatic modes. I regard the presentational as a more derivative pragmatic mode (among many others).[22]

Where the communicated purpose is informational – as with the newspaper notice – the originator communicates a conviction of some kind, indicating that she does so in order to make the addressee share this conviction. Where the communicated purpose is directive, the originator communicates a desire of some kind, indicating that she does so in order to make the addressee comply with her wish.

An example of a directive written composition is the recruitment advertisement for the British Army reproduced here (figure 3). The advertisement illustrates, at the same time, that the concrete communicated purpose may well exhibit both informational and directive tendencies. Behind this advertisement one can discern both a wish to inform the addressee of certain circumstances and a wish to give rise to certain actions on the part of the addressee. In this case, the directive purpose probably dominates. The advertisement stands out, above all, as the offering of an opportunity to obtain more information about the career of a British Army officer by posting the attached coupon. The factual information, though quantitatively dominant, has in reality a subordinate function. It is there to show that we have good reasons for contemplating an army officer's training and thus for obtaining more information about it.

Elements of Presentational Discourse

When Axelsson produces "The Freedom of Light," and when Updike produces "Pygmalion," they are not conveying convictions that we are expected to share or wishes that we are expected to fulfil. They are conveying, instead, complex fantasies meant to be experienced as literature, and we now face the question of how the communicated purpose should be characterized in cases like these.

In fact, I have already answered that question by describing, in the last chapter, what the reader of literature does, and is expected to do, in reading. I shall, however, recapitulate that description, adapting it to the special context of this chapter by transforming it into a description of a special type of linguistic communication.

I mentioned, at an earlier stage, Nicholas Wolterstorff's account of what the writer of fiction, the "fictioneer," is occupied with, an account with

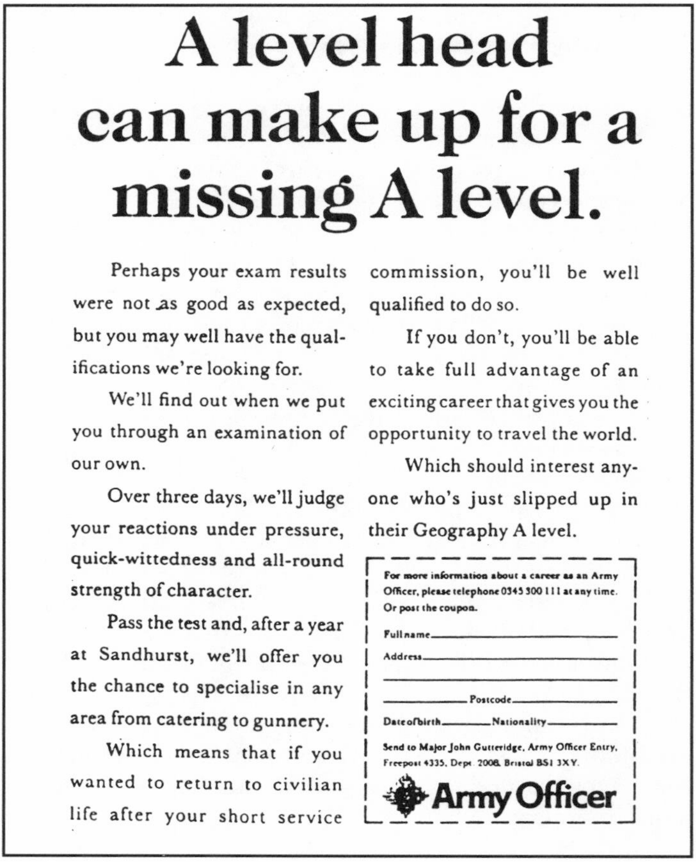

A level head can make up for a missing A level.

Perhaps your exam results were not as good as expected, but you may well have the qualifications we're looking for.

We'll find out when we put you through an examination of our own.

Over three days, we'll judge your reactions under pressure, quick-wittedness and all-round strength of character.

Pass the test and, after a year at Sandhurst, we'll offer you the chance to specialise in any area from catering to gunnery.

Which means that if you wanted to return to civilian life after your short service commission, you'll be well qualified to do so.

If you don't, you'll be able to take full advantage of an exciting career that gives you the opportunity to travel the world.

Which should interest anyone who's just slipped up in their Geography A level.

For more information about a career as an Army Officer, please telephone 0345 300 111 at any time. Or post the coupon.

Full name_____

Address_____

_____Postcode_____

Date of birth_____ Nationality_____

Send to Major John Gutteridge, Army Officer Entry, Freepost 4335, Dept 2008, Bristol BS1 3XY.

Army Officer

Figure 3
Recruitment advertisement for the British Army
(*Guardian*, 18 August 1990)

which I largely concur. Wolterstorff says that "the stance characteristic of the fictioneer is that of *presenting*. The fictive stance consists of *presenting*, of *offering for consideration*, certain states of affairs – for us to reflect on, to ponder over, to explore the implications of, to conduct strandwise extrapolation on. And he does this for our edification, for our delight, for our illumination, for our cathartic cleansing, and more besides. It's as if every work of fiction were prefaced with the words 'I hereby present that ...' or 'I hereby invite you to consider that ... '"[23]

Thus, according to Wolterstorff, when Updike publishes "Pygmalion" he conveys certain states of affairs – let us say the conditions in the world of the story – to his readers. I should like to say, instead, that Updike conveys a fantasy whose core content is made up of the conditions in the world of the story.[24] What is really important here, however, is that the communicative content of a work of fiction is, as it were, meant to afford satisfaction to a reader in and by itself. The reader is supposed to reflect on the communicative content, which is presumed to prove cognitively, sensually, or emotionally rewarding. In my opinion, this constitutes in reality the composition's communicated purpose. Acknowledging Wolterstorff, I call a communicated purpose of this kind "presentational."

The author of a presentational composition conveys an intentional state – most typically a fantasy, as in the case of Updike's "Pygmalion." The content of a fantasy does not agree with empirical reality, and in that sense a fantasy is unreal. On the other hand, encountering a fantasy, having a fantasy presented to one, is an altogether real experience, and it is important to bear this in mind.

The unceasing interpretation of impressions from the outer world, and the evaluation of their relevance to ourselves, is an absolute necessity for us humans. It requires no specific decisions and no conscious thought: "Appraisal of an event's significance is neither deliberate nor a conscious process." A reader encountering a literary fantasy thus inevitably reacts, and just as inescapably she evaluates its relevance to herself in one way or another.

The reader enters into the content of the fantasy, conscious of the fact that the conveyance to her of the fantasy forms part of a communicative intention. She reacts to the communicative content, and to the act of conveying it, her reaction involving an appraisal of the encounter's significance for herself.[25] So much can be gathered already from considering the conditions of communicating and general truths about human nature. Just how the reader's evaluation comes about and what it consists in is a more speculative question.

In chapter 2 I suggested that the genuine encounter with a literary work initiates processes of many kinds in the reader. I also pointed to a type of process which I find especially important in this connection. The encounter with the work brings to consciousness, or gives rise to, beliefs in the reader. The encounter with Updike's "Pygmalion" should, for example, tend to bring to consciousness or give rise to beliefs of many different sorts, most significantly perhaps to beliefs about love, art, our attempts to control our own existence, and so forth. The encounter, then, brings to consciousness or gives rise to pictures of reality, to evaluative beliefs about the world's character. Such pictures of reality possess direct relevance for ourselves (and thus an emotional dimension): they imply images of the world's demands on us, and of the opportunities and restrictions conditioning our lives. I have assumed, further, that the pictures of reality intimated to us by literary works typically represent a reality accommodating enough to be at least bearable. I have not, however, attempted an overall picture of what one can do when reading literature within the framework of literary practice. In addition, my picture of presentationality, of presentational discourse and its underlying communicated purpose, is a sketch rather than a detailed drawing. (The same could be said of my description of informational and directive discourse.)

This description of how presentational discourse works is to be understood as being at the same time, essentially, a description of the fundamental mechanisms of literary communication. I do not, like Wolterstorff, wish to associate presentational discourse exclusively with fictionality. In my opinion one can, if certain explicit reservations are introduced, approximately equate "presentational" with "literary."[26] The reservations in question are important ones, however. Only if one is thinking, roughly, of the literature of the last two centuries – the time in which our present concept of literature has existed – is it possible to see all literature as presentational.[27] One has to confine oneself, further, to literature belonging to the most central literary genres – to novels, short stories, poems, plays, and the like. There are a number of other, clearly non-presentational genres – for example, speeches, prayers, and travel books – often considered literary, although more peripherally so than the epic, lyric, and dramatic genres.[28] Some other, minor reservations could also be introduced. However, I shall not, here, enter into the detailed relations between presentationality and literariness.[29] (The literary works discussed in this book are all presentational.)

Informational, directive, and presentational communication could be said to constitute three different language games. To put it simply, informational communication amounts to the conveyance to the addressee of the fact that one has a certain conviction, the implicit expectation being that the addressee will take over this conviction (which will benefit her directly or indirectly). Directive communication amounts to the conveyance to the addressee of the fact that one has a certain wish, the implicit expectation being that the addressee will fulfil this wish (which will benefit her directly or indirectly). Presentational communication amounts to the conveyance to the addressee of the fact that one finds oneself in a certain intentional state – in the most typical case, that one has a certain fantasy. The implicit expectation is that contact with the communicated content will prove rewarding for the addressee; for example, make her create or bring up gratifying ideas about reality.

Communicating a factual belief is accordingly never the main point of a presentational composition (but always of an informational one). What the presentational composition is conveying functions, among other things, as *a basis for the reader's creation or bringing to consciousness* of beliefs about reality. Unlike informational or directive compositions, presentational discourse is thus *indirect* in an irreducible fashion. The notice about the Conservative candidate *communicated* precisely that conviction which the reader was expected to take over, and the army recruitment advertisement *communicated* precisely that wish which the reader was expected to fulfil (the wish that the reader, if interested, should request more information about an army officer's training). What is *communicated* by Updike's "Pygmalion," however, is a fantasy for the reader to process; she must, herself, discover its possible relevance to her picture of reality and consequently to herself.

It is true that informational or directive compositions also often function as bases for readers' associations and processing, i.e., for the creation or bringing to consciousness of beliefs by indirect means. The notice about the Conservative candidate has perhaps made some young Tory with political ambitions modify her picture of a party career, thereby slightly changing her assessment of her own future prospects. And the formulations in the recruitment advertisement about "an exciting career that gives you the opportunity to travel the world" may have made imaginative readers create concrete close-ups of possible situations in their own futures, pictures on the dividing-line between anticipations and daydreams. The eliciting of associative processing is, however, not a central element of the communicated purpose of an informational or directive composition. Only presentational compositions have this as their (implicit) main purpose.

There is an element of idealization in the description of the three language games just given. As suggested earlier, one and the same verbal composition may well exhibit informational, directive, and presentational tendencies simultaneously (while being normally, nevertheless, clearly dominated by one of these pragmatic modes). In my context, it would, however, seem unwarranted to enter more deeply into that problem, adducing borderline cases and discussing their modal status.

I shall, instead, now leave the presentation of the three pragmatic modes. As indicated above, I approximately equate presentationality with literariness-in-the-modern-sense. Thus I have already accounted for my view of the differentia specifica of the literary work, for its uniqueness as a linguistic phenomenon.

Fictional Utterances

In speaking of literary communication, I have applied and developed a pragmatic philosophy of language of the Gricean kind. Grice's thinking has successively become quite influential within analytical literary aesthetics. Mostly, however, it is being utilized differently; it has been exploited particularly in explaining the nature of fictional discourse.

I am thinking, here, above all of Gregory Currie's analysis of fictionality, particularly as it was presented in his *The Nature of Fiction* (1990).[30] Currie starts from ideas of communication, communicative intentions, and communicative acts inspired by Grice. Based on these ideas, he defines fictional communication and fictional utterances.[31] Currie describes the central element of the author's stance in connection with a fictional communicative act as follows: "The author intends that we make-believe the text (or rather its constituent propositions) and he intends to get us to do this by means of our recognition of that very intention" (30).[32]

According to Currie's analysis, then, what turns "The Freedom of Light" and "Pygmalion" into fictional texts is Axelsson's and Updike's communicative intention that we readers make-believe the text's constituent propositions. Substantially the same analysis of fictionality is put forward in Peter Lamarque and Stein Haugom Olsen's *Truth, Fiction, and Literature* (1994).[33] This analysis must in fact be said to represent the currently prevailing view of fictionality within analytical aesthetics.

There are two things I wish to make clear with regard to this particular analysis of fictional utterances. First, I would like to emphasize that fictionality and presentationality are different matters. For that reason, an analysis of fictionality is not necessarily in competition with my analysis of presentationality, or vice versa. Second, I want to demonstrate that my view of fictionality nevertheless differs from that of Currie, Lamarque, and Olsen.

"The Freedom of Light" and "Pygmalion" are fictional compositions[34] and at the same time presentational compositions. There is a sense in which *all* fictional compositions are presentational: they convey representations (fantasies, in this case) meant to arouse more or less determinate associations in the addressee and to benefit her in this indirect fashion.

The converse, however, does not hold true. There are non-fictional presentational compositions. Many poems faithfully describe existing realities. Their content is not, in any relevant sense, invented. They are not communicated for the sake of informing, however – they would not have been poems in that case – but (implicitly) for eliciting associations, for constituting a cognitive-emotional incitement. (Robert Lowell's "Father's Bedroom," dealt with in the next section, is to all appearances one such poem.) Seen from this angle, fictional compositions form a subdivision of the presentational.

From a linguistic and communicative point of view, moreover, fictionality is clearly a less fundamental phenomenon than presentationality. The latter is connected with the communicated purpose, with the very point of the communicative act. Fictionality is rather a type of possible means for the originator who wishes to communicate a content with a presentational point. In effect, fictional compositions fulfil a presentational purpose, only using different means from non-fictional presentational texts. The fictional text ("The Freedom of Light," "Pygmalion") serves its presentational purpose by conveying fictions, representations with an invented content. The non-fictional presentational text ("Father's Bedroom") copes with the same type of task by conveying representations corresponding to actual reality.

This account should be provided with a qualification, though: fictionality may be transformed into a kind of indirect informationality or directivity. My favourite example of this is my own first textbook in philosophy, the German-Swedish philosopher Konrad Marc-Wogau's *Philosophical Discussions* (*Filosofiska diskussioner*, 1955), a rendition of a series of philosophy lessons in the Swedish upper secondary school. These take the form of discussions between a group of pupils and their philosophy teacher about various fundamental philosophical questions. The book is a fictional composition: the persons and the utterances are all made up. Marc-Wogau's true purpose, however, is to familiarize the reader with a number of philosophical problems, with some of their proposed solutions, and with important arguments for and against the proposals. In these circumstances it is natural to say that Marc-Wogau has given presentationality an essentially informational turn. His presentational composition is first and foremost calculated to call forth in the addressee ideas about empirical facts: the idea that the questions referred to are important philosophical problems, that such-and-such solutions to these problems have been proposed, and so forth. Marc-Wogau has thereby created something which must – in spite of its indirect, fictional form – undoubtedly be classified as informational discourse.

Analogously, presentationality may be transformed into indirect directivity. On this point the best examples are moving pictures rather than texts: I am thinking of the use of fictional compositions in television advertising. The compositions in question are likely (or at least meant) to produce positive ideas about certain commercial products.

As a consequence the compositions function, at bottom, directively: as invitations to buy these articles.

Because of these complications, not all fictional compositions can, in the final analysis, be classified as presentational discourse.

Even so, fictionality and presentationality are closely related. I shall not enter into my own views of fictionality in this context.[35] As already indicated, however, I wish to explain why I do not subscribe to Currie's, Lamarque's, and Olsen's definitions. This is important for me, since the spirit of their influential description is incompatible with my own understanding of literary communication.

The principal point in Currie's analysis, previously mentioned, is the identification of an attitude that the author wants the reader to adopt. She is to "make-believe the text (or rather its constituent propositions)." Or, formulated in other words: "We are intended by the author to *make believe* that the story as uttered is true" (18).

Let us take "Pygmalion" as an example. According to Currie's analysis, we should not be perceiving what is said in "Pygmalion" as true, but still be *pretending* that it is so.

Currie never explicitly explains what pretending that a fictional story is true amounts to. Nor do Lamarque and Olsen; in this tradition, "make-believe" or "make believe" is in reality treated as a fundamental, unanalysed concept. It appears obvious, however, that Currie, Lamarque, and Olsen are thinking of a more specific attitude in the reader than the rather general one which I have described as the standpoint expected from the reader in connection with presentational discourse.

As I see the matter, the reader of "Pygmalion" identifies the fantasy communicated by Updike and the communicated purpose, while at the same time reacting to this reconstructed content. I suppose, among other things, that the reader comes into contact with the communicated fantasy. She makes herself a representation of its content, a representation involving Pygmalion's being married to Gwen, and so on.

(1) The reader imagines that Pygmalion is married to Gwen (etc.).

On this point, Currie, Lamarque, and Olsen regard the reader as doing something more. As demonstrated by the last quotation, Currie sees her as, at least, also imagining that it is *true* that Pygmalion is married to Gwen (etc.). Thus:

(2) The reader imagines that it is true that Pygmalion is married to Gwen (etc.).

The difference between (1) and (2) may appear minimal, but it is not. According to Currie, the reader must evidently imagine (despite knowing it to be untrue) that Pygmalion and Gwen really exist, and hence that they exist in the same world as she does. Unlike me, Currie thus conceives of the reader as moving, herself, in her fantasy, into the fictional world of the story, where it would, in principle, be possible for her to meet Pygmalion and Gwen face to face.[36] Or, perhaps, the reader is thought, with the same effects, to imagine Pygmalion and Gwen as actually existing, as part of our surrounding reality. Currie writes: "When we make believe the story we make believe that the text is an account of events that have actually occurred. ... Thus it is part of the make-believe that the reader is in contact, through channels of reliable information, with the characters and their actions, that the reader learns about their activities from a reliable source. To make-believe a fictional story is not merely to make-believe that the story is true, but that it is told as known fact" (73). Lamarque and Olsen offer essentially the same analysis.[37]

We have seen that presumptions (1) and (2) are associated with partly diverging pictures of the reading of fiction. I myself regard the reader of "Pygmalion" as being confronted with representations according to which Pygmalion is married to Gwen (etc.), representations communicated by Updike for presentational purposes. For the reader of "Pygmalion," these representations serve as sources of associations (in ways to be discussed later). All this takes place in the real world; there is no need for the reader to imagine that she finds herself in the fictional world, or that Pygmalion, Gwen, and the others form part of empirical reality. Currie, Lamarque, and Olsen would say, however, faced with the "Pygmalion" example, that the reader does not merely imagine Pygmalion, Gwen, and their relationship. She also imagines herself as occupying a place in the fictional world, listening to, or reading, statements about Pygmalion and Gwen, statements altogether true and genuine in that world. Or, perhaps, the reader imagines that Pygmalion and Gwen are not fictional creatures but real living Americans, and that she is just being told a true story about them. The difference between my analysis and that of the Walton-Currie tradition has a number of further consequences for the theoretical comprehension of literature, one of which will have to be commented on in a later chapter.[38]

Presumption (1) is the weaker one (in the technical, philosophical sense of "weak"). Currie, Lamarque, and Olsen certainly accept the truth of (1) just as I do, but they also make further assumptions. These are in fact assumptions about which elements constitute essential parts of the reading of fiction in accordance with the rules of literary practice, and as such I see them as untenable. For my own part, when I read "Pygmalion" or similar literature I do not imagine myself as being inside the fictional world, listening to a true story about Pygmalion and Gwen or similar characters. Nor do I imagine that the fictional characters actually exist, so that I might in principle encounter them in real life. Yet, I am no doubt a reasonably competent reader of fiction.[39] (Currie, Lamarque, and Olsen could of course maintain that I *unconsciously* imagine being in the same world as Pygmalion and Gwen. But what justification would there be for advancing such a hypothesis?)

Currie, Lamarque, and Olsen essentially employ Walton's analysis of fiction as involving games of make-believe. Walton's main argument in support of his theory is that it solves a number of important theoretical problems. In my view, that is not true – the assumption in (1) is sufficient to do the job – but this is not the place to present an overall evaluation of Walton's theory.[40]

Robert Lowell's "Father's Bedroom"

The picture of communication and understanding in and outside literature just provided also has consequences for the view of literary interpretation, literary meaning, and literary works. In the next chapter, I shall point out those further implications. I shall work my way step by step towards an answer to the question of the literary work's genus proximum: What kind of object, concretely, is the literary work or the literary text? First, however, I wish to summarize and concretize my view of communication and understanding. In that connection I shall have recourse to a short poem: Robert Lowell's "Father's Bedroom."

Robert Lowell's book *Life Studies* (1959) contains among other things a series of autobiographical poems. Three of these centre on Lowell's father's death: "Terminal Days at Beverly Farms," "Father's Bedroom," and "For Sale." "Father's Bedroom" reads, in extenso:

> In my Father's bedroom:
> blue threads as thin
> as pen-writing on the bedspread,
> blue dots on the curtains,
> a blue kimono,
> Chinese sandals with blue plush straps.
> The broad-planked floor
> had a sandpapered neatness.
> The clear glass bed-lamp
> with a white doily shade

was still raised a few
inches by resting on volume two
of Lafcadio Hearn's
Glimpses of unfamiliar Japan.
Its warped olive cover
was punished like a rhinoceros hide.
In the flyleaf:
"Robbie from Mother."
Years later in the same hand:
"This book has had hard usage
On the Yangtze River, China.
It was left under an open
porthole in a storm."[41]

The detailed description of the father's belongings – the kimono, the sandals, the bedside lamp, the book – draws the reader's attention to the father, making his absence, though unmentioned, very palpable. It is not explicitly said that the father is dead, but it is quite natural to understand the poem in this way when encountering it in its context in *Life Studies*; in addition, certain features of the text seem to support such a reading. For example, the formulation that the lamp is "still" raised on Hearn's book about Japan suggests that a change has occurred which has made the arrangement superfluous. Furthermore the poem has a nakedly descriptive character, and the short irregularly stressed lines make its rhythm slightly inhibited and abrupt in comparison with natural talk or more fluent lyric diction. I believe that the reader tends to sense both features, in this context, as symptoms of depression. It is as though they bore witness to an inner paralysis making it impossible to speak of other than outward and tangible matters, or to strong feelings restrained only with effort.[42]

The poem's first seven lines contain no verbs, so the scene remains, for a while, indeterminate with respect to tense and placing in time. First the locality is defined. The following five lines, then, strike the keynote of the poem in their extreme facticity: they consist in a simple enumeration of blue objects. The first of these, the blue threads on the bedspread, are said, however, to be "as thin as pen-writing." The reference to writing by hand (anticipating the writing on the flyleaf at the end of the poem) may evoke the impression that hidden personal messages are embodied in the objects.

As already indicated, the colour blue is made prominent in the opening lines: the word "blue" occurs four times. Thoughts of the colour's association with sadness come easily to mind, and we are no doubt justified in feeling that the blue strikes an emotional chord of that tone.[43] But the colour is probably also connected with the personality of the father, a former naval officer – one commentator speaks of the "naval blue-and-white" of the bedroom.[44] Perhaps the blue may even be associated, in a broader fashion, with Lowell's family and its life-style.[45]

In line 8 the poem is given a fixed tense, the past, thereby acquiring the character of a description of a recollected room. This happens in the poem's central part, following on the introductory lines and leading up to the picture of the volume beneath the lamp. At the end of the text, that volume and the writing on its flyleaf are the centre of attraction. Lowell's father was in fact presented with *Glimpses of Unfamiliar Japan* by his mother as a child, and perhaps that book contributed to his choice of a naval career, leading to his serving, during the First World War, as the commander of a gunboat on the Yangtze River.[46] Because of the book's intimate connection with the father, and the comparison of the book's exterior to wrinkled or furrowed skin, the idea of the book may tend to coalesce, for the reader, with the idea of the father, badly knocked about by life.

The complex representation conveyed to the reader of "Father's Bedroom" cannot be called a fantasy. It appears more natural for the reader of *Life Studies* to assume that the poem gives a substantially reliable, though carefully edited, description of the actual interior of Lowell's father's bedroom at Beverly Farms. Most likely, a complex *conviction* (about aspects of a bedroom interior) is being conveyed, not a complex *fantasy*. (As I underlined in the last section, literature is not necessarily fictional, at least not in the sense of its content's being invented.)

In this chapter I have been trying to explain how the communication of an intentional state to an addressee is arranged: one somehow makes it natural for the addressee to infer that one wishes to make it natural for her to infer that one finds oneself in precisely that state. Lowell communicates the complex conviction in question by initiating the production and publishing of sheets of paper patterned with printer's ink in accordance with his specifications. A literate addressee with a command of English will then inevitably interpret these patterns of printer's ink as representing complexes of characters which represent, in their turn, English words carrying a conventional meaning. Therefore she can – starting from her knowledge of English, of the world, and of the relevant context – reconstruct Lowell's communicative intention in broad outline, thus coming into contact with the complex conviction he intended to convey.

If one were to account for the entire content of Lowell's communicative intention, the whole intended meaning of "Father's Bedroom," it would be natural to indicate, first of all, what states of affairs actually obtain according to the complex, communicated conviction. It is obviously part of the poem's intended meaning, for example, that there was a bedspread with thin blue threads in Lowell's father's bedroom, that there were also blue-spotted curtains, and so on. But the world of the poem is not simply a collection of facts. It consists of facts seen in a certain light. In my brief comments on Lowell's text I indicated a number of features likely to arouse more or less specific associations modifying the impression of the poem. I mentioned, among other things, the attention to the father's belongings, the blue elements, the creased book volume, the simile "as thin as pen-writing," the use of the word "still," and the very rhythm of the poem. The associations elicited by such elements create a special cognitive and emotional point of view; they throw a special light on the bedroom interior, as it were.

Having described the poem's world and the implicit perspective on it, one has not, however, given an exhaustive account of the intended meaning. I have maintained that literary communication exhibits a special, presentational pattern. In connection with literature, the communicated content is not understood as information to be assimilated or as specifying a state which is to be made real. Instead, it is implicitly taken as the point of departure for a kind of associative processing. It is included in the poem's intended meaning that the communicated content is to be understood in this presentational spirit. A full description of the intended meaning could therefore begin: "Lowell presents that .... "; then the vacant space would be filled with a perspectival account of the poem's world.

Apart from the intended meaning, there is also the reader's application to consider. I have said that the reader inescapably reacts to the communicated content: she inevitably evaluates the relevance to herself of her encounter with the physical object and with the specific communicative intention to which the object testifies. On the basis of the communicated content, she creates or brings to consciousness a conviction, a picture of reality. The reader's reaction to the poem may certainly be more or less adequate, and not all associations contribute to the building up of an adequate reaction. But let us, for now, avoid entering into that complex of problems (which will be dealt with in chapter 6).

"Father's Bedroom" may be said to have death as its theme. (I do not contend that every other thematic characterization would be incorrect, just that it is at least reasonable to see death as the theme of the poem.) The poem provides a picture of what it is like when a father (or perhaps more generally anyone) dies. Or if we foreground, instead, the feelings of the poem's speaker, the poem provides a picture of a person's attitude towards his father's death (or towards death). If we accept the picture as possible, or perhaps even as representative in some sense, we automatically allow it to acquire implications for ourselves. For then we implicitly regard the picture as having something to say about the conditions – the risks and possibilities – of life, and hence also of our own lives.

The reactions of a reader can hardly be reproduced in words. Being confronted with exactly this poem is a unique experience. It arouses memories, convictions, hopes, and fears, all with emotional tones of their own. As emphasized earlier, such an experience eludes exact description. Furthermore, it goes without saying that the character of the experience must be supposed to vary appreciably from reader to reader. For those two reasons it is impossible to single out one specific reaction to the poem as being the "right" one. One may of course characterize one's own reaction, or attempt to describe a type of reaction one sees as exemplary from an aesthetic point of view. But as literary practice arguably leaves a great deal of latitude, it still appears unavoidable that quite different reactions to the poem may fall within what is de facto understood as the scope of the adequate. If I were to account for my personal, spontaneous reaction, I would say that I accept Lowell's partial picture of death, perhaps even letting it influence my own views. I feel that death is portrayed, through the low-key or depressive mood expressed, as an absence, hard to understand and weighing us down. The absence stands out as difficult to comprehend not least because of the palpable presence of the paraphernalia in the room. (It is, in addition, as though the absence had sharpened the senses, thus making the exquisite observations of the room's interior possible.) The picture of death emerging before me is not in itself of a positive character; nevertheless it has room for the alien and absurd in death without being out-and-out frightening. A description like this can, however, only give a limited idea of an experience – and moreover I would, as already indicated, be inclined to see many types of experiences of the poem as being adequate from the literary point of view.

My reactions as a reader certainly comprise other elements as well, and some of these are purely aesthetic, or at least seemingly so. I enjoy Lowell's control of his means of expression. I appreciate his skilful use of rhythm, his play with real and imaginary pen-writing and with contrasting colours, with time and timelessness. One reason for placing cognitive considerations in the forefront here, however, is that this poem depends on its representational content to a large extent, the representations moulding, so to speak, the basic frame making the aesthetic qualities possible. I shall have to reserve for much later (chapters 8–10) my discussion of the general question of the interrelationship between form and thought.

4 Meaning and Text

The Concept of Meaning

The concepts "text," "interpretation," and "meaning" played no important part in the previous discussion. In fact, I refrain from assigning a structural role to these concepts in my theory. I regard them as wide, all-embracing terms of only indirect interest in an analysis striving for clarity and precision. Concepts like "text," "meaning," and "interpretation" are bound to appear to be of central importance to those who think in terms of a folk theory of communication, that is in terms of the transportation and container metaphors. According to folk theory, the author creates a text that literally possesses a meaning, and to interpret the text is to describe or investigate that meaning. However, this view of the matter, apparently so plausible, appears fatally superficial to me.

Let us begin with the concept of meaning. In the last chapter I gave an account of how linguistic communication works and of what understanding of texts and utterances consists in. One might say that I sketched a process of creating and understanding meaning – but none of the interacting factors included in my sketch can, strictly speaking, be identified with the *meaning* as it is usually comprehended. One is reminded of the point in chapter 1 at which it proved possible to describe, broadly, what happens when emotions arise – i.e., the emotion process – while the identification of a specific factor in the process as the actual *emotion* remained highly problematical.

Several of the elements appearing in the communication process are natural candidates for the role of being *meaning* itself. The originator's communicative intention is one central factor, and I have spoken of its content as *the intended meaning*. I have said, further, that the addressee attempts to reconstruct the intended meaning,[1] at the same time inevitably evaluating the communicated content. The whole of her reconstruction and evaluation – or if one wishes, the content of her experience of meaning – is another conceivable candidate for the role of *meaning*. I shall call that content *the applicatory meaning*.

The addressee reconstructs the intended meaning largely by exploiting her own and the originator's mutual knowledge of linguistic conventions, of *the conventional meaning* of words, phrases, and constructions used by the originator. The conventional meaning of a text, its general import as determined by linguistic conventions, is naturally a third major candidate for the role of being the text's *meaning*.

These, I believe, are the only really serious contenders,[2] and obviously none of the three can be identified with *meaning* as traditionally imagined. At first sight, perhaps, conventional meaning strikes one as the most promising alternative. But we know that one and the same sequence of spoken or written words may mean entirely different things in different contexts, despite the fact that a word-sequence has a fixed *conventional* meaning. For example, "He gave a brilliant performance" is a linguistic formula with a given conventional meaning. Nevertheless, it can be employed to express highly dissimilar propositions: it may be used about different persons and about performances on different occasions, and it may be uttered seriously or ironically. In the ordinary concept of meaning, a serious and an ironic utterance of the sentence would clearly be conveying different meanings.

Applicatory meaning agrees even less well with popular conceptions of meaning: we do not normally think of a text as capable, in principle, of having an unlimited number of non-identical meanings. Nor does the originator's intended meaning let itself be identified with meaning pure and simple, for an author may simply make an error in writing, overlooking it even in the proofs. Let us imagine, for example, that Lowell's true intention was to tell us that the bedside lamp in his father's room was resting on volume one of *Glimpses of Unfamiliar Japan*, though he came, through various oversights, to let "volume two" be written instead of "volume one" even in the printed version. That would not make "volume one" the actual meaning of the words "volume two" in the poem: de facto, we do not use the concept of meaning in that manner.

It appears impossible, therefore, to identify any element in the communication process with meaning-in-the-traditional-sense-of-the-word. This, I contend, is due to the fact that the ordinary concept of meaning is founded on an ultimately untenable folk model of the mechanisms of communication. On closer inspection, the notion of meaning disintegrates into a series of more homogeneous and precise concepts. In speaking of meaning in the following, I shall normally be referring to one or other of these more determinate entities, not to meaning in general.

Discerning and distinguishing different kinds of meaning, and describing their interrelations, could be carried a long way. In this context, I have confined myself to distinguishing between intended meaning, conventional meaning, and applicatory meaning. I would, however, also like to introduce the concept "symptomal meaning."

Apart from the communicative intention, there are a number of other causes and reasons underlying an agent's communicative act. These are of different kinds and belong on different levels of abstraction: on being curt with you, for example, an agent may perhaps be said to be governed by the habits of his class, or by his feelings of superiority, or by his wish to put a quick end to the conversation. Some of the causes and reasons can be inferred from the act, or from its traces: the utterance or text. The utterance or text constitutes a symptom of the existence of these underlying circumstances, which make up its symptomal meaning.[3]

The text of "Father's Bedroom" may be read as a symptom of Lowell's feelings for his father. Herbert Leibowitz writes, about the three poems concerning the father's death and about "Commander Lowell": "The emotions are reticent, as if Lowell felt a perturbed forgiveness and stern love for his father, difficult to express."[4]

If the poem, as Leibowitz understands it, faithfully reflects Lowell's feelings at the time of writing, these feelings are love and forgiveness for the father. In that case, this love and this forgiveness form part of the poem's symptomal meaning.

It is another matter that Lowell's actual attitude towards his father appears to have been complex. I cannot refrain from quoting Ian Hamilton's characterization of Lowell's feelings, both the real-life emotions and those expressed in the poems: "Lowell liked to think of his presentation of his father as 'tender,' but only in the elegiac poems that appear in the fourth section of *Life Studies* does pathos outweigh ridicule. And even here the evidence of Lowell's drafts suggests that ridicule could as easily have been outweighed by something close to hatred."[5]

Theories of Literary Meaning

My description of the communication process is far from uncontroversial. Many would give wholly or partly different accounts of the process, the divergences having, in many cases, repercussions on the view of the concept of meaning. I lack the space, here, for a really in-depth defence of the standpoint I advocated above. But I shall comment on some of its most serious competitors, briefly explaining why I do not endorse any of them.[6]

A common idea of linguistic communication ascribes the decisive role in the communication process to the language system, the communicative code. I am thinking of the view that the sender encodes what she wishes to say in accordance with the rules of the language, known both to her and the addressee, thus making the coded message accessible to the addressee, who decodes it by applying the same code backwards, as it were.[7] What determines the meaning of a sentence is linguistic and communicative convention, the "public conventions of usage,"[8] as Monroe C. Beardsley states in his well-known argument for this standpoint, which I call "conventionalism." Its fundamental idea is that meaning is a function of the text's formulation and the rules of the language. "Take Lowell's 'Father's Bedroom,' and apply public conventions of usage to that text!" the consistent convention-alist would say. "What results is the meaning."

Beardsley's approach to the communication process is representative of the New Criticism, which maintained, among other things, that the literary work is an autonomous object, the author's intentions being consequently irrelevant for someone reading the work as literature. Those who attached more importance to the author's meaning often replied that the conventions of language are too indeterminate to define a work's meaning.[9] This is indisputably a valid objection. For that reason, in later versions of conventionalism the conventions of language are often supposed to supply the text merely with a kind of general meaning, the reader being then more or less free to fill in the details. (This is a line which has enjoyed popularity both among structuralists and analytical philosophers.)[10]

According to my description of the communication process, however, the text and the rules of language do not together *determine* meaning. They constitute *indications* – extremely important indications, certainly – used by the reader in his attempts to get to the intended meaning (which he is expected to react to). In my opinion, this analysis is superior to that of conventionalism in several respects.

The fundamental problem with conventionalism is, in my view, its disregard of the difference between linguistic formulations in themselves and language in use.[11] "Charlie's ill" is a correct English sentence, its conventional meaning being that someone called Charlie is ill. Understood simply as a sentence in English, as a combination of English linguistic material, "Charlie's ill" possesses only the conventional meaning just described. That meaning is, of course, at least essentially, a function of the combination of words itself and the conventions of language. So conventionalism is eminently suitable for the analysis of conventional meaning, the meaning of linguistic formulations in themselves. But when sentences are actually used, produced, uttered – as they are in the production of a literary work[12] – they convey a content far transcending the conventional meaning. If I were actually to utter the sentence "Charlie's ill," addressing my wife, my act would normally be both intended and understood as expressing the statement that our budgie, Charlie, is ill. Likewise, if the mother of a boy named Charles were actually to utter the sentence addressing her husband, she would normally intend it, and he interpret it, as stating that their son Charles is ill.

The addressees certainly do not produce these interpretations by starting from the conventional meaning ("Someone called 'Charlie' is ill"), filling in extra content as they please.[13] It appears obvious that the addressees are, instead, trying to understand what the speaker means (though they must, indeed, use their knowledge of the utterance and of linguistic conventions as points of departure in doing this). In fact, a fundamental linguistic convention requires that the addressee should attempt to comprehend the speaker's communicative intention. As Renate Bartsch says in an analysis of the norms of language: "All specific linguistic norms are justified relative to the highest norm of communication, which is: 'Express yourself in such a way that what you say is recognizable and interpretable by your partner in agreement with what you intend him to understand.' And, correspondingly, for the hearer it is: 'Interpret such that interpretation will be in agreement with what the speaker intends.'"[14]

According to this analysis, one is *obliged* to attempt to reconstruct the sender's intended meaning if one is to comply with the norms of language in interpreting the message.

For my part, I see literature as following normal communicative conventions on this point – a natural standpoint, it would seem, literature being a kind of language use. The conventionalist will certainly argue that the linguistic supernorm invoked by Bartsch is out of the running precisely because literature is involved. But it reasonably rests with her to adduce good arguments for that assumption, something which appears difficult.[15] The meaning of a literary work is – like the meaning of any utterance – more determinate than linguistic conventions alone can make it. Linguistic conventions are fuzzy – though words, phrases, and constructions have their semantic spectra, it is difficult to point to really precise conventions for how these are to be combined into more comprehensive meaning structures. For that reason, considering linguistic conventions alone yields imprecise results, even where the text's meaning is unequivocal. Think of the formulation "Robbie from Mother" on the flyleaf dedication in Lowell's "Father's Bedroom"! The book evidently belonged to Lowell's father, so *he* must be the "Robbie" referred to (not the author himself). In reason, that reference to the father forms part of the poem's meaning. It is easy then to explain, by invoking considerations of what the author may have wished to convey, why "Robbie" must be supposed to refer to Lowell's father. The linguistic formulations in themselves, however, obviously do not form a sufficient basis for an explanation of the reference. It is difficult to imagine, let alone specify, a system of linguistic conventions of such general scope that, when applied to this poem, they would have as their unambiguous corollary that "Robbie" implies a reference to Robert Lowell's father and not to himself.

Irrespective of their determinacy or indeterminacy, the conventions of language may, moreover, always be violated, stretched, exploited, or played with[16] – another reason why conventionalism appears untenable. It is possible, for instance, to communicate quite the contrary of what one's utterance conventionally means: all that is required is a sufficiently clear indication that one is speaking ironically. To believe in the possibility of ascertaining the presence of irony by means of the application of general rules, without guesses about sender intentions, would without doubt be to cherish illusions.[17]

Conventionalism constitutes, in itself, an important view of the bases of literary meaning and of what literary interpretation amounts to. Apart from that, however, several other theories of meaning and interpretation also contain an element of conventionalism. Theories focusing reader response, for example, often make the assumption that a text in itself may carry at least a rudimentary meaning, which it is then, to a large extent, up to the reader to make complete and concrete. In such cases, the allegedly autonomous part of the textual meaning is often construed along conventionalist lines.[18]

But conventionalism and its offshoots do not reign supreme. According to Stanley Fish's radically addressee-orientated theory in *Is There a Text in This Class?* (1980), the reader, or more precisely the interpretive community, is responsible for creating meaning. In reality, Fish starts from the incontestable fact that every literate reader inevitably and spontaneously experiences an encountered text as carrying such and such a meaning, normally being unaware of any preceding process of interpretation. Fish then contends (groundlessly, as I see it) that there is in fact no text and no meaning prior to the reader's experience; for him, texts and all other things in the world "are made by the interpretive strategies we set in motion."[19] It is certainly correct that the reader is constructing (or reconstructing) meaning in her encounter with the physical object representing the text. But the crucial question for an understanding of meaning and interpretation seems to me to be *what* "interpretive strategies" the reader is making use of in that connection, and Fish essentially avoids that question. To my mind, as a consequence, his way of looking at the matter contains very little concerning the theory of literary meaning and literary understanding. Fish would, for example, be unable to explain why it is justified to read the word "Robbie" in "Father's Bedroom" as referring to Lowell's father. When we are confronted with that question, it would be beside the point for us to appeal to the fact that this is indeed how we construe the text, and that our interpretative practices might well have been different. What the question demands from us is a specification and explanation of the content of the interpretative practices that we actually do adhere to. I believe that we are entitled to take it for granted that all competent readers in relevant interpretive communities would construe the reference of "Robbie" in very much the same way, as referring to the father. In doing so, they would, presumably, be following similar principles. And the question is: *what* principles?

Theories which choose the author's communicative intention as their starting point exemplify another type of non-conventionalist standpoint. Theories of this kind are usually called "intentionalist," and a radical version of such intentionalism is met with in P.D. Juhl's *Interpretation* (1980). The central idea in Juhl's book is that a text's meaning is identical with the content which the author intended to communicate.[20] In this form, intentionalism seems patently indefensible, simply because the author's pen may slip. To return to an example used earlier, let us imagine that Lowell intended to describe the bedside lamp as resting on volume one of *Glimpses of Unfamiliar Japan*, but happened to write "volume two" instead of "volume one" by mistake. Juhl's theory would imply, then, that the expression "volume two" in the poem actually means "volume one."[21] But as I have already said, it appears obvious to me that this is not how we actually utilize the concept of meaning.

E.D. Hirsch's well-known variant of intentionalism – first set out in his book *Validity in Interpretation* (1967) – steers clear of that difficulty, but at an appreciable cost. For Hirsch, meaning is identical with the content that the author intended to communicate *provided that this content lets itself be communicated by means of the chosen linguistic formulations.*[22] Hirsch is apparently striving to attain a sensible compromise between intentionalism and conventionalism. His proposed solution is, however, beset with considerable difficulties. What happens, for example, if the author makes an error in writing, as we imagined that Lowell did when writing down the words "volume two"? The consistent answer from Hirsch ought to be, I think, that the author's formulation will in that case be *devoid of* meaning, and once again I would like to maintain that the concept of meaning is not, de facto, understood in that spirit. In addition, we can of course never feel entirely sure that the author has in fact managed to find formulations suitable for expressing his communicative intentions. Accordingly, it would be a further and still more embarrassing consequence of Hirsch's standpoint that we can never be totally assured that a given, seemingly normal text has any meaning whatsoever.

The view of communication I am advocating here brings together features from conventionalism, reader-response criticism, and intentionalism. The reader is seen as encountering a purely physical object, the physical text. Her knowledge and experience enable her to utilize the text as an indication of the author's communicative intentions. In that, the reader is creating meaning in the sense that she is reconstructing the intended meaning to the best of her ability and reacting to that meaning. So far I agree with reader-orientated theories. But there are also evident and important connections between my analysis and conventionalism, for I certainly do not deny that the reader, in reconstructing meaning, must first and foremost be exploiting the linguistic signs represented by the physical text. At the same time, however, I regard the reader as essentially aiming at an understanding of (and a reaction to) what the author wished to convey. So it is obvious that my theory also has crucial points in common with intentionalism.[23]

The Concept of Text

According to the picture of communication implied by everyday language, a speaker's words and an author's text are physical phenomena containing meaning. The words are physically audible or visible and at the same time full of import. We are thus used to speaking as if words and texts had an exterior and an interior: a purely physical surface, but also an inner cavity, as it were, more or less filled with meaning. This pattern also, by and large, underlies our intuitive thinking about verbal compositions.[24]

That being so, we are used to thinking and speaking of the literary text[25] as a separate, independent physical object full of meaning. The text is something which can be created by an author and read by a reader, much as a physical inscription may be created and read, and, just like the physical inscription, the text is found outside the author and reader; it has, as D.E.B. Pollard once aptly put it, an "extracranial" existence.[26] It is not merely physical, though. It is also supplied with a text in the sense of a sequence of signs – it consists of definite sentences, words, or graphemes in a definite order – and above all with a meaning.

It can be very difficult to emancipate oneself from the transportation and container metaphors that have such a firm hold on our thinking about communication. It comes quite naturally to us to say of a letter that it is lying before us on the table, that it contains several spelling mistakes, and that it is full of humorous observations. But only physical objects can be lying on tables – and how is it possible for a physical object literally to contain spelling mistakes or humorous observations? Language makes us create a picture of the letter which is, strictly speaking, absurd. Nevertheless, that picture has had a profound impact even on philosophical and linguistic reflection about the ontology of verbal compositions.

Naturally, then, it has also influenced our thinking about the nature and the mode of being of literary texts, making the literary text stand out as a genuinely existing physical object fitted with a text (i.e., a sign-sequence) and a meaning. It also comes quite naturally to us to say of a text like Lowell's "Father's Bedroom" that it is actually there before us, that it opens with the words "In my father's bedroom," and that its lines "have the factual crispness of reportage" while being at the same time "charged with complicated feelings."[27] I would maintain, however, that what we are physically confronted with is merely a physical object indicating to literate English-speaking persons, via its traces of printer's ink, the words and the meaning Lowell intended them to reconstruct. As a physical object it cannot literally contain feelings; it cannot even, literally, contain words.

The last contention may sound extreme. As an absolutely extracranial physical object, however, a letter or a copy of a poem may be said to consist simply of white paper with traces of ink, printer's ink, or the like. The traces *represent* graphemes, and indirectly words or sentences. But it is not the case that the traces in themselves *are* graphemes, words, or sentences. To determine what words are written "on" the paper, we must interpret, not merely inspect, the textual object before us. The traces of ink or printer's ink are physical facts; not so the graphemes, words, or sentences.

It is well known, in principle, that there is a distinction to be made between *graphemes* ("written characters") on the one hand and *physical features representing graphemes* on the other.[28] But this distinction is seldom respected when texts and communication are discussed, and I find it appropriate to inculcate it by means of an example. In the late 1970s, a fibula from about 50 BC, now known as the Meldorf fibula, was found in a museum in Schleswig-Holstein in northern Germany. Engraved on the object were physical marks representing, to all appearances, a sequence of four signs. According to an early hypothesis, these marks represent runes intended to be read from right to left, thereby forming the word form "HIWI" meaning, approximately, "to the housewife." Another reading, however, soon entered into competition with that hypothesis. It was maintained that the marks represent, instead, an inscription in the Latin alphabet meant to be read from left to right, standing for an inflected form of a name, "IDIN," and meaning "to Ida" or "to Idda."[29] To the best of my knowledge, the exact interpretation of the sign-sequence is still a controversial issue; I shall, however, not go into the later discussion. What interests me here, of course, is the relation between the physical traces and the sequence of written characters.

In the case of the fibula it appears obvious that the physical traces are found, literally, on the object. Having precisely these marks is an internal property of the object, whereas what graphemes are represented by the traces is a question of interpretation. No inspection of the fibula, however meticulous, will in itself be sufficient to decide whether the marks "are" runes or Latin letters, for strictly speaking the fibula does not *contain* letters or runes. It is true that we can speak of certain letters (or runes) as being written "on" the object, but in doing so we make use of a variant of the container metaphor. "Containing" definite letters (or runes) is in fact not an internal property of the object but a relational property, a property grounded in the fibula's relationships with other phenomena. The relevant relation in this connection must, at bottom, be the one between the physical traces and the engraver's communicative intention. The disunity among linguistic experts is no doubt to be understood basically as a dissension about how the traces were originally meant to be taken. If the traces were intended to be interpreted as Latin letters, then Latin letters is what they "are," and conversely, the traces "are" runes if the engraver intended them to be interpreted in that manner.

The example demonstrates the basic importance of the author's communicative intentions for the understanding of texts. Already the very establishing of the sign-sequence to be interpreted rests on an implicit assumption about those intentions. True, one might be inclined to see the fibula as a very special case and suppose the situation to be fundamentally different where "Father's Bedroom" is concerned. But that would be mistaken. Imagining a copy of the poem – the physical textual object, part of a book page with traces of printer's ink – as literally containing Latin letters or English words is simply not reasonable. We would not be saying that English words and sentences are written "on" the page unless we were tacitly assuming that the author intended the traces of printer's ink to be interpreted thus. The real difference in this respect between the fibula and the poem consists in its being, as far as "Father's Bedroom" is concerned, not debatable but overwhelmingly clear what system of writing the author intended to employ. In the case of "Father's Bedroom" we know for certain that we are dealing with Latin letters; nothing could be more obvious to us. That this is *evident* does not, however, make it *a physical fact*.

According to the container metaphor, a text (in the sense of a work) is a physical object supplied with a text (in the sense of a sign-sequence) and a meaning. That is also how the white paper with the traces of printer's ink appears in our spontaneous experience. It acquires embodied expressivity thanks to our automatic, unreflecting interpretation of the physical marks. It is as though the very words (and not merely some squiggles in need of interpretation) were written on the paper and as if the meaning, too, existed there, outside ourselves, as something simply encountered.

The account of the process of communication presented in the last chapter makes it possible to draw another, less contradictory picture of the nature of texts. In the simplest case of written literature imaginable, the author communicates with his audience by producing a *physical object* – for instance, a page of handwriting which can be made available to interested readers. The paper exhibits physical traces – for instance, patterns left by a ballpoint pen. These traces represent a *sign-sequence* – for instance, a sequence of English words and punctuation marks arranged into lines and stanzas. Author and reader expect the physical object to make it possible for the reader to reconstruct the sign-sequence and, in the next step, the *intended meaning* that the author wished to convey to her (and then use this intended meaning to initiate a literary experience).

Generally, a further complication is added: the physical object produced by the author is made manifold. Where printed literature is concerned, the author normally supplies a manuscript, an *original*, for copying. Manifolding amounts to the production of *copies* of the original, that is, the production of new physical objects intended to represent the same sign-sequence (and, ultimately, the same intended meaning) as the author's original. It is naturally possible to reiterate the process: copies may in their turn be copied, and so on.

I am not acquainted with the manuscript or manuscripts behind "Father's Bedroom." I take it for granted, however, that Lowell supplied Faber and Faber, the firm which first published *Life Studies*,[30] with a physical, written manuscript, an *original* representing a definite *sign-sequence*. The firm then ordered the making of a large number of *copies* of the original, copies intended, by definition, to function as carriers of the same *intended meaning*.

One may feel tempted to inquire what, then, is the real "Father's Bedroom": the original, the copies, the sign-sequence, the intended meaning, or something else? But that is precisely the question we should refrain from asking. The idea that a definite object that is the text exists – here: a definite object that is "Father's Bedroom" – belongs within the framework of the contradictory folk theory of communication. In my analysis of the communication process – let us call it "the alternative approach" – there is in reality no room for the concept of a text as traditionally understood. The analysis allows, in the end, only for physical objects – original manuscripts together with their copies (and copies of copies ...) – and for the sign-sequences and meanings (intended meanings, conventional meanings, symptomal meanings, and so on) conveyed by these physical objects.

The alternative approach has the same capacity as the folk theory for expressing everything usually formulated as statements about literary texts,[31] but the alternative formulations will, of course, differ somewhat from the more familiar ones. One possibility is making the original the starting point of the alternative idiom. To demonstrate the strategy, let us call the original of "Father's Bedroom" the "Father's-Bedroom-original."[32] After that, common types of statements about "Father's Bedroom" may be rephrased as statements about the Father's-Bedroom-original, or about (one or several of) the copies of (the copies of ...) that original, or about the sign-sequence or meaning (in one or another of the relevant senses of the word) associated with that original or its copies. For example, the three statements:

(1) "Father's Bedroom" was first published in 1959.
(2) "Father's Bedroom" opens with the word "In."
(3) "Father's Bedroom" contains a description of Lowell's father's bedroom.

could be formulated, respectively,

(1') Copies of the Father's-Bedroom-original were first published in 1959.
(2') The English word "In," spelled with a capital "I," is the first word of the sign-sequence represented by the Father's-Bedroom-original and by all correct copies of (copies of ...) that original.
(3') Mental representations of the appearance of Lowell's father's bedroom form part of the intended meaning which the Father's-Bedroom-original, and every correct copy of (a copy of ...) that original, were created to convey.

The alternative way of formulating the statements is obviously more circumstantial. Its advantages are on the theoretical plane, its chief merit being that it renounces operating with the contradictory fiction that there are texts, i.e., physical objects containing non-physical constituents like sign-sequences or meaning. As a consequence, the alternative approach gives us a far better chance of thoroughly understanding and describing how literature works. The folk theory is downright unsuitable for such purposes, entangling us in deeply paradoxical ideas about what we have got into the habit of calling the literary text.

Theories about How Texts Exist

There are several different current conceptions about how texts exist, just as there are divergent current opinions on the nature of meanings. Much as in connection with the concept of meaning, I would like to comment on some of the most important alternatives to my own standpoint, explaining why I cannot endorse them. I have written extensively on this matter elsewhere, and I refer the reader to my earlier publications for a more detailed presentation of my views.[33] In the present context, I shall have to confine myself to a crude sketch of the state of the art and of my own attitudes.

As a rule, the discussion of how literary texts[34] exist, of the concrete identification of the literary work, has been conducted in philosophical aesthetics – linguists and students of literature have in fact had relatively little to say about the subject. Therefore the problem has usually been brought up as part of the more comprehensive question about the mode of existence of works of art (a topic which is not, in that general form, on my agenda). One may speak, roughly, of three different current approaches to the problem. I shall call them the "Amalgamation Theory," the "Type Theory," and the "Elimination Theory."

For the amalgamation theorist, the arresting problem is the fact that a physical object – the painting's canvas, the book's white paper – is spoken of as if it possessed properties of meaning. In the foregoing I have, in Reddy's spirit, dismissed as absurd the idea that physical communicative objects, such as physical copies of books, may literally *exhibit* meaning. The amalgamation theorist views the situation differently. He contends that such a thing as a text represents an indissoluble amalgamation of physical and semantic properties, being "a material something animated by something,"[35] "a physical-interpretational thing."[36] According to the amalgamation theorist, the idea of the existence of such "animated" signs is fundamental to our thinking. The physical and the semantic elements "cannot possibly be separated";[37]

if they could, this would anyway destroy the "useful ambivalence"[38] of the corresponding notions.

As one can see, the amalgamation theorist accepts the folk theory's picture of literary works as physical objects supplied with meaning. He is undoubtedly correct in maintaining that we do in fact employ the indicated mode of thought. But I cannot unreservedly share his conviction that we do so with justice. It is true that the popular picture of literary texts – as well as common parlance, reflecting that picture – is useful in many contexts. The brevity and smoothness displayed by sentences (1), (2), and (3) when compared with sentences (1'), (2'), and (3') forcibly demonstrate the "useful ambivalence" of the folk theory fictions. It is my contention, however, that the folk-theory is in reality self-contradictory – for example, the text is presented as being at the same time physical and non-physical – and that its logical inconsistencies prevent us from constructing a satisfactory analysis of the nature of literature and literary understanding as long as we let the folk analysis form part of our theoretical framework. I maintain, thus, that the folk-theory picture of the text, while useful in everyday contexts, is profoundly unfruitful for literary theory.

As we have seen, at least some amalgamation theorists would reply that it is *impossible* to consider meaning as an element distinct from the physical communicative object; the two "cannot possibly be separated." To my mind, however, that idea is simply unfounded. It is naturally true that there is utterance meaning in the physical text as long as one adheres to the folk-theoretical framework. However, nothing prevents us from designing other, logically more defensible pictures of linguistic communication. Earlier I described the communication process, and also pointed to the entities capable of replacing the text as referent (physical manuscripts and copies, a sign-sequence, meaning). Those descriptions separate physical text from utterance meaning, and doing this presents no difficulties.

In reflecting on how a work of visual art exists, one is confronted, first and foremost, with the difficulty of explaining how the work's physical properties hang together with its properties of meaning; the amalgamation theory is an attempt to solve that problem. In the discussion of those arts where there are, normally, many equivalent and exchangeable exemplars of the work – music and literature, for example – another problem has been in the forefront. There are many copies of the work, and each individually appears to *be* the work. When I open the Umeå University Library copy of *Life Studies* and read "Father's Bedroom," precisely *that* literary text is, undeniably, before me. But I know that "Father's Bedroom" also exists in many other places at the same time. How can that be? "Father's Bedroom" is presumably an individual, particular object, so how can it appear in several places at once?

There are those who simply put logic to one side, asserting that a literary text is simultaneously one and many.[39] But the usual way of attacking the problem is slightly different. The type/token distinction first mounted by Charles S. Peirce is brought in, and it is maintained that the literary text is a type.

It is customary to introduce the type/token distinction with the aid of examples taken from the sphere of language. In "Father's Bedroom," the word "blue" occurs four times. Let us say that the word "blue" in itself is a *type*, while each individual occurrence of the word represents a *token* of that type. A distinction of this kind is needed in several contexts. If, for instance, we are to check how many words "Father's Bedroom" contains, we have to know whether to count the number of word-types or the number of word-tokens. In the latter case, but not in the former, the word "blue" should be registered four times.

The type/token distinction, however, can be applied to non-linguistic objects as well. The Swedish flag may be said to constitute a type, concrete individual Swedish flags being tokens of that type. Likewise, the Mitsubishi Lancer can be regarded as a type, concrete individual cars of that model presenting themselves, then, as tokens of the type. Or the dog might be said to be a type having concrete individual dogs as its tokens – and so forth. The thinkers I call type theorists hold that literary texts are types. In their eyes, "Father's Bedroom" is a type, individual copies of the poem constituting tokens of that type. For a long time now the Type Theory has been the most widely embraced idea about the existence of literary texts.[40] I myself, however, can see serious objections to the Type Theory.

It is true that the concept of a type is a philosophical construct. But it nevertheless appears clear to me that the conception of types is bound up with a popular, pretheoretical strategy for generalizing. That strategy could be described in the following fashion. When it is a matter of generalizing about such things as the characteristics of dogs, one creates a phantom object, the dog, letting that object represent every qualitatively normal dog. All the qualities of a normal dog – for example, the quality of having four legs – may be ascribed to the dog; accordingly, the dog has four legs. Since partly different properties can be attributed to normal dogs, the dog acquires, in some respects, rather complex features. There are dogs both in Europe and in America, for example, so we must accept that the dog exists on both continents at once.

The type theorist is no doubt right in believing that a strategy of this sort is employed in our thinking about literary texts. As "Father's Bedroom" appears in ordinary language and everyday thought, the text could indeed be characterized as a type. First, the poem has every property possessed by a correct copy of it. We may have the poem before us and read it; the poem opens with the words "In my father's bedroom"; the poem describes Lowell's father's bedroom; and so on. Second, the poem also has rather complex characteristics in some respects, just like types in general. Despite its being a single and unique object, for example, it exists in several thousand copies.

The fundamental problem with the Type Theory, as I see it, is that a type is an illogical construct. To serve its purpose, a type has to appear to be simultaneously one and many, and to be simultaneously abstract and concrete. A given type – "Father's Bedroom," say – is evidently an *abstract* object and *one* abstract object. At the same time, however, if the type is to serve its generalizing purpose, it must be possible to ascribe physical properties to it – properties that can rightly be ascribed to individual, concrete objects only. Therefore the type acquires a paradoxical character. "Father's Bedroom" is an abstraction – and yet we may have the poem before us and read it. The Swedish flag is an abstraction – and yet it has colours: it is blue and yellow. The Mitsubishi Lancer is an abstraction – and yet it has four doors (five in the hatchback version).

The Type Theory faithfully reflects the popular picture of a literary text. But I contend that the popular picture does not permit us to construe a rationally defensible account of the nature of literature and literary understanding, while a good alternative representation can certainly be found. Assuredly, we often need to generalize about objects in reality – but it is not necessary to do this by means of types. We may replace them with sets and with predicate calculus. Instead of saying

(4) The dog has got four legs.

we could say

(4′) All normally equipped dogs have got four legs.

or, using a more stringent formulation,

(4″) It is true of all x that if x is a normally equipped dog, then x has got four legs.

This is more circumstantial but liberates us from the dependence on abstractions having physical properties and being simultaneously one and many. That was indeed, in principle, the strategy I used in translating, in the last section,

(5) "Father's Bedroom" opens with the word "In."

into

(5') The English word "In," spelled with a capital "I," is the first word of the sign-sequence represented by the Father's-Bedroom-original and by all correct copies of copies of ...) that original.

(5') may be formalized into

(5″) It is true of all x, that if x is the Father's-Bedroom-original, or if x is a correct copy of (a copy of ...) that original, then x represents a sign-sequence where the English word "In," spelled with a capital "I," constitutes the first word.

Strangely enough, however, the type concept's logical respectability has seldom been questioned[41] – in part, no doubt, because the differences between types and sets have been underestimated or overlooked.[42] Serious efforts have also been made to explicate the type concept by clarifying, partially at least, the logic governing the relations between the type and token properties.[43] The general feeling seems to be that the type concept is fruitful but insufficiently analysed.

In practice, the Type Theory and the Amalgamation Theory are not mutually exclusive. At least where literary texts are concerned, the amalgamation theorist too confronts the task of explaining how the work of art is capable of "animating" several physical objects at once. In that connection, the Type Theory represents a convenient option. And the type theorist, for his part, has to be able to answer the question what the literary text is a type *of*. If "Father's Bedroom" is indeed a type, is it a type of physical object, a type of sign-sequence, or what? Evidently, one possibility is to say that the text is a type of "animated" physical object.

That is, essentially, the solution chosen in one of the best-known theories about the existence of texts, that of Joseph Margolis. According to Margolis, in connection with a work of art, such as a literary text, we are dealing with a kind of significant object "embodied" in physical things (the text's copies) that constitute tokens-of-the-same-type (copies of the same text). Contrary to the usual practice, however, Margolis holds that types do not have a separate existence – speaking of tokens as tokens-of-the-same-type is, for him, simply to emphasize an essential association that exists between them.[44]

The third theory about the existence of texts, the Elimination Theory, is of a quite different kind. In the last section, I propagated a variant of that theory when I pointed to a way of breaking with the folk theory of communication and speaking of literature and literary understanding without making use of the folk assumptions.

The starting point of the Elimination Theory is the idea that the notion of a text is in itself contradictory, the text being simply a fiction practical in everyday contexts. As far as I know, the Elimination Theory was first put forward by Richard Rudner in a 1950 article. Though Rudner certainly admits that we speak as if works of art really exist, he regards the talk of art works as a "convenient shorthand,"[45] a useful way of expressing oneself. He sees no reason to take our formulations at face value and presuppose that there exist definite abstract entities functioning as the referents of work-names like "Father's Bedroom." Rudner also attempts to show that we might in principle eliminate all reference to works of art by translating formulations mentioning works of art into synonymous formulations that do not.

Rudner gained some followers, notably Jay E. Bachrach,[46] but on the whole the Elimination Theory has aroused little interest. This may have something to do with the patent defectiveness of Rudner's and Bachrach's formulations of their views. Demonstrating the viability of the Elimination Theory is a matter of proving that all that can meaningfully be said about literature may be said without using concepts denoting literary texts. One has to make it credible that all meaningful statements formulated as assertions about literary works can in principle be "translated" into a language lacking the conception of a literary text. However, Rudner and Bachrach do not have at their disposal a sufficiently developed alternative to the folk theory, a sufficiently rich and coherent alternative "language." As a consequence, their attempted translations prove unfortunate.[47] I contend that my own version of the Elimination Theory, sketched in the last section and presented in greater detail in other contexts, is capable of being used to rephrase all meaningful statements about literary texts into more rational formulations.

Conclusion

In this chapter I have argued, among other things, that literary works of art, literary texts, do not exist in the sense usually assumed. True, there are separate communicative objects independent of the minds of author and reader: the sheets of paper with traces of writing or print making up the copies of the text. But those objects are physical things, and cannot accordingly contain thoughts or feelings. As for form, no doubt they have a certain form, but they do not possess form in the relevant sense, i.e., literary form. The ideas and feelings must be found, in reality, in the author and in his readers, while literary form – as I shall endeavour to make clear in the next part of my book – is an aspect of the communicated complexes of thoughts and of the linguistic expressions used in conveying them.

This standpoint may seem unfamiliar and odd, but it should not, after all, be difficult to take in. There are authors, actions performed by authors, and mental processes occurring during writing. Likewise, there are readers, actions performed by readers, and mental processes occurring during reading. Moreover, we know that there are physical objects – such as sheets of paper with traces of writing or print – which mediate between author and readers. Is it really conceivable that there is in addition, *over and above* these entities, a separate object outside author and readers – the literary text?[48]

Perhaps not. But it may still be difficult to abandon the conviction that a literary text, such as Lowell's "Father's Bedroom," is a genuine, separate, extracranial object. As I observed earlier in this chapter, everyday language lends support to that conviction, and so does our spontaneous impression of encountering, in reading, an actual object existing outside ourselves.

What we really do in reading, I maintained, is reconstruct and react to an intended meaning, starting from the physical traces on the paper and from our own knowledge and experience. In that connection we might indeed be said, in a sense, to encounter a genuine, external object. At least we form an idea of such an object: the author's intended meaning.

Nor is it unusual for the text to be identified with its meaning, often – by theorists regarding intended meaning as essential – more precisely with its intended meaning.[49] This is certainly an unreasonable identification – one can read the text but not the author's intentional states; unlike the author's intentional states the text contains so many pages; and so forth.[50] But still there is a grain of truth in the idea. When reading, we are confronted with a meaningful whole which appears to exist, and to have its cause, outside ourselves. The meaning in question (which is not in fact encountered but hypothetically reconstructed) is of course not an extracranial object: it is the author's intended meaning. But it may well be the literal encounter with the physical copy of the text and the seeming encounter with a meaning that, together, make us feel that our reading brings us in contact with an object both physical and mental, the text, existing outside ourselves.

Let us consider it proved that texts do not exist, at least not in the form and sense usually intended by laypersons and students of literature alike. Is this, then, an important fact? Or is it rather an esoteric detail in literary aesthetics, devoid of major theoretical or practical consequences?

I myself find the observation momentous. It changes the basis of our understanding of the literary communication process, of the nature of literary interpretation, and (of course) of what is sometimes called the literary object. In the following chapters I shall be attempting to demonstrate this, emphasizing particularly that the differently constructed perspective alters the picture of literature's cognitive, emotional, and formal aspects.

PART TWO

Aspects of Literary Experience

5 Conveyed Thoughts in Literature

Introduction

The outline of a theory of literature in the first part of the book has laid the foundations for the second part's inquiry into the interrelationship of the cognitive, emotional, and formal aspects of literature. An inquiry of the latter kind makes it necessary to raise a number of basic questions about thoughts, feeling, and form. Essentially, four types of problems will be dealt with. What *is* a thought (what is a feeling, what is form)? How is it possible for thoughts (feeling, form) to *get into* the literary object? How are thoughts, feeling, and form *interrelated* in literary wholes? And what *role* do thoughts (feeling, form) play in literature – what function or functions do they have?

As concerns thoughts – the main topic in this chapter and the next – I have in reality already taken up some of the four problems in the first part of the book. Thus, I have touched upon the question of what a thought is. In chapter 1, I said that intentional states constitute an important part of our experiences. Being in an intentional state may involve seeing a midnight blue Ford Scorpio coming towards one, or knowing London is the capital of Great Britain, or picturing to oneself a future holiday in Athens. Being in an intentional state is to have perceptions, or ideas, or imaginings, or the like. I said, further, that intentional states comprise mental representations (pictures of realities, for instance, *a midnight blue Ford Scorpio is coming towards me …*) presenting themselves to consciousness in a special psychological mode (for instance, as a genuine perception: … *and this is something which*

I am actually seeing). With "thought" I am referring to an intentional state or a mental representation. I use "thought," as a convenient but less exact term, in contexts where the difference between the two referents lacks proper significance.[1]

This, of course, does not constitute a concrete explanation of what a thought is. I shall simply leave aside the question of the true nature of an intentional state or a mental representation, just as I did in chapter 1. It is evident that people have ideas about the world around; most of us are convinced that the earth is round, that two and two make four, that stealing is wrong, and so on. Structures with this content are somehow stored in our minds – so much can be said even without knowing precisely how the relevant structures are constituted and maintained. In many contexts, we need a way of speaking of such structures and contents, however insufficient our understanding of their nature may be. My way is to speak of them as being thoughts – intentional states or mental representations – and that is all I wish to say about what a thought is.

Problem number two, the question of how thoughts get into litera-ture, was treated, indirectly, in chapters 3–4. Linguistic communication entails the conveyance of thoughts from speaker or author to listener or reader (in a special, non-literal sense of "conveyance"). I have endeavoured to describe the basic mechanisms behind that conveyance, pointing out, at the same time, the naturalness of conceiving literature too as a kind of linguistic communication (with a distinctive, "presen-tational" character). In fact, my analysis also offered an explanation of how thoughts get into literature: the essence of literary communi-cation quite simply *consists in* the conveying of thoughts from author to reader. What is being conveyed in connection with Lowell's "Father's Bedroom" is, on the most elementary plane, a complex of mental representations of the interior of a certain room.[2]

As already indicated, the word "convey" carries a figurative meaning in the last paragraph. I do not hold that any literal conveyance of thoughts from author to reader is taking place. On the contrary, in drawing my picture of communication in the last two chapters I have consciously dissociated myself from the transportation metaphor. I have not been maintaining that the author literally clothes his thoughts in words, that the words form a kind of container with the thoughts being its contents, that the words are transferred to the reader, and that she literally assimilates their content. In consequence I am not willing to say, either, that the thoughts exist inside the literary object, i.e., inside the literary work or the literary text. For the literary object, as we are accustomed to conceive of it, is in fact the transport metaphor's verbal container with the thoughts – the intentional states, the mental representations – as its contents.

Instead, according to my picture of (written) communication, the author communicates thoughts by producing physical objects or having them produced – as Lowell produces the manuscript of "Father's Bedroom" and initiates the production of further copies of the poem. The entities concerned are, in themselves, just material objects, neither more nor less. They have, however, been supplied with physical marks intended to enable the reader to reconstruct (and react to) the thoughts that the author is attempting to make her reconstruct (and react to). In my version, therefore, the thoughts – the representations of Lowell's father's bedroom – are not found in any object existing outside author and reader. The only possible object of that kind, the book or page, is in my analysis a physical object, such objects being, of course, incapable of containing thoughts. In my view, some of the relevant thoughts are found in the author – the intentional states whose character he wishes to communicate to the reader and the mental representations he intends the reader to reconstruct from his physical signs. Other relevant thoughts appear in the reader; in her we find the representations which she believes the author to have intended to communicate to her, as well as the representations emerging in the reader's further processing of the communicated content. It is in that manner, as aspects of states in the author's and reader's respective minds, that thoughts enter the process of literary communication.

I find it practical to postpone the discussion of my third problem – how thoughts are associated with feelings or with literary form – to later chapters. It will be taken up in connection with the treatment of feeling (chapter 7) and form (chapters 8–10).

The last of my four questions about thoughts concerned their role in literature, their function or functions in such contexts. Formulated in that fashion the question is large indeed, and I shall not discuss it in all its ramifications. It appears both possible and interesting, however, to offer a few observations about the functions of thoughts in literature.

The most important circumstance of all has already been touched on: thoughts constitute the very core of what is "conveyed" from author to reader in literary communication. Literature's medium is language, and language almost always has a representational content.[3] Attempts to create non-linguistic literature have certainly been made, especially within dadaism and kindred movements, but those attempts are relatively peripheral phenomena.[4]

To put it simply: literature *has to* contain mental representations, since it is unimaginable without them. Without materially distorting the facts one can say that the writing and reading of literature *are identical with* the presentational linguistic communicating of thoughts, of mental representations enveloped in intentional states. Accordingly, the mental representations and the intentional states form the very basis of most literary effects, cognitive, emotional, and formal. This will become increasingly apparent.

It is natural to treat literature's affective and formal values at a somewhat later stage, in connection with feelings and form. The cognitive dimension of literature, however, will be made the topic of a number of comments in this chapter and in chapter 6. First I shall enter into the thoughts emanating from the author and their cognitive significance, commenting particularly on the problems surrounding truth in literature but also pointing to the presence of expressed but non-communicated authorial convictions. In the following chapter I will proceed to the reader's processing. What does the reader make of the thoughts, whether communicated or simply expressed, and why does she process them the way she does? This question leads on to problems concerning the concept of theme and literary thematization, problems surrounding the reader's identifications, and so on.

Uwe Johnson's Jahrestage

The fact that literature possesses a cognitive dimension becomes especially obvious in connection with broad realistic novels, so a text of that type will now be introduced: *Anniversaries: From the Life of Gesine Cresspahl (Jahrestage: Aus dem Leben von Gesine Cresspahl*, 4 vols., 1970–83), a work by the German author Uwe Johnson (1934–84).[5] This novel will play an important role as a literary example in the following, especially in this chapter and in chapter 6.

The episodes related in *Anniversaries* take place during the course of exactly one year, between 20 August 1967 and 20 August 1968.[6] The protagonist is a German woman, Gesine Cresspahl, thirty-four years old at the beginning of the novel, who, having left East Germany and worked in West Germany for a time, is now living in New York with her ten-year-old daughter Marie and working as a foreign-language secretary at the main office of a major bank.

The vice-president of the bank, de Rosny, decides that Gesine Cresspahl – whose Eastern European background is a relevant qualification in this connection – is a suitable person to play a part in the bank's discreet contacts with the new, reformist government of Czechoslovakia, a government interested in loans from the West. Gesine prepares herself for this mission in various ways; among other things, she has to take private tuition in Czech. When the novel ends, in the afternoon of 20 August 1968, Gesine and Marie find themselves in Denmark, on the eastern coast of Sjaelland, about to resume their journey to Prague later the same day. Gesine does not know, of course, that the Soviet Union and its allies will occupy Czechoslovakia during the night.

This brief résumé could be said to trace, very superficially, the most important strand of external action running through the novel. To be sure, the novel is full of events, and these are partly quite dramatic. For one thing, Gesine's fiancé – the émigré East German physicist Dietrich Erichson ("D.E."), working for the U.S. Air Force – is killed when his Cessna crashes in Finland. In fact, the book introduces an entire little world of people, settings, and events.[7] Summaries of the story do not, however, say anything really significant about *Anniversaries*; this is not a novel where day-to-day events are the centre of attraction. Nor is it a psychological novel. Actually, *Anniversaries* is a creation that is not easy to present.

The novel is calm and matter-of-fact in style and realistic in content, but in a certain sense it has a fractured form. *Anniversaries* consists of a series of dated sections, one for each day, about Gesine's life during the year in question – 366 one-day sections in all, 1968 being a leap year.[8] (The only portion outside this frame is a brief introductory section describing Gesine during her holiday on the Atlantic coast in New Jersey.) This does not mean that the novel has the form of a diary. Even if an "I" who is Gesine[9] or the narrator[10] occasionally appears, the normal form is third-person narration from a point of view close to Gesine's perspective.[11]

The English title, *Anniversaries*, is the closest possible translation of the German *Jahrestage*. The German word has, however, a prominent association lacking in the English noun. If the English word for "anniversary" were "yearday," and the translation of the novel were entitled *Yeardays*, Johnson's intentional ambiguity would be captured: the novel describes the days of one year, and each of these days is an anniversary.[12] No day is without memories of the past or questions about the past.

The one-day sections that build up *Anniversaries* differ widely in size and organization, but one still senses an underlying common pattern. To give an idea of what a one-day section can look like, I shall quote the very first, that of Monday, 21 August 1967, in extenso. I also include the end of the brief opening section. When we encounter Gesine, she finds herself on the train carrying her from her New Jersey holiday resort back to New York.

The train rumbles leisurely up to little station squares; commuters in business suits emerge from the dimness beneath the roofs, each alone with his brief case; on the train they lower their seat backs and settle down to sleep. Now the sun is licking the rooftops, throwing fistfuls of light over the lower-lying countryside. The branch line between Gneez and Jerichow led at a distance past villages; the stations were like children's red blocks with gabled, tarred roofs, a scattering of people waiting outside with shopping bags. The high-school students positioned themselves on the platforms in such a way that by the time they got to Gneez they were all in a group in the third and fourth compartments behind the baggage car. It was along this route that Jakob learned the railway business. In his black smock Jakob looked down from his caboose so tolerantly onto the group of school kids, as if unwilling to recognize Cresspahl's daughter. At nineteen perhaps he still classified people by their social status. From New Jersey's scummy brown marshes across long-legged trestle bridges the train sways into the Palisades and down into the tunnel beneath the Hudson to New York, and she has already been standing quite a while among the weekenders and commuters lined up in the center aisle, occasionally moving forward six inches all poised for the race to the train door, the escalator, the labyrinthine construction fences of Pennsylvania Station, over to the West Side subway, the Flushing line, onto the escalator, out from under the blue vaulting to the corner of 42nd Street by Grand Central Station. She must not reach her desk more than an hour late, and that only today, after her vacation.

AUGUST 21, 1967   MONDAY

Clearing skies in North Vietnam enabled the Air Force to attack targets north of Hanoi. The Navy bombed the coast with aircraft and fired eight-inch shells into the demilitarized zone. In the south, four helicopters were shot down. The racial disorders in New Haven continued yesterday with arson, broken store windows, looting; an additional 112 persons have been arrested.

Beside the stack of newspapers waits a little cast-iron dish, and the vendor's arched hand swoops down over it before she has even had time to throw down the coin. The man's eyes are hostile; people have snatched his money once too often in passing by on the street.

So that's what I let my neck be shot up for, lady.

The body of the American who failed to return to his Prague hotel last Wednesday evening was found yesterday afternoon in the Vltava River. Mr. Jordan, aged 59, was an official of the Jewish charity organization JOINT. He had gone out to buy a newspaper.

The bottom of Lexington Avenue is still in shadow. She remembers the taxis jostling each other in the morning on the wide street, prevented from turning by a traffic light, its red exploited by pedestrians to cross the one-way street going east, its green allowing them to hold up the waiting cars. She does not hesitate to defy the traffic signal. She has been coming here since time out of mind, elbows pressed to her sides, intent on the rhythm of the people walking next to her. She avoids the blind beggar clinking his outstretched mug, grunting surlily. Again she cannot make out what he says. She is walking too slowly, her gaze wanders, she is preoccupied with her return. Ever since she has been out of town the wail of sirens has been suspended between the high, windowed towers, swelling, dying away, raucously erupting beyond more distant blocks. From the side streets fierce hot light strikes the avenue. Her eyes on the dazzling cement, she walks along beside a black-marble base facade that mirrors the colors of faces, painted metal, canopies, shirts, store windows, dresses, in muted echo. She turns aside into a white-lit passage from which ammonia steams into the open, released bite by bite through the narrow spring door. This entrance is known only to the staff.

She is now thirty-four. Her child is almost ten. She has been living in New York for six years. She has been working at this bank since 1964.

I imagine: under her eyes the tiny grooves were paler than the tanned skin of her face. Her hair, almost black, cut short all around, has become lighter. She looked half asleep; she has not spoken much to anybody for some time. She did not remove her sunglasses until she had passed beyond the glinting door panel. She never wears her sunglasses pushed back into her hair.

She was barely amused by the rage of the drivers who are victimized day after day by a traffic light on Lexington Avenue. She had arrived in this country by car, a Swedish sedan that had been eaten away by snow salt for two years at the foot of 96th Street, across from the three garages. She has always taken the subway to work.

I imagine: during the lunch hour she again reads that yesterday afternoon a man was rowing on the river in Prague and, on reaching the May First Bridge, found lodged in one of the water barriers a Jew from New York who had left his hotel to buy a newspaper. (She has heard that in Prague English-language newspapers are sold only in hotels.)

You American? Hlavní nádrazí drive, this station, before, Wilsonovo nádrazí. Sta-shun. Woodrow Wilson!

She would have had to say Yes, since she had an American passport in her handbag. She has forgotten the name in the passport. That was in 1962.

I imagine: in the evening, under a sky already stripped of light, she emerges from the 96th Street subway station onto Broadway and sees, framed in the arch below Riverside Drive, a green open space, beyond the frayed greenery of the park the flat river whose hidden shore makes the river seem to spread like a lake in an August forest in dry, scorched silence.

She lives on Riverside Drive in three rooms, below the treetops. The indoor light is pierced with green. To the north, in the midst of dense clouds of leaves, she can see the lamps on the bridge, beyond them the lights on the parkway. Dusk sharpens the lights. The sound of engines runs together in the distance and pounds in steady waves through the window, like ocean breakers. From Jerichow it was an hour's walk to the beach, past the marsh and then through the fields.[13]

The description of Gesine Cresspahl's life could be said to consist of three basic components, discernible already in the passages cited and then returning, in varying proportions, in most later one-day sections. One element is the depiction of Gesine's everyday life. This depiction, in its constant recurrence, also creates, bit by bit, a fragmentary but many-sided portrayal of New York, or at least of Manhattan – seen, above all, from streets, subways, place of work, home, and restaurants – and of American phenomena.

The news matters a lot to Gesine. She follows it primarily in the *New York Times*, which she buys on her way to work and starts reading in the subway. Among the topics particularly occupying Gesine are the war in Vietnam, violence and racial conflicts in America, and the political developments in Germany and the Communist countries. Gesine by no means prefers the Eastern bloc – after all, she has abandoned East Germany for the West – but her reservations about the USA and American values are also obvious. Despite the relatively impartial tone, it becomes evident that Gesine deprecates the Vietnam War and sympathizes with the Czech endeavours to establish a socialism with a human face, a sympathy combined with misgivings about Czechoslovakia's political future.

The flow of news, especially political and criminal news, can be said to constitute the second basic component of the novel, the third being Gesine's personal and family history: the account of her parents, of her surroundings during the years when she was growing up, and of her earlier life. Gesine comes from a small (fictitious) place, Jerichow, near (the fictitious) Gneez in the (real) province of Mecklenburg on the Baltic coast of Germany.[14] Associations with Mecklenburg often come through in the text – as in the opening of the quoted passage, where the sights of the boarding commuters and of the villages along the railroad seem to call forth memories of the journeys between Jerichow and Gneez during her schooldays. (In the account of Gesine's visual memories we also catch a glimpse of the great love of her life: Jakob, Marie's father, who died before the birth of his daughter.) That is one of the ways in which Gesine's personal history is narrated, fragment by fragment, in different one-day sections: chunks of memory material appear, reasonably understood as representing retrospective thoughts engrossing Gesine. In addition, Gesine recounts the Cresspahl family's history to Marie at odd moments, at Marie's request, so that this knowledge will survive even when Gesine herself is dead.

Thus, Gesine's everyday life is permeated both with the news stories of the day and with her own and Germany's past, this complex whole being presented in an exceedingly concrete and nuanced way. The resulting description is original and multifaceted. The clear and tangible picture of Gesine's existence tends to expand into an image of a historical and existential predicament shared by us, the readers. It is interesting and instructive to ask oneself whether Johnson's *Anniversaries* "says" anything about reality and, if the answer is yes, how we are able to identify its message. In this chapter and the next I shall repeatedly revert to various aspects of those problems.

The Distribution of Cognitive Work between Author and Reader

It is, indisputably, a widespread idea that great literature has something to say about the world. I do not introduce this notion merely to reject it; in my opinion it brings into focus one of literature's most important properties. It is not advisable, however, to take this everyday concept altogether literally. If one accepts it at face value, one would have to ask oneself what a novel like *Anniversaries* actually says, and attempt to point to statements somehow expressed in the book. That, however, is a strategy which can only lead to disheartening results: if one looks for distinct and interesting statements, in *Anniversaries* or in other important literature, one does not find many. The propositions it is possible to extricate are either assertions about trivial details or sweeping, more or less banal, generalizations. Worse still, they could always have been formulated and substantiated more clearly and convincingly in a non-literary context.

One should not conclude from this that literature's cognitive potential is negligible.[15] What has been demonstrated is merely that propositional truth – the putting forward of literally true statements about reality – only plays a subordinate part in literature. Cognitive significance, however, is a much more comprehensive phenomenon than propositional truth.[16]

As I see it, literature may indeed affect the reader's understanding of reality substantially, for good or ill. One of its ways of doing this is by communicating thoughts. One might say, slightly metaphorically, that literature communicates pictures of reality, or pictures of a merely fictitious reality. The pictures initiate cognitive processing of various kinds in the reader, a processing likely to effect larger or smaller displacements in her apprehension of reality or the adding of new conceptual resources to her cognitive repertoire.

To my mind, literature's cognitive significance does not emanate from statements or from constructs similar to statements. It comes into existence in the reader's processing of the thought material created and communicated by the author. As it is important to have a clear conception of the character of this interplay, let us attempt to describe the special nature of the "statements" about reality conveyed by literature (and by other representational arts).

When a person's ideas about the world are changed in some respect, this of course is a result of her active thinking, conscious or unconscious. She has been thinking; she has been processing a material of impressions, and in consequence her picture of reality has undergone at least *some* alteration. Accordingly, the reader's processing of the communicated content is undoubtedly a key factor connected with literature's acquisition of cognitive significance.

But the reader's processing is evidently also important when we read non-fiction or are confronted with explicit statements purporting to be true. The reader evaluates the credibility of the statements, adjusting her picture of reality correspondingly. The occurrence of mental processing in the reader, then, is naturally not peculiar to literature. But we do not acquire new convictions through non-fiction in precisely the same way as we do through literature and the other representational arts.

John Hospers once tried to define how art affects our experience of the world by falling back on Bertrand Russell's distinction between two kinds of knowledge: knowledge by acquaintance and knowledge by description. More precisely, Hospers – not without cause finding it problematic to say that art really affords *knowledge* – connected on to Moritz Schlick's further elaboration of Russell's idea: Schlick and Hospers distinguish between *knowledge* of something and *acquaintance* with this something.

Let me make the distinction clearer with an example of my own. We can form an idea of New York by spending a day strolling its streets (which acquaints us with New York or, in Russell's version, affords knowledge by acquaintance), or by reading, for example, Murray Schumach's article about New York in the *Encyclopaedia Britannica*[17] (which provides knowledge of New York or, in Russell's version, knowledge by description). The idea introduced by Hospers – in *Meaning and Truth in the Arts* (1946)[18] – is that the representational arts can offer us acquaintance with things, while science gives us knowledge about them.

Hospers's idea is untenable for several reasons. The objection carrying most weight in our context is simply that, in fact, art and literature do *not* provide acquaintance with reality in the required sense. In reading Johnson's *Anniversaries* we are not literally transported to New York; we are no more placed face to face with the city than we are when reading Schumach's article: the reader acquires direct, unmediated acquaintance only with printed pages in a book. Moreover, even *if* art and literature could have afforded acquaintance with reality in the intended sense, what would have been the point? A stay in New York also gives acquaintance with the city. Are art and literature really to be understood as a mere substitute for real life, a suitable replacement when the thing itself is beyond our reach?

Having made those critical remarks I hasten to add that there is, nevertheless, a sound and important intuition behind Hospers's analysis. In order to see this we have to consider more closely the differences between learning from real life, from literature, and from non-fiction.

We may learn things through direct confrontation with the corresponding reality – for example, learn things about New York through being in the city. But the reason we are learning in a case like that is naturally not that New York *states* something, literally *says* something to us. It is we who are *independently observing and drawing conclusions* from what we are seeing. We may establish through methodical or accidental observation that there is a large library at the corner of Fifth Avenue and 42nd Street. New York does not tell us this; it is we who are noticing it. In a somewhat similar fashion we may learn things about New York from Johnson's text.

Think, first, of Schumach's article about New York in the *Encyclopedia Britannica*. It constitutes a piece of informational discourse. Essentially, Schumach is making assertions: essentially, he is conveying ideas about the city to us, vouching for their correctness. We acquire new convictions about New York by identifying and believing the statements communicated to us.

Anniversaries, on the other hand, is a presentational composition, not an informational one. In presenting the text, Johnson is not asserting anything[19] but displaying an invented world, introducing representations of a fictitious reality. We acquire new convictions about New York (if we do) by drawing conclusions based on our confrontation with Johnson's invented New York and on the fact that Johnson communicates precisely these representations to us. If we acquire the conviction that there is a subway station at 96th Street with at least one exit onto Broadway (cf. the end of the earlier quoted portion of

Anniversaries), this is not because Johnson *states* that. It is because we draw the conclusion, from the complex of thoughts communicated to us, that there is such a station, or was in 1967. (Johnson communicates the thought that there is such a station, and we have reason to believe that he is acquainted with the localities and that he lacks a motive for inventing precisely this detail.) In that respect, our conclusions about reality drawn from *Anniversaries* – conclusions about New York, or about how it feels to be suffering from painful wartime memories, or about what attitude one should adopt towards oppression that one is unable to do anything about – are reminiscent of conclusions founded on our immediate experience of the world around. They come into existence not through our acceptance of the truth of statements but through our confrontation with, and processing of, other kinds of material. What is relevant here, then, is not distinguishing between knowledge (by description) and (knowledge by) acquaintance but between *convictions based on the acceptance of other people's statements* and *convictions based on our own observations and conclusions*. If literature affords new convictions about reality it does so, essentially, by making new ideas of the latter kind natural.

It is important to remember, however, that our observations and conclusions in connection with literature are *guided* in a way they normally are not in our encounters with actual reality. Our experience of Johnson's New York is, unlike our experience of the real city, an experience of an *invented* reality *conveyed through language*. This means, among other things, that the experience of Johnson's New York, unlike strolling in the real New York, puts us in contact with something *prearranged for us by someone else*. The author, Johnson, has prepared the object of our experience beforehand in order to elicit more or less determinate impressions and associations in us. True, Johnson affirms nothing. Metaphorically he might be said to let us visit, in our imagination, a made-up world.[20] But that world is a world of his own making, calculated to give rise to experiences of a more or less determinate kind. In her cognitive processing of the communicated content, the reader is far less guided and dependent than when she is confronted with assertions, though much more so than when she is facing empirical, non-manipulated reality. What we apprehend when reading literature occupies a curious intermediate position between determinate, identifiable statement and mute, unamended reality.[21] If we acquire new convictions, we have obtained them through our own observations and conclusions, but they have nevertheless arisen in an encounter with carefully prearranged material.

The outcome of that encounter depends both on the reader and on the cognitive material with which she is confronted. In this chapter I shall, as already indicated, deal particularly with the cognitive material that the reader encounters (i.e., the material reconstructed by readers reading in accordance with the rules of the practice).

The cognitive material that the reader is faced with may be divided into two kinds: the communicated and the uncommunicated. I shall first speak of the communicated material, coming back to the uncommunicated elements later in the chapter.

This chapter has revolved round the observation that the author communicates thoughts to his readers. The thoughts involved may be fantasies but also convictions, wishes, and so on. With *Anniversaries*, the relevant thought complex is, principally, a web of fantasies: imaginings concerning Gesine Cresspahl, her actions, the content of her consciousness, the milieus in which she finds herself, and so forth. The reader is required to perform a good deal of processing if she is to profit cognitively from the *fantasies* communicated by the author; such processing will be commented upon mainly in the next chapter. But as I said before, the thoughts communicated by an author may also be *convictions*, and the author sometimes appears to guarantee the truth of these. In such cases the author seems to be making genuine statements, true or false. Thus literature may apparently be true or false in the most literal sense – at least in places.

The question of literature and truth is a much-discussed problem of literary aesthetics. I shall devote a couple of sections to outlining an analysis of the problem, starting from the vantage point of linguistic pragmatics.

Statements in Literature: John Searle's Analysis

Can literature really convey truths to the reader? In that case, what are the communicative mechanisms that make such conveyance possible? And does the conveyance of truth have an important role to play in literature? These are three central questions about literature and truth, perhaps the most central of all, and they will be the centre of attention in the next few sections.

In chapter 3 I reproduced a newspaper notice about the selection of John Sykes as the Conservative candidate for a British constituency. I do not doubt the factual information contained in the notice; I feel convinced of the trustworthiness of the assertions (1990) that John Sykes is thirty-three years old, that he is a company director from Huddersfield, and that he has been selected as the Conservative candidate for the seat of Scarborough and Whitby. In asking my questions about literature and truth it is conveyance of truth in this simple and straightforward sense of "truth" that I am thinking of. I am considering propositional truth, and the conveyance of true statements, whether by explicit or implicit means.[22] I do not treat of truth as a property of reality itself, nor do I use "true" in the sense of "important," "deeply moving," or the like.[23] (In order to avoid misunderstanding, it should be added that I take into consideration the fact that literature may be important or moving. I do this, however, under other head-words than "truth.")[24]

A proposition – or, as I prefer, a mental representation of reality – is true when it corresponds with the actual facts. To convey a truth is to communicate a true statement, a statement introducing a true mental representation. I regard those remarks as tautologous, as merely specifying what we usually put into the idea of truth and true statements. I shall not pose the question of whether it is at all possible for our statements to correspond with actual facts and what such correspondence, in that case, consists in. There is, I should say, an everyday understanding, however vague, of what is required for a statement to be true. (Think of the question of whether the information about John Sykes in the newspaper item is true or not!) Where the concept of truth is concerned, my reasoning will remain on the plane of these vague everyday conceptions. Probing the philosophical problems surrounding truth – for example, asking in what sense statements may be said to be true – would carry us much too far. What I want to discuss here is, instead, simply whether literature can communicate true statements just like texts of other types. The question what it means to say that a statement is true is a far deeper problem – whose actual relevance to aesthetics may well be negligible.[25]

Is it possible, then, to communicate true or false statements by publishing a piece of literature? The most widespread opinion is, unquestionably, that the answer is yes.[26] That view is not universally prevalent, however,[27] and I find this quite understandable. One's standpoint on the matter must depend, I think, on what meaning one chooses to give to the word "statement."

Starting from pragmatics, more specifically from speech act theory, John Searle has provided an interesting analysis of what a statement is. As Searle sees it, in order for something to be a statement it must first of all be a linguistic *utterance* with a *propositional content*. (When translated into the terminology I am using here, this means, approximately, that a mental representation – a conviction or the like – has to be communicated by linguistic means.) Secondly, the propositional content must be conveyed with an assertive force. (In my terminology: the communicating of the conviction has to possess an informational communicative function.) According to Searle, the latter involves two things. On the one hand it implies that the originator vouches for the concordance between the things said and actual reality; on the other, that his doing so constitutes *the very point* of his communicative act.[28] "Point" – the closest counterpart of which in my conceptual system is "communicative function" – is in reality used by Searle as an undefined fundamental concept.[29] One can glimpse the idea that the most important raison d'être of an utterance makes up its point, and that no more detailed explanation could clarify the term any further.

Searle is among those who maintain that literary works may contain statements. This comes out in his article "The Logical Status of Fictional Discourse" (1975). That article is a well-known – and much-criticized[30] – attempt to analyse fictional discourse from the vantage point of speech act theory, Searle's main idea being that fictional discourse consists of *merely pretended* speech acts. It is not necessary to discuss this aspect of Searle's theory here, but he also holds that genuine speech acts, for example, genuine statements – may occur in a work of fiction. For Searle, statements may form part of a literary work, but not of its fictional story. "Sometimes," he writes, "the author of a fictional story will insert utterances in the story which are not fictional and not part of the story. To take a famous example, Tolstoy begins *Anna Karenina* with the sentence 'Happy families are all happy in the same way, unhappy families unhappy in their separate, different ways.' That, I take it, is not a fictional but a serious utterance. It is a genuine assertion. It is part of the novel but not part of the fictional story ... A work of fiction need not consist entirely of, and in general will not consist entirely of, fictional discourse."[31]

Thus, according to Searle the first sentence of Tolstoj's *Anna Karenina* (2 vols., 1875–7) supplies an example of a genuine statement contained in a literary work. Searle's approach may seem sound enough. But it is not without inherent problems.[32]

Evidently, Tolstoj communicates a representation, a propositional content: roughly, that *all happy families are similar to one another, while all unhappy families are unhappy each in their own way.* But can he be said to vouch for the content's agreement with reality? And if so, is this vouching for the content's truth really *the very point* of communicating the content?

The latter may appear doubtful. Part of the purpose of a part-utterance[33] – i.e., of an utterance forming part of a larger utterance whole, as Tolstoj's opening sentence forms part of *Anna Karenina* – is no doubt always to contribute to the constructing of the whole. Supporting a larger compositional structure may in actual fact sometimes be the most significant function of a part-utterance. And one may ask whether the purpose of fitting the sentence "Happy families are all happy in the same way, unhappy families unhappy in their separate, different ways" into *Anna Karenina* as its first sentence[34] was not, above all, simply to provide the novel with a suitable opening.

For suitable it is, introducing the topic of happy and unhappy families, thereby creating the expectation that the work will deal with family life – presumably with an unhappy family, since this is presented as a more varied and consequently more substantial subject. Perhaps the sentence, through its general form, also makes the reader expect the subsequent narrative to shape itself into a description of life and manners – a description capable of being, in a sense, generalized, and thereby conducive to moral insight. Both features appear adequate and meaningful in the context. And considerations of this kind may be supposed to have played a prominent role in the decision to incorporate the sentence into the novel, since it is difficult to imagine that Tolstoj would have inserted the sentence mainly because he wished to share some factual beliefs about happy and unhappy families with his readership. (We are, after all, speaking of a work of imaginative literature.)[35]

But in that case Tolstoj is not using the sentence to make a statement in the Searlean sense: if the main reason for introducing the sentence in question is not to vouch for the truth of its content, then the sentence does not have an assertive point. And that is not all. If literal truth is not Tolstoj's principal consideration at this point, then perhaps he takes the liberty of saying something he does not entirely believe. (The sentence may of course be effective from a literary point of view without being true. What is required with regard to veracity, if the sentence's artistic effectiveness is to be preserved, is perhaps rather its not being apprehended as unreasonable by the reader.)

It is certainly *possible* for a part-utterance contained within a larger textual whole to be a genuine statement. For example, an article about Uwe Johnson in an encyclopedia of literature opens with the following biographical information: "Johnson, Uwe, *20.7 1934 Kammin/ Pomerania, now: Kamién Pomorski/Poland, +23.2.1984 Sheerness-on-Sea/Kent (England)."[36] This is obviously a (complex) statement. True, an important part of its function is to contribute to the building up of a larger whole, an introduction of Uwe Johnson. But the introduction of Johnson is a piece of informational discourse, its main point being to convey the most relevant information about the author, also purely external facts such as the ones just cited.

According to the theory of literature's presentationality, literary compositions are always a different matter. Texts like Tolstoj's *Anna Karenina*, Johnson's *Anniversaries*, or Lowell's "Father's Bedroom" have not, essentially, been written with a view to communicating true statements; they have another, more intricate, communicative function. The author may no doubt communicate pictures of reality of whose facticity he himself is apparently convinced: "Father's Bedroom" is a good instance of this. But the *point* of a literary composition cannot very well consist in conveying empirical truths. So the communicating of empirically correct pictures of reality must have a subordinate function, as a means of solving a more comprehensive task which is, in itself, of a different kind. And then it stands to reason that we are no longer dealing with statements in Searle's strict sense, no matter how similar to statements the part-utterances in question may appear.

Statements in Searle's strict sense are conceivable in literature only where we are dealing with part-utterances breaking out, as it were, of the work's aesthetic whole and being employed for more or less competing, purely informational purposes. At the end of *Anniversaries*, at a point where Gesine's recapitulation of her own personal history has reached the partition of Germany after the Second World War, Johnson with implicit approbation produces a letter from Thomas Mann to the East German party secretary Walther Ulbricht, a letter where Mann takes strong exception to the summary trials in Waldheim in the summer of 1950. In adducing the letter, Johnson carefully indicates that he is quoting – this is even one of the quotations in Johnson's novel for which information about the copyright is given in the text itself.[37] Technically, the memory of Mann's letter and its formulations should presumedly be thought to appear in Gesine's consciousness, there forming part of her continuous processing of the past. Yet the quotation – like some other passages in the one-day sections of the novel's last month – threatens to disengage itself from the epic context and become an element in an independent historical discussion. Thus it tends to acquire the character of a statement: an assertion that Thomas Mann wrote this, that he condemned the Waldheim trials in precisely these words.

If Searle's concept of a statement is applied – and that notion "statement" seems reasonable to me in all essentials[38] – then statements, and consequently propositional truth, can appear in literature only in contexts where the literary work tends to lose its literary character and its sense of being a united whole. The conclusions drawn from that observation may vary. One may simply accept Searle's definitions, affirming in consequence that literature cannot contain proper statements as long as it is being true to its native presentational character. There is much to be said in favour of such a standpoint, in spite of its somewhat uncommon content. Another possibility, however, is to opt for a weaker concept of a statement than that of Searle. One may, for example, content oneself with the requirement that a person stating something has to introduce a picture of reality while vouching for its facticity, and thus do without the proviso that the person's vouching for the truth of the things said must also be the *point* of his utterance. In that case one should, in all likelihood, be speaking of statements also in connection with Lowell's lines

> The broad-planked floor
> had a sandpapered neatness.

There is something reasonable in this approach,[39] but also something dubious: the basic purpose behind Lowell's lines obviously differs from that of an ordinary, non-literary statement, and our knowing this clearly colours our perception of his utterance.

In other words, my discussion of whether literature can convey truth to the reader has not led to any clear-cut answer. Certainly one can introduce truths, true pictures of reality, by means of literary works. This can be done because it is possible for literature to communicate representations. But the mere communicating of a correct picture of reality can hardly qualify as a conveyance of truth. The picture of reality must, reasonably, in some sense be *asserted* – and not, for instance, introduced as being *negated* or *just possible* – for conveying of truth to be said to take place. If the author is vouching for the facticity of the true picture of reality, that should be enough. But in practice it is difficult for the reader to feel certain of the author's actually doing so unless it is obvious that the author's *main reason* for introducing the picture of reality is to inform.

What is important in this context, however, is not to give a definite answer to the question whether literature may contain statements and consequently truth. As we have seen, that problem stands out as, basically, a question of definition, each positive answer necessarily being stipulative to a significant extent. What is worth emphasizing is the fact that the literary, presentational context lends a peculiar character to the things said, associating them with special purposes undermining, to a certain degree, the assertive character one may eventually wish to ascribe to some of the formulations. If one feels inclined to insist that statements may in fact be found in genuinely literary contexts, one nevertheless has to admit, I believe, that their affirmative character is weakened and somewhat dubious. We are dealing with "aetiolations," as John L. Austin once put it,[40] not really with full-blown assertions.

Implicit Utterances in Literature

When speaking of assertions in the last section, I was consistently referring to manifest, explicitly formulated utterances. But the author may also employ more indirect ways of communicating an assertion, a fictional utterance, or some other type of content. He might use figures of speech, or irony, in conveying the content. And he could also produce indirect utterances by relying on what are called indirect speech acts,[41] or via connections built up in the fictional discourse itself, and perhaps by other means as well. I lack the space for a comprehensive exemplification of these phenomena, so I shall restrict myself to making just a few remarks about implicit utterances, remarks especially important in my context. I shall use implicit assertions as examples and start from a poem by the English author Philip Larkin (1922–85).

The poem in question has a sarcastic and conversational tone frequent in Larkin's poetry. It was written in 1972, the year of the author's fiftieth birthday, and went unpublished until after his death. It is called "The View," and I reproduce it in extenso.

> The view is fine from fifty,
> Experienced climbers say;
> So, overweight and shifty,
> I turn to face the way
> That led me to this day.
>
> Instead of fields and snowcaps
> And flowered lanes that twist,
> The track breaks at my toe-caps
> And drops away in mist.
> The view does not exist.
>
> Where has it gone, the lifetime?
> Search me. What's left is drear.
> Unchilded and unwifed, I'm
> Able to view that clear:
> So final. And so near.[42]

While the first two stanzas are metaphorical, the third and last is by and large formulated in literal, relatively unequivocal terms. Life has vanished without a trace, says Larkin.[43] And he adds: "What's left is drear." At first, that formulation seems to refer to life: to what is left of Larkin's "lifetime," which has just been mentioned. When one reads on, however, the reference starts to shift to death. When Larkin says that what is left is "So final. And so near," it is obviously death, the end of life, that he is confronting.[44] With those words the field of vision, and thus the "view" referred to in the title, are transferred in an unexpected fashion from past to future and consequently from life to death. "My death is something final, and it is not far away," says the last sentence of the poem.

When formulated like this, the assertion in question is rather trite. In the poem, however, Larkin succeeds in making death's nearness and definitiveness striking and substantial. He does this, above all, through the two opening stanzas, which introduce the poem's theme – life's successive passing and possible ways of viewing it – in a way preparing for the final effect.

In the first and second stanzas, aging is metaphorically described as mountain climbing, which gives rise to a small coherent system of metaphors: the age of fifty is a special peak (or perhaps only a special point on the mountainside?) commanding a fine view, people over fifty are experienced climbers,[45] and so on. Larkin maliciously fashions these metaphors into abstract, scentless alpine clichés – "fields and snowcaps / And flowered lanes that twist" – undermining the climbers' optimistic message by branding it as cheap rhetoric. And when, immediately afterwards, he puts their statement to the test, it is quite predictably proven false: "The view does not exist."

In the third stanza, the poem's fundamental metaphor – now seriously discredited – is so much in the background that one may get the impression of its having been definitively discarded. Nevertheless, since the metaphors associated with mountains and seeing have played a major part in the poem, it is easy for Larkin to revive them in the final lines. And there they return, with a certain element of surprise, making death's nearness and definitiveness *seen*. That gives death a much more palpable and insistent presence than it would have in a prose translation ("what is left of life is, in reality, only death").

The proposition in which I have taken an interest ("My death is something final, and it is not far away") is not explicitly formulated in the poem but expressed in a split-up, indirect manner. (This is yet another of the many circumstances nuancing the impression created by the assertion, but considerations of space prevent me from entering into a more detailed interpretation of the assertion, let alone of the whole poem.) Still, I would call the assertion explicit rather than implicit. The poem, however, also provides a good instance of an implicit assertion. I am thinking of the (rather peripheral) assertion made in the first two lines of the poem. Literally, they tell us that *experienced climbers say that the view is fine from fifty*, and indirectly they no doubt express, approximately, the assertion that *those who can talk from experience say that people of fifty have a pleasing perspective on their lives*.

Just like the opening sentence of *Anna Karenina*, this assertion – or "assertion" – should no doubt be seen principally as a literary device; Larkin can hardly have worried much about its literal, empirical truth. What interests me right now, however, is not the utterance's character of an assertion but the fact that the utterance is implicit. I want to use the utterance as an example in making three simple observations about implicit utterances in literature.

First: The difference between explicitly and implicitly conveyed contents is not of major *theoretical* significance. As I see it, there is a fundamentally important dividing line between what the author *says* and what *reveals itself* in what he says: between thoughts *communicated* by the author and thoughts that are *uncommunicated* but still conveyed to the reader. Both explicitly and implicitly conveyed contents are communicated by the author; both form part of what he wishes the reader to infer that he wishes the reader to infer. Wholly explicit utterances provide the reader with clues that are as good as possible to the content of the communicative intention; implicit statements simply supply clues that require more interpretation. When reading Larkin's lines "The view is fine from fifty, / Experienced climbers say," we automatically understand from the linguistic material and the textual and cultural context that Larkin wishes to communicate to us, within a presentational frame, that experienced climbers praise the view from fifty. Furthermore, it is a less obvious conclusion that, by the content explicitly conveyed, Larkin implicitly wishes to impart that those who can talk from experience say that people of fifty have a pleasing perspective on their lives. But we certainly follow the same strategy when we draw that conclusion, thus identifying Larkin's implicit statement: given the language, the textual context, and the cultural context, we find it reasonable to assume that Larkin wishes to communicate this implicit content to us. So there is a difference of degree rather than a difference in kind between the explicit and the implicit, and in actual cases the limits indeed often appear fluid. Think, for example, of the half-explicitly, half-implicitly formulated assertion at the end of Larkin's "The View": "My death is something final, and it is not far away."

Second: though the distinction between explicit and implicit statements may not be very important from a theoretical point of view, there are practical differences which deserve attention. Indirectly formulated statements are naturally on the whole more elusive than explicit ones. As regards assertions, even explicit assertions are as a rule more or less vague or imprecise – this applies, for example, to the assertion that *those who can talk from experience say that people of fifty have a pleasing perspective on their lives.* The group of people mentioned has no entirely clear boundaries. Is it possible to specify an absolutely exact minimum age required for membership, and if so, what age is that? And are we being told that *all* the people in question entertain the opinion referred to, or that *most* of them do, or that at least *some* of them hold the view? Indirectly formulated assertions introduce additional problems, since almost without exception there will be more than one conceivable way of transforming them into explicit assertions. In connection with "The View," the combination of words "experienced climbers" can be given a large number of partly different translations of about equal plausibility, and so can the phrase "The view is fine from fifty." The gist of this, the simple but important point, is that indirect statements are less clear, more open, than explicit ones. They give more interpretative scope to the reader.

Third: even if there were one and only one correct way of translating a certain implicit statement into an explicit one, the implicit statement would not, because of that, be reducible to the corresponding explicit version. There are considerable differences between "Experienced climbers say that the view is fine from fifty" and "Those who can talk from experience say that people of fifty have a pleasing perspective on their lives." Even if the former statement had said implicitly exactly what the latter says explicitly, it would still have utilized other linguistic means for doing so, and in consequence it would have had somewhat different connotations.[46] As readers we register, and are influenced by, not only the statement made but also the means by which it is made and the connotations surrounding the statement. In chapter 1 I pointed out that the interpretation of a perception does not, so to speak, obliterate the material from which the interpretation started: interpretations on different levels may coexist in consciousness, each in its own way contributing to the global perceptual impression. In seeing two equally high trees, one closer and one further off, we do not perceive the trees as occcupying equally large parts of our field of vision, and yet we experience them as being equally big. In seeing green grass in the shade of a tree we clearly perceive the grass as something grey while nevertheless interpreting it as being green. Similar cases abound in the interpretation of language. In reading the opening lines of "The View" we are fully aware that Larkin is speaking of views from a mountain, and yet we are at the same time interpreting him as talking about perspectives on a life. This gives a different impression from an encounter with the explicit assertion "Those who can talk from experience say that people of fifty have a pleasing perspective on their lives." And the difference in impression is of vital importance, not least in a literary context.[47]

The Limited Role of Truth in Literature

We have seen that literary works may communicate assertions, at least etiolated assertions, and that such assertions can also be conveyed implicitly and hence indirectly.

One sometimes encounters the idea that literary works, regarded as wholes, normally communicate implicit assertions, and that these constitute the most essential content of the work – its "message," thesis, or theme. In fact, Searle takes up a standpoint of this kind in "The Logical Status of Fictional Discourse." He maintains that fictional discourse is made up of *merely pretended* speech acts and is thus faced with the problem of explaining how non-serious, merely apparent assertions can be of interest to the reader. Searle's answer is that the author, in putting forward his pretended assertions, is, as a rule, somehow making genuine assertions in an indirect fashion: "serious (i.e. nonfictional) speech acts can be conveyed by fictional texts, even though the conveyed speech act is not represented in the text. Almost any important work of fiction conveys a 'message' or 'messages' which are conveyed *by* the text but are not *in* the text. Only in such children's stories as contain the concluding 'and the moral of the story is ... ' or in tiresomely didactic authors such as Tolstoy do we get an explicit representation of the serious speech acts which it is the point (or the main point) of the fictional text to convey."[48]

The formulations ("message," "moral," "didactic," and so on) suggest that Searle believes the implicit speech acts constituting the work's "message" to be, in the first place, assertions. So we are confronted, here, with an extremely clear instance of a cognitively orientated standpoint on what literature is and does: the point (or the main point) of a work of fiction is thought to be, above all, the conveyance of assertions to the reader. This is an idea which has not enjoyed much popularity in reputable literary aesthetics since the Second World War,[49] and it is certainly difficult to take it seriously today. Nevertheless, I find it important to discuss the standpoint.

The gist of the idea at issue is that literary works of fiction, taken as wholes, normally convey implicit assertions, this being the actual main point of the works. In my view – which is, here, in complete agreement with that prevalent in contemporary literary aesthetics – that idea is simply erroneous. One could perhaps find a few literary works of fiction that do answer Searle's description – despite the fact that I cannot, myself, think of any obvious instance, I do not regard it as impossible that such works exist.[50] However, typical literary works of fiction are assuredly of a different nature.[51]

My analysis of literary discourse as being essentially presentational is of course irreconcilable with seeing the conveying of assertions as the main point of literary works. And the idea that literary discourse normally has an informational communicative function is indeed, in my opinion, entirely untenable. Devastating criticism could be levelled at the conception, but it is not necessary to do so in this context, since I wish to reject at the outset the idea that fictional literary works, taken as wholes, are normally conveying assertions. Consider Updike's "Pygmalion," which can be regarded as a rather ordinary literary work of fiction in the respects relevant here. What would be the assertion or assertions conveyed by "Pygmalion" taken as a whole?

In discussing "Pygmalion" in chapter 2, I said that it is natural for the reader to associate the story with the idea of love as self-seeking, or of art as a farce, or of our efforts at mastering reality as vain and presumptuous. One could attempt to base a definition of the work's message on such observations. But what message or messages, then, should the story be said to convey? "Male love is egoistical, and this is to the detriment of both woman and man"? Or: "There are those who try to remodel their partners in accordance with their own ideals, but no good comes of that"? Or: "Our attempts at comprehending and mastering reality always fail"? Or something else?

I should say that none of the alternatives mentioned represents an assertion that Updike is in fact making via his story. Making an assertion involves, at least, communicating a conviction and vouching for its truth. But according to my analysis of communication there are no grounds for saying that Updike is in fact communicating any one of the convictions indicated while at the same time vouching for its truth. Asserting something implies at least, if one follows my analysis, indicating to the reader, with deliberate transparency, that one entertains the corresponding belief and guarantees its correctness. Thus, for asserting to occur, one has to intend to make it possible for the reader to infer that one is, with deliberate transparency, indicating to her that one entertains the belief in question and vouches for its truth. And as I see it, the reader of Updike's story cannot possibly infer, from the text and the context of its publication, that Updike is indicating, with deliberate transparency, that he has any one of the convictions at issue and guarantees its truth. (So either Updike made no attempt to assert something, or else he failed signally in his assertive endeavours.) There is a multitude of partly different beliefs that could, with about the same amount of justification, be said to be reflected in the story. The ones just indicated are merely three among many. And each of them could, moreover, be produced in lots of slightly varying versions: "All male love is egoistical ... ," "Some male love is egoistical ... ," " ... at least in the USA of the 1980s ... ," and so on. All these alternatives are more or less reasonable approximations of thoughts that are, in some sense, brought to life by the story. But none of the thoughts appears to me to be *communicated* and *asserted*. I cannot find that Updike has indicated to me, the reader, with deliberate transparency, that he does in fact hold the belief and guarantee its correspondence with actual reality. Or, looking at the matter from another angle: if we insist on speaking of implicit assertions conveyed by the story as a whole, we will have to water down the concept of an assertion to such a degree that the story will prove dizzyingly rich in vague, disparate, and somewhat vacuous assertions.

Thus I deny that literary works of fiction, texts like Updike's "Pygmalion," do convey implicit assertions when taken as a whole. It is perhaps natural to raise objections at this point. Is it not quite sensible to think that the story actually says, roughly, that love is egoistical, or that art is a farce, or that our attempts at mastering reality are both presumptuous and unavailing? Yes, it is sensible – or at least not unreasonable. But the crux of the matter is: what should it be taken to mean that the story "says" this?

What I have disputed is that the story *implicitly asserts* it. My point of view should be easy to grasp if one recalls what was said, earlier in this chapter, about the distribution of cognitive work between author and reader. In my version, the author of fiction first and foremost presents a material of fantasies to the reader. The reader processes the material; she uses it as a basis for observations and conclusions. But her activity is directed by the author, to some extent, for by his choice and arrangement of material he has encouraged the reader to make observations and draw conclusions along lines he has more or less clearly anticipated. With reference to that analysis I would willingly concede that Updike's story "says" things about male love in the sense that it *is liable to give rise to* certain reader observations and reflections about male love (and, for that matter, about a good many other phenomena as well). I would even admit that the story was no doubt *more or less intentionally constructed in precisely such a fashion that it would be liable to give rise to* such observations and reflections in the reader. I insist, however, that to write in such a manner is to do something considerably vaguer and more open-ended than to formulate an assertion, even an implicit one.

Literature can communicate assertions, at least etiolated assertions, both explicitly and implicitly. Consequently, literature may also convey truth via assertions – at all events it can do so *in a certain sense*. But the conveyance of literal truths plays no prominent role in literature.

The central function of literature simply is not that of imparting information.

In chapter 3 I singled out presentationality as the most important characteristic of literature. It is true that political or didactic literature, in extreme cases, does verge towards informational discourse. But it still remains an obvious fact that practically all works that are *literary* in the central, contemporary sense of the word are presentational compositions. It follows from this that the conveying of true assertions plays only a subordinate part in literature.

The close association between literature and presentationality means that literature is not a profitable medium if one's main purpose is to supply literally true assertions. Although a novel or poem may convey assertions, the very fact that the assertions appear in a work of literature tends to undermine them and make them more imprecise. It suffices to think of Lowell's "Father's Bedroom." As far as I understand, Lowell's poem gives a truthful description of his father's bedroom, and a competent reader cannot, I believe, avoid the assumption that it was in fact Lowell's ambition to do so. (*Life Studies* contains many pieces bearing an autobiographical stamp, and in its place in that collection "Father's Bedroom" makes a rather more autobiographical impression than it does here in my book, detached from its original context.) Still it is natural for the reader to feel less confident of the actuality of the facts in question than if the corresponding information had been given in a biography of Lowell. The reader knows that the imparting of factually correct information is, at the most, a subordinate objective of Lowell's in the lyrical context. This being so, she also knows that Lowell might see it as justified to be careless with truth, within certain limits at least, if this would make it easier for him to attain his principal, literary goals.[52]

Saying that truth plays a subordinate role in literature is not the same as saying that it plays no part at all. Again, "Father's Bedroom" is an instructive example. It is one thing to create an invented version of the interior of a father's bedroom immediately after his death. The (purportedly) truthful rendering of the interior of the bedroom of one's own father immediately after his death is something quite different. I do not claim that an act of the latter sort must, in itself, of necessity be more artistically significant. But I maintain that the human import of the two communicative actions differs considerably. Accordingly, the reading experience – the experience of being confronted with the respective communicative action – will be different in the two cases, and certainly in an artistically significant way. So truth may serve, among many other things, as an instrument of artistic expression, truth being capable of releasing literally relevant effects that cannot be achieved by other means. The self-exhibiting character of *Life Studies* was apparently very important, both positively and negatively, for the literary impression that Lowell's collection of poems made on its audience.[53]

Expressed but Non-Communicated Thoughts

The reader not only encounters assertions and fictional statements but also draws conclusions about thoughts in the author that are not communicated but still find expression in the work. In this way, too, the reader may come in contact with author convictions she has the opportunity of making her own.

Thus in reading a work like Johnson's *Anniversaries* it is difficult not to have one's picture of reality modified on a number of points. In part, the modifications involve the reader perceiving elements of the fictional account as realistic and trustworthy, and hence her acquiring new, or more precise, ideas about New York, about Germany in the interwar period, and so on – a mechanism that I pointed out earlier.

One may ask how important this phenomenon should be judged from a purely literary point of view. The question is worth considering, but I shall postpone my answer to the next chapter, where I can allot more space to it. For the moment, let us instead dwell upon the fact that modification of belief does indeed appear in connection with much literature. It is interesting to reflect somewhat further on how such modification comes about, and these matters also have a bearing on literature's relation to truth. For one has, no doubt, in speaking of literature's truth-conveying capacity, often referred also to ideas that are not communicated but still manifested.

Using *Anniversaries* as an example, one has ample opportunity to discuss the phenomenon of expressed but non-communicated thoughts. I should say that *Anniversaries*, in spite of its presumably rather massive cognitive influence on the reader, does not, on the whole, formulate any assertions, not even etiolated assertions.[54] Those who have read the novel may, however, feel inclined to disagree. One could point to an abundance of passages that must be understood as based upon notices or articles from the *New York Times*, such as the following, opening the one-day section concerning Wednesday, 23 August 1967: "Yesterday the Air Force flew 132 missions over North Vietnam. A caption under a picture of the wreckage of an airplane in Hanoi states that the Communists claim this to be aircraft shot down by them. The photo was important enough for the front page, but it is not until page 6, overshadowed by news from Jerusalem, that we find the official announcements of the death of forty servicemen, only the dead from New York and surrounding areas being mentioned by name, fifteen lines of local news."[55]

But this is not assertion, at least not explicit assertion. We must not say that we encounter assertions just because we meet with declarative sentences whose conventional meaning links up with actual reality. The crux of the matter is how the sentences are employed: whether they are being used to convey assertions or not. And what Johnson is doing here is of a more complicated structure than one might be able to see right away: Johnson is rendering the contents of a fictive person's consciousness. By introducing the sentences cited he makes it the case in the fiction that Gesine learns from the *New York Times* that the U.S. Air Force flew 132 missions over North Vietnam on 22 August (and so on). He asserts nothing – not that the U.S. Air Force flew 132 missions over North Vietnam on that day, or even that the *New York Times* reports this. What he does is add a few new strokes of the brush to his painting of a fictional world.[56]

It is another matter that the competent reader is likely to get the impression that the factual information reported could indeed be found in the *New York Times* of 23 August 1967. *Anniversaries* contains much detailed and plausible information about what was said in the *New York Times* on certain definite days during the year in question. It is natural for the reader to make the (correct) assumption that Johnson has been utilizing actual newspaper copies as a source. And why should Johnson have wished to mislead us concerning their content? What sense would that make? If the reader lets herself be convinced by Johnson's accounts of the contents of the *New York Times* – as I take it for granted most of his readers do – this is no doubt due to implicit considerations of the kind suggested.

So the reader faced with the quoted passage will probably conclude that Johnson has the conviction that the U.S. Air Force flew 132 missions on the day at issue (and so on). According to my analysis, that conviction is not *communicated* by Johnson. It is, instead, a conviction which a consideration of the pragmatic situation and the communicated content makes it natural to ascribe to Johnson. I shall say that it is reflected in the communicated content, that it is "expressed" there.[57]

Certainly readers often sense that a given conviction finds expression in the author's formulations. If the reader believes the author to be well informed on the point in question, she will tacitly take over his conviction. In my opinion this is a cognitively important mechanism. Whether we find its effects relevant or not from an aesthetic point of view, they contribute substantially to making it possible for presentational compositions, in literature as well as in the other arts, to take an active part in the forming of our picture of actual reality.

Here it should of course be added that, as we all know, it is problematical to use literature as a source of knowledge about actual reality. I am not principally referring to the possibility that the author may err, or that he may deliberately try to mislead us, since those are risks that we always run as addressees. Instead, I am thinking of the special, additional problems that arise when we process pictures of reality communicated via literature. These problems emanate from the fact that the author, by letting his composition stand out as presentational discourse, has exempted himself from the normal obligation to tell the truth. Certainly he can, without jeopardizing the overall presentational character of his work, bind himself to be relatively veracious by presenting the content as wholly or partly documentary. That is what Lowell is doing in "Father's Bedroom," and what Johnson does with the *New York Times* material in *Anniversaries*. (If Lowell's bedroom interior or Johnson's news stories proved to be pure fabrication, the reader would, in my opinion, have a right to accuse the author of malicious deception.) But not even an author who markedly lays claim to documentary reliability thereby waives every right to poetic licence. Moreover, it is difficult to say exactly how liberal a use of invention and imagination is compatible with a given degree of emphasized documentary ambition, and it is often even more difficult to know how the author himself regards that matter.

The last-quoted passage from *Anniversaries* illustrates these problems too, as the information given is not to be relied on in every detail. The news about 132 Air Force missions in Vietnam is certainly found in the *New York Times* of 23 August, but it concerns Monday 21 August, not Tuesday 22. In addition, the description of the photo combines – or confuses – two different pictures in the copy in question: one of a plane in Hanoi reported to have crashed and one of a plane outside Hanoi supposedly shot down. And so on. It is hard to say whether the reader is being misled in an unjustified fashion, or to determine what lies behind the deviations from the facts – has Johnson seen it as desirable and legitimate to make minor alterations in the underlying states of affairs, or has he just been careless?[58] What is certain, however, is that the factual information conveyed is not one hundred per cent correct, despite the text's documentary appearance.

I have now discussed a clear and simple supposed example of expressed, non-communicated thoughts. But the example is also trivial. Let us heighten the degree of complexity somewhat by studying a later passage in the one-day section concerning 23 August 1967, an account of the first meeting between Gesine's father and mother (as imagined by Gesine). The father, Heinrich Cresspahl, born in 1888, a native of Malchow in Mecklenburg, has emigrated to London, where he runs a small but successful joiner's workshop. In 1931, during a brief stay in Germany, where he is unpleasantly affected by the poisonous social and political situation, he happens to see the young Lisbeth Papenbrock on a Sunday excursion. He falls in love, and so postpones his voyage home. In the passage to be quoted, we find ourselves in a garden restaurant. Cresspahl has followed the Papenbrocks there and observes them from a distance.

In 1931 my mother was twenty-five, the youngest of Papenbrock's daughters. In family photos she stands at the back, hands clasped, head slightly to one side, unsmiling. One could tell she had never worked other than to please herself. She was about medium height, like me, wore our hair in a knot on the nape of her neck, dark hair, falling loosely around her small, docile, somewhat sallow face. She was looking worried now. She seldom raised her eyes from the tablecloth and kneaded her fingers as if she were at a loss. She was the only one to notice that the man, who was watching her levelly without nodding, had followed them from the Priwall ferry to the linen draper's, to the nearest free table in the garden. Old Mr. Papenbrock leaned back with his whole weight in his chair and nagged at the waiter, or his wife, when other tables were served. My grandmother, silly sheep, said, as if she were in church: "Yes, Albert. Of course, Albert." The waiter stood beside Cresspahl and said: "Not that I know of. Weekend. A lot come up from Mecklenburg. Good families. Yes, sir."

> I was pretty, Gesine.
> And yet he looked more like a workman.
> We had an eye for such things, Gesine.

Cresspahl was waiting for the ferry to Priwall when the Papenbrocks came and stood in the front row; on the ferry he stood leaning against the barrier, with his back to them. On the other side he let them go past him to Albert's delivery truck and soon disappeared among the people walking along under the dense foliage of the residential street. In the evening Cresspahl drove back to Mecklenburg in a rented car, through Priwall, past Pötenitz Bay, along the coast to Jerichow. When my father's boat sailed from Hamburg for England, he took a room at the Lübeck Arms in Jerichow.[59]

The passage gives a glimpse of Germany in the 1930s, and as before there is every reason to believe that the description is by and large trustworthy: that Uwe Johnson was, on the whole, well informed, and that he had, in all essentials, the ambition of being true to reality even in details.

The reader is, however, confronted not only with the author's convictions about empirical facts in external reality. In *Anniversaries*, as in all great literature, the reader encounters a sensitivity with a character of its own and a view of life, unique in its finer nuances, that are not easily defined. I shall revert to that fact in later chapters. At this stage I merely wish to point out that the author's strategies for perceiving and his general outlook on life also belong to the elements in the novel that are expressed without being communicated.

On some points, one might argue that the ideas that I have called *expressed but non-communicated* are in reality *asserted*. Is it in fact the case that Johnson, via his earlier cited summary of news from the *New York Times*, actually asserts that the newspaper states that 132 missions against North Vietnam were carried out on 22 August 1967? What Johnson directly does by means of his linguistic formulations is, admittedly, to *pretend* that this is how Gesine understands the matter. But could he not be said to be thereby *asserting*, indirectly and implicitly, that the *New York Times* gave the corresponding information?

As we have seen, it is not altogether obvious what is a prerequisite for an assertion – especially not in cases so special as that of implicit assertions in fiction. It takes stipulations to fix an exact boundary, and there is more than one such stipulation that can be given a reasonable motivation. So there is perhaps no good, unequivocal answer to the question of whether Johnson actually makes the implicit assertion that the *New York Times* states that the U.S. Air Force flew 132 missions against North Vietnam on 22 August 1967.

This does not mean, however, that all the things that are, in my analysis, non-communicated but still expressed could instead be regarded as asserted. I would say, for instance, that the last quotation from Johnson reflects the conviction that it was possible to take a passenger steamer from Hamburg to England in 1931. But it does not seem natural to me to say that Johnson *asserts* this. He communicates a fantasy about Cresspahl deliberately missing his boat from Hamburg to England. The conviction that there was such a line in the 1930s is, in my opinion, expressed, but to me at least it appears impossible to maintain that the conviction itself is communicated. In that case it is, a fortiori, also impossible to maintain that its content is asserted.

Traditional Analytical Theory of Literature and Truth: The Conventionalist View of Meaning

Having pointed to the existence and importance of expressed but non-communicated thoughts, I have completed the introduction of my own standpoint on conveyed thoughts in literature. That subject has, however, always been central in literary theory, under one designation or the other, and I would also like to say a few words about how my views differ from competing conceptions. A real assessment of the various attitudes that have been adopted from Plato and Aristotle onwards is of course out of the question. I shall content myself with a concise indication of how my analysis relates, on the one hand, to traditional theories about literature and truth in analytical philosophy and, on the other, to some ideas about the symbolic character of literature orientated towards semiology or structuralism.

Both traditions – and, generally, earlier thinking about these problems – normally build on a theory of meaning of the kind that I have called "conventionalist." The conception of the literary work or text is, ultimately, inspired by the container metaphor – the work is seen as a physical object containing meaning – and it is taken for granted that it is the conventions of language that turn the work's words and sentences into bearers of a determinate semantic content. A quotation from John Hospers (1946) provides a good illustration of the kind of meaning theory that I am referring to: "When we state the meaning of a word or phrase, we are stating what the word refers to, what it has come by convention to stand for. This is doubtless the main sense in which the word 'meaning' is used."[60]

Much could be said about this doctrine, which today is obsolete (though many non-specialists speaking of meaning still obviously consider it valid). I would merely like to point out, as one of its shortcomings, that it identifies meaning (in the word's main sense) with conventional meaning. According to this view, a sentence is by convention paired off with a meaning which is at the same time the meaning of utterances of the sentence. It is true that the latter element of the doctrine does not become evident in the adduced citation, but it emerges in other contexts. In 1960, for example, Hospers, then still an adherent of conventionalism in the theory of meaning, said this: "The meaning of a sentence does not vary with the use to which it happens to be put on a particular occasion. In particular, the meaning does not vary with either (a) the feelings of the speaker, which it may express, or (b) the response which it evokes in the listener."[61]

In the first quotation from Hospers, the sentence's meaning was identified with its reference, with what the sentence stands for. What, then, do words or sentences "stand for"? According to a time-honoured opinon they stand for real objects, real situations, or the like, and it is, broadly speaking, that (untenable)[62] idea that Hospers was advocating in 1946.[63] A more common idea is that the meaning of a declarative sentence is the statement, or proposition, that the sentence conventionally "expresses" or "conveys." That idea, too, is at least hinted at in Hospers's 1946 account.[64]

In the conventionalist's view, a declarative sentence is paired up with a statement (a proposition), i.e., with an (asserted?) picture of reality that either does or does not correspond to actual reality, and to utter the sentence is, in principle, to make the statement. Declarative sentences in literature are of course somewhat recalcitrant to such treatment. They often give rise to phenomena difficult to fit into the predetermined system. For instance, such a sentence as "In 1931 my mother was twenty-five, the youngest of Papenbrock's daughters" is about non-existent people or objects, but the sentence is not, because of that, untruthful, since the reader well knows that the persons or objects concerned are invented. In traditional analytical literary aesthetics such sentences are called "fictional sentences." According to one view of the matter, such fictional sentences are false, since they introduce a picture of reality that does not correspond to the facts. According to another analysis, they are neither true nor false, since they introduce a picture of reality that is not asserted: because they make no claim to truth they should not be characterized as true or untrue.[65]

The approaches just accounted for do not belong wholly to the past; the same basic thought patterns can be met with in some theorists even in the 1980s and 1990s. But the situation has nevertheless changed considerably, especially since the 1970s. A closer attention to the reader's role has tended to discredit the container metaphor, making it harder to believe that meaning is embodied in a work or text impervious to reader operations. Moreover, the breakthrough of linguistic pragmatics, and the new insights into the functioning of language in actual communication which it brought about, have undermined the traditional convictions described above.

There are, above all, two differences between the conventionalist picture of conveyed thoughts in literature and my own analysis influenced by linguistic pragmatics. A fundamental divergence is that I operate with a somewhat different view of the mechanisms of communication and as a consequence also with another concept of meaning. As I see it, it is impossible to equate meaning with conventional meaning – for example, to equate the meaning of the utterance of a sentence with the meaning of the sentence uttered. Various utterances of one and the same sentence may differ in meaning. Consider the sentence "Yesterday the Air Force flew 132 missions over North Vietnam." Even if "Yesterday" is taken to mean "22 August 1967," and "the Air Force" is interpreted as "U.S. Air Force," different uses and different imports remain possible. The sentence could obviously be utilized to communicate the assertion that the U.S. Air Force flew 132 missions over North Vietnam on 22 August 1967. But it might also be uttered – in a context which makes the sentence stand out as a quotation from the *New York Times* – to communicate the assertion that the *New York Times* stated that the U.S. Air Force flew 132 missions over North Vietnam on 22 August 1967. If I am correct, Johnson uses the sentence in a third way in his *Anniversaries*: to make it a fact in the novel's fictional world that Gesine Cresspahl learns that the *New York Times* for 23 August 1967 says that the U.S. Air Force flew 132 missions over North Vietnam on 22 August 1967. And it is certainly possible to imagine yet other ways of using the sentence.

Clearly, it is entirely unjustified to assume that the conventional meaning of a sentence must coincide with the meaning of an utterance of the sentence. If one makes that assumption, one will be forced to maintain that "Yesterday the Air Force flew 132 missions over North Vietnam" carries the same meaning in all the three situations just suggested. Such a standpoint would obviously prevent us from characterizing the meaning of concrete, actual occurrences of the sentence in a nuanced fashion, thus depriving us of the tools required for the analysis of assertions, of truth, in literature. Simply, a declarative sentence in literature which is, according to its conventional meaning, conveying a proposition without fictive elements does not necessarily express a true or false statement. We may be dealing with an etiolated assertion – Tolstoj's "Happy families are all happy in the same way, unhappy families unhappy in their separate, different ways" – or with an act of implicit pretence, as in connection with Johnson's "Yesterday the Air Force flew 132 missions over North Vietnam."[66]

A second and in literary contexts equally important difference between a pragmatic and a non-pragmatic approach is the following. In my analysis, the constitution of meaning is seen as depending on teamwork of sorts between originator/author and addressee/reader. Using the undifferentiated concept of meaning – although I actually prefer, as the reader will remember, to speak of more precise kinds of meaning – one could say that the reader contributes to the making of meaning. In fact in the end, according to my theory, it is the reader's application which creates the more subtle and humanly important elements of literary meaning ("applicatory meaning"). In the conventionalist analysis, on the other hand, meaning is regarded as somehow objectively associated with the work or text by force of linguistic conventions. It was certainly clear to traditional analytical aesthetics that literature does not simply tell a story or give vent to a feeling, that something more, something elusive but deeply significant, is evoked by the literary text. Given the conventionalist theory of meaning, however, it appeared self-evident that the more profound elements of meaning had to be conceived as contained in the work itself. What appeared as a still unresolved task was the demonstration of the special conventions, the uninvestigated semantic mechanisms, bestowing this deeper significance on the work.

The difference just mentioned makes itself strongly felt also concerning the relationship between literature and ideas. As for myself, I have been speaking of a distribution of cognitive labour between author and reader, and representing much of what is "said" by literature as being, in the final analysis, produced by the reader (a point dealt with in more detail in the following chapter). For the conventionalist, however, it is natural to suppose that literature communicates all that it "says" by virtue of some conventions of meaning shared by a whole cultural community. A conventionalist analysis is liable to find that literature's deeper import is objectively "implied" by, or can be objectively "derived" from, literature's more manifest, convention-bound meaning.

Traditional Analytical Theory of Literature and Truth: The Idea of "Implied" or "Derived" Truths in Literature

A literary, fictional account – such as Updike's description of Pygmalion – is not in itself true. But if one views the matter from a conventionalist perspective one may, as I just indicated, cherish the hope of finding conventions which transform the literary fiction into a bearer of a convention-bound deeper meaning. One may hope, accordingly, that it will be possible to establish that fictions conventionally stand for assertions not explicitly made, for implicit propositions – preferably, of course, for interesting and significant propositions.

Several attempts to point out such mechanisms – in some cases very expert attempts – have been made by analytical aestheticians of a conventionalist persuasion. I myself naturally regard their endeavours as ultimately unsuccessful. The fundamental deficiencies of the strategy manifest themselves in that the philosophers concerned cannot in fact point to conventions capable of doing the work expected of them. In my view, they cannot even make it credible that such conventions exist. I shall comment, briefly and sketchily, on a few analyses of this conventionalist kind.

In his essay "Implied Truths in Literature" (1960), John Hospers asked himself whether literary works may not in fact, in some sense, imply truths over and above those that are eventually explicitly communicated by the work. Hospers considered five types of implication, discussing their significance in this connection. He paid special attention to a type which I shall call here "implication by suggestion" and which he saw as an important source of truth in literature.[67] In the essay, Hospers understands the content implied by suggestion as something which is convention-based and lies *in* what is said or written, thus being independent of the author's intentions and the reader's response and accessible to whoever is "at all aware of the English idiom."[68] Hospers emphasizes that literary works "are able, through the delineation of character and the setting forth of situations which are followed through in the details of the plot, to suggest *hypotheses* about human behavior, human motivation, human actions, and sometimes about the social structure."[69] As I understand, it would be in the spirit of Hospers's analysis to say that a work like Updike's "Pygmalion" among other things implies by suggestion that male love is egoistical.

A problem on which I have touched earlier is that "Pygmalion" could, to all appearances, just as well be said to convey implicitly a multitude of different, though more or less closely related, assertions: "All male love is egoistical … ," "Some male love is egoistical … ," " … at least in the USA of the 1980s … ," and so on. Hospers sees the problem clearly, wishing to solve it by accepting, in principle, *many* such variants as being implied by suggestion. He writes: "A frustrating and at the same time fascinating aspect of complex works of literature is their resistance to a single interpretation, in that many propositions seem to be implied, some of them contradicting others. The work would be far less rich in texture without this feature. Nor need any of the conflicting interpretations be wrong; both of two contradictory propositions may really be suggested by a work of literature, and though of course they cannot both be true, they may both really be implied, and both may live in aesthetic harmony in the same work, giving it a kind of piquancy by the very tension which is thus set up."[70]

I can see at least two serious objections to Hospers's standpoint. One has to do with the absence of evidence: I do not think that Hospers provides us with good reasons for assuming that the content which he considers to be implied by suggestion does in fact form part of *the work itself*. Hospers presumes that conventions creating implications can be found, but he does not actually make an attempt to demonstrate their existence, explain how they operate, or describe any such convention, so his view of the matter is provided with no real foundation.

The second objection concerns the aesthetic substance of Hospers's idea. I would say that the idea has embarrassing aesthetic consequences.

Hospers must find a way of handling the problem that such a large number of assertions are apparently implied by suggestion, as well as the even more dramatic difficulty that a text can, in his opinion, imply mutually incompatible statements, even statements that contradict each other. He attempts to resolve the problem by accepting incompatibilities and tensions on the grounds that these, basically, make works more interesting, more complex.

The argument may sound plausible. But it is worth noting that we are not speaking, here, of a work's *containing thoughts or attitudes contradicting each other* without unequivocally endorsing any of these (as we are when talking of dialogism in Bachtin's sense). We are speaking about cases in which a work is *making mutually incompatible statements* about reality, albeit implicitly. Propositions contradicting each other cannot of course both be true at the same time (as Hospers carefully points out). So works comprising mutually incompatible statements about reality must consequently be conveying genuine statements about reality that are false.

That circumstance, it seems to me, is liable to cast doubts on Hospers's theory. In describing the kind of complexity at issue as aesthetically rewarding, Hospers, perhaps without noticing it, is turning the literary conveyance of seriously intended empirical self-contradictions (and hence empirical falsehoods) into a factor contributing to a work's aesthetic value. It appears obvious to me that something has gone wrong in his argument. The basic error, I believe, consists in his seeing the conflicting propositions as forming part of the work itself. (My analysis – according to which the conflicting propositions are not elements of the work itself but produced by different readers on the basis of the work's non-asserted picture of reality – avoids similar difficulties.)

In an ingenious and in many ways clarifying essay, "On Literary Truth" (1968), D.H. Mellor argues that literary works often convey generalizations not explicitly formulated in the text.[71] The phenomena that he has in mind are reminiscent of Hospers's implications by suggestion. Mellor, too, is conscious of the problem that many generalizations rather similar to each other seem to be produced, some true and others false. Mellor takes it for granted, however, that one can determine exactly which of the similar propositions are being conveyed by the work, and he presupposes that this is done by the aid of conventions.[72] Thus he demonstrates a firm conventionalist conviction, but he has seemingly little to offer us by way of argument apart from that assurance. Just like Hospers, Mellor avoids specifying any relevant conventions; he does not even make any real attempt to indicate their structure.[73]

Later discussion of the problem of literature and truth in analytical aesthetics affords some more concrete ideas about mechanisms enabling us to derive from literature propositions not explicitly made. In *Fictional Narrative and Truth* (1984), for example, L.B. Cebik takes it as his starting point that utterances are associated with presuppositions. A sentence such as "Smith answered the telephone" is said to presuppose, among other things, generalizations like "Telephones are things to be answered," "Smith is a being capable of answering requisite things in the requisite way," and "Smith knows what to do when telephones require answering";[74] according to Cebik, truths may be presupposed by literary works and can therefore be "derived" from the works.[75] As is obvious already from the quotations, there are several internal weaknesses in Cebik's account.[76] There is, however, no reason to scrutinize them here, since Cebik's view of the implications or derivations differs considerably from both Hospers's and Mellor's. According to Cebik, the propositions "derived" should not be seen as assertions made by the work,[77] and besides, Cebik is well aware of the triviality of those propositions. Where literature's really important cognitive contributions are concerned, Cebik invokes the reader's participation as a constitutive factor,[78] and his ideas will be commented on in the next chapter.

On the whole, it is common in modern analytic literary aesthetics to accentuate the reader's importance in actualizing the cognitive potential of literature. "The point is that whatever cognitive elements a literary work may properly be said to be sources of are not to be found already in the finished product (a book) but can sometimes be generated in a particular performance of the work (a reading),"[79] says Peter McCormick in his *Fictions, Philosophies, and the Problems of Poetics* (1988). That is a representative pronouncement.

Other Ideas about the Symbolic Relation in Literature

If only their main outlines are considered, the ideas from analytical philosophy discussed in the last section fit into a much more comprehensive pattern in literary aesthetics. Literary texts are traditionally seen as not merely having a manifest meaning – not merely telling a story, expressing the poet's feelings, and so on – but as also possessing some kind of deeper significance. And it has long been regarded as self-evident that this significance objectively belongs to the text. (Just like the container metaphor, to which it is related, the conventionalist theory of communication has a long history as a fundamental element of our thinking about the conveyance of meaning.) So the literary text has appeared to be a symbol somehow associated with an implicit, deeper import.

Hospers's and Mellor's contributions, with their talk of implications by suggestion or of implicit generalizations, are two attempts in analytical philosophy to explicate the relation between symbol and deeper significance. But other schools of thought have faced basically the same problem. In a more modern guise, the problems have been with us at least since Hegel's aesthetics, where it is, as I have stressed earlier, a fundamental idea that art lets spiritual realities emerge in a sensuous form. (Cf. the discussion of concrete universality in chapter 2.) The Hegelian complex of problems, as I also noted, has lived on not least in Marxist aesthetics – understandably enough, since Marxism historically developed from left-wing Hegelianism. In Marxist aesthetics, the concrete universality of art has traditionally been conceived as depending on art's typifying character: the literary work has been thought to portray typical characters in typical circumstances, thus letting the essential qualities of reality become evident.

Viewing the matter in some such fashion, one is, in principle, confronted with the same problem as Hospers and Mellor. What is called for is an explanation of how the sensuous artistic configuration is related to a deeper significance, how the concrete picture of human life can be associated with its more universal content. No really satisfactory answers to such questions have been proposed by the Marxist tradition.

Let us imagine that, in approaching the problems, we presuppose that the deeper significance can be derived from the literary object itself. That is taking the container metaphor at face value, presuming that the literary object does exist such as we normally conceive of it. But let us disregard that problematical assumption for the moment.

We are faced, then, with two major tasks. The problems consist in providing a clear description of the relation existing between object and import, and of demonstrating how the import can be inferred from the object. The attempts at explication that I know of fall short on one or both points.

Hospers's theory of implication by suggestion is already fuzzy as a description of the relation – a property which it shares both with Hegel's notion of the sensuous appearance of the Idea and with the analysis of typification and generalization in Marxist literary theory. On the other hand, Mellor and some other analytical aestheticians of our day give a comparatively comprehensible account of the relation, at least in so far as they describe it as purely conventional: we are supposed to be able to infer the deeper import from the literary object with the aid of a system of conventions. What has not been forthcoming, however, is the formulation of specific conventions actually making it possible to derive the deeper import from a literary object of a given description.

Some may believe newer schools, such as modern semiotics, to be in possession of a solution which avoids reference to the reader's associations, her meaning-creating activities. I cannot find, though, that such optimism is justified. Jurij Lotman, for example, in conceiving of art as a secondary modelling system, and of the literary work of art as a model of reality,[80] seems to be caught in the same net as Marxist aesthetics in this respect. We comprehend, in principle, the nature of the relation between a model and the reality described. But for a relation of that kind to come into existence, it has first to be made clear what reality the model should be understood as portraying, and by what projection rules we are expected to move from the model to the realities represented. In connection with literary works, those conditions simply are not met. What actual realities are described in "Pygmalion," "Father's Bedroom," and *Anniversaries* – and according to what projection rules? That is of course left largely undecided, and consequently Lotman's idea about art and literature as modelling systems cannot be developed into a semantic explanation of how literature acquires a deeper import.

Further analogous examples could be adduced, but what is important to me is the principle itself. Before leaving the issue, however, I would like to mention another well-known approach to the theory of symbols, that of Nelson Goodman.

A *symbol* (sign) is usually said to *symbolize* (refer to) a *referent* (something designated, an import). In his theory of symbols, Goodman analyses various *types* of symbolization or, as he normally says, "reference," denotation and exemplification among others.

It might appear natural to expect Goodman's elaborate and interesting system to have the capacity to explicate the relation between the literary object and its deeper import. And in a sense, it has. But one should realize that Goodman's system was not at all designed for *interpreting* symbols. Goodman provides, essentially, a classification and an analysis of the types of relations between symbols and their referents. In order to apply the system to, say, the relation between "Pygmalion" and its deeper import, we must first know both "Pygmalion" and its deeper import. Then, perhaps, "Pygmalion" will prove to be *exemplifying* its deeper import (instead of *denoting* it or the like). But to recover the deeper import in the first place, we will have to interpret the story, and Goodman's system is not helpful there, nor was it meant to be.

Let us choose exemplification as an example. In order to understand the concept of exemplification, one may think of a salesperson showing a sample of a linoleum floor covering to a customer. The sample refers (in Goodman's sense) to a certain pattern, a certain colour, a certain texture, by exemplifying them. It exemplifies them by having, itself, that pattern, colour, texture. Formulated more generally and formally: An object O exemplifies a feature f if and only if O possesses f and O refers to f.[81]

Literary works are supposed to have the capacity for exemplifying features in this sense. It would thus not be alien to the nature of an analysis along Goodman's lines to claim that "Father's Bedroom" exemplifies distress.[82] But in order to know what "Father's Bedroom" exemplifies, one must of course first have *interpreted* the poem. An object often has all sorts of properties (in Gooodman's nominalist terminology: it often exemplifies all sorts of labels). And not all the properties possessed by the object are exemplified. As Catherine Z. Elgin expounds the matter: "Interpreted according to different systems, a single object may exemplify different labels ... Under one interpretation the sample on the paint card exemplifies 'teal blue'; under another it exemplifies 'made in Baltimore.' Under one interpretation an abstract painting exemplifies a pattern of light and shadow. Under another it exemplifies 'bourgeois decadence.'"[83]

What is true of exemplification applies to other types of reference too. Goodman's system may, at best, help us to characterize the relation between a symbol and its import once the import has been determined. It does not place at our disposal any conventions that could assist us in covering the distance between the knowledge of the symbolic object and the understanding of its meaning.[84]

6 The Reader's Thematization and Application

Introduction

The core phenomenon in linguistic communication is that thoughts are, in a certain determinate sense, "transmitted" from the originator to the addressee, who in her turn is expected to process the thought content conveyed.

Literary communication, too, follows this general pattern. It differs from other linguistic communication in its intended communicative function, in the fact that the processing foreseen is partly of another kind. In terms of literature, the picture of reality presented, the thoughts introduced, are not meant to be taken as a correct picture of actual reality or as a depiction of a situation that it is incumbent on the addressee to make real. Instead, the point of transferring the picture of reality is to conjure up, via associations, valuable thoughts, feelings, or experiences of form in the addressee.

For now, I would like to concentrate on the cognitive aspect of literature – which, according to the analysis that I shall be introducing step by step, is also axiomatic, at least from a *systematic* view. The conveying of thoughts, of pictures of reality, is a prerequisite for the conveying of feelings and forms, but not vice versa. (That is not necessarily to say that the cognitive aspect of literary experience is more *aesthetically* important than the affective or form-orientated.)

In the last chapter, I focused on the originator's contribution to the literary experience: on the thoughts communicated by the author or disclosed through his communicative act. The reader attempts to reconstruct these thoughts, essentially the communicated thoughts, the reconstruction then forming the basis of what I shall call the "post-communicative" part of her processing. Ultimately, the reader's post-communicative processing is the source of her literary experience.

So far I consider my analysis to be obviously correct: it is easy to bring forward good arguments in its favour, and appears to be difficult to contest its soundness in a coherent fashion. There are, however, a number of pressing attendant questions concerning the cognitive aspect of literary experience. These problems lead us on to ground that is, for various reasons, less firm. In this chapter I shall raise some such issues that are of particular importance.

It is quite natural to ask: what, more specifically, is the reader doing when processing the material conveyed to her? I have given a very broad answer to the question in chapter 2.[1] I said, there, that the reader's processing may assume many different forms, but I also referred to a certain cognitive-affective processing pattern as being fundamentally important and a natural basis of the understanding of the reader's response. The processing pattern consists in the reader connecting the things read with real life, much as if her reading were governed by questions like "Is reality as it is described here?" "In that case, what are the consequences for me?" and "Can I learn something from the human attitudes depicted or expressed?" In this chapter I shall, among other things, expand my account of the processing pattern with the aid of some new concepts and observations.

Another important question is concerned with problems of validity. Can the reader follow any maxim she likes in her post-communicative processing? In all I have said up to now, it has sounded as if the reader of literature were in principle at complete liberty to process and experience the conveyed thoughts just as she wished. But can this really be true? Are there not rules of sorts, implicit but accepted de facto, even for the reader's post-communicative processing? I shall also take up that question and propose an answer.

A third problem of considerable aesthetic importance concerns the cognitive benefit afforded by literature. In chapters 2 and 5, we saw that the ideas conveyed by literature have the power to affect our view of the world in a variety of ways. And it seems obvious that literature may also incite ideas about actual reality via the associations aroused in the reader and then processed by her. But the same, of course, is true for ordinary, non-literary discourse. One has to ask oneself, here: is it possible for literature to be the source of an understanding of reality which is, in some sense, sui generis, or does literature provide essentially the same kind of understanding as informational discourse, only less efficiently? That is the third problem to be discussed in this chapter.

The issues will be considered in the order in which they have been introduced. I shall first supplement the picture of the reader's post-communicative processing given earlier, and then discuss whether the processing is governed by any special norms. To make the purport of my analyses more concrete, I shall bring them to bear on the reading of Johnson's *Anniversaries* and on different ways of understanding the novel. In the course of my argument, I shall also compare my stand-point with other ideas about how the reader's post-communicative pro-cessing operates and how the theme of a literary text is to be identified. Finally, I shall comment on literature's peculiarity as a source of knowl-edge and on some other theorists' explorations of that problem.

Thematization and Application

In a text like Johnson's *Anniversaries*, the reader is faced with a comprehensive and complicated picture of reality. According to my theory of literature as presentational discourse, she is expected to engender benefit for herself – cognitive, emotional, or formal/aesthetic – from that picture.

At least where *Anniversaries* is concerned, it is not immediately clear what features of the picture the reader is to focus on. The novel does not seem to possess an unequivocal message, a clearly definable point. It may be interesting to know that Johnson was not, himself, prepared to single out any definite main theme in *Anniversaries*, let alone a moral. He insisted that what he was doing was telling a story.[2]

One of the specifications of what Johnson expected from a novel, a story, is found in his article "Proposals for the Testing of a Novel" ("Vorschläge zur Prüfung eines Romans," 1973).

> So what is the novel good for?
> It is an offer. You get a version of reality.
> It is not a society in miniature, and it is no model acccording to scale. It is not a mirror of the world, nor a reflection of it; it is a world to be held up against the real world.
> You are invited to compare this version of reality with the one entertained and utilized by you yourself. Perhaps the other, the different gaze fits into your own.
> Defend your independence till the last page of the book. If what the novel tried to say is explicitly spelled out, it is high time to rid oneself of the book. You have the right to demand a story. Delivering a quintessence or a moral is breaching the agreement. The promise of a novel implies the promise of a story.
> What is to be said about it, is for you to say.[3]

In an approximately contemporaneous interview with Manfred Durzak, Johnson again emphasizes the same point: "A story is ... something that is being told, not a message." And he adds, referring directly to his own writing: "When I am narrating, what is important for me is not that the reader says, with recognition: That is how it is, and that is how we live, which may certainly no doubt be an enjoyment, a pleasure which is not to be discarded. But for me it is a matter of a second level, of the recognition and the question after all involved in it: Yes, things are such as it is written there, that is how we live. But do we want to live that way? That, again, transfers the message back into the reader's reaction. I can only show him something and hope that he gets something out of it."[4]

Johnson's statements – by no means original in themselves – agree well with the general picture of literary communication given earlier. According to Johnson, the author introduces some kind of picture of reality, expecting the reader to react to it; a basic pattern for the reader's anticipated response is indicated by the questions "Do we live like that?" and "Do we want to live like that?" The parallels with my outlook are obvious.[5] (Compare, for instance, the four processing questions that I formulated in chapter 2 and in the introduction to this chapter: "Is reality as it is described here?" and so on.)

After this parenthetical account of Johnson's own view of the "agreement" between author and reader, let us revert to the reader of *Anniversaries* and her post-communicative processing of the book. As a reader, one is expected to derive literary pleasure from the picture of reality conveyed by the novel. How, then, is it possible to get anything out of *Anniversaries*?

I would like to recount my own first experience of the earlier parts of the novel, roughly at the time of its original publication. I believe that I read the first two volumes, appearing in 1970 and 1971 respectively, in the years 1971–2, being then twenty-five and twenty-six years old and a graduate student of Swedish and Comparative Literature. The book gave me a great literary experience. What especially caught my attention was the Gesine figure and Gesine's everyday existence in New York. Now, long afterwards, I would like to describe my reaction by saying that I was fascinated by what I saw as an exceedingly concrete and convincing description of a meaningful and attainable life. The political and the private, world events and everyday life, appeared as integrated and equally important aspects of Gesine's situation. Despite various pressures – from her memories, her professional life, her responsibility for the child – Gesine functioned and kept herself resilient and candid, apparently in motion towards some goal, realizable or not. The lustre and enticement of the description of the metropolis helped to make the novel inspiring. I was absorbed and all but overwhelmed. It did not matter that I was unused to reading German and only little by little began to achieve an almost complete understanding of the meaning of the words themselves.

This reading can hardly be called exemplary – it seems fair to see it as perceptive and dedicated but at the same time rather one-sided. But it is not the reading's reasonableness that I wish to discuss just now. It is, instead, the question of how the structure of such post-communicative reader processing can be described in a simple and adequate fashion. I shall distinguish three central elements: focusing, non-self-orientated associating, and application.

When confronted with communicated literary thought material, the reader will, first, attend to certain features or aspects of the material, perceiving them as the most interesting ones. It is this foregrounding of certain aspects of the communicated content that I call "focusing." In my first reading of *Anniversaries* I can be said to have focused on Gesine-as-she-is-living-in-New-York.

Second, the material focused on gives rise to reader associations, to conscious or unconscious thoughts. Thus my first reading of *Anniversaries* apparently occasioned thoughts picturing Gesine's way of mastering reality as admirable and worth emulating. It is its forming of such, so to speak, "secondary"[6] representations that I characterize as "non-self-orientated associating." I distinguish, then, between "self-orientated representations," representations where the person having the representation herself forms part of its content, and "non-self-orientated representations." (Compare the self-orientated representation that *I am looking out of the window* with the non-self-orientated representation that *a lane is leading across that field*.) My thought as a reader that *Gesine's way of mastering reality is admirable and worth emulating* is the product of non-self-orientated associating: it constitutes a secondary representation in which I myself do not form part of the content.

Third, the reader brings the non-self-orientated associations to bear on her own self. As already said, on my first reading of *Anniversaries* I saw the novel as holding out a concrete, realizable example of a life worth living. What I had in mind for myself was naturally not an existence as a bank employee in New York, unmarried and with one child. But it still seemed possible to construct a model of a liveable life from Gesine's situation. Let us schematically describe the essence of my application as the thought (the self-orientated representation) that *it will become possible for me to lead a life similar to Gesine's, and if leading such a life I would feel happy*. No wonder I was enchanted with the novel.

The word "thematization" is my overall designation of the reader's focusing and her non-self-orientated associating. In my choice of term I am influenced, of course, by normal critical parlance, usually designating as the "theme" that which is the centre of attraction of the literary work: its main subject or leading idea.[7] As regards the term "application," I have, basically, taken it from Hans-Georg Gadamer.[8] In my view, thematization and application normally form an essential part of the content of the reader's post-communicative processing.

Focusing, non-self-orientated associating, and application are not of course to be understood as three separate, consecutive phases of the reader's processing. I conceive of them as being woven together in the reader's continuous active contemplation, during her reading, of the things read.[9]

It must be emphasized that my account of thematization and application should not be taken as an attempt to describe what the competent reader is always doing in her post-communicative processing of literature. Her processing may assume many forms. As I see it, however, actual processings by readers may often be regarded as specific (often partial, but on the other hand often expanded) realizations of a given basic pattern. It is that basic pattern that I have attempted to define.

Lesser, Gadamer, and Nussbaum on the Reader's Creative Agency

Conventionalists and intentionalists (such as Beardsley and Juhl in their best-known contributions) do not perceive the reader as being genuinely creative in her processing. As we will see later, they conceive of what I call thematization as purely an actualization of something already implicit in the literary text, and what I call application they would regard as in principle an unnecessary outgrowth of the literary experience. Similarly, it would be natural for a deconstructionist to find the text, not the reader, to be the real agent.[10] In this respect, I have been introducing controversial ideas when speaking of a post-communicative processing consisting in focusing, non-self-orientated associating, and application.

On the other hand, however, a considerable number of twentieth-century theorists of literature have maintained that the reading of literature always also involves a further cognitive and emotional elaboration of the text on the reader's part. The succession could be said to start with Freud, who argued, in "Creative Writers and Day-Dreaming," that a literary experience comes into existence essentially through the reader's imaginative identification and through her exploitation of the work's fantasy material for her own personal use (cf. chapter 2). Simon Lesser is one of the thinkers who have developed Freud's idea further. In *Fiction and the Unconscious* (1957) he contended that several unconscious processes take place during the reading of fiction. He saw two of these as "active" forms. On the one hand he considered that the reader unconsciously takes part in the story, projecting herself, as it were, by means of identifications, into the story world. On the other hand he thought that the reader creates her own stories inspired by the fiction communicated to her, that she "analogizes." "In the first of these 'active' forms of response," says Lesser, "we unconsciously participate in the stories we read; in the second, we compose stories structured upon the ones we read (or upon parts of them) which give us an opportunity to relive or alter our actual experience or act out dramas revolving around our wishes and fears. The last-mentioned kind of response, the creation of stories parallel to the ones we read in which we play a part, I call analogizing."[11]

Lesser obviously imagines that the reader associates from the work to things that have happened, or might happen, to herself, developing that aspect of her response into a satisfactory self-orientated fantasy in narrative form.

Lesser's theory of the reader's unconscious processing, inspired as it is by psychoanalysis, naturally leaves less room for cognitive elements than my own analysis. But the factors that I call focusing and application can be discerned too in Lesser; he clearly sees the reader as picking out something in the story (focusing) and letting those elements give rise to satisfactory self-orientated fantasies (a kind of application). I myself conceive the process as being more flexible and often of a more discursive character – I imagine, above all, that the reader is able to find traits in the literary picture of reality that, for her, arouse interesting thoughts about actual reality (for example, the thought that a life like Gesine Cresspahl's is liveable and attractive). Lesser does not pay much attention to such reality-testing, non-self-orientated associating.[12] Moreover, I find it unwarranted to presuppose that the reader's application necessarily assumes the form of a narrative with herself as protagonist. I make the more limited presumption that the reader's application always involves self-orientated representation (more or less comprehensive and complex).

On the other hand, some theories of the reader's post-communicative processing lay *more* stress on cognition than my own. This is true of Hans-Georg Gadamer's extremely consequential statements about application in his *Truth and Method* (*Wahrheit und Methode*, 1960). Gadamer criticizes the traditional idea that hermeneutic work consists simply in a reconstructing of meaning, in "making intelligible what others have said in speech and text." He contends that texts make truth-claims and that we cannot therefore, in our interpretations, content ourselves with the observation that the originator meant so-and-so. We must not disregard the underlying claim to truth or validity, for "indirectly, wherever an attempt is made to understand (eg scripture or the classics), there is reference to the truth that lies hidden in the text and must be brought to light. What is to be understood is, in fact, not thought as part of another's life, but as a truth."[13]

If the claims of the teachings of the Bible – or, for that matter, of the words of a parliamentary act – are to be met in concrete reality, an element of application must come in, an assessment of how the intentions behind the text may be implemented in the specific existing situation. Since Gadamer perceives a corresponding problem of historical mediation in connection with the literary or scholarly text, he finds a corresponding need for application there too.[14] Consequently he considers that "understanding always involves something like the application of the text to be understood to the present situation of the interpreter."[15]

Gadamer's analysis of application is relatively easy to comprehend where directive discourse is concerned: laws, decrees, requests, and the like. It is more difficult to see how it could be applied to informative discourse – for example, to scientific research reports – or (which is more relevant in our context) to imaginative literature. A more thorough elucidation of the problem, though, would require a discussion of Gadamer's concept of truth and of his view of literature, which would, in this context, take us too far.

A superficial examination already shows, however, that the tenor of Gadamer's analysis differs appreciably from that of the model introduced in the last section. Three dissimilarities stand out as especially significant. First, and expressed in my terminology: Gadamer locates the theme in the work itself; with Gadamer, the beginning of the reader's post-communicative processing is "the truth that lies hidden in the text." That is a point on which my analysis directly conflicts with Gadamer's. Second, Gadamer tends to regard the interpreter as obliged to subordinate herself to the claims of the work, her task seemingly consisting in helping the work's truth to prevail in her own situation. Third, the psychologizing indigenous to my model is foreign to Gadamer's analysis. What the work has to offer, according to him, is "truth" or "validity," not an amorphous personal benefit. All in all, I believe that application in Gadamer's rather specific sense can profitably be regarded as a subtype, peculiar in certain respects, of what I call thematization and application.

The model in the last section is, however, close to the view of reader processing represented by Martha Nussbaum in her essays in *Love's*

Knowledge (1990). There Nussbaum repeatedly alludes to the phenomena that I call thematization and application. It is true that she does not try to introduce a distinct theory about those subjects, and the observations in her essays – written over an extended period of time – may point in partially different directions, making her statements somewhat vague and contradictory. I also have reservations about her tendency to see so much of the cognitively significant representations connected with a literary work as located in the work – as, literally, statements by the author, literally truths in the text. Nussbaum sometimes speaks in highly Gadamerian terms (without directly referring to Gadamer), saying things like "We are invited to find the truths of the text applicable to our human lives."[16] It is, however, quite obvious that my views of thematization and application are closely related to the ideas that Nussbaum expresses in such statements as the following: "the moral activity of the reader ... involves not only a friendly participation in the adventures of the concrete characters, but also an attempt to see the novel as a paradigm of something that might happen in his or her own life."[17]

In more recent analyses first and foremost by Susan Feagin and Gregory Currie, Lesser's and Nussbaum's talk of reader "participation" is replaced with observations about the reader's "simulating." I shall comment briefly on Feagin's and Currie's analyses later on (see the section "Empathy and Identification" in chapter 7 below). I could also have cited a large number of further examples of current ideas about the mechanisms underlying the reader's post-communicative processing. In fact, a few more standpoints on the question – those of Norman Holland and Richard Rorty – will be touched upon later in this chapter, in my discussion of whether thematizations are in need of rational justifications. A comprehensive survey of the field would, however, require a separate book.

What I introduced in the last section was not a general theory, valid always and everywhere, about how the reader's post-communicative processing is constituted. I described something I regard as a basic pattern capable of being made manifest in various ways, of being realized wholly or in part, of being enriched with further elements, and so on. My brief discussion of Lesser's, Gadamer's, and Nussbaum's standpoints is calculated, primarily, to demonstrate that my model is indeed versatile and adaptable. I do not have to deny the existence of analogizing, as described by Lesser, or of application, such as Gadamer conceives of it. Those types of processing can be understood as special cases covered by my model. My principal objection to Lesser and Gadamer is, rather, that their respective characterizations of the reader's post-communicative processing are too definite and one-sided

– they leave no space for the actually existing variation. The same type of criticism could be levelled at several other standpoints, even at Nussbaum's. For in fact she tends (as the adduced quotation suggests) to see it as mandatory on the reader's post-communicative processing to include "an attempt to see the novel as a paradigm of something that might happen in his or her own life."

There is much more to be said about the fundamental mechanisms of thematization and application, but this is not the proper time or place for it. Some details in the picture of these phenomena will, however, be added at later stages in my presentation. Thus, later on in this chapter I shall, as already said, take up the question of whether certain thematizations may be unacceptable. Then I shall also give a succinct account of how my analysis of the validity of thematizations tallies with current scholarly and critical views. Moreover, I shall, at the end of the chapter, place the discussion of thematization and application in a larger context. The question of the nature of thematizations and applications will also play a significant part in later chapters, particularly in chapters 7 and 9.

Themes in Johnson's *Anniversaries*

I shall now pass on to the question of the extent to which the reader is free to make whatever thematizations and applications she chooses, and the extent to which she is, in contrast, restricted by the rules of literary practice. At this point it seems wise to consider concrete examples, and therefore I shall introduce some statements from various critics and scholars about the themes in Johnson's *Anniversaries*.

The choice of material requires an explanation. What I want to discuss is the rules of literary practice, the implicit expectations behind the readings performed by ordinary readers. But the statements I am going to refer to come from *critical* and *scholarly* contexts, and so their relevance for my topic may be questioned. (It is obvious that the ordinary reading of literature, literary scholarship, and literary criticism are three somewhat different games, so to speak, governed by somewhat different norms.)[18]

Judged according to stringent rules, the observations about themes adduced below do not in actual fact possess any immediate relevance in my context. They are something other than reports about more or less reasonable reader thematizations; in their respective contexts they are, among other things, implicitly making larger claims to validity and general interest. But they are nevertheless indicative of possible ways of reading the novel, ways that might well be realized in the readings of ordinary readers (and are perhaps actually realized as such when the respective scholars or critics are themselves reading *Anniversaries*, off duty as it were). It would have been methodically correct, but too laborious in my context, to collect instead a material of reactions from the general reader of *Anniversaries*.

To get to my point, however, *Anniversaries* can be seen from many angles. The Johnson specialist Bernd Neumann has said, with much justification, that "*Anniversaries* is to be understood as a closing of the books, an historical chronicle, a political book, and an 'existential' text."[19] In practice, however, critics and scholars have been more limited than that in their thematizations. In fact one gets a simplified but convenient survey of the reception of *Anniversaries* if one subsumes different conceptions of the novel under Neumann's four headings. Some may be said to have read *Anniversaries* as a historical chronicle, while others have apprehended it as a political book and yet others have perceived it as a closing of the books or as an existential text.

A flexible description of the differences between these readings may be given in terms of differences in focusing or in non-self-orientated associating. As far as focusing is concerned, there seem to be two main types of readings. Some readers centre their interest on Gesine and Gesine's handling of her problems (as I did in my original reading). In that case, only a secondary role in the experience of the novel will be allotted to the description of society (Johnson's contemporary USA, German conditions from the 1930s to the 1950s or perhaps even 1960s). In a reading of this kind, those descriptions represent, respectively, an insistent reality and a burden of painful recollections that Gesine is obsessed by and is constantly processing. To others, however, the description of society is the principal thing, while Gesine becomes of secondary interest, primarily functioning as an optical instrument, as it were, with whose aid Johnson creates the desired perspective on German and international twentieth-century history.

Apparently German and non-German scholars have tended to make slightly different focusings.[20] Even if the dissimilarities should not be exaggerated, I believe it is fair to say that the German reactions to *Anniversaries* foreground its historical and political themes to a greater extent than the British or American reception, where the interest in the novel's psychological and existential aspects is instead, arguably, more prominent.

Even if one is focusing on the description of society, especially the description of the developments in Eastern Germany from the 1930s to the 1950s, the representations in the novel may still of course give rise to differing thematizations. And in fact, the non-self-orientated associations of critics and scholars do vary considerably. An important source of difference is the level of generality of the associations that Johnson's fictive pictures of reality are permitted to arouse.

Some commentators seem to have taken the courses of events accounted for, the fictive and factual occurrences in Mecklenburg, New York, and the world, as first of all projecting a picture of twentieth-century history and politics. To illustrate that type of reading, one may point to some of Michael Bengel's remarks about the novel. Bengel writes: "Johnson's *Anniversaries* conveys a chapter not only of German history, above all concerning the time from 1931 to 1961, but also it conveys a contemporary scene, today itself a piece of history: that of the years 67/68."[21]

It is worth noting that Bengel intends this as an indication of a feature of the book that he sees as quite central and as connecting on to "the theme of the whole body of Johnson's work." He describes that theme as follows: "It is, now, certainly not the division of Germany; it is that only as a special case of the redistributions in Europe after the war. But it is something that could, to be sure, be called the theme of his life: The war and its consequences (and, on one level of *Anniversaries*, also its background)."[22]

This is, certainly, a generalizing reading of the novel. But there are those who carry the processing further, seeing *Anniversaries* less as a historical chronicle than as a political book. They thematize, above all, the political ideas discernible behind the novel's depiction of the period between the wars and of its own age. In doing so, they may of course differ in their conclusions and evaluations. In an early analysis – presented during the long break in the publication of *Anniversaries* between volumes 3 and 4 – Neumann argued that *Anniversaries* expresses a political resignation that was alien to Johnson's first novel, *Speculations about Jacob* (*Mutmassungen über Jakob*, 1959).

For Gesine learns to live hopelessly conscious of her inevitable "homelessness" in Bloch's social sense of the word, brave and free from all illusions, as it were, and still always haunted by the painful memory of the irrevocably lost Mecklenburg "home." Where the treatment of this theme in *Speculations* was not only forward-looking in a concrete Utopian fashion, but also characterized by an ironical distance, in *Anniversaries* it unfolds its whole nostalgic and therefore suspicious – and, besides, specifically German-intimate – sweetness. For what *Speculations* still brought together in a synthesis – the social and the natural, the belonging to the same extent to nature and society, the socially satisfactory and moreover natural life, thus the concrete Utopian fulfilment of what the early bourgeoisie promised and capitalism then denied – breaks up in petty bourgeois sentimentality in *Anniversaries*.[23]

Neumann finds that *Anniversaries* shows us people helplessly determined by their social situation, and that the reason for this is that "the
Utopian intention" has disappeared.[24]

Even if one is making very similar focusings in *Anniversaries*, however, one may construe the novel differently. To Ulrich Fries, *Anniversaries* is also unambiguously a political book. He speaks of "the proper,
the political content of *Anniversaries*," and it becomes clear that he
sees "*Anniversaries* as an essential contribution to the understanding
and the inner mastery of German history."[25] Nevertheless Fries formulates (in a book from 1990) an alternative to Neumann's views:

> Neumann demands from Johnson's novel an indication of a positive line of
> action, a bringing out, in the description of the world, of the elements that
> will lead to its improvement. He presupposes that they exist. It must escape
> him, therefore, that the novel has made it into an implicit assumption that
> precisely these elements have been lost historically. ... Consequently it is not
> the failure of the labour movement that is, in itself, the theme of the novel;
> it is rather the backdrop against which it is demonstrated – certainly with
> the aid of people with great human resources – that there is room for the
> individual to assert himself. ... Giving in to the merely actual situation
> represents quite the reverse of the political ethics in *Anniversaries*.[26]

Also if Gesine is focused on, rather than the societies in which she has
lived, there are several different possibilities of proceeding from there
with one's thematization. Before I comment on this, however, my
description of the novel's content has to be enlarged.

Gesine suffers not only from political homelessness. She also had in
her past a number of painful and some truly terrible separations. Her
mother, a deeply religious person looking on Nazism with more and
more despair, committed suicide as a consequence of a chain of events
triggered by the pogrom of 9–10 November 1938. Jakob Abs –
Gesine's unforgettable beloved, Marie's father – was killed in 1956, in
mysterious circumstances, while crossing the area of railway tracks
around the central station of Dresden. (And Dietrich Erichson, whom
Gesine in 1968 is about to marry, dies in Finland, in a crashed Cessna,
in August that year, just before the end of *Anniversaries*.) In leaving
the German Democratic Republic, she has also become separated from
her father, with whom she had a close relationship, and he dies in
1962. Moreover, her break with East Germany has made it impossible
for her to return to her native Mecklenburg, which is never absent
from her mind. Towards the end of Johnson's novel, Gesine's love for
the landscape of her childhood breaks through in a passage often

commented on, right in the middle of a description of the friendship between Gesine and Anita Gantlik in 1951.

Since their visit to Barlach's house by the lake island of Güstrow, the students Gantlik and Cresspahl had come to a mutual agreement, a clandestine understanding. Both had taken their distance from art criticism as dispensed by the subject specialist Selbich, found one another on the ridge of Heather Hill, where a slope begins, well known to the children of Güstrow as a sledding place in season, but opening to the eye, too, a sweeping view of the island in the lake and the gently rising land beyond the water, sparingly set with backdrops of trees and roofs, radiant, for the sun had just managed to oust some somber rain clouds: a sight that I pray may be with me in the hour of my

We don't care a hoot if you find this a bit overcharged, comrade writer! You are going to write this down! We are still able to withdraw from your book this very day. Up to you to figure out what kind of things we keep in mind in case of death.[27]

There is never any question of returning to Mecklenburg. But at the very end of the novel a contact with the past is established. Gesine and Marie have arranged a meeting on their way to Prague with Gesine's aged English teacher from Gneez, Julius Kliefoth, in a hotel on The Sound, near Copenhagen.[28] They walk on the beach. The last paragraph of *Anniversaries* reads: "As we walked along the beach, we got into water. Shingle rattled about our ankles. We held each other by the hand: a child; a man on his way to the place where the dead are; and she, the child that I was."[29]

Each of the three figures constitutes a link in a chain of generations. It is easy to find something hopeful in this ending, to see Kliefoth, Gesine, and Marie's togetherness as instancing a continuous flow through history of positive human resources. We know, though, that we are looking at a fragile chain. Gesine and Marie are on their way to Prague and Gesine's problematic mission, and Kliefoth to the place where the dead are. So this ending is hardly the logical terminal point of an action, but rather a minute of stillness, a frozen moment as it were, in an ongoing process. One may emphasize the fellowship almost emblematically presented by the novel's ending, or one may, on the contrary, stress the fact that this togetherness is temporary, at least in an outward sense, and that it will be sundered in the very next hours.[30]

Let us now revert to the possibilities of thematization for the reader of *Anniversaries*.

A reading bringing Gesine into focus easily becomes a reading based on identification.[31] It appears obvious that Johnson, too, must have identified with Gesine in some sense; in many respects, her life story is reminiscent of Johnson's own.[32] Johnson, too, knew what war, occupation, and separation are like – the dramatic loss of close relatives, the exile. Johnson, too, had a profoundly serious political commitment. And Johnson had had to see his most important political hopes – to all appearances, substantially the same as Gesine's – come to naught. The author's personal involvement in his story has naturally been made into a major point by some commentators. Thus Hans-Bernhard Moeller has characterized *Anniversaries* – cynically but not without credibility – as "the social, political and historical self-psychoanalysis of Uwe Johnson, the Mecklenburg Proust."[33] This could be called a "closing-of-the-books reading" of *Anniversaries* – admittedly in a sense somewhat different from Neumann's; Neumann no doubt had in mind, primarily, the book's character of a final, comprehensive treatment of the all-pervading themes of Johnson's œuvre.

It is open to discussion whether the reader of *Anniversaries* is really supposed to thematize the character of Johnson's own engagement in the story (I shall return to this question). But it is possible to detach Gesine's work with the processing of her memories from so private a biographical frame. Colin Riordan has given it a wider, more exemplary import. He refers to Alexander and Margarete Mitscherlich's *The Incapacity for Mourning* (*Die Unfähigkeit zu trauern*, 1967) – presumably well known to Johnson – whose thesis was that the West Germans had, in a way fraught with momentous consequences, avoided coming to terms with their political past: they are said to have failed to bring the memories from the Nazi era to life and to integrate them, through a process of mourning, into their experience of the world. Riordan understands *Anniversaries* as a model for such a process of mourning (into which – I suppose – the German reader is expected to be able to enter through identification with Gesine). He writes: "The most important first step is remembering; the Mitscherlichs express the hope that 'ein Wiedergewinnen von Erinnerungen könne uns helfen, aus dem Geschehenen zu lernen' ['a winning back of memories might help us to learn from what has occurred'] (p. 84). *Jahrestage* is nothing if not a working model of that very process, and, as such, a model of *Trauerarbeit*, with Gesine as the subject. ... *Jahrestage* suggests a mode of behaviour which would enable all Germans to understand, not only intellectually but also emotionally, how the present division of their country came about, and accept the responsibility and the consequences for that. Only with such acceptance can there be hope for the future."[34]

However, the focusing of Gesine may (like the focusing of the description of society) form the basis of more and more general thematizations. Rolf Becker has ascribed to Gesine's work at mastering reality a more general, more universal and existential, import than Riordan. "Once again," he tells us, "Johnson develops his great theme: How is it possible to lead a decent life, how can one express a just opinion and speak the truth in a world of constraining systems enmeshing us in obligations on all sides, with its ideological illusions and party-determined norms of linguistic expression? How is one to live with the 'consciousness of an existence in nearness to guilt' of which no change of land and state can relieve Gesine?"[35]

Such readings tend to emphasize the character of *Anniversaries* as "an 'existential' text," an understanding of the novel which finds an even more pronounced exponent in Reinhard Baumgart. Baumgart's interpretation, however, represents a type of reading that contrasts with the pattern that I have hitherto described. Baumgart is not really focusing on Gesine, or on the description of society, but rather on the narrator's way of viewing and evaluating (something that might perhaps be said of Becker as well). To Baumgart, the novel has no message admitting of formulation ("it proves nothing, is not in movement towards any ethics or any useful application"):[36] the breadth and exactness of the narrating has – he imagines – successively emancipated the book from the theses that Johnson was possibly intent on propounding when beginning the project. Baumgart stresses the gravity and bitterness of the picture of reality; the fourth volume is said to display "a disillusion impossible to live with, one that may neither be accepted nor forgotten."[37] The counterpoise acting in the novel is created, according to Baumgart's view, by the incorruptible exactness of the viewing and formulating itself, and by the eye for the sensuous and human values of everyday life. Johnson "tries to offer resistance to the anonymizing, levelling process of history already through language"; he "insists on all still discernible distinctions."[38] "But the novel also tries another strategy against the work of politics destructive to humans: over hundreds of pages it sings a Song of Songs of everyday life, it extols and honours it as a last zone of shelter, as a pocket of resistance for the value of the private human being. As if it were a question of re-creating, from language, a small spot of earthly Utopia."[39]

Expected Understanding

The determinations of theme in the last section give no wholly representative picture of what has been said about the themes of *Anniversaries* – that was never my purpose, and I have in fact entirely passed over several important critical contributions. Nor do I intend to choose among the interpretations of theme, or even to assess them critically. I repeat that they were brought in as illustrative material. They are meant to be of help in answering the question of the extent to which the reader is free to thematize and create applications as she likes, and the extent to which she is, eventually, bound by the rules of literary practice.

It is my spontaneous conviction that the reader normally enjoys much liberty in her choice of thematizations and applications, but that the rules of literary practice nevertheless place some restrictions on her readings. Not all ways of reading *Anniversaries* are compatible with the practice; I can easily think of readings that I myself would reject as being bizarre or incompetent.

My analysis of literary communication, as it has been presented so far, comprises no elements suggesting that the reader's post-communicative processing is not completely free from external constraints. What has to be introduced, then, is an idea about the sorts of restrictions that circumscribe the reader's post-communicative processing and what motivates those restrictions.

Such an idea is presented in this section and the next. In this section, I shall introduce the concept of expected understanding, a notion necessary for my further argument. In the next section I shall summarize my view of what makes a thematization acceptable and provide some arguments to support my view.

Jokes are presentational compositions, despite their being texts of a non-literary kind.[40] In connection with jokes – a type of text no doubt related to simple literary genres – the basic structure and the fundamental rules of thematizing seem clear, at least to my mind. For that reason, in some contexts, I shall use jokes as examples when discussing how the thematization of literary texts operates and with which principles it eventually complies. Most important, I shall exploit one such example for introducing the concept of expected understanding.

Let us make use of a joke retold by Freud in *Jokes and Their Relation to the Unconscious* (*Der Witz und seine Beziehung zum Unbewussten*, 1905). In the joke we encounter two Galician Jews, and it is important to know that Galician Jews were ill famed for their presumed unwillingness to have a bath: "Two Jews met in the neighbourhood of the bath-house. 'Have you taken a bath?' asked one of them. 'What?' asked the other in return, 'is there one missing?'"[41]

Let us imagine the joke being told in an actual situation in Freud's time. It stands to reason that the joke would, in such a case, constitute a presentational composition. A (fictional) picture of reality is introduced, and it is made mutually manifest that the picture neither lays claim to being literally truthful nor seeks to influence the addressee to realize the corresponding situation. The joke's implicit raison d'être is, rather, that it is meant to be in some sense intrinsically gratifying to enter into the picture of reality introduced and to process it.

But that is not all. We cannot say that the addressee is free to process the picture of reality introduced just as she pleases. In the imagined situation it will be obvious both to speaker and hearer, and so become mutually manifest, that the speaker is telling a joke. The purpose of a joke is to be funny. Consequently it will become mutual knowledge that the speaker is laying claim to introducing a picture of reality which it is amusing to enter into and to process.

That circumstance may still be regarded as an element of the communicated content. The informative, directive, and presentational function are *types* of communicative functions. And as I pointed out in chapter 3, every utterance may be said to possess its own *unique* communicative function. The communicative function of the telling of the joke is, when classified crudely, simply a presentational function. When we describe it in a more individualized fashion, it may be said to be a presentational function of a special sort: that of jokes. (The individualization of the description could be carried much further, but that would be purposeless in this context.) The pretensions to funniness are implicit – according to this analysis – in the very communicative function of the telling of the joke. It is included, then, in the communicated utterance meaning of the narrative act that the narrator manifests the aspiration to be amusing. (An understanding of the communicative function forms part of the understanding of the communicated utterance meaning.)[42]

Thus far we are dealing with intended and reconstructed meaning. But when we leave language and the level of pragmatic verbal understanding behind us, there are also frameworks within which the addressee is expected to move. This creates the phenomenon that I call expected meaning.

I have said that the teller of a joke implicity claims that it is potentially amusing to acquaint oneself with her utterance. This is only a special instance of a general, basic requirement of communicative acts: they have to be relevant to the addressee, to have something of interest to offer him.[43]

Any speaker or writer implicitly claims that it is, in some respect, interesting to be informed of the content of her words. So it must naturally be incumbent on the originator to make sure that her utterance is interesting enough in those respects relevant to her type of text. The teller of a joke, for instance, must apprehend the joke as being funny enough (otherwise she abuses the hearer's confidence). And this presupposes, of course, that she herself has an idea about its funniness. She must have tested the quality of the joke, so to speak: assessed its funniness from the point of view of the addressee and evaluated the joke as being funny enough. In brief, the originator must see something funny in the joke. And her expectation is, certainly, that the addressee will see this funny aspect as well and appreciate it.

Formulated more generally: any originator expects the addressee to process her utterance in such a fashion that he perceives the features that the originator implicitly sees as its interesting aspects, and so that he also perceives that precisely those features are the aspects meant to be interesting. If the addressee succeeds in doing this, his understanding is within the scope of what I call "the expected understanding." In connection with the joke related by Freud, the addressee realizes the expected understanding if, and only if, he sees the point of the joke.

Not even where jokes are concerned does the expected understanding have to be clearly defined. What is amusing in the Jewish joke adduced by Freud? As Freud himself suggests in his commentary, it is perhaps not so much the linguistic misunderstanding, the circumstance that Jew number two misapprehends the word "take," interpreting it as used in its most concrete sense. It is, presumably, rather the fact that the taking of baths appears to be so alien to Jew number two that he cannot even handle the concept of a bath and tends to understand the phenomenon as some kind of removable physical object.[44] But perhaps one should, over and above that feature, also notice the fact that Jew number two seems to be so fixated on external belongings, on nothing being missing or stolen, that he has problems with placing the word "take" in contexts other than entirely concrete ones. So there might be room, within the scope of the expected understanding, for several slightly different ways of comprehending the joke.

In connection with a literary work like Updike's "Pygmalion," the expected understanding will naturally be far more vague and open-ended. Nevertheless it appears obvious to me that an expected understanding is associated with Updike's story too, even if it is more diffuse. What is expected to be interesting in the story is undoubtedly the man's psychological manipulations of his women and the results of those manipulations. As we have seen earlier, it is hardly possible to discern a wholly determinate message or an exactly defined point in the story. But if someone, say, attended primarily to the erotic motifs, reading the story as a piece of soft pornography, he would decidedly have placed himself beyond the scope of the expected understanding.

The Validity of Thematizations

I can now formulate my basic views on the validity of thematizations. In my opinion there is, in *one* sense at least, a limit to the reader's freedom to thematize and create applications. *The competent reader of literature is expected to perceive, and to take into consideration in her post-communicative processing of the things read, what the expected understanding is likely to have been.* I shall endeavour to explain and motivate this compressed thesis.

The reader has a right to expect the author to have seen to it that her literary text has values to afford to its audience – a cognitive, emotional, or formal-aesthetic benefit. It is certainly rational of him to be looking for that benefit, the intended literary use being the sole source of values prepared in advance that the text offers.

There are, however, hardly any really specific literary conventions to help the reader realize the pleasures which the text was calculated to engender. In practice the reader will have to read the poem, story, or novel, reconstructing the communicative content and focusing, thematizing, and applying features that he finds especially conspicuous or especially interesting. That, in any case, is how I think it is done when I am reading literature, and that is also what I believe happened on my first reading of *Anniversaries*.

In many cases, the reader (at least the trained, professional reader) could describe the aspects thematized and applied by himself as the "theme" of the text, its real subject or message. On my first reading of *Anniversaries* I might well, in Becker's spirit, have defined the theme of the novel as the question of how one is to lead a decent life in today's world.

As I indicated in the last section, I believe that the boundaries of the expected understanding are often rather indistinct in connection with literature: the expected understanding is *not really precise*, or it cannot for other reasons be demarcated with exactitude. Consequently it is often hard to say whether or not a given reading is within the scope of the expected understanding. But there are certainly cases where a reading is outside the scope: what the reader finds striking or worthwhile may be highly idiosyncratic. Let us imagine, for example, a child psychologist who, in his reading of *Anniversaries*, mainly pays attention to the descriptions of children – of Gesine in Jerichow, of Marie in New York – thematizing and applying these and deriving much personal benefit from doing so. Johnson can hardly have intended *Anniversaries* to be understood as a novel about the conditions of childhood. Would the child psychologist's reading, accordingly, be unacceptable?

I wish to distinguish, here, between several different cases. If the child psychologist does not realize that there is what I call an expected understanding associated with a literary text, then he is an incompetent reader. Likewise, he behaves incompetently if he perceives the existence of the phenomenon of expected understanding but believes that *Anniversaries* is meant to be understood as a description of children. In both cases I would say that he does not quite know what he is confronted with. He is not enough trained in the practice of reading literature, or not familiar enough with the literary genre or tradition in question, to see what the text is expected to have to offer. There is, however, also a third type of possible situation. The child psychologist may understand the novel as a comprehensive fictional picture of reality carrying both political and existential implications, but what really fascinates him may nevertheless be the novel's descriptions of children. In that case, I would say, there is nothing wrong with the competence underlying his reading. Therefore I would not like to maintain that his reading – and by that I mean his overarching comprehension of *Anniversaries*, including his comprehension of the expected understanding – misses the point of the book. The thing is simply that he is making non-expected focusings in the text. I shall put it that he is "transcending" the expected understanding. In a transcending reading, the reader oversteps the boundaries of the expected understanding (whether or not he realizes what the expected understanding is). Conversely, I speak of a reading staying within the scope of the expected understanding as "matching" that understanding.

As I see it, then, we implicitly expect the reader of literature to identify the expected understanding of the text. If he fails in this, his reading will be incompetent (more or less; naturally we are dealing here with a gradual phenomenon).[45] A competent reading is, however, not obliged to remain within the confines of the expected understanding. Readings transcending it may well be acceptable.

Readings transcending the expected understanding are not *necessarily* acceptable, though. They may in principle be bizarre, irrational (something that readings matching the expected understanding never are). If, for example, a reader first and foremost thematizes and applies the sound structure of *Anniversaries*, his reading will no doubt be strange enough to be called unacceptable. His focusing will stand out as irrational because of its arbitrariness and irrelevance. Still, I do not think that we would be dealing, in the case at issue, with a breach of the specific rules of the reading of literature. The problem with the reading is rather that it offends against general principles of rational behaviour. To bring in an example from a very different area: there are normally no rules stipulating how an employee should get to and from work. So creeping to work would not contravene a regulation – but on the other hand it would be so startlingly irrational that it would be regarded as a sign of mental derangement and in that sense as abnormal.

I have been speaking about the thematizations of ordinary readers and their acceptability conditions. When a critic or scholar points to the theme of a literary text (as Becker explicitly did with *Anniversaries*), I see the matter somewhat differently. Such a definition of the theme appears to me to involve a claim to make an objective and well-founded observation about the text (and that is not the case where private thematizations are concerned). Discussing the conditions under which a critic's or scholar's identification of the theme is tenable would, however, carry me too far (it would not even be within the scope of my subject).

My statements about the acceptability of thematizations are of course intended as descriptions of reality, not as methodological decrees. I am attempting to discern and account for the norms and expectations actually governing the practice of reading literature. The practice is, however, far from being clear and unequivocal. True, it can be analysed relatively simply and convincingly in some respects, but it is hard to pin down in others. The rules for the validity of thematic interpretations belong, no doubt, to the elements that are very difficult to observe and describe.

It is important to bear in mind that the logic of thematization is uncertain and ambiguous. I can, however, see several reasons for believing that the analysis given above is essentially correct.

First, I find that the analysis is intuitively plausible, and that its plausibility emerges clearly if the analysis is applied to simple presentational texts like Freud's Jewish joke (as told in an actual situation in Freud's time). The analysis indicates that the addressee does not process the joke competently unless she gets the point that appears to have been intended. If she sees the point, her reception will be acceptable (as long as no other, extraordinary elements are added). If she does not realize that there is a point to be found, or if she obviously apprehends the wrong "point" as the intended one, she behaves as an incompetent recipient of jokes. If she gets the point, but lets other aspects of the joke come to the forefront in her experience – if, for example, her first interest is in the question of whether any anti-Semitism lies behind the telling of the rather coarse Jewish joke – her reception will transcend the expected understanding but nevertheless be competent and acceptable. I see this as a reasonable way of describing some of our intuitions about the correct and incorrect handling of jokes and – extrapolating these observations – of presentational compositions generally.

Second: According to my analysis, there are normally several more or less different readings that fall within the often wide and fuzzy frame of the expected understanding. Thus the analysis makes comprehensible how there can be more than one acceptable interpretation of a literary text. At the same time the analysis implies the possibility of unacceptable interpretations – "incompetent" or "irrational" interpretations. It also explains what is wrong with such interpretations. In the more complicated case – for example, the incompetent but rational understanding – the reader does not choose the interpretation presumably expected. That is to say that she does not, to all appearances, correctly understand what she is faced with, what expectations and claims the author is carrying with him to their encounter. So my analysis provides an explanation of the situation at hand as the most prevalent intuitions about interpretation construe it: an explanation of the fact that there are normally both acceptable and unacceptable interpretations of a literary work, and that no single interpretation is the only correct one.

Third, I regard it as a considerable strength that the analysis is based on an overall view of literary communication supported by a contemporary pragmatic philosophy of language. It follows from current pragmatics that there has to be an expected understanding in connection with presentational texts. Principles of rationality, and the interactive character of communication, make it reasonable to assume that the addressee is supposed to register that expected understanding and to take it into account in one way or another.

Consequently, my theory about the validity of thematizations seems to me to possess a fair amount of prima facie credibility. I would also contend that it is more reasonable than the other current ideas about thematic interpretation. I shall attempt to substantiate this claim in the next section.

Other Theories about the Validity of Thematizations

When someone identifies the theme of a literary work, is she then making an observation that may be true or false? It is the answer to that question, and the motivations behind it, that differentiate among various theories concerning the validity of thematizations.

The answers may be divided into three main groups. Some theorists are what I call "objectivists" when it comes to assessing the validity of thematic identifications. They hold that a determination of a text's theme is either right or mistaken (though it may not always be possible to decide which). Others are "relativists." For them, all determinations of a text's theme are a priori according to rule (even if they are prepared to find some thematic interpretations odd). A third group, to which I myself now belong, could be called "believers in 'interpretative scope.'" The proposers of such answers think that a literary text usually gives the reader a greater or smaller scope for construing its theme. All interpretations within that scope are acceptable (and there is normally no absolutely correct identification of the theme), while other understandings of the text are unacceptable.

Consistent conventionalists and intentionalists such as Beardsley and Juhl are naturally objectivists in the sense stated above.[46] According to Beardsley, the theme of a work is a "general idea" or "concept" tying together elements in the work.[47] And in 1981 Beardsley is still clearly of the opinion that the themes of a work are to be found *in* the work and have to be determined, just like the rest of the work's meaning, "by appealing to the potentialities of meaning ... given the lexis and syntax."[48] Juhl takes up a related position, though he regards the author's intentions, not the conventions of language and reading, as responsible for the meaning of the literary text.[49]

It is easy to see what constitutes the basic weakness of objectivism in the theory of thematic interpretation. As soon as one examines the reception of an ordinary literary text, one finds partly different readings, and these may normally be combined or varied so that they form an immense number of slightly different interpretations of the work's theme. (That, above all, was what I wished to illustrate by citing a number of different thematic interpretations of *Anniversaries*.) It appears impossible to find a governing principle behind the practice of reading literature, a principle that would permit us, when confronted with a literary text, to reject as unacceptable all thematizations except one. What I am saying is not simply that I cannot detect any *consciously* accepted principle of that kind. I cannot see that the practice of reading *in fact* builds on any such principle, with or without the knowledge of those involved. The two objectivist strategies that immediately suggest themselves – saying that readers attempt to read in accordance with the author's intentions or that they attempt to read in accordance with the conventions of reading – will obviously not yield the desired result. Even if one were willing to conceive of thematization as being wholly governed by the author's intentions, one would face the problem that her intentions are not, normally, sufficiently unequivocal. The difficulties emerge quite clearly in our chosen example, for if Johnson is to be believed, he wishes the reader to enjoy complete liberty in his processing.[50] Nor can the conventions of reading reasonably be supposed to be sufficiently exact. Serious attempts to specify conventions followed in reading (above the level of the reconstruction of verbal meaning) characteristically come up with conventions that are imprecise and mutually unintegrated.[51] Thus a determinate, correct thematic interpretation of a literary text cannot, normally, be expected to exist: there is no reasonable explanation of how such an interpretation would be possible.

The reason for this is, naturally, according to my analysis, that only a relatively indeterminate expected understanding is associated with a literary text. Consequently I regard the basic objection just put forward as being valid for thematic interpretations from critics, scholars, and ordinary readers. At least where thematizations from ordinary readers are concerned, there is the additional argument that even rather out of the way readings – readings transcending the expected understanding – may well be acceptable.

This last idea may perhaps be provocative. My impression is, however, that competent readers often depart from the intended perspective in their readings. When I myself now read *Anniversaries*, my attention is drawn not least to Johnson's attitudes and diction and to what I perceive of as his attempt to build a fiction interpreting and explaining his own life experience. Given the familiarity with *Anniversaries* that I now have, this is actually the aspect of the novel most conspicuous to me when I read for literary satisfaction. Undoubtedly, the aspect falls beyond the frame of the understanding that Johnson expected and hoped for. Nevertheless I am not prepared to regard my present way of reading *Anniversaries* as less competent or acceptable than my original one – or than the rather neutral way in which I read on my second, probing, perusal of the work around 1990.[52]

I know of no empirical investigation into the characteristics of the expert reader's reading of literature. In the field of the visual arts, however, there is a relevant study – Michael Parsons's *How We Understand Art* (1987) – accounting for how viewers ranging from preschool children to art professors respond to art. I would say that in this study two things stand out as especially characteristic of the experts' experience of art: a problematization of the expected understanding and a special interest in the artist's underlying will to achieve expression and his difficulties in realizing it. (In both respects, the experts' experiences, in reason, transcend the artist's intentions.) The people interviewed by Parsons were viewing and commenting on works of art; the comments cited by Parsons as being "especially characteristic"[53] of the most expert viewers are:

– It seems to me that it breaks out of the limitations of the style by emphasizing the flatness of the surface.
– It has a kind of tired feel to it. I can't be sure if it's because I'm tired of seeing that kind of thing, or if he got tired of painting it.
– In the end the style is too loose, self-indulgent. I don't like that. I want more self-control.
– I go back and forth on this. I used to think it too rhetorical; now I vibrate to it again.[54]

Relativism is, naturally, one of the alternatives to objectivism in the theory of thematic interpretation. It is also a standpoint which I myself abandoned relatively recently. As late as a few years ago, I held the opinion that the reader's creative, post-communicative processing could not be judged correct or incorrect – contrary, of course, to her communicative processing, her attempts at reconstructing the author's communicative intentions.[55]

What has made me change my views is the simple insight that there are thematizations which have, de facto, been unequivocally branded as incorrect by the interpretative community. Where *Anniversaries* is concerned there exists a thematic interpretation rejected, to the best of my knowledge, by everyone (except, perhaps, by its originator). The interpretation in question was put forward in 1978 by Roberta T. Hye.[56] Its leading idea is that the American present in the *Anniversaries* is to be understood as a repetition with variations of the German past, the novel saying that everything repeats itself. Hye formulates "the central theme" of *Anniversaries* as the statement that "the present time is a varied repetition of the past"; she perceives the novel's "main theme" as being that "the past repeats itself in the present times."[57]

The natural objection to Hye's interpretation is that it conflicts with the spirit of Johnson's novel. Hye exaggerates a certain, limited aspect of the novel, unjustifiably turning it into the centre of attraction. It also appears unwarranted to say, even, that Johnson describes the past as being repeated in the present. In my view, some formulations in Baumgart – who has captured Johnson's exactitude and feeling for nuances particularly well – pinpoint the deficiencies of such an understanding of *Anniversaries*: "Johnson's own construction, his parallel narratives from the Nazi time in Mecklenburg and from the year in New York during the war in Vietnam, invite comparisons only to insist on the differences. ... the careful, patient narrative makes it clear that the discrimination of minorities and of the 'wrong' races then and now can be the same only to demagogy's erratic, impatient vision."[58]

In describing the practice of thematic interpretation one has to note as a fact that some interpretations of themes, Hye's among others, are simply rejected as unjustified by the interpretative community.[59] An interpretation may be irrational, or it may – like Hye's – be rather normal but still, when it comes to the point, appear entirely unconvincing.

As I see it, the above analysis gives a more credible explanation than a consistently intentionalist or conventionalist one of what makes Hye's reading of *Anniversaries* unacceptable. Her reading does not fall within the scope of what may be assumed to be the expected understanding, though Hye herself, to all appearances, believes it to.

A relativist in the theory of themes must of course maintain that an interpretation like Hye's is acceptable (though not necessarily discerning or interesting). A relativistic approach to thematic interpretation is advocated, principally, by reader-response critics and by pragmatists.

The main idea of such relativists is extremely simple: As readers we encounter a text which we experience each in our own way, and questions of right or wrong do not arise. That idea can, however, manifest itself in various forms. In chapter 4 I touched upon a version that has attracted much attention, that of Stanley Fish; here, I shall comment briefly on some formulations by the pragmatist Richard Rorty and by Norman Holland, a reader-response critic orientated towards psychoanalysis.

Rorty is critical of attempts to distinguish between the *interpretation* of texts and the free, creative *use* of them. Things have no essences, he points out, so no way of handling a text could run counter to its nature. A screwdriver may be used just as well for prying open cardboard boxes as for driving screws, and the text has no more a priori restrictions on its field of application than has the screwdriver.[60] The reader always places the text against a *special* background, thus achieving *special* meaning effects, and different readers will naturally place and understand the text differently. "Reading texts is a matter of reading them in the light of other texts, people, obsessions, bits of information, or what have you, and then seeing what happens. What happens may be something too weird and idiosyncratic to bother with ... Or it may be exciting and convincing ... It may be *so* exciting and convincing that one has the illusion that one now sees what a certain text is *really* about. But what excites and convinces is a function of the needs and purposes of those who are being excited and convinced. So it seems to me simpler to scrap the distinction between using and interpreting, and just distinguish between uses by different people for different purposes."[61]

Rorty is of course right about our fundamental freedom to use a text just as we choose: who could stop us from doing that? In my view, however, Rorty is missing the point when he insists on that self-evident freedom. The question I find interesting is what reading literature actually consists in: how we do in fact read, and are indeed expected to read, literary texts.

Nothing prevents me from utilizing a chessman for cleaning my ears, but acting in that manner is not playing chess. Correspondingly, I can do whatever I wish with the four volumes of Johnson's novel, but if I am to be said to *read* them I have to work with the text in the way implicitly expected by Johnson (and by our entire culture), attempting to identify sentences, intended meanings, communicative functions, and so on. And in my judgment, the traditional practice of reading literature envisages the employment of certain special strategies even in the post-communicative processing of the things read. Therefore, quite contrary to what Rorty says – and notwithstanding the text's lack of an essence – it appears to me to be an obvious fact that what we call interpretation *is* a special and privileged type of use of the text.[62]

Starting from a wholly different point, Norman Holland comes to results very similar to those of pragmatism. Holland distinguishes between two levels in the process of interpretation, a more universal and a more subjective one, much as I distinguish between reconstructive communicative processing on the one hand and creative post-communicative processing on the other. Holland, however, conceives of the reader's thematization and application of the picture of reality conveyed to her as being governed by her free associations. Faced with the fictive material, the reader, because of her distinctive personality, associates in a characteristic way calculated to maximize her pleasure and minimize her discomfort. As a logical consequence of that way of looking at the matter, Holland finds all interpretations on this level acceptable.[63]

Holland, too, disregards the fact that the reader encounters the text well aware of its having been created by another person and of its being intended to afford literary satisfaction if processed in the fashion foreseen. Holland emphasizes the reader's creative processing of the text, but he ignores the reading's character as a "negotiation with a human mind other than our own."[64] He sees the text's meaning as being created exclusively by the reader (like the meaning of a natural object, one might say, or the meaning associated with a Rorschach inkblot). According to Holland the finding of thematic unity in a text is due to the reader's psychological need for security which impels her to integrate the work.[65] Holland does not consider the possibility that the experience of thematic unity could arise because of the reader's attempts to discover the profitable way of apprehending the text that she takes for granted the author has in readiness for her. In common with other theorists orientated towards pragmatism or reader response – Fish, Rorty, and others – Holland overlooks the elements of re-creation of meaning present even in the reader's post-communicative processing, consequently landing in relativism.

I find myself much closer to the outlook that Joseph Margolis – a believer in interpretative scope in the sense indicated earlier – advocates in his *Art and Philosophy* (1980). Margolis, who has constructed an analysis of his own of the nature of art works and literary texts,[66] thinks that one often cannot point to overall principles for drawing the line between what is and what is not included in the literary work. True, there is much that can positively be declared to form part of the work; such things make up the subject of what Margolis calls "descriptions" of the work. (To say that *Anniversaries* is mainly set in New York, for example, would be to *describe* the novel in Margolis's sense.) "Interpretation," on the other hand, has subjective connotations.[67] Nevertheless, this does not imply that interpretations cannot be rationally discussed. Margolis makes a comparison with scientific theories that cannot be definitely corroborated: theories about the origin of our solar system, of life, and so on. At best, such theories possess considerable plausibility, given our present knowledge, but several competing theories may be plausible at the same time. Correspondingly, several interpretations of a work, diverging among themselves, may be plausible, or so Margolis thinks: "in principle, plural, non-converging, even incompatible hypotheses may be defended as interpretations of a given artwork."[68] There are, however, important differences between a plausible interpretation and a plausible scientific hypothesis. Above all, questions of interpretation are undecidable in principle, not only in practice.

At the same time, Margolis considers that some interpretations may be rejected as conflicting with the describable properties of the work.[69] Thus – to give a brief summary of his standpoint – he maintains that some interpretations are unacceptable while others are plausible, but that an interpretation can never be shown to be true.[70] So far, there are marked similarities to the conception for which I am arguing. There would, however, be significant differences between Margolis's standpoint and mine, even if interpretation in Margolis's sense were exactly identical with what I call ascription of themes. My account of texts, communication, and meaning is essentially different from that of Margolis.

The closest conterpart in my conceptual system to what Margolis calls the work is the communicated content, i.e., the intended meaning, or, if one likes, the reconstructed meaning. I can detect no *logical* obstacles to the determination of the communicated content. As I see it, however, the theme of a literary text does not exist in "the work itself" (does not form part of the communicated content proper) but is supplied by the reader (who, to be sure, is then acting under certain restrictions). This is perhaps my most conspicuous single departure from Margolis's views.[71]

Literature as a Source of New Thoughts

It is time to start gathering together the different threads that have been running through chapters 5 and 6.

I have said that thoughts, mental representations, play a key role in literature, since the content "conveyed" in literary communication is a complex of mental representations. The reader attempts to understand what representations the author intended to communicate. But the communicated content, the reconstructed meaning, also gives rise to secondary representations in her. In typical cases she focuses on determinate aspects of the communicated content and forms associations based on these (non-self-orientated associations), associations which in their turn are the source of applications, of self-orientated imaginings. I have claimed that the reader is, on the whole, perfectly free in her thematization, i.e., in her focusing and her non-self-orientated associating. True, her thematization will stand out as incompetent if she does not understand how the text is meant to be read, i.e., if she fails to make a reasonable identification of the expected understanding.

When speaking of thoughts in literature, it is also natural to discuss literature's importance for our understanding of our lives. In the last chapter I maintained that literature may contain genuine statements – at least for certain definitions of "statement" – and thus in principle affect our understanding of reality by conveying true and asserted propositions. But I characterized as more important in practice the power of literary descriptions to influence us by making it reasonable for us to assume that such-and-such states of affairs actually prevail. If one believes Johnson to be both well informed and interested in giving a description of New York that is correct in many respects, then one is in a position to extract much detailed information about the city from his *Anniversaries*.

But literature may also exert an influence on the reader's ideas about reality in a third way: through her own thematization and application. I shall set aside the rest of the chapter for comments on that fact. My argument supplements (or, on some points, recapitulates), observations in chapter 2.

"As readers," says Cebik, "we may revise our worlds according to an author's invitation and its interaction with our existing framework of concepts and beliefs."[72] The fictional world described in the work may give rise to definite ideas about reality in the reader; naturally, it may even have been created expressly to do so. The same goes for the attitude to the fictional world, or to elements of it, that is communicated by means of the text. The latter factor is easy to overlook where prose is concerned, but it often emerges clearly in poetry. In Lowell's "Father's Bedroom" it is no doubt in the first place the speaker's implicit attitude to his father's death, not the described room in itself, that constitutes the starting point of a skilled reader's thematization and application. In such cases it is of course not quite natural to assert that literature gives us knowledge. It would be more to the point to say that literature functions as a cognitive impetus.[73]

In recent years, several philosophers have endeavoured to explain *how* it is possible for literature to become a cognitive impetus.[74] Two accounts that appear especially lucid and multifaceted to me are David Novitz's argument in his *Knowledge, Fiction, and Imagination* (1987) and Peter Lamarque and Stein Haugom Olsen's discussions in *Truth,*

Fiction, and Literature (1994).[75] For the moment I shall mainly concern myself with Novitz, dealing with Lamarque and Olsen later.[76]

Novitz is among those who find it possible for literature to provide knowledge by conveying genuine, true statements.[77] In his treatment of the problem of literature and knowledge, however, he puts the stress on the more comprehensive idea that literature may function as a cognitive impetus.

In his exposition of the subject, Novitz overlooks the fact that the reader encounters not only a fictional world but also a communicated attitude to that world. He therefore does not observe that the communicated attitudes may provoke reader reflections, as in connection with "Father's Bedroom." (Nor does he notice the part that can be played by expressed, non-communicated thoughts.) As regards the fictional world as a cognitive impetus, however, Novitz has many relevant observations to make.

According to Novitz, there are several different ways in which literature functions as a cognitive impetus.[78] For example, a feature of the fictional world may induce the reader to form the hypothesis that a corresponding feature may be found in reality – the text may suggest a supposition about an empirical fact.[79] Novitz is thinking here, no doubt, partly about cases such as the one where the description in *Anniversaries* gives rise to suppositions in the reader about the actual New York, i.e., about cases which I would analyse differently.[80] It is, however, obvious that a text may also suggest, in the way intended by Novitz, hypotheses about reality that do not answer to factual empirical beliefs apparently held by the author himself. Novitz discusses, for example, the possibility that a reading of Dostoevskij's *Crime and Punishment* (*Prestuplenie i nakazanie*, 1866) may lead the reader to reflect that "human selfishness is frequently lost in times of ordeal."[81]

Novitz also conceives that we may acquire "values, attitudes, and skills of one sort or another, as well as empathic beliefs and knowledge"[82] from reading literature. As regards "skills": in a text, we can often discern strategies employed by the characters, and it is possible for us to adopt those strategies ourselves. To continue drawing on *Anniversaries*: the reader is supplied with a detailed description of how Gesine folds her *New York Times* in order to be able to read it on the subway train.[83] We could easily take over that manner of folding newspapers. As regards "empathic beliefs and knowledge": as sympathizing readers we form a vivid idea of what it must be like to grow up and live on with experiences like Gesine's in one's heart. And concerning "values" and "attitudes": when entering into the world of the work, we learn of choices with which the characters are faced. This brings to life for us the question of how one should act in situations of those types. We are forced to bring our own values and attitudes to the fore, perhaps to adjust them or make them more precise.[84]

Novitz also attempts to describe how the reading of literature may give rise to a new outlook on reality in the reader. His idea is, roughly, that features of the fictional world may lead the reader to form comprehensive hypotheses about reality. This is where the *Crime and Punishment* example comes in:

> if because of Dostoyevsky's novel one believes that human selfishness is frequently lost in times of ordeal, one may come to think of ordeals not just as a threat to human life and limb, but as a way of overcoming one's self-centerdness.
>
> Clearly, then, the factual beliefs which we acquire from fiction may challenge and undermine our normal ways of construing the world and understanding ourselves. They may furnish us with new ways of articulating our experiences, and with new ways of classifying and relating the objects and affairs which surround us. As a result we may come to perceive qualities of, and similarities between, objects and events, where these were previously unnoticed. It is in this way that fiction at times enables us to "rearrange" our world, to "re-model" it and fashion it anew.[85]

Novitz points to an impressive number of natural cognitive effects of reading literature.[86] Nevertheless, there is yet another type of such possible effect that deserves special mention. It is that where the literary description contains a combination of traits that may not perhaps occur together in reality (and so cannot provide us with new "factual beliefs"), but that still impresses itself on the reader's mind, coming to function, in the future, as a point of reference for her. Thus in Updike's "Pygmalion" we meet with a manipulative, in a sense sterile, male figure described in a memorable fashion. Reading the story supplies one with new material for the comprehension and comparison of males. It may, so to speak, enrich one's conceptual resources with the notion "behaving like the protagonist of Updike's 'Pygmalion.'" The acquisition of such a concept enables one to employ a new distinction in experiencing reality, thereby making that experience more nuanced, potentially at least. And that, in its turn, is of course a step forward intellectually, just as one advances in the understanding of music or the connoisseurship of wines when learning to utilize new distinctions which aid one in better distinguishing the structure of a symphony or the gustatory components of a claret.[87] The intellectual gain is of course small, taken in itself. But if you think of the literary texts that we normally read as having this kind of distinction- or concept-creating effect in a number of different respects, it lends some substance to the idea that it is possible for literature to enrich our comprehension of reality. Literature may, as it were, supply us with a nuanced and relevant material of samples with which to compare the realities encountered. And thanks to that, it can help us to perceive aspects of real situations that we would otherwise have missed.

I cannot remember having seen this cognitive literary effect described in an exact manner. But approximations of it are common in analytical aesthetics. I believe that it is precisely this effect that makes Hospers say, about the metaphors in T.S. Eliot's "Rhapsody on a Windy Night" and "Morning at the Window," that "they capture an essence, an aspect of the perceived world; and the insight we get from them enriches our subsequent perception of the world around us."[88]

Another approximation, it seems to me, is Nelson Goodman's idea that art and literature *exemplify* or *express* phenomena found in reality, and that in doing so they serve a cognitive interest (that should not be imagined as being divorced from affective or sensuous factors).[89]

The Special Character of Literature's Cognitive Effects

We have seen that the reading of literature may involve cognitive benefit in several different ways. Even so, many would say that this aspect of literature is in reality uninteresting. Literature is unable to afford any knowledge that cannot be better and more solidly supplied by non-literature, so giving cognitive benefit cannot be literature's real mission. Making the cognitive aspect the centre of attraction would be to reduce literature to a way of conveying knowledge – something which literature is not and lacks the adequate qualifications to be.[90]

That approach has a certain narrowness to it, resting as it does on the tacit assumption that correct convictions about reality (or true propositions, or true statements) constitute the standard by which cognitive value is to be measured. It is in fact possible to regard the matter from another angle.[91] In chapter 2 I observed that man can be regarded as "a perceiving and behaving system," a creature receiving impressions from her surroundings and using these impressions as bases of her own activity. Irrespective of whether one is reading non-fiction or imaginative literature, one passes through a genuine experience, taking in and processing impressions in a way that affects the conditions of one's own subsequent behaviour. I have contended that the experience of reading about Gesine Cresspahl's actions may affect one's ideal in life to some extent. And I have said that familiarity with Updike's "Pygmalion" can furnish us with new distinctions, making it possible for us to interpret other people's behaviour in a somewhat different fashion. In both cases, of course, we derive cognitive benefit from our reading, but not in the form of new, correct beliefs. The cognitively relevant effects consist, rather, in the creation of new ideas or distinctions that, perhaps, to some small extent, alter our motivation, our way of looking at things, our later conduct.

Naturally, the reading of non-fiction also makes us modify our ideas, systems of distinctions, evaluations, and behaviour. But it is not evident that it must, in that respect, be totally superior to literature from a cognitive point of view. True, it goes without saying that non-fiction has a far better chance than literature of conveying truths in the strict sense (true propositions, true assertions, true convictions), and that it is able to convey every single truth-in-the-strict-sense that literature can. On the other hand, non-fiction will not necessarily, in every respect, be a more efficient means of changing our view of the world and our actions. And it appears perfectly obvious that non-fiction *cannot* convey (or inspire the forming of) all the representations that literature can.

In one of its interpretations, the last remark is a truism. Almost without exception, literature is presentational while non-literature is in the informational or directive mode. Already because of that, literature communicates complexes of representations that are characteristically unlike those of non-fiction. And for that reason the experience of literature must differ from the experience of non-literature to some extent: it is the experience of another type of entity. No confrontation with non-literature can be wholly like the confrontation with such objects as Updike's "Pygmalion" or Johnson's *Anniversaries*.

Thus, experiences of literature are of a special nature. But that is almost self-evident. It is more interesting to ask whether literature's distinctiveness is significant from a *cognitive* point of view. Does literature contribute to our orientation in reality in a way that non-literature cannot do (although non-literature has of course, conversely, other cognitive resources that literature does not possess)?

In my analysis, it is the fact that a literary text is a *presentational* verbal composition that, fundamentally, determines its peculiar nature. I would like to add that the literary text is also in most cases *concrete*. It is usually about particular people, events, or actions as met with at a certain moment and in a certain place. For instance, all my main examples of literary texts, "The Freedom of Light," "Pygmalion," *Anniversaries*, "Father's Bedroom," and "The View," are of that type. Literary texts that do not deal with particulars at all are in fact rare.

For brevity's sake, I shall call a representation of something concrete – a particular person, situation, and so on – a "concretum-representation." Normally, literature conveys concretum-representations, and we are meant to bring these representations to life through our focusing and our associating, and to base our applications on them. On reading Updike's "Pygmalion" we build up conceptions of the Pygmalion-man who appears in the story. And implicitly we are expected to focus on the Pygmalion-man and form ideas about his behaviour, ideas applicable to the realities surrounding us.

After those preliminaries, I can introduce my explanation of why literature contributes to our orientation in reality in a way that is not open to non-literature. *Encountering a concretum-representation in a piece of presentational discourse is an experience that cannot be replaced by any other experience as a cognitive incitement.*

I have described above how the confrontation with Updike's Pygmalion-man supplies us with material for comparison which may, to some extent, affect our future interpretations and assessments of people in the real world. Could not a piece of informational discourse, then, serve the same purpose? Not really, I think; not unless we (mis)read it as literature.

The description of the Pygmalion-man brings us face to face with an example of possible male behaviour. One might think that a piece of informational discourse portraying the behaviour would perform the same service. We could begin "There are men who want women to adapt wholly to their wishes," then complete the account with one or another precise description of a type of male conduct. But such a solution will not work. The piece of informational discourse will simply differ from the concretum-representation in question in its cognitive effects. Let me explain why.

As I see it, the main reason is that the presentational concretum-representation is introduced precisely in order to serve as the basis of focusing, associations, and application. In that capacity it cannot, naturally, be replaced by any other representation. If two representations are to afford *exactly the same possibilities of focusing* or to have *exactly the same potential as a source of associations*, then of course they will have to be *exact counterparts*.[92]

At this point, one may wish to make the objection that informational compositions, too, can be concrete. The newspaper notice about John Sykes, my main sample of informational discourse, already communicates concretum-representations. In a newspaper story – which is certainly a piece of informational discourse – the representations may even be vivid and pictorial, just as in Updike's "Pygmalion." And the reading of newspaper stories could no doubt have indirect cognitive effects reminiscent of the ones I have described in connection with literature. Let us imagine a newspaper report about a family where the parents are unemployed, and as a reader a mother who, herself, runs the risk of becoming jobless. It would of course be natural for that reader to associate from the things reported to her own situation, more or less as if she was reading a literary narrative with similar content. What would the crucial difference consist in?

The principal difference lies in the fact that as a reader of the newspaper report, but not as a reader of the literary narrative, she would be transcending the expected understanding. The report is written with a view to informing the reader about a jobless family, and thereby, indirectly, about the actual conditions of families affected by unemployment. But as a reader she thematizes (ex hypothesi) the facts connected with her own situation, and her application squarely concerns that situation. So she does not let her reaction be governed by the information communicated, as in a reading within the scope of the expected understanding. She utilizes the text as a releaser of associations, much as if it had been a literary text (but here without the support of the communicative intention behind the text). No wonder that there is no clear contrast to literature.

This was an abstract explanation of why presentationally understood concretum-representations have a unique character as cognitive incitements. Their peculiar character is, however, also describable in more observational terms. It appears obvious, for instance, that concretum-representations arouse more associations in us than abstract representations do, and associations more directly related to ourselves and our own lives.[93] Therefore, literature's concretion makes it richer in associations than non-particular discourse, and, because of literature's presentationality, associating is relevant for the processing (unlike the case in connection with a piece of informational discourse). As Lesser writes: "Fiction lends itself to analogizing because of the extreme connotativeness of its episodic language."[94]

Concretum-representations understood in the presentational vein have other interesting cognitive peculiarities as well, but the ones that I just pointed out are, to my mind, their most significant characteristics. They make it possible for literature to function, among other things, as a kind of thinking – "the Western equivalent of meditation," it has been said[95] – where we implicitly or explicitly ponder more or less comprehensive approaches to life and the consequences they may possibly bring in their wake.[96]

The experience of literature is of course – I want to repeat this – at one and the same time a cognitive experience, an emotional experience, and an experience of form. In chapters 5 and 6, I have isolated the cognitive aspect (which, incidentally, I regard as being in a certain sense basic). Now it is time to move on, to attempt to add more dimensions to the picture of the reader's experiences before the text.

7 Literature and Feelings

Introduction

My reasoning concerning the cognitive dimension of literature in chapters 5 and 6 has laid the necessary foundation for my analysis of the place of feelings in literature. As I suggested earlier, there are four basic questions that I wish to ask regarding literature and feelings. What is a feeling? How is it possible for feelings to get into the literary object? How are the feelings in the literary object related to the thoughts and the form also present there? And what function or functions do feelings have in literary contexts?

In chapter 1, I touched on the question what a feeling is, describing it as a pleasure or discomfort accompanying a mental representation. I also surmised that feelings are normally,[1] ultimately, caused by memories of pleasurable or unpleasant physical sensations – I imagine that it is possible for representations such as perceptions, memories, or anticipations to bring to life, directly or indirectly, recollections of past pleasure or pain. As regards emotions – which are not, in the terminology of the psychology of emotion, the same thing as feelings – I reported the definitions of some theorists and commented that it appears difficult to determine the concept of emotion in a way both productive and faithful to common parlance. As I suggested in chapter 1, I myself see the concepts of the emotions (happiness, fear, admiration, and so on) as supplying standardized explanative descriptions of our feelings. An emotion is such and such a pattern of pleasure or discomfort (eventually also an accompanying pattern of such and such physical sensations) *with such and such a causal background*. Fear, for example, may be analysed as marked discomfort (in more pronounced cases accompanied by palpitation) caused by anticipation of the risk of serious misfortune for oneself. (Note that I do not include the mental representation of the risk in the emotion proper, as emotional cognitivists generally do; in my analysis, the emotion itself lacks a cognitive component. Cf. chapter 1, "A Sketch of a Theory of Emotion.")

Feelings – and a fortiori emotions – have a motivating effect. If I am afraid of being assaulted, I will avoid being in lonely places in the city after nightfall; if I am proud of having been elected to a certain board, I will not without powerful reasons ask to be relieved of the commission, and so on. The motivating effect of feelings makes understandable our need for concepts describing and explaining feelings, i.e., concepts of emotions. Knowing something about a person's emotions is knowing something about how he or she is disposed to act, and that of course is of vital importance in one's dealings with the person.

So much about what a feeling is. The question of how it is possible for feelings to enter into the literary object is the literary version of a time-honoured aesthetic problem: "how a feeling can be got into an object."[2]

Traditionally, the situation is understood as involving a paradox that should be resolved. As viewers, readers, or listeners we are inclined to say that such and such a feeling exists in the painting, the text, or the piece of music. But at the same time we realize that only living creatures can have feelings, and we are certain that art works are physical objects or, as regards literary texts and pieces of music, at least not biological organisms. So how can the feeling be got into the object?

A fairly common answer is that we, as viewers or readers, project our feelings, the feelings arising in us when we process the work, onto the art object. We then, *illusorily*, experience the feeling as already existing in the external object itself.[3] My own conception is somewhat different,[4] but I too hold that the affective character of the art object is illusory. In my depiction of the literary communication process, only the physical sign object itself (the copy of the text: for example, the paper with printer's ink) is a genuine, external object between author and reader. That object cannot literally be said to contain any emotions. Just like the thoughts, the feelings must in reality exist solely in the human participants in the communication process: the author and the reader. The author has feelings, and he communicates feelings. Feelings then arise in the reader both in connection with the reconstruction of the communicative content and in connection with the post-communicative processing, i.e., the thematization and application.

According to the approach to the concept of feeling just recapitulated, a feeling consists in a pleasure or discomfort accompanying a mental representation. Here we can find the starting point for an answer to the third question, or at least for an explanation of how feelings are linked up with thoughts in the literary process. Self-orientated representations are normally emotionally coloured, i.e., they are to a greater or lesser extent pleasurable or unpleasant. As we have seen in chapters 5–6, thoughts are being conveyed and worked on during the literary communication process. In the course of that process, self-orientated representations are brought to the fore for several different reasons, and literature thereby acquires an emotional dimension. (The relations between feelings and form will not be taken up until the next chapter.)

As regards the function or functions of feelings in literary contexts, my view is that feelings serve, above all, as some kind of evaluation. This is an attitude not normally adopted, but it often comes very close to being so in contemporary emotion theory – "my emotions reveal whether I see the world or some aspect of it as threatening or welcoming, pleasant or painful, regrettable or a solace, and so on," says William Lyons.[5] The reader's feelings demonstrate, among other things, how she evaluates the possibilities in life around which she revolves in her application of her reading. When I read Johnson's *Anniversaries* for the first time, it was precisely my positive feelings towards a life like Gesine's that proved that, in some sense, I found Gesine's life worth emulating.

Having indicated above the lines along which I want to answer the four questions posed in the opening of this chapter, I shall now devote the rest of the chapter to developing and defending this preliminary, general sketch of my standpoint.

The next four sections describe more concretely how feelings arise while the author is communicating and the reader receiving and processing. There follow three sections offering a more nuanced discussion of the question of the function of feelings or emotions in literary contexts. After having thus clarified and substantiated my standpoint I shall, in the last four sections of the chapter, take up some foreseeable critical objections to it. That will simultaneously give me the opportunity to position my analyses in relation to modern aesthetic theories about literature and feelings in a more systematic manner.

The Author's Feelings and the Feelings "in the Text"

In chapters 5 and 6 I pointed out that thoughts are involved in literary communication and processing in many ways. There are thoughts being communicated by the author which for that reason become an element of the literary communication taking place. The reader attempts to reconstruct the communicated thoughts, but he also produces thoughts of his own in his post-communicative processing of the things read, thoughts that thus come to be elements of his literary experience. It is convenient, therefore, to distinguish between *the author's non-communicated thoughts* (thoughts that she is entertaining without communicating them), *the author's communicated thoughts* (as intended or as reconstructed), and *the thoughts elicited in the reader in connection with his reconstruction, thematization, and application.* And regarding feelings and emotions, we require exactly the same type of distinctions.

The author's non-communicated feelings constitute a phenomenon analogous with the author's non-communicated thoughts. Let us take Robert Lowell's "Father's Bedroom" as an example. Lowell must be supposed to have had various feelings, perhaps also various emotions (sorrow, admiration, triumph ...), in the course of his more or less protracted composition of the poem. Despite the fact that these feelings are, by definition, not communicated, feelings in this category may affect the reader's experience, for they can be expressed without being for that reason communicated. In chapter 6 I observed that non-communicated thoughts may find expression in the text: as readers we can sometimes clearly see, or believe that we see, that the author has certain definite convictions, in spite of the fact that he does not appear to have wished to communicate them. Correspondingly, we can sometimes apprehend, or gain the impression of apprehending, that the author has certain uncommunicated feelings or emotions. This is, in principle, the same phenomenon as when we think that we detect, in an everyday situation, thoughts or feelings that our conversation partner harbours without wishing to convey them (her hidden scepticism, her unintentionally displayed admiration, and so on).

To the extent that Lowell's feelings are neither communicated nor otherwise expressed in the text, they will of course remain unnoticeable to a person who merely reads his poem, and so they will not be likely to have any impact on the experience of "Father's Bedroom."[6] However, when a reader perceives, or believes that she perceives, expressed but non-communicated feelings, this has every chance of influencing her literary experience. Expressed but non-communicated feelings, real or apparent, may affect her reading experience positively or negatively, and they may do so whether the author wants them to or not. Cases of several different types could be introduced and discussed at this point, but I do not want to enter more deeply into the subject. The issue is far from being unimportant, but it is subtle and specific and not so crucial that it cannot be avoided.

The author's communicated feelings form a parallel to the author's communicated thoughts, and naturally they are part of the communicative content (the intended or reconstructed meaning). Neither thoughts nor feelings can literally be transmitted from author to reader. In both cases, the "transmission" consists in the author's indicating that he has the thoughts or feelings, in his intentionally inviting the conclusion that he wishes to communicate that he has them.

As I see it, communicating feelings is doing a rather intricate thing. In my analysis, feelings must always be communicated by implicit means, since only thoughts can be explicitly conveyed. If one says something like "I feel very sad today," it is not a feeling (of sadness) that is being explicitly communicated, but a thought, the *representation* that one is feeling low-spirited. If one wishes to communicate the *feeling* of dejection, it is perhaps most natural to deliver one's utterance in a depressed tone while making it obvious that the depressed character of the tone is deliberate. The communicating of feelings, thus, demands mastery of relatively sensitive, non-conventional nuances of expression. (Nevertheless, practically all people possess that power to express themselves, at least in speech.)

I would say that in "Father's Bedroom" Lowell communicates sorrow for his father's death. If one expresses oneself in the way Lowell does in the poem, one makes it natural for a reader to draw the conclusion that one is feeling sorrow. The diction, for example, indicates a feeling of loss in the speaker. I am thinking, above all, of his implicit surprise at the fact that his father is gone while everything else is untouched, combined with the impression of a depressed state of mind conveyed by his somehow naked and numbed description of reality.[7] By using such means – presumably with intention – Lowell makes it natural for the reader to draw the conclusion that he wishes the reader to draw the conclusion that he feels sorrow at his father's death. Therefore, we have reason to assume that Lowell wishes to *communicate* sorrow at his father's death.

In cases like "Father's Bedroom" we are accustomed to speaking as if the feeling of sorrow existed *in the poem*, in the text itself as it were. Thus Herbert Leibowitz says of the suite of poems of which "Father's Bedroom" forms part: "The lines have the factual crispness of reportage but underneath they are *charged with complicated feelings.*"[8]

It is, however, naturally, the transportation metaphor that we make use of in thinking of the text as something that literally *contains* meaning, feelings among other things, or in speaking of lines in a poem as if they were physical objects literally carrying emotions, literally *charged* with complicated feelings. It is important to see more deeply than the transportation metaphor allows us to. What are usually called the feelings "in the text" – the sorrow in "Father's Bedroom" and the like – are certainly, above all, the communicated feelings: the ones that the author intended to communicate or that the reader understood him as intending to communicate.

I said earlier that feelings in connection with literature must in reality be found in the human participants in the literary exchange: in the author or in the reader. With regard to existence, the communicated feelings occupy a difficult intermediate position. They are ideas of feelings, the semblance of feelings, but not necessarily in themselves feelings that exist or have existed.[9] "Father's Bedroom" communicates sorrow at Lowell's father's death – but this in itself does not guarantee that Lowell really did feel sorrow. It is possible, perhaps even likely, that he did, but it is not certain, and the question of whether he really did is of limited literary relevance. As everyone knows, we are able to communicate ideas and feelings that we do not actually hold or have, and to do so in a literary context is not normally seen as reprehensible.[10] Nor is there a guarantee that the communicated feelings will really arise in a reader reading the poem in an adequate manner. Correctly reconstructing what feelings the author is communicating is one thing, taking them over is certainly something else. It is true that the poem is apt to give rise to a rather complex feeling in the reader, an emotional state where the quality of sorrow may be prominent. But this does not alter the fact that if we read "Father's Bedroom" and understand that Lowell communicates sorrow at his father's death, we will not necessarily, because of that, feel sorry ourselves (about Lowell's father's death or about anything else).[11]

The author's non-communicated feelings, on the other hand, whether expressed or not, must evidently be genuine feelings in the author. Also *the feelings arising in the reader in connection with her communicative reconstruction and her post-communicative processing* actually exist. It is to those that the rest of the chapter is devoted.

Before passing on to the reader's feelings, however, I wish to add that in talking about the feelings "in the text" we are not necessarily thinking of the author's communicated feelings. Another possibility is that feelings *described* in the text are being referred to.[12] A text often contains descriptions of the feelings or emotions of the invented characters. Thus Sun Axelsson's "The Freedom of Light" contains descriptions of the protagonist's fear or anger: "In the nights, the endless nights, something horrid was digging itself out in her consciousness. It was a fear so annihilating that she could only endure it sitting upright in her bed, her hands around her knees and her head inclined. It bustled about around her. It tore at her. It meant to force her to lift up her face, walk up to the mirror, and look. There was a very wrathful person inside wanting something from her."[13]

What we, as reconstructing readers, are primarily faced with in such cases are not, however, *feelings*, not even communicated feelings. We are faced with communicated thoughts – *representations* of feelings, *descriptions* of human emotions.

Causes of the Reader's Feelings

I have assumed that the reader's feelings come into existence, principally, because his reconstruction and processing of the communicative content elicits self-orientated representations implicitly related to memories of pleasure or pain. Several different mechanisms may be thought responsible for such elicitation.

It is possible to maintain that self-orientated representations should already arise in the reader's work with the identification and interpretation of the very words of the text. As early as here the reader has to draw on his experience, in the final analysis on situations where he has come across these words before. But the emotional charges that do, eventually, arise in this fashion are no doubt weak, diffuse, and conflicting among themselves.

When the reader is reconstructing the communicative content, he is confronted with pictures of reality. Whoever reads "Father's Bedroom" is imagining a certain, definite bedroom. Again the reader must make use of his experience of life to understand the situations that are being described and their implications. He must "enter into" the depicted world, as the phrase goes. On this point, it appears realistic to assume that the reader's self-orientated memories, ideas, and anticipations are made topical in a way that brings in material carrying a more pronounced emotional charge.

In a fictional narrative it is, moreover, often the case that the motives of the people involved are left undescribed. Then the reader must, herself, construct an explanation for their behaviour if she is to be able to follow the story. In "The Freedom of Light" it is said of the woman, during her most difficult period: "Now she was dressed very strangely, without any genuine relation to her self. However something told her that she should remember not to dress like an old woman."[14]

Here the reader himself has to supply an explanation for why the protagonist avoids dressing like an old woman. The most natural assumption seems to be that the woman wishes to insist, before herself and others, that she is not old yet. In spite of her depression she still wishes to be seen as a fairly young woman, which suggests that she is, at heart, still interested in attracting men's attention to her and in being loved. To arrive at this interpretation of the protagonist's aspirations and her way of experiencing herself – an interpretation which is of course important for an understanding of the later course of events – the reader must "enter into" the woman. She must, without explicit support from the text, form an opinion of how the woman is thinking and feeling. In doing that, the reader will have to make use above all of her own experience of people's evaluations and reactions (including her own): of memories, self-orientated imaginings, and so on.

These deliberations should make it clear that the reader's attempt at understanding the communicative content may already arouse feelings in him. A possible, complementary explanation is that it may be inherent in human nature to react with emotional reflexes of some sort to certain types of perceptions and fantasies, without the perceptions or fantasies having to undergo any further cognitive processing.[15] An explanation along such lines appears, however, less credible to me where literature is concerned than in connection with an art like film, where the perceptions and fantasies communicated normally become more concrete and insistent.[16]

Naturally, the post-communicative processing, too – the thematization and, above all, the application – is likely to have an emotional impact (as I pointed out above in chapter 2). One obvious way of reading "Father's Bedroom" is to focus on, associate around, and then apply Lowell's way of speaking of the bedroom scene and the attitude towards his father's death that his diction helps to convey. When reading in that manner, one is implicitly reflecting on Lowell's attitude. On some level one is asking the question: Is this a natural (or reasonable; or common) attitude to take to death (or the death of one's father; or the death of a person close to one)? The processing of such questions must revive different kinds of earlier experiences of one's own. And certainly the resulting conception of how one could or should relate to death will, in its turn, acquire emotional consequences, whether it involves an idea about death that is new to one or simply an inculcating of death's actuality. If one really contemplates the significance of death, that will lead to the formation of emotionally coloured ideas about one's own death, the death of one's intimates, and so on.

Empathy and Identification

It is not yet possible to give a well-founded scientific description of the mechanisms responsible for the arousal of feelings in the reader during his reading. My sketch in the preceding section was fairly sweeping and hypothetical. It shares those properties, however, with the treatments of the subject by other theorists, and my account seems more coherent and credible, at least to me, for reasons I shall give at the end of this chapter.

Before carrying my argument further, however, I should like to comment briefly on the two concepts of empathy and identification, which often play an important role in theoretical explanations of the reader's feelings.

As regards "empathy," I shall be very succinct. It is a widespread assumption that the reading of literature presupposes something called "empathy" or "participation." The concept of empathy ("Einfühlung") was launched in late-nineteenth-century German aesthetics.[17] In contemporary literary criticism and aesthetics, the notion of empathy is encountered, principally, in the form of the idea that the reader always participates in the fictive literary events or is emotionally involved in them. In the last chapter I cited Simon O. Lesser's contention that "we unconsciously participate in the stories we read" and Martha C. Nussbaum's reference to the reader's "friendly participation in the adventures of the concrete characters."[18]

Among the phenomena mentioned in my analysis, the ones most naturally described as the reader's "empathy" or "participation" are his registering of the situations portrayed and his interpolating, emotion-activating interpretations of such things as the hidden thoughts, feelings, and motives of the characters. I shall, therefore, let the word "empathy" refer to such registrations and interpretations. (Of course I do not mean that the reader *actually enters into* the fiction, that he *literally participates* in it. The concepts of empathy and participation are based on metaphors that are frequently taken much too literally;[19] something it is important to avoid.)

In some contemporary analyses – for example, in recent contributions by Susan Feagin, Gregory Currie, and Kendall Walton – the phenomenon of empathy or reader participation is discussed in terms of "simulation." The meaning of this may vary; each of the three philosophers just mentioned views the reader's supposed simulation somewhat differently.

Feagin seems to believe that readers react emotionally to texts for various reasons, and that the simulation basically consists in the empathetic reader's ascribing to a fictional character her own emotional responses while reading.[20] I myself, of course, would prefer another explanation. I think that the reader, among other things, imaginatively enters, more or less, into fictive characters, and that this is one of the reasons why representations potentially charged with feeling arise in her.

Currie's understanding of the empathizing with fictional characters hinges on his theory of fiction reading as a make-believe reading of a factual account, a theory that I do not subscribe to and that I criticized in chapter 2 above. Currie sees the reader of fiction as simulating a person reading the story as a non-fictional and well-informed narration;

according to him, the reader of fiction thereby acquires "off-line versions of his [sc. the imagined reader of the factual account] (relevant) beliefs and desires."[21] Apart from my reservations concerning the theory of fiction as make-believe fact, I also think that both the imagining of, and reflection on, figures implicitly known to be fictional is of a character that cannot be explained as the make-believe understanding of those figures as real. However, I lack the space, here, to argue for that conviction.

Irrespective of its exact formulations, I feel generally uneasy with the idea that emotional responses to fiction are grounded on simulation – provided, of course, that the idea is taken not metaphorically but at face value. As I see it, there is undoubtedly an element of simulation in the reader's activities, since she must no doubt, as part of her response, form impressions of a kind about what it would be like to be in the fictive character's shoes. In my opinion, however, to talk of simulation in this context is to exaggerate the reader's (normal) degree of involvement with the fictive character and to underestimate the multiplicity of her intellectual operations in the act of reading. The reader registers the fictive state of affairs, attempts at least partially to understand the fictive characters' situation from within, and goes through a continuous process of reflection, attended by feelings, over the representations that her reading and reflection confront her with. To my mind, "simulation" is too blunt a word to cover these complex occurrences in a felicitous way, and is even too one-sided and definite to describe adequately the nature of the reader's "entering into" the fictive characters.[22] This reservation is valid, I think, even in connection with less complicated and, to my mind, more natural analyses (like Walton's)[23] of how empathetic intercourse with fiction can be understood as a variety of simulation.

Enough about empathy and simulation. As regards the concept of identification, it is rooted in Freudian thought. In psychoanalytic theory, "identification" denotes a process of extensive imitation, a process of assimilating oneself to someone or something in one's surroundings constituting the object of the identification.[24] Freud himself was, however, prepared to use "identification" in the literary domain as well. In "Psychopathic Characters on the Stage" ("Psychopathische Personen auf der Bühne," 1904, first published in 1942), an early manuscript reminiscent of "Creative Writers and Day-Dreaming" in its general view of literature, he argues that the dramatist and actor let the viewer "*identify himself* with a hero," i.e., let him enter a fantasy where the viewer is, himself, the hero.[25]

Other psychoanalytically orientated theorists also see the reader's identification as an assuming of roles that the text has in readiness for her. Later Freudian theory has, however, widened the scope of Freud's view of literary identification in other respects. After the breakthrough of ego psychology, the literary text has often come to be seen as a compromise formation affording satisfaction, in various ways, to id, ego, and superego, thus helping the ego to keep the play of psychodynamic forces reasonably balanced. It has become natural, then, to regard the reader's identification as being more multifaceted: it is often thought that the reader can identify, in different ways, with various characters in the work at the same time, so that a person following Shakespeare's *Romeo and Juliet* is perhaps partially identifying with Romeo, the nurse, the monk, the prince, and Mercutio (the example is Norman Holland's).[26]

The concept of identification has, however, become part of our general critical vocabulary. It has not for a long time been exclusively associated with psychoanalytic literary research.[27] Actually, talk of the reader's identifications often does not seem to imply more than the reader perceiving similarities between herself and some fictive character or characters and her taking this as a starting point in her thematization and application.[28] Sometimes one may even get the impression that all the reader's emotional involvement in the story is understood as a matter of identification.[29]

Conversely, the concept of identification is sometimes given a more precise and more theoretically pretentious interpretation, which may lead one to regard its use in aesthetic contexts with suspicion. Thus Noël Carroll, in his "Art, Narrative, and Emotion" (1997), points out that a reader's or viewer's artistically relevant emotions hardly coincide with the feelings of any fictive character. He therefore denies "the possibility that emotional identification characterizes the general mechanism or structure that elicits the audience's emotional response to narrative fiction."[30] Although Carroll's remarks are no doubt true as they stand, however, there seems to be no need to demand such a remarkable amount of explanatory power from the concept – or, indeed, to presume that there is *any* single, reasonably precise and circumscribed "general mechanism or structure" of the kind suggested.[31]

The concept of identification has long been an important instrument for theorists wishing to draw attention to the fact that readers are constantly making connections between the things read and their own lives. Such reader activity is not of course a matter of identification in the strict psychological sense,[32] but in reality the term nowadays often covers a wide spectrum of connections between the reader's textual understanding and his emotionally charged self-orientated representations. Thus, as several times before in this book, we come up against an established concept which is too broad and imprecise to be useful in our context without prior clarification. For me, the really important thing is to point out that the phenomena usually referred to as identification are elements of what I describe as normal communicative and post-communicative processing on the reader's part. It appears to be especially common to use "identification" about what I see as various types of application.

My judgment about the literary concept of identification may strike the reader as too dismissive. Perhaps it is natural, after all, to apprehend what we call identification as a determinate, definable psychological phenomenon. When we read a fictional narrative, it sometimes happens that what befalls a fictional character seems to affect us emotionally as directly as if it concerned ourselves. It may be hard to believe, then, that there is in fact an unconscious thought process mediating between our registration of the story content and our emotional reaction. Do we not often identify with fictive characters in some more literal and positive sense?

That is of course hard to say. But some of the mechanisms usually taken for granted in the psychology of reading could help to explain these enigmatic impressions of absolute immediacy. Teun A. van Dijk and Walter Kintsch have maintained that anyone who reads a text builds up an idea of what constitutes the text's central content. This idea of the text, which can naturally be modified all the time, is held constantly accessible in the reader's working memory. It functions as a frame of understanding, a "control system," governing her continuous interpretation of new, incoming sequences of the text. The general context does not, thus, have to be recovered anew for each new stretch of text; it is constantly available.[33] One could imagine that a certain definite connection *fictive character – thematized realities – relations to the reader's interests*, having once been coupled up as it were, could correspondingly be kept active in working memory so that it would not constantly have to be constructed from scratch. That would help to explain the impression we sometimes get that the destinies of a fictive character are immediately associated with our own interests.

The Reader's Feelings and the Temporality of Reading: The Example of Suspense

When reading a text, literary or non-literary, among other things one solves the problem of forming an overall idea of a whole, coherent complex of meaning. This is a fact of which psychologists of reading are well aware. According to Marcel Adam Just and Patricia A. Carpenter, "[w]hat distinguishes a text, whether it is a children's story or an editorial, from a collection of unrelated sentences is the cohesion of the underlying ideas. To understand a text, a reader must not only make sense of each sentence in itself, but he must also determine its relation to the preceding portions of the text. He must determine the relations among the events, objects, and facts that are described by the text and *construct a representation that integrates the information.*"[34]

It is normally assumed that, from the very first moment, the reader attempts to form a conception of the general semantic whole, a conception then continuously modified or revised in the course of his reading.[35]

In describing the reader's conception of the textual whole as the main content of her reading experience, one is giving a basically static picture of reading. The *process* of reading and the continuous alteration in content in the reader's evolving experience are relegated to the background. My own picture of reading has hitherto been of that static kind. Even if I have repeatedly referred to the processual character of reading, my interest has essentially been focused on particular instants during reading or on the reader's overall conception of the text.

To understand the feelings that arise in the reader, it is sometimes sufficient to refer to his empathy with the fictive characters at a given moment, or to the focusings, associations, and applications based on his reconstruction of the text's meaning. But there are also feelings in the reader that we cannot comprehend without considering the temporality of reading, the fact that the communicated complex of mental representations is reconstructed *in a fixed order.* Successiveness may give rise to many important and subtle emotional effects.[36] I shall confine myself, here, to commenting on a comparatively robust and simple mechanism, the one responsible for suspense, for exemplifying succession-dependent emotional effects. Suspense is built up step by step and, in the end, dissolved; in order to understand the phenomenon of suspense one must consequently take into account that reading constitutes a process with an extension in time.

Thrillers, of course, are texts where suspense is of utmost importance. I shall make use of Frederick Forsyth's first novel, *The Day of the Jackal* (1971), as an illustrative example.

"The Jackal" is, in the story, the cover name for a professional London-based assassin. In 1963, the ultra-nationalist, secret revolutionary organization OAS hires him to murder the president of France, Charles de Gaulle. The French government has recently given up Algeria, and as a result the political situation in France is tense. The death of de Gaulle would be likely to spark a civil war. Several attempts by OAS to assassinate the president have been unsuccessful, mainly because of the extremely efficient security arrangements protecting him. The novel describes the Jackal's preparations for the murder and, in a parallel narrative, how the French superintendent Claude Lebel, whom the forewarned French authorities have invested with extraordinary powers, does his best to find out who the Jackal is and thwart his plans. The novel ends in a mansard apartment in Rue de Rennes in Paris. Great festivities are being held in the city; it is the anniversary of the liberation of France after the Second World War. In the Place du 18 Juin, only 150 yards away, de Gaulle is decorating war veterans with medals. Unknown to himself, he is in the hairline of the Jackal's telescopic sight. At the last moment, however, Lebel reaches the room where the Jackal is, and a life-and-death struggle ensues. It is easy to imagine how many opportunities for creating suspense this plot offers, and the possibilities have been skilfully exploited in Forsyth's novel.

Noël Carroll has analysed suspense as an emotion associated with the need to have a question answered: "Suspense arises when a well-structured question – with neatly opposed alternatives – emerges from the narrative and calls forth what was earlier referred to as a simple answering scene (or event). Suspense is an emotional state that accompanies such a scene up to the point where one of the competing alternative outcomes is actualized."[37]

Carroll's basic idea is simple but undoubtedly correct. If the reader is to feel suspense, it is necessary for her to ask herself, "What will happen?" When that question has eventually been answered, her suspense will be dissolved. Creating and exploiting suspense consists in arousing a desire to know, maintaining it by various means, and finally appeasing it.

In its general structure (an expectation of one kind or another is raised and kept up, and then fulfilled or frustrated), this explanation is in fact applicable to all literary effects rooted in the temporality of reading. However, this interesting merit represents, simultaneously, a weakness in Carroll's analysis, considered as an analysis specifically of suspense: Carroll provides a general, basic explanation of effects exploiting the temporality of reading rather than a specific explication of suspense. "Suspense" in the quotation could just as easily be replaced with "curiosity," but suspense and curiosity are not identical. Suspense – and I am not thinking, now, of the emotionally positive suspense that is in reality eager expectation – could be characterized as temporally extended fear before an approaching, decisive event. Fear is the unpleasurable anticipation of serious thwartings of one's own interests. Consequently, a person feeling fear finds herself in a situation where she perceives herself as being under some kind of threat. Carroll's definition should be supplemented, then, above all, with the stipulation that the reader has to experience a sort of fear in order to be said to be in suspense.

Since it is the temporality of reading, and the emotional effects occasioned by that temporality, that are of interest in this section, I could break off my discussion of suspense at this point. I shall, however, comment briefly on the question of how the reader can come to experience suspense, i.e., a sort of fear, when reading *The Day of the Jackal*.

Let me first say that the reader is naturally aware that the reading of Forsyth's novel involves no *real* threat to him. His suspense will therefore be somewhat different from that experienced when facing real, expected danger, and the reading experience itself will no doubt, normally, even be pleasurable. (I shall revert to the latter, seemingly paradoxical circumstance later in this chapter.)[38]

Fantasies may, however, through their associations, be connected with the real desires and fears of the fantasizer. Therefore, conflicts within the frame of a fantasy, and their developments, can symbolically come to stand for conflicts in which the fantasizer finds himself and their possible outcomes. As regards *The Day of the Jackal*, the assassin obviously violates fundamental social norms in his disrespect for the inviolability of human life and for that which holds society together. So it is natural to expect the reader to associate the Jackal with social disintegration and with threats to his own interests. (The reader's well-being requires that the social fabric is not torn to shreds, that uninhibited violence is not allowed to rule.) This points to one possible explanation for the fact that a reader may feel suspense in reading *The Day of the Jackal*. The reader does not want to be made to accept as a credible picture of reality that society cannot defend itself against fatal attacks on its foundations. So he follows the narrative in suspense: indirectly, it is about a threat to his vital interests and its chances of actualization.

Effective suspense stories build on two opposing forces being played off against each other in the fiction, as the Jackal (and the OAS) and Lebel (and the French government) are made to enter into a deadly conflict in *The Day of the Jackal*. The usual basic pattern of such a story is that one of the forces represents values expected to be perceived as good, while the other force, conversely, stands for negative values. (Thereby a force that the reader must experience as a threat is mobilized, and also a force counteracting the threat.) The kinds and degrees of goodness and badness of the conflicting forces may vary from story to story. In *The Day of the Jackal*, we have a political thriller where the theme of power is prominent, which probably strengthens associations with certain types of threats while making others less likely. In this case, moreover, the evil side has been made attractive to some extent. Forsyth has equipped the Jackal with superior skills and a willpower that it is natural to admire, and has also allowed many of the events to be seen from the assassin's point of view.

I believe that the mechanisms already discussed, especially empathy and application, basically explain why the reading of the novel is apt to create a strong emotional experience of suspense. Undoubtedly, different readers of *The Day of the Jackal* react differently, and if they feel suspense this may be for somewhat different reasons. It appears likely to me, however, that the reader's emotional absorption (if any) will in part be owing to application, to the circumstance that the occurrences described symbolically constitute an attack on (or a struggle between)[39] important interests in himself. Presumably, it will also be due to empathy, to the fact that emotionally charged self-orientated representations will automatically be raised when the reader is acquainting himself with the many dramatic situations in the novel. This suspense can then be increased, decreased, and variously modulated by Forsyth, before he finally dissolves it.

The Reader's Feelings: Their Functions

I have already said that, in my opinion, feelings function as evaluations of a sort. When one is feeling a marked sympathy or a marked loathing for a person, that certainly manifests how one appreciates him or her.[40] Feelings in the face of literary representations function in the same manner: as evaluations of situations or options.

Let us consider the end of Axelsson's "The Freedom of Light." The fictive events conclude in the protagonist's finding a carnal and spiritual love which liberates her from her anguish and self-contempt. If that ending fills us with positive feelings, feelings of satisfaction, it may do so on various grounds. The reason could be that we are entering into the situation as it can be imagined to appear from the protagonist's angle, and that this creates feelings of satisfaction (stemming, ultimately, from memories). Or the path may have led via focusing and non-self-orientated associating. We could, implicitly, have asked whether genuine love is indeed possible and answered it in the affirmative. This bright picture of reality, with its promises of possible happiness for ourselves and those we care for, could then have given rise to positive self-orientated representations. But in both cases the feelings constitute *evaluation*: the evaluating of situations like the one in which the story's protagonist ends up, or the evaluating of an aspect of our human condition.

The story's ending could certainly also fill us with discomfort. Perhaps we think that the picture of reality conveyed is false – that the woman's difficulties are being overcome in too facile a manner, or that the idea that love can solve all our problems is just a pious (or impious) fraud. Then we assess negatively both Axelsson's literary act and the understanding of reality which she seems to invite. But in such a case, our feelings also make up our most basic attitude to the realities rendered topical for us by the text.

It is a common idea within the philosophy of emotion that an essential connection exists between feelings (organized into emotions) and evaluations. Normally, however, that connection is not understood in the way advocated here. As we saw in chapter 1, William Lyons in his 1980 book defined an emotion as "a bodily state caused by ... an evaluative attitude," while Patricia S. Greenspan has determined it as "comfort or discomfort directed towards evaluative propositions."[41] My view of the matter differs partially. Certainly, feelings are elicited by mental representations – for example, by perceptions of a reality that, as memories and anticipations tell us, risks causing us pain (cf. the wasp example in chapter 1). But these comparatively simple and concrete representations are not in themselves "evaluative attitudes" or "evaluative propositions." Evaluations in the latter sense – propositions like "That wasp is dangerous" – are not the *causes* of our feelings. On the contrary, they are *founded on* our feelings. The idea "That wasp is dangerous" is a registration, on the level of relatively abstract thought, of the fact that the wasp is experienced with fear.[42] As regards evaluative content, the idea is merely an explicit representation of what is already implicit in the spontaneous, preverbal feeling. It is the feeling itself that constitutes the real instance of *evaluation*.

It is true that Lyons and Greenspan are speaking of emotions, not simply of feelings. However, that does not remove the objection to their analyses that I just made. An emotion is, in my view, a pattern of feelings (and, eventually, of physical sensations) with such and such a causal background. I could agree with Greenspan that emotions are "compounds of two elements: affective states of comfort or discomfort and evaluative propositions spelling out their intentional content."[43] In the wasp example, the fear consists in an affective state (intense discomfort) caused by the possibility that the wasp may sting. Since that possibility calls forth intense discomfort, it is eo ipso evaluated as negative. Its negative value may well be expressed in an evaluative proposition: "That wasp is dangerous." But it is not *that proposition* but *the facts on which the proposition is partly based* (simple concrete representations that involve perceiving the wasp as potentionally liable to sting) that release the feelings and make it possible to speak of the occurrence of an emotion, fear. Nor can I regard the feelings as *directed at* the evaluative proposition; it seems impossible for feelings to possess object-directedness.[44] To the extent that the discomfort in the wasp example can have a directedness ascribed to it at all, the discomfort must in reason be said to be directed at the wasp or at the prospect of being stung by the wasp (thus being discomfort at the wasp, or at the risk of being stung, not at a proposition).[45]

I consider, then, that the principal function of the reader's feelings in the face of the text is to assess the realities raised in her communicative and post-communicative processing. Even if this standpoint is not altogether original, it diverges from the traditional view of the role of feelings in connection with art and literature. For a considerable period during the nineteenth and twentieth centuries, it was common to think that art and literature were a communication of feelings, that the very function of the arts was the conveyance of somehow valuable emotional experiences. Thus Hermann Lotze says, in his *History of Aesthetics in Germany* (*Geschichte der Ästhetik in Deutschland*, 1868): "It is not the case that it [sc. aesthetics] has to separate our feelings from pure aesthetic judgment ... but on the contrary aesthetics has to draw all feelings into its domain in the double conviction that an aesthetic judgment is only the expression of a feeling – since it is only in the feeling, and not in itself, that this value exists –, and that, in addition, *each* feeling represents the actualization of a value, the expressing of which would constitute an aesthetic judgment."[46]

A well-known idea of Lev Tolstoj's, propounded in *What Is Art?* (*Čto takoe iskusstvo?* 1897), is that the essence of art and literature consists in the communication of feelings: "*To call up in oneself a feeling once experienced and, having called it up, to convey it by means of movements, lines, colours, sounds, images expressed in words, so that others experience the same feeling – in this consists the activity of art. Art is that human activity which consists in one man's consciously conveying to others, by certain external signs, the feelings he has experienced, and in others being infected by those feelings and also experiencing them.*"[47]

Kindred theories, based on the idea of art and literature as an expressing of feelings, played a central role in British and American aesthetics up to the middle of the twentieth century. In the literary field, it is particularly natural to call to mind I.A. Richards's views, influential in many respects. According to Richards's *Principles of Literary Criticism* (1924), literature is characterized by a specific, "emotive" use of language. Unlike the language encountered in scientific contexts, literary discourse is not principally meant to refer to objects but to give rise to feelings and attitudes: it is "used for the sake of the effects in emotion and attitude produced by the reference it occasions."[48] (As we all know, it is still a rather widespread conviction that literature should, above all, afford emotional experiences.)

I shall not, here, embark on a discussion of the aesthetics of expression of the late nineteenth and early twentieth centuries; its weaknesses have often been exposed.[49] This aesthetics, obviously, diverges from mine in several respects. It differs in its view of the nature of feelings and emotions and of their role in art and literature, and also in its conceptions of the mechanisms behind the emergence and "transmission" of feelings and emotions. But a closer inspection of ideas like those of Lotze, Tolstoj, and Richards would nevertheless reveal important points of contact with my theory; in all of these analyses, for instance, cognitive and affective elements tend to merge. I shall come back to this.

The Problem of Tragic Pleasure

But let me first make an apparent digression. Speaking of *The Day of the Jackal*, I observed that if suspense is in reality a kind of fear, then there is something paradoxical about the fact that we may enjoy suspense. That remark touched on a classic aesthetic problem, that of explaining how it is possible for the reader to appreciate texts that, judging by their content, would seem liable to provoke painful feelings.

The paradox emerges for the first time in Western aesthetics as early as in the passage in Aristotle's poetics where Aristotle says of the tragedian that "the poet should create the pleasure which comes from pity and fear through mimesis."[50] That such pleasure does not appear paradoxical to Aristotle himself may perhaps be explained by his conviction that well-made imitations afford knowledge, and hence satisfaction, even when they represent objects that it would have been painful to observe in real life.[51]

A well-known later treatment of the same problem is David Hume's in his essay "Of Tragedy" (1757). The idea behind Hume's proposed solution is that the painful feelings aroused by tragedy are eclipsed, and even converted into positive feelings, by the pleasure deriving, on the one hand, from imitation itself (here Hume is on the same track as Aristotle), and, on the other, from the genius with which the imitation has been performed and from the beauties of diction and rhythm.[52] There are also several present-day explanations.[53]

It is worth noting that Aristotle does indeed imagine that there is "*pleasure* which comes *from pity and fear*" (my italics). In the same spirit, Hume speaks of the "*pleasure*, which the spectators of a well-written tragedy receive *from sorrow, terror, anxiety, and other passions, that are in themselves disagreeable and uneasy*" (my italics).[54] Thus, Aristotle and Hume do not simply say that we may appreciate a tragedy *despite* the fear that it arouses. Their idea is, more specifically, that fear, pity, and so on *contribute* substantially to the pleasure that we derive from our encounter with the text.

Aristotle and Hume clearly presuppose that it is a central aim of a literary text (here, a tragedy) to give us pleasure. If one does not share that assumption, one does not have to regard it as especially strange that we sometimes appreciate literature which arouses painful feelings. If one adopts a mainly cognitive view of literature – and thus sees literature primarily as a source of knowledge of a special kind – one may content oneself with saying that a person wishing to know reality will inevitably gain a knowledge of its painful aspects as part of the bargain. Considered from this angle, the appreciation of literature that arouses painful feelings will appear no more enigmatic than the fact that people find satisfaction in watching the news on TV in spite of the frequently unpleasant content. For my own part, however, I find good reasons to reject all-out cognitivism in literary theory (cf. chapter 5 above).

Aristotle and Hume also presuppose that the arousal of feelings such as fear and pity *contributes* to the pleasure derived from the text (apparently, they even regard it as a necessary condition of such pleasure). This assumption, too, may of course be questioned. There is, so to speak, a "coexistentialist" view of tragic pleasure. It diverges from Aristotle's and Hume's "integrationalist" standpoint in contending that the painful feelings *merely coexist* with the pleasure that the text provides.[55] To the coexistentialist, the negative feelings (fear, pity, and so on) are not pleasurable in themselves, nor do they make a positive contribution to the net pleasure that the text gives us. Carroll, thus, has argued that the pleasure afforded by horror films and horror literature emanates from aroused and satisfied curiosity, while the feelings of horror are a kind of spin-off and unproductive in themselves.[56]

Spontaneously, I find it counterintuitive to think of the fear that works in the horror genres are calculated to arouse as having such a relatively superficial relationship to the psychological benefit afforded by the works. For my own part, I am more prepared to adopt an integrationalist attitude to the problem of tragic pleasure. My general argument about literature's possible functions also provides some grounds for an integrationalist view of the matter.

I have stressed that literature often conveys a kind of perspective on existence (indirectly, via its expected understanding). In doing so it cannot, naturally, pass over the problematic aspects of reality – at least not in so obvious a fashion that the text will appear naïve to its intended audience. On the contrary, the ability to incorporate an acute awareness of the tragic aspects of life without making the overall effect unbearable is, to a certain extent, the gauge of a text's quality – or, at least, it is a feature frequently found in the most artistically respected literature.

Anniversaries is a good example in this connection. A reader entering into Gesine's experiences of painful separations and of stupid and brutal political repression can hardly avoid letting feelings of sorrow and frustration arise, specially since one cannot very well question the realism of Johnson's descriptions. As I emphasized in the last section, I see such feelings as evaluations of the realities emerging before the reader. Without the feelings of sorrow and frustration, the reader would not, basically, have appraised the corresponding aspects of reality as negative. Life's tragic side would have been included in her reception only nominally, not as *being experienced* as tragic. In that sense, the feelings of sorrow and frustration are in fact necessary if the experience of reality that the text instils into the reader is to have any significant depth.[57]

Furthermore, I believe that *Anniversaries*, despite its tragedies, has all the necessary qualities to afford net pleasure in an adequate reading. A concrete reading experience naturally includes many elements, so there is no real reason to believe that the feelings of sorrow and frustration will necessarily determine the overall impression. In fact, I think that the text has the chance of conveying a perspective on reality that can be experienced as both tenable and consoling (or at least bearable).

If one experiences the picture of reality conveyed by *Anniversaries* as being tenable, this is no doubt due, to a large extent, to its inclusion of the tragic aspects of life: suffering, death, dashed hopes, wasted opportunities. If the tenability of the perspective on reality is conducive to the novel's giving net pleasure, and if the reader's experience of sorrow and frustration indirectly helps to make the perspective on reality seem tenable to her, then her feelings of sorrow and frustration indirectly contribute to the pleasure that she derives from *Anniversaries*.

With that explanation I have in fact outlined one integrationalist way of viewing tragic pleasure; one view where the tragedy constitutes a condition of the emotional benefit.[58] I do not maintain that feelings of sorrow and frustration involve, *in themselves*, any positive benefit for the reader, nor do I contend (as Hume did) that the tragedian's aesthetic forming reverses their nature. My idea is that sorrow and frustration may, while retaining their character of being painful, form necessary parts of (constitute indispensable partial emotions within) an overall emotional experience which itself, all in all, has a positive rather than negative affective charge.

It is a fact that even texts like *Anniversaries* – texts that present what is, at a cursory glance, a very dark picture of reality – can be read with mental satisfaction. They may, as I just explained, convey a perspective on reality which can be experienced as both tenable and consoling (or at least bearable). It is perhaps not so difficult to understand how they can represent a tenable perspective. But what do their comforting qualities consist in?

One can hardly give a general answer to that question. One has to expect different readers, and readers from different times and cultures, to diverge in their habits of thought and feeling. Also, no doubt, different psychological mechanisms come to the forefront in connection with different texts. Further, these psychological mechanisms are difficult to ascertain in an objective fashion; consequently, the answers must be more or less speculative, even when a definite reader in a definite situation is being discussed.

In spite of these strong reservations, I shall point to some cognitive and emotional mechanisms that may be in operation when positive reading experiences develop in the face of texts that one would like to call dark or tragic. I shall continue using *Anniversaries* as a principal illustrative example. By and large, my explanations link up with various more or less traditional ideas about the psychology of artistic and literary experience. They are, however, formulated in the way that I myself find most reasonable.

Aristotle regarded it as a general truth that humans find pleasure in imitations. He explained this by contending that imitations provide knowledge.[59] His explanation could be supplemented with the reflection that pictures of reality serve, to some extent, to make it more susceptible of human control. Even if the picture's content is in itself depressing, the successful representation still gives us a better survey of the things described and so far helps us to understand them. If we understand a thing, we have a better chance of acting on it. The feeling of having understood something hitherto uncomprehended is therefore naturally combined with an experience of enhanced capability, of increased power over one's existence, and consequently with some pleasure. (Mechanisms of that type could conceivably be active while we are reading *Anniversaries*. The novel obviously has the ambition of throwing light on comprehensive wholes, making them possible to survey and comprehend: twentieth-century German history, conditions in New York, a modern human life.)

A literary picture of reality can also, via the reader's thematizations, convey an experience of an overall coherence in life, of basic patterns in our existence, that gives us the feeling of being a part, even if insignificant, of a larger whole. Such an experience may be a relief and consolation, throwing the awareness of our own life, with its individual disappointments, into the shade. The impression of being contained in a larger, meaningful context may uplift us. Historically, the idea that aesthetic, not least tragic, pleasure is related to a way of seeing that transcends the limitations of the self and liberates us from its sufferings is especially associated with the views of Nietzsche and Schopenhauer.[60] (On a banal level, aspects of this conception are reflected in the idea that the reading of literature can offer a salutary escape from reality.) The comforting thought of the individual becoming merged in a larger whole can be glimpsed in *Anniversaries*, especially clearly in the final scene of the novel, where Marie, Gesine, and Kliefoth let themselves be seen as links in a chain of generations.

Other, more specific explanations of the literary satisfaction are also possible where literary pictures of *painful* realities are concerned. As readers, we withstand the confrontation with tragedy; as readers of *Anniversaries* we endure facing what Baumgart called "a disillusion impossible to live with, one that may neither be accepted nor forgotten." That may give us a positive picture of our own ability to put up with the trials of our existence, and consequently some satisfaction. Greenspan has attempted an explanation, along lines reminiscent of these, of how we can extract pleasure from the viewing of horror films. Her idea (which to me appears more credible than Carroll's) is at heart integrationalist. What is pleasurable according to Greenspan is not the fear in itself, but the fact that we are *released* from it: "it is not the release of fear itself that is pleasurable, at least in immediate terms, but the fact that one is soon released *from* it. The overall feeling is discomfort yielding to comfort – a kind of 'roller coaster' sensation that is pleasurable on the whole. ... In some such cases fear may be essential to an overall experience that is pleasurable: the experience of fear followed by relief or accompanied by a sense of immunity to danger gained by facing danger repeatedly in imagination or in real life."[61]

It should be remembered, here, that in the final analysis it is we readers who regulate what and how we thematize and apply. If we can, we no doubt avoid bringing up realities so frightening or unpleasant that we are not able to handle them even in the well-protected reading situation. We only expose ourselves to thoughts that we can bear to think.

Hume found that the very *form* of literature affords pleasure through its beauty and elegance. A distantly related explanation has been given by psychoanalytical thinking about literature for nearly a hundred years: the text's fascinating form attracts our conscious attention, while our unconscious procures satisfaction for itself from the fantasies that the text has in readiness for us.[62]

I shall not discuss the functions of form until chapters 8–10. It is, however, natural to relate pleasure connected with "the exercise ... of ... noble talents, together with the force of expression, and beauty of oratorial numbers"[63] to admiration of the ordering intelligence behind the structuring of the text, ultimately of man's ability to control a subject-matter. The human capacity for mastering reality to which the command of form testifies, and which the reader can feel that she herself shares in some degree, should of course have the chance of arousing positive feelings.[64]

I have suggested four possible reasons – among many – why even tragic texts may afford satisfaction. (On the whole, my explanations point to general sources of literary pleasure.) To be on the safe side, I repeat that my argument is speculative. It is, however, obvious that we can also benefit emotionally from texts that paint a very dark picture of reality, and how to explain such benefit is an important problem of literary aesthetics. It is worth reflecting on, even if conclusive and exhaustive answers are beyond our reach.

A Cognitive-Emotive Model of Literature's Function

In chapter 2 I described how literature can be conceived as affording a combined cognitive and emotional benefit. As I see it, literature can convey a perspective on life that one can experience both as tenable and as emotionally rewarding or at least bearable. This idea fits a cognitivist view of literature in so far as literature is seen as supplying a perspective that makes our existence comprehensible to us (while being at the same time acceptable from an emotional point of view). It also fits an emotive view of literature to a certain extent, since it regards literature as giving us emotional satisfaction (via the conveyance of a perspective on reality which makes it understandable to us). The model of literature's function that was introduced in chapter 2 is thus a kind of cognitive-emotive model.

Chapters 5 and 6 paid special attention to the cognitive component of literary experience. In that connection I also discussed the sense in which a literary text can be said to convey a perspective on existence. I stressed that the conveyance is normally not effected by way of explicit or implicit assertions, but through the text's inviting a definite type of creative processing from the reader ("expected understanding"). Here in chapter 7 I have added the emotional aspect of the reading of literature to my account. I have, above all, described the reader's feelings as her implicit standpoint on the realities that the literary text brings to her mind. In the final analysis, the reader's feelings constitute her evaluation of the perspective on life that emerges before her.

It is important to remember that my cognitive-emotive model does not claim to account for how all literature functions. I believe, rather, that I am describing how many literary works can reasonably be supposed to function (and are, perhaps, implicitly intended to function) for many readers. The model captures some very general and basic features of my own reaction to texts like "The Freedom of Light," "Pygmalion," "Father's Bedroom," *Anniversaries*, and "The View"; perhaps I myself in fact read all sorts of literary texts with the type of basic expectations suggested by the model. But many have testified that their reading of literature, or some varieties of literature, starts from entirely different premises, and I do not pretend to have the right to declare invalid, generally and a priori, their testimony or their way of dealing with literary texts. There must be room for different types of assimilation of literature – at least, that appears to follow from my view of the reading of literature as a practice that is only moderately well defined.

Yet I think that the model is valuable. After having been supplemented with a consideration of the role of form in literature (in chapters 8–10), the model will indicate how the cognitive, affective, and formal sides of literature can combine to create the values that, so I believe, much literature has for many readers. One could say that the model starts from basic components of literary communication – thought, feeling, form – and shows how they may work together. It is not my intention to deny that the components may also be put together in somewhat different ways, or that other effects will then ensue. But the model from which I start here could be taken as basic, and other structurings of the literary building blocks could be understood as transformations of the model.

Even if one believes that these contentions are correct, it is natural to object that descriptions of the functions of literature could conceivably take other models than mine as basic, a strategy that would render my own model merely one of many possible secondary transformations. That I do not deny. True, I believe that my model captures a common and important function of literature, but I do not want to exalt the model into, in one sense or another, the most essential description that can be given of what literature provides us with. For me, the real point of introducing the model is different. I do not merely wish to demonstrate what thought, feeling, and form in literature concretely consist in and how it is practically possible for them to combine – I also want to give an idea of how such a combination can be functional from an artistic and human point of view. The model helps me to do this.

My cognitive-emotive model should be seen as, in itself, highly flexible. Literature, and literary experiences falling within the model's frame, can be closer to the emotive pole: psychological satisfaction may be pushed to the forefront; values such as suspense, humour, or sex may be capitalized on. Or the orientation may, on the contrary, be mainly cognitive in nature: what is offered can be documentary realism or an existential interpretation of the human predicament, and pleasure in the ordinary sense can be given low priority. As long as the striving for truth and vision is coupled with consideration for the human bearability of the perspectives, and as long as the seeking of enjoyment and courage in facing life takes into account the credibility of the perspectives on life conveyed, one is moving within the frame of the model. Consequently, "the frame of the model" delimits a rather large space; as I already said, both my experience of *Anniversaries* and of "The Freedom of Light" can be accommodated there.

Naturally, whether the perspectives emerging in the reading experience will be found cognitively and emotionally acceptable does not depend on the text alone, but also on the reader. What one reader perceives as a tenable and comforting perspective on life may appear to another as the result of puerile and wishful thinking, revolting in its flight from reality. And a perspective that one reader takes as tragic-cathartic may appear to another insupportably dreadful.

As one can see, it is part of the idea behind the model that a text may fail to produce the desired effect not only because the reader finds it too removed from reality but also because it comes to be apprehended as, literally, hopeless. As I pointed out in chapter 2, the reading of literature, understood in the spirit of my model, is meant to produce satisfaction, just as playing is expected to do according to Winnicott's analysis. Let me quote Winnicott again: *"Playing is essentially satisfying. This is true even when it leads to a high degree of anxiety. There is a degree of anxiety that is unbearable and this destroys playing."*[65]

It is not a coincidence that Winnicott's name should come up. The idea that literature conveys the picture of a reality obliging to humans is spiritually allied to Winnicott's descriptions of "transitional phenomena" belonging to a "domain" that exists "between" self and surrounding reality. According to Winnicott, it is also in that domain that playing and cultural activities are enacted.

If we are to believe psychoanalytical theory, it is frightening for the baby to come to understand, little by little, that the mother has a separate existence, that she is physically divorced from the baby and in principle beyond its control. As Winnicott sees the matter, the "good enough" mother fulfils the baby's wishes sufficiently often for a "domain" to come into existence where the child's wishes and the actual nature of reality overlap. The security that this domain represents is indispensable for the child if its creative fantasy is to develop normally.[66] The conviction that the world is in principle sufficiently obliging to us instils, one might say, an optimism that makes possible a creative attitude, a searching for the lines along which the desires of the self and the nature of reality can be brought into harmony.

The forging of a tolerably good correspondence between desires and reality is one of our constant preoccupations. Mental capacity that is not required to meet the instant's pressing needs is largely invested in the invention of ways to bring about such correspondence. Here one may think of planning in everyday life, of science, of religion, and of art and literature.

It is not surprising, therefore, that various cognitive-emotive theories have, at different times, held an important place in the philosophy of the arts. Aristotle moves along such lines in his poetics – it suffices to think of his idea that imitations, even imitations of the hardly bearable, give knowledge and by that means pleasure. The modern view of the arts, including literature, that began to take shape in the eighteenth century was still connected to Aristotle's. The conveying of beauty was placed in the centre of the idea of art, especially the imitation of beautiful nature,[67] and thus, in practice, the depiction of realities pleasurable to humans. The nineteenth-century German idealist aesthetics apprehended both humanity and nature as spiritual and saw their unity as revealed not least in art. According to Hegel, religion, art, and science move in the same sphere, "in which the *one* concrete totality comes home to the consciousness of man as his own essence and as the essence of nature. And this one genuine actuality alone evinces itself to him as the supreme power over the particular and the finite, whereby everything otherwise separated and opposed is brought back to a higher and absolute unity."[68] It is this tradition of thought that is still alive, albeit in a subdued form, in Lotze's *History of Aesthetics in Germany*, the idea "that the connected whole of the existing world agrees with the impressionability of the spirit, that the connections between things are made, and can be made, in such forms that their impression occasions an harmonious exercising of the soul's activities: all this being-for-one-another of world and spirit is the great fact that we enjoy in the feeling of beauty, a fact in the general order of the world which forms the independent object of our admiration and our aesthetic enjoyment."[69]

Thus the feelings that art conveys, according to Lotze, are feelings contributing to our orientation and adjustment in existence: feelings of satisfaction before the experiential fact that man and world, spirit and nature, form a harmonious union.

There is also a cognitive aspect to the kinds of aesthetics of expression developed by Tolstoj and Richards. For them, too, great art has the role of conveying feelings that help us towards an adequate orientation and adaptation in life – even if they differ in their ideas about existence and about the right way of living. In his aesthetic treatise, Tolstoj regards genuine art as "a means of transferring Christian religious consciousness from the realm of mind and reason to the realm of feeling, thereby bringing people closer, in practice, in life itself, to the perfection and unity indicated to them by religious consciousness."[70] Richards, who presupposes no specific ontological or ideological system, maintains that the feelings conveyed in literature instil attitudes to real life, at best adequate, balanced attitudes. According to him, it is in such terms that "all the most valuable effects of poetry must be described," and in fact Richards conceives of the conveying of literary fictions as "the chief means by which our attitudes to actual life may be adjusted."[71]

As I have repeatedly pointed out, I have not yet really got on to the formal side of literature, to what is traditionally seen as its *aesthetic* aspect. Before taking up literary form in chapters 8–10, I would, however, like to discuss some of the possible objections to the depiction of literature's emotional dimension given here.

At least two types of objections appear natural in the light of traditional literary criticism and aesthetics. They both amount to the accusation that I have, in my analysis, conflated the emotional side of literature with the reader's everyday feelings during her reading.

First, there is a well-established opinion according to which only the feelings found *in the text* are aesthetically and artistically relevant.[72]

Second, it is possible to contend that the aesthetically and artistically relevant feelings – whether or not these include the reader's feelings – must be feelings or emotions of a special type: emotions of a specifically *aesthetic* nature. My account makes it seem as if we were dealing, instead, with the usual everyday feelings or emotions – with sorrow, fear, admiration, and so on in the perfectly ordinary sense of those words. More particularly, many would no doubt feel inclined to object that I mistakenly describe the reader's feelings as being directed at actual realities: at objects, situations, or people in the outer world.

I shall conclude the present chapter by dealing with these two objections, devoting one section to the first one and three sections to the second.

The Ideas of Objective Correlatives and Embodied Emotions

In anglophone aesthetics it has often been maintained that when the reader reads adequately, his feelings are determined by the text. The feelings that are found "in the text" will then be regarded, from a literary point of view, as the only relevant ones. The emergence in the reader of feelings other than those determined by the text will be perceived as an irrelevant side-effect.

T.S. Eliot's idea about objective correlatives plays a significant role for this tradition. Eliot introduced the notion of an objective correlative in his essay "Hamlet and His Problems" (1920) in order to indicate what he saw as the principal weakness of Shakespeare's *Hamlet*:

> The only way of expressing emotion in the form of art is by finding an "objective correlative"; in other words, a set of objects, a situation, a chain of events which shall be the formula of that *particular* emotion; such that when the external facts, which must terminate in sensory experience, are given, the emotions are immediately evoked. If you examine any of Shakespeare's more successful tragedies, you will find this exact equivalence; you will find that the state of mind of Lady Macbeth walking in her sleep has been communicated to you by a skilful accumulation of imagined sensory impressions; the words of Macbeth on hearing of his wife's death strike us as if, given the sequence of events, these words were automatically released by the last event in the series. The artistic "inevitability" lies in this complete adequacy of the external to the emotion; and this is precisely what is deficient in *Hamlet*.[73]

According to Eliot, then, the literary author who wishes to express a feeling must produce a description ("a set of objects, a situation, a chain of events") which, when read, immediately results in the evocation of the intended, specific feeling. It seems as if "objective correlative" could be defined – more clearly but less arrestingly – as "literary, textual stimulus with a specific emotional effect."

I would say that Eliot's concept has a decisive weakness. Eliot presupposes a largely reliable coupling between the hearing or reading about a certain situation and the experiencing of a certain feeling, but so reliable a coupling simply does not exist. We are not all alike; complex individual processing intervenes between the registering of an impression and the emergence of a feeling. Therefore, feelings certainly do not have objective correlatives, if "objective correlative" is understood in so uncompromising a manner as Eliot's.

After having introduced the idea of objective correlatives, Eliot provides examples of the phenomenon. He says, first, that some details in Shakespeare's *Macbeth* skilfully communicate to us Lady Macbeth's state of mind.[74] Here, it is explicitly a matter of the *reader's* experience. Eliot no doubt wishes to maintain – translated into my terminology – that Shakespeare skilfully facilitates the reader's "participation," her "entering into" Lady Macbeth. (As before, I would like to object that different readers are likely to experience different feelings, even if the readers are highly competent.)

In a next step, Eliot describes the message informing Macbeth of his wife's death as an objective correlative releasing *Macbeth's* sorrow. Thus Eliot suddenly shifts from speaking of the reader's altogether real feelings to reasoning about the fictitious feelings of literary characters. This introduces a troublesome ambiguity making Eliot's concept of an objective correlative even more difficult to understand.[75] (As far as I can see, Eliot is of the opinion that we readers or viewers take the description of Lady Macbeth's death as a convincing cause of the feeling that arises in Macbeth and finds expression in his following lines. The basic fault with *Hamlet* is that we cannot, correspondingly, take Hamlet's experiences as convincing causes of his feelings, as these find expression in his words and deeds.)

Eliot's idea about objective correlatives is an obvious influence behind Monroe Beardsley and William Wimsatt's "The Affective Fallacy" (1949), the key text in the tradition I now discuss. Beardsley and Wimsatt distinguish between "the poem itself" on the one hand and the reader's feelings, "the psychological effects of the poem," on the other.[76] The latter are seen as being devoid of literary significance. The feelings that are found in the text itself, however, are aesthetically important and possess a considerable amount of objectivity:

> Poetry is characteristically a discourse about both emotions and objects, or about the emotive quality of objects. The emotions correlative to the objects of poetry become a part of the matter dealt with – ... presented in their objects and contemplated as a pattern of knowledge. ... Poetry is a way of fixing emotions or making them more permanently perceptible ... Though the reasons for emotions in poetry may not be so simple as Ruskin's "noble grounds for noble emotions," yet a great deal of constancy for poetic objects of emotion ... may be traced through the drift of human history. The murder of Duncan by Macbeth ... has not tended to become the subject of a Christmas carol. In Shakespeare's play it is an act difficult to duplicate in all its immediate adjuncts of treachery, deliberation, and horror of conscience. Set in its galaxy of symbols ... this ancient murder has become an object of strongly fixed emotional value.[77]

The notion of objective correlatives appears, principally, in the formulation about "emotions correlative to the objects of poetry"; the choice of *Macbeth* as an example was probably also influenced by Eliot.

Almost thirty years later, Stein Haugom Olsen still mentions Wimsatt and Beardsley's ideas about literature and feelings with assent in *The Structure of Literary Understanding* (1978). Building on Anthony

Kenny's philosophy of emotion, Olsen then characterizes the literary text as being logically linked with the author's emotions:

> The work is a criterion for the emotion. An analysis of the work will ... also be an analysis of the relevant emotion since the nature of the work determines the nature of the emotion. The author creates an expression of his emotions by creating an object towards which they can be directed. The creation of this object is at the same time an articulation of the emotions involved. The emotions are defined only by working out an object which is their target. The reader may by studying the object gain insight into the emotion which lies behind it, and, indeed, if he is sensitive enough, he may succeed in recapturing the emotion by letting the work become an object for his own emotions. In this way, literature may educate the reader not simply by letting him recognize intellectually the nature of a complex emotion, but by making it possible for him to recapture the emotion himself.[78]

In the context of the present work it is quite unnecessary to analyse in detail the passages from Wimsatt and Beardsley and from Olsen. I shall therefore content myself with a few general observations.

Both quotations concern what I have called "the feelings in the text" – in reality, the feelings that the author attempts to communicate to his readers ("The author creates an expression of his emotions"; Olsen) or the feelings explicitly or implicitly described in the text ("a part of the matter dealt with"; Wimsatt and Beardsley). As I have made clear earlier in this chapter, I do not deny the existence of such "feelings in the text." I see them, mainly, as feelings that the author has wished to communicate (according to the reader's understanding of the text). There are, however, important differences between my view of these feelings and the standpoint found in Wimsatt and Beardsley and in Olsen. If one disregards the dissimilarities between our respective ways of looking at the nature of feelings and at the basic mechanisms of the communication of feelings (dissimilarities that I will leave aside here), two principal differences are involved.

The vital point is my contention that the feelings arising in the reader during her post-communicative processing, her thematization and application, form a necessary part of an adequate literary experience. (The reasons for this view should be obvious from chapters 3, 4, and 6 and the introduction to this chapter.) Neither Olsen nor Wimsatt and Beardsley propose any arguments against this standpoint. They point to the existence of "feelings in the text" – an existence that I do not deny – and seem to take it for granted that these feelings, and only these, are relevant from a literary point of view. The reason for this is, no doubt, that their thinking on this point is firmly grounded on New Critical assumptions about the autonomy of the literary work.

This is a significant divergence between us. In comparison, it is less consequential that Wimsatt, Beardsley, and Olsen also ascribe a much higher degree of *precision* to the literary communication of feelings than I do. I would not say, at least not without careful reservations, that the text's formulations make the feelings in the text "strongly fixed" (Wimsatt and Beardsley) or "defined" (Olsen), or that the text "determines" these feelings (Olsen). The idea of objective correlatives, of literary stimuli releasing reliable and precisely determined emotional reactions, still makes itself felt in the theories of Wimsatt and Beardsley and of Olsen.

Where Wimsatt and Beardsley are concerned, a third difference also comes into play: Wimsatt and Beardsley draw on the transportation metaphor, seemingly imagining that the feelings of which they are speaking can be found *in* the text in some genuine sense – embodied in it, as it were.[79] They speak as if objects could *literally* possess emotional properties ("the emotive quality of objects"). Since literature describes objects with emotional properties, emotions in literary texts become "a part of the matter dealt with." The feelings relevant in literature are found, somewhat surprisingly, "in their objects," i.e., in the depicted objects constituting their objective correlatives. The feelings even appear to have been made "permanently perceptible."

True, there are philosophers of art who do, in practice, defend the transportation metaphor. Gene Blocker rejects the idea that a person ascribing feelings to a work of art is, in reality, merely projecting her art experience onto the physical object that released it. Blocker seems to trust everyday language: "Emotion as it appears in the work of art is not isolated from that work, but internal to it, that is, an autonomous part of a public work of art."[80] And Joseph Margolis finds it natural to speak of texts (with their meaning, emotional qualities, literary form, and so on) as "embodied" in physical copies of the text.[81] To me, this is holding on to an obviously metaphorical way of expressing oneself instead of creating the more literal understanding that is so needed within the theory of art and literature.

Feelings for Fictitious Characters: A Paradox and a Proposed Solution

In the philosophy of emotion, emotions are commonly conceived as being logically associated with convictions. One cannot be proud of one's looks unless one believes that one is good-looking. One cannot be afraid of getting Alzheimer's disease if one does not believe the disease exists. One cannot feel pity for the homeless of Stockholm if one does not believe that there are homeless people in Stockholm, and so on.

Against that background, it becomes difficult to comprehend how we could possibly have feelings regarding fictitious characters. In 1975, the philosopher Colin Radford published an article calling attention to this problem. According to Radford, we may indeed feel for fictitious characters. We can pity Anna Karenina in Tolstoj's *Anna Karenina* in spite of our knowledge that she is a creature of fiction. Radford asks himself how this enigmatic, seemingly paradoxical and irrational fact is to be understood. He examines various possible explanations but finds none of them acceptable. "I am left with the conclusion," he writes, "that our being moved in certain ways by works of art, though very 'natural' to us and in that way only too intelligible, involves us in inconsistency and so incoherence."[82]

Since then, the paradox described by Radford has been discussed extensively in British and American aesthetics.[83] The central question in that discussion has been whether we can indeed have feelings or emotions vis-à-vis fictitious characters, and if so, how that circumstance may be reconciled with the philosophy of emotion and its system of assumptions. This discussion affects my theses about literature and feelings in several ways. I have not, for instance, allowed for the possibility that we may feel for non-existent persons. Is that a flaw in my account?

In order to make the question more concrete, I would like to introduce an example taken from reality. At one time I was reading C.S. Lewis's Narnia books aloud to my daughter, who was then nine years old. It often came naturally to her to comment spontaneously on the events in the book while I was reading, or to ask questions about the story. In the beginning of *The Last Battle* (1956) we are told about an ape, Shift (a gorilla, in the Swedish translation), who is described as being sly, ugly, and wrinkled, and a kind but simpleminded donkey, Puzzle, whom Shift calls his friend but of whom he is, in reality, merely taking advantage. Shift's behaviour towards Puzzle worried my daughter more and more. She finally and completely lost her patience with Shift at the very moment it became evident that he was, for selfish reasons, going to trick Puzzle into dressing up as, and impersonating, the lion Aslan, the magical but seldom seen animal that in the Narnia world functions as an analogue of God. My daughter immediately exclaimed, indignantly: "You nasty gorilla! You selfish thing and gorilla!"[84]

Undeniably it is convenient to say, here, that my daughter was angry with Shift. And so we are confronted with Radford's paradox. How can one get angry with a gorilla that – as one is well aware – does not exist? (There is no reason to believe that my daughter was conflating fiction and reality. She knew perfectly well that Lewis's Narnia stories were altogether made up; her understanding of them was, even, deep and full of nuances.)

As my discussions earlier in this chapter make obvious, however, I myself find it unwarranted to analyse emotional reactions in the face of literature as being in fact directed at fictitious characters. What happened in the above example was, I imagine, that my daughter was suddenly overwhelmed by feelings of indignation on seeing what Shift was about. Her attentive following of the narrative may have involved the creation of vivid imaginings of what it is like to be made the instrument of another's lust for power and to be cheated and compromised. And through thematization and application she may have identified the story as dealing with bullying and manipulation and related it to memories, anticipations, and fantasies of her own. I suppose that it was from sources like these that her feelings of indignation welled.

My opinion is, thus, that it may be natural to *say* that my daughter got angry with Shift (it is brief, expressive, presumably also true to her spontaneous perception of the situation), but that it is not reasonable to take such *modes of expression* quite literally. In reality my daughter was, for various reasons, filled with indignation. She herself apparently interpreted this indignation as anger with Shift; at any rate, she attempted to abreact it through an utterance formed as an insult to Shift.[85] But readers do not actually feel for fictitious characters. If their feelings or emotions can at all be said to be directed at something, the objects are persons or circumstances in real life.

There is an extensive and sophisticated discussion about feelings about fictitious characters, and the analysis of how literature is related to feelings forms an important part of my project. For those reasons, I find it necessary to enter somewhat more deeply into the subject of Radford's paradox. But let me first give my own formulation of the problems at issue.

As I suggested earlier, the key question can be couched in these terms: "Is it possible for us to have emotions that are directed at fictitious characters? (Can we feel pity for such creatures, love them,[86] be angry with them?) Why, or why not?"

In discussions of that question, however, a number of underlying problems are brought to the surface. I perceive them as, essentially, problems of two separate kinds: on the one hand factual problems concerning the biological and psychological mechanisms responsible for our feelings, and on the other conceptual problems concerning the exact content of the concept of an emotion. (In the ongoing discussions, the distinction between what I call feelings and what I call emotions is often blurred; I regard this as one of the major shortcomings of the current debate.)

The relevant factual problems could be summarized in the question: "What makes precisely these feelings arise in the reader in precisely this connection?" As I have devoted much space to that problem earlier in the chapter, there is no need to reiterate the analysis (centred on the concepts of empathy and application).

There is certainly much that needs to be explained regarding the actual mechanisms behind our feelings. But what makes it possible to create a *paradox* concerned with *fiction and emotion* is, I would say, exclusively the fact that the concept of an emotion is partly indeterminate.[87] I shall therefore comment on "emotion" in somewhat more detail before I start examining the discussion about Radford's paradox. My aim is not to suggest an exact definition of "emotion," but simply to clarify the situation by pointing to some inner tensions in the corresponding notion.

I have analysed an emotion as feelings seen as having a specific causal background: fear as feelings of discomfort aroused by the anticipation of serious setbacks to one's interests, and so on. I would like to add that we do not speak of an emotion unless our instantaneous global experience has a *marked* character of pleasure or discomfort or both, but further conditions hardly need to be introduced in this context. It is, however, a common idea that an emotion must also have an object. Fear is then required to have a "directedness," to be fear *of* something more or less determinate.

A specification of what it is for an emotion to be *directed* should by rights build on an analysis of the nature of what is usually called intentionality, and intentionality is a difficult notion. One option, however, is to say that an emotion is directed towards the object (if any) that the emotion makes it natural to seek or avoid. I have described emotions as feelings-cum-explanations. In connection with a negative emotion like fear there is, normally, an object that constitutes the reason to anticipate setbacks to one's own interests – like the wasp in the example used earlier. The natural reaction is to remove or avoid that object (kill the wasp or move out of its way); the emotion could then be said to be directed towards the wasp. When we are dealing with a positive emotion like love, there is normally an object to which one is attracted. The natural reaction is to attempt to establish a close relationship with the beloved person; the emotion could then be said to be directed towards him or her.

But directedness could of course be explicated in other terms. And there are also theorists who explicitly deny that emotions necessarily have an object (and so directedness).[88] I myself have not required directedness from emotions, but have still left open the possibility that directedness is always there. In fact, I would be inclined to hold that the feelings forming the basis of an emotion will often have many different objects. If the indignation with which the story of Shift and Puzzle filled my daughter was directed towards something, I believe that it had *many* different (real) objects.

Another problem in connection with the concept of an emotion, and the most crucial one where Radford's paradox is concerned, is whether we should allow for the possibility of emotions directed towards fictitious entities. If one goes by the analysis of directedness just sketched, emotions evidently cannot have objects that the experiencing person perceives as being fictitious. We cannot, for logical reasons, seek or avoid, counteract or promote, objects or persons that we believe to be non-existent. On the analysis of "directedness" just introduced, then, only a person who confuses fiction with reality can be literally said to pity Anna Karenina or to be angry with Shift. But it is no doubt possible to construct other interpretations of "directed-ness," interpretations that would allow the literal having of emotions vis-à-vis fictitious characters.

This brief discussion of two aspects of the concept of an emotion will be of help when we reflect on the literature about Radford's paradox. But it also provides a perspective on the question of the existence of specifically *aesthetic* emotions.[89]

It appears natural to me to say that there are no specifically aesthetic *feelings*. As I see them, the feelings entering into a literary experience are in themselves ordinary feelings of pleasure and discomfort. On the other hand, the experience of *Anniversaries* or of "Father's Bedroom" clearly differs from most experiences met in non-aesthetic contexts. When I now read those texts, frustration and sorrow are relatively prominent elements of my reading experience (constituting part-emotions, as it were, within the total affective whole). But joy and satisfaction are also conspicuous, for reasons that I attempted to indicate in the section about tragic pleasure. The character of my experience is certainly also affected by my awareness of the fact that I am reacting to a presentational text, not to unmediated realities. All in all, my total experience is of a type that it is difficult (but perhaps not impossible) to encounter in a non-aesthetic context. Because of that, it may be reasonable to say that the feelings in question build up

– taken together, with their complex global character – a special, aesthetic emotion (a complicated pattern of feelings, occasioned by the reading, without any homogeneous directedness). I do not, however, allow for aesthetic emotions in a more pregnant sense: I do not believe that there is a special type of feelings, aesthetic feelings, occasioned by experiences of nature or the arts and capable of crystallizing into aesthetic emotions when manifest enough.

This standpoint on the existence of aesthetic emotions is not very original in its main features; it is, for instance, reminiscent of that of R.G. Collingwood.[90] Nevertheless, it goes without saying that much remains to be discussed in connection with the nature of aesthetic emotions. In addition, the subject is closely associated with the question of the existence of specifically aesthetic experiences, and so with some of the most fundamental problems of aesthetics in general. These matters also hold great interest for the theory of literature, but for several reasons I am not able to deal with them in a defensible manner in this book.

Paskins and Charlton on Feelings for Fictitious Characters

The discussion about Radford's paradox is much too extensive to be penetrated in any detail here. I shall confine myself to commenting (in this section) on the views most resembling my own and (in the next section) on a couple of the best known and most influential analyses.

Some theorists have maintained that readers do not actually feel for fictitious characters: the feelings and emotions arising during reading are in reality directed towards real people. The earliest and best known contribution in that vein is Barrie Paskins's brief and sketchy article "On Being Moved by Anna Karenina and *Anna Karenina*" (1977). The cardinal point in Paskins's analysis is the idea that pity for fictitious characters like Anna Karenina "is, or can without forcing be construed as, pity for those people if any who are in the same bind as the character in the fiction."[91] Paskins's attitude is similar to the one that I have adopted, but for obvious reasons I cannot endorse his analysis as it stands.

Paskins's main idea is that in experiencing what we tend to call feelings for fictitious characters we are in fact feeling for real people. Paskins, then, needs to explain for *which* real people we are feeling. His answer is that our feelings concern all those who find themselves in the same predicament as the characters in the fiction.

My view of the matter is somewhat different. I contend that reading occasions thoughts, secondary representations – above all via empathizing and application – and thereby also pleasure and discomfort (likely to be associated, in the final analysis, with memories). So the reading stimulates thinking about reality, mainly unconscious thinking, and the thoughts are tinged with pleasure and discomfort in various ways. It may sometimes be a question of such specific and concerted ideas about reality that it becomes natural to regard the feelings as, in fact, feelings for specific existing people. But the ideas aroused are no doubt often more heterogeneous than that. I doubt, for example, that it is justified to analyse my daughter's reaction to Shift, the fictive gorilla, as anger directed towards quite definite individuals in the real world.

Moreover, there is a presumably irremediable fault with the analysis that Paskins suggests – for it must reasonably sometimes be the case that *no* real people actually find themselves in the same predicament as the characters in the fiction. Paskins attempts to get around that problem by introducing the reservation "if any." But pity for Anna Karenina surely cannot be reinterpreted as pity for real persons unless such real persons exist. So the insertion "if any" stands out as a logical blunder.

In a essay published in 1984, William Charlton, among other things, took up and revised Paskins's analysis. Charlton, too, is dissatisfied with Paskins's "if any" clause, but on somewhat different grounds. Charlton writes:

> The real objection [against Paskins's analysis] is that we can feel for real people only if we know who they are. The notion of a person who is not any particular real person but not a purely fictitious person either is incoherent. You can feel for your sister who is married to an unattractive man, or for your aunt, whose lover had to give up his career; you cannot feel just for real people if any who are or have been in these predicaments. The analysis of "We feel for Anna" which I am proposing here is not that we categorically pity hypothetical persons; it is that we hypothetically desire to benefit real persons. Our state of mind is expressible by "If any of my friends had a husband like Karenin or a lover like Vronsky, would that I might be able to help her do what is best."[92]

As I just underlined, Anna-Karenina-like people cannot serve the purpose that Paskins had in mind unless they do in fact exist. I believe that this is what Charlton wishes to point out. His actual formulations, however, appear less fortunate to me. For it seems self-evident that we can also be said to feel pity for complete strangers (for example, an unknown person whom we see being run over by a car in the street, or the victims – unfamiliar to us as individuals – of an air disaster we read about in the newspaper). Besides, Paskins does not actually allow for hypothetical people, individuals neither real nor fictitious. (It is not the Anna-Karenina-like people in themselves, but their existence, that is hypothetical according to Paskins's account.)

As regards Charlton's own analysis, briefly summarized at the end of the quotation,[93] it, too, is spiritually allied to mine. Both Charlton and I imagine that the reader in the Anna Karenina example identifies a situation like Anna's as *possible in real life* and realizes what it would mean, cognitively and emotionally, if such a situation were actualized.

Naturally, there are also considerable differences between Charlton's analysis and my own, and consequently reservations on my part. I think, for example, that Charlton tends to make emotions too cognitive. Thus, in the quotation above, he identifies pity for Anna Karenina with a certain type of wish. But I would not say that to have a wish is, in itself, to have a feeling or an emotion. In any case, Charlton only takes an interest in the cognitive content of the wish, not in its physical or affective character. In consequence pity, as Charlton describes it, sounds more like a kind of thought than like a kind of feeling or emotion.

In addition, both Paskins's and Charlton's analyses have a certain narrowness that I myself have attempted to avoid. In their present shape, the analyses seem applicable only in connection with formally realistic literature, only when situations falling under the same descriptions could arise in reality. Consequently, the analyses will hardly explain my daughter's anger faced with the idea of Shift. It is certainly not anger with real gorillas, nor does it appear natural to explicate it along Charlton's lines: "If one of my friends came to Narnia, and were enticed by a malicious, talking gorilla into impersonating a lion god, would that I might properly berate that gorilla."[94]

More differences could be pointed out. And of course one could ask Paskins and Charlton for more thorough analyses of the concepts of feeling and emotion and of the mechanisms responsible for the reader's feelings.

Both Paskins and Charlton would deny that readers' emotions can be directed towards fictitious characters. True, they would not mind speaking of pity for Anna Karenina, but they would understand that simply as *a mode of expression.*[95] Both Paskins and Charlton perceive apparent feelings for fictitious characters as being, in reality, directed towards real people.

It is not a new idea that we are actually feeling for phenomena in real life when we seem to have feelings for fictitious things and characters. An early formulation of the idea is found in Samuel Johnson's "Preface to Shakespeare" (1765): "Imitations produce pain or pleasure, not because they are mistaken for realities, but because they bring realities to mind. When the imagination is recreated by a painted landscape, the trees are not supposed capable to give us shade, or the fountains coolness; but we consider, how we should be pleased with such fountains playing beside us, and such woods waving over us."[96]

More examples from the past could be adduced.[97] And in the twentieth century, of course, it has been a central idea in psychoanalytical criticism that the reader's feelings are due to the fact that the text stirs up wishes and fears related to his own life.

In the analytical-aesthetic discussion about Radford's paradox, however, considerations like these play a very subordinate role. Views like Paskins's and Charlton's are normally considered entirely untenable (though many seem ready to accept that feelings towards real people may well form part of our emotional reactions during the experience of fiction).[98] Gregory Currie, especially, has subjected Paskins's analysis to uncompromising criticism.

Currie gives an account of Paskins's idea that pity for Anna Karenina is "pity for those people if any who are in the same bind as the character in the fiction." (Currie's own principal literary example in this connection is Henry James's *The Turn of the Screw.*) Currie thinks that he can see two weaknesses in Paskins's analysis.

> Paskins' qualification "if any" is rather problematic; what if there aren't any, or – more to the point – what if I don't believe there are any? But the basic flaw in this and similar suggestions is that they sever the *normative* connection between our responses to fiction and the fictions they are responses to. Responses to fictions are to be assessed as reasonable or unreasonable according to how well or how badly they are justified by the events of the story. And we can be persuaded that our responses to a character are inappropriate, because we have misunderstood some aspect of the story. Admiring the courage and determination of the governess is reasonable, at least in part, because of what is said to happen in *The Turn of the Screw.* Admiring courageous and determined people in general is justified in quite other ways. So admiring the governess cannot *be* admiring courageous and determined people in general.[99]

It is certainly justified to criticize Paskins's "if any" clause. I do not, however, accept Currie's second objection.

The basic fault with his argument is easy to see. Currie takes for granted (in the antepenultimate sentence in the quotation) what he should by rights be proving: that we can indeed feel for fictitious characters – for example, admire the governess in *The Turn of the Screw.* It is true that if it *is* in fact possible to admire the courage of the governess – as Currie quite simply presupposes – such admiration cannot concern real courageous people. The fact that the admiration is justified in another manner is only one of many signs of its not being identical to admiration for similar persons in real life. But on the other hand, if one *cannot* literally be said to admire the governess – and Currie has not shown that one can, merely taken it for granted –, then Currie's argument lacks the necessary foundation.[100] In fact, the cardinal, contested point in the discussion about Radford's paradox is precisely whether we can really with justice be said to feel for fictitious characters – for example, to admire James's governess. (After all, she does not in reality exist, nor, consequently, does any courage or determination on her part, so what is there to admire?)

These remarks suffice, I believe, to demonstrate that Currie's argumentation is inconclusive. There is, however, another line in his reasoning on which I would like to comment in some detail. Currie says that there is a *normative* connection between what is said in *The Turn of the Screw* and the reader's response. According to my own analysis earlier in this book (especially chapters 3, 4, and 6), this is true only in part. The reader is no doubt obliged to try to understand what the author wishes to communicate – so far, an adequate understanding must be governed by the text. But I have contended that an adequate reading of literature also possesses a creative element, since it includes a thematization and application that the text makes possible but does not really regulate.

Naturally, the *reader's* feelings do not form part of what is communicated. In consequence, the reader's emotional response cannot be a pure reconstruction of the communicative content (and it is hard to see any reason to deplore that fact). So where the reader's feelings are concerned, it is out of place to postulate a relatively straightforward normative connection between text and response.

Actually, Currie sometimes allows the reader to "sever the *normative* connection" in question. According to him, the "sensitive" reader always identifies "what emotion is expressed in the work," but if he is also a "refined" reader he responds "congruently," i.e., as the postulated normative connection dictates, not to each and any piece of sentimental trash but "only to works that have a certain kind of merit."[101] In my view, however, this admission is far from doing justice to the freedom of emotional response that competent readers are in fact granted by literary practice.

Currie's presupposition of normativity is, I believe, representative for contemporary analytical aesthetics. For instance, Currie's requirements on adequate emotional reader response have recently been taken up and developed by Paisley Livingston and Alfred R. Mele, who differentiate them rather than relaxing them.[102] My view of the matter is palpably different, because of my insistence that application is distinct from reconstruction but is still a necessary (and certainly an implicitly expected) element in an artistically competent response to a literary work.

Let me make my position more concrete with the help of an example. Gesine Cresspahl in Johnson's *Anniversaries* is, in a certain sense, portrayed as being sympathetic: she is described in a way that indicates that the person narrating *Anniversaries* perceives her as being sympathetic. According to my analysis, this is part of what the reader should comprehend. If the reader does not see that Gesine is portrayed as sympathetic, he misunderstands the text. To perceive that Gesine is decribed as sympathetic is not, however, in itself, to feel anything. It is to have a mental representation of a part of the communicative content of *Anniversaries*.

True, the description of Gesine may, then, fill the reader with sympathy or dislike (or leave him indifferent). But such reactions can hardly be called correct or incorrect. The reader may have respectable reasons for his negative feelings, even if he perceives that the narrator is attempting to place Gesine in a favourable light. Consider Peter Demetz's murderous criticism of "the elder Gesine" – the bank employee, the reader of the *New York Times* – in his review of the fourth volume of *Anniversaries*: "Frankly: I would not like to share an apartment with the elder Gesine, the one in New York (but gladly with her younger self, the skinny schoolgirl in a new black coat). The elder Gesine has been transformed into a kind of machinery of consciousness and narration reproducing day by day the contents of the *New York Times* and, moreover, seemingly believing that the Czechs staged their Prague spring only to deliver her from her disappointments in life; she, too, in her sterile fashion, is one of the German female dreamers who wish to triumph ideologically only in places where they do not find themselves."[103]

Demetz can hardly have missed the fact that Gesine is drawn with sympathy in Johnson's novel. But Demetz is of course still at liberty to experience her character as unsympathetic. Had Currie been right in stating, without reservations, that there is a "*normative* connection between our responses to fiction and the fictions they are responses to," a critical reading like that of Demetz would be indefensible. But as I see it, such a reading may very well be competent, compatible with the practice of reading literature, despite the fact that it must of necessity transcend the author's intentions. For my part, I find Demetz's perception of the text both competent and interesting (its divergences from my own reading notwithstanding).[104]

Walton, Lamarque, and Scruton on Feelings for Fictitious Characters

My reason for devoting close attention to Paskins and Charlton, and to Currie's criticism of Paskins, is the affinity between my standpoint and those of Paskins and Charlton. I wanted to indicate the similarities but also the differences, and I wished to refute an important critic of this type of thinking. The rest of the discussion about Radford's paradox will be treated more summarily. I shall point to three other, better-known proposals for a solution and explain briefly why I do not endorse them. Space will not permit a detailed analysis and discussion.

In a series of publications culminating with the book *Mimesis as Make-Believe* (1990), Kendall Walton has maintained that the viewing of art, the reading of literature, and so on exhibit certain analogies with children's games of make-believe. Thus in playing cops and robbers, children create a world of make-believe where it is fictional ("true in the fiction") that some of them are police, others villains. It is possible to use props in the game – it may be fictional that a certain stick is a firearm. According to Walton, we employ literary texts as props in games of make-believe.[105] In connection with literature, the game of make-believe typically consists in the reader's pretending that she herself forms part of the fictive world that she imaginatively constructs on the basis of the text, and that a trustworthy person in that world is telling her the story of the invented characters.[106]

According to Walton, then, when reading *Anna Karenina* we find ourselves, in our fantasy, inside the fictional world. This being so, we perceive – in our game of make-believe – Anna and her sufferings as real. This occasions feelings in us, in this case feelings that Walton would characterize as "quasi pity": "Realizing it to be fictional that Anna Karenina suffers misfortune, it is fictional that we are aware of her suffering, and we experience quasi pity as a result. This, perhaps, is approximately what makes it fictional that we pity her."[107]

Mutatis mutandis, Walton would also make use of the same analysis in connection with other emotions than pity and other texts than *Anna Karenina*. So Walton, too, denies that we can have emotions directed towards fictitious characters. His position is that we cannot genuinely pity Anna since she is not real. True, we experience feelings while reading about her, feelings reminiscent of pity. If we wish, we can utilize these real feelings as props of a kind. We can, in our game of make-believe, take them as a justification for saying that we pity Anna. The feelings may thus help us to make it fictional that we pity Anna.

In reality, however, the feelings merely constitute something pity-ish: quasi pity.

The view that the reader of literature is engaged in a game of make-believe of a special type is central to Walton's analysis of feelings for fictitious characters. I myself do not share his view.[108] As a reader, I never imagine myself inside the world of fiction; to fantasize in that vein would appear irrelevant to me, not to say inappropriate. Does this mean that my way of dealing with literature is incompetent? I do not think so (and my conviction is strengthened by the fact that several other experienced critics of art and literature have also raised substantially the same objection).[109] It is imaginable, of course, that I enter the world of fiction in an unconscious fantasy and so unwittingly. But I can see no need to make that assumption; unlike Walton,[110] I am of the opinion that the character of our reading and experiencing of literature can be explicated without its help.

Thus I do not believe that the playing of such games of make-believe as Walton describes does in fact enter as a desirable or necessary element into the practice of reading literature. For that reason, among others, I cannot concur with Walton in his analysis of emotions occasioned by the reading of literature or in his explanation of how the reader's feelings arise.

Radford took it for granted that we do sometimes have emotions directed towards invented characters. That intuition has also been predominant in the later discussion. Several theorists seem to have anchored their analyses to their spontaneous phenomenological experience of fiction, and consequently to regard it as incontestable that we can feel for the fictitious.[111] Their problem, then, has been to explain how such a thing is in fact possible.

Peter Lamarque has taken as his point of departure the fact that in experiencing literature we actually do come into contact with something real: a linguistic composition and ideas about invented characters. In an article from 1981, he contended that we do not, as Walton thinks, enter into the world of fiction, but that we interact with the fictitious characters in *our own* world ("it is *in the real world* that we psychologically interact with them").[112]

"How can fictional characters enter our world?" Lamarque asks. "What is it in our world that we respond to when we fear Othello and pity Desdemona? My suggestion, which I shall work out in detail, is that fictional characters enter our world in the mundane guise of descriptions (or strictly senses of descriptions) and become the objects of our emotional responses as mental representations or, as I shall call them, thought-contents characterized by those descriptions. Simply put, the fear and pity we feel for fictions are in fact directed at thoughts in our minds."[113]

In his 1981 essay, Lamarque did not really discuss the psychological mechanisms behind the reader's feelings – the question of why the ideas inspired in her can give rise to fear and pity. Lamarque has returned to the analysis in several later contributions – most recently in his *Fictional Points of View* (1996) – without changing it substantially.[114] The 1996 book contains a new feature, however, which I welcome. Lamarque now emphasizes that the reader's "sympathetic imagining of what it would be like to be in just such a predicament"[115] helps to explain the fictional story's emotional impact on her.

Lamarque wishes to demonstrate that the talk of feelings for fictitious characters can be analysed in a way that makes it logically unexceptionable. But the attempt still remains problematical. The basic fault with Lamarque's proposed solution is, as I see it, that fictitious characters obviously *cannot* enter our own world – for the plain reason that they do not exist. It is *logically* impossible to interact with fictitious characters in the real world, as Lamarque expects us to do.[116]

Lamarque supposes that fictitious characters enter our world as thought contents. But saying that they "enter" our world is defensible only if the expression is taken as metaphorical. True, it is because of our encounter with linguistic formulations in the text of *Anna Karenina*, and through them indirectly with the thoughts which Tolstoj communicates with their help, that ideas about Anna Karenina come into existence in our minds. But the fact that an idea about Anna Karenina arises in us does not imply that Anna Karenina, the fictitious character, enters our world. Lamarque implicitly identifies *Anna Karenina, the fictitious character* with *the content of our thoughts about Anna Karenina*, i.e., with *mental phenomena in us, aspects of our actual thoughts*. But that identification is unwarranted. One could say that Lamarque conflates the representational content of our mental picture with the subject-matter that the picture is about, which is much like conflating, say, the Napoleon-representation in David's well-known portrait of Napoleon on horseback with Napoleon himself. In fact, our emotions would not be directed towards Anna Karenina even if they were directed at the content of our thoughts about her.

But is Lamarque at least right in holding that it is the content of our own mental representations that we fear and pity when reading literature? Walton has presented several natural objections to that idea.[117] I myself would like to ask, on this point, how Lamarque conceives of *directedness*, what he means by saying that our feeling is "directed at" our thought content. If the object of a feeling is understood, basically, as the object that the feeling makes one want to manipulate – the option that I considered earlier –, then pity for Anna or anger with Shift cannot be directed at thought content: it is not thought content that we would like to help or punish. To substantiate his claim that our feelings for the fictitious are directed at the content of our own thoughts, Lamarque would have to make explicit his view of "directedness" and explain why it should be preferred to (seemingly) more ordinary ways of understanding the concept.[118]

Several other theorists have also argued that we can in fact have feelings for fictitious characters. Roger Scruton did this as early as in a contribution antedating Radford's 1975 article.

Scruton points to the fact that the reader of literature or viewer of art normally reacts with empathy before the situations described (though Scruton does not use the word "empathy"). The reader imagines the situations, imagining, in that connection, how she would have felt if she had found herself in such a situation in real life.

Scruton would be willing to characterize as "pity for Anna" the feelings that we experience when our adequate reading confronts us with Anna's misfortunes. He would, however, classify the emotion as merely imagined, just like the situation described. Scruton writes, of the art viewer: "In the only sense that matters we might … say that the emotion he feels in response to the picture is the 'same' as (and classified by reference to) the emotion he would feel towards the depicted situation. For his feeling towards what he sees *in* the picture is, like his perception itself, only 'unasserted.'"[119]

There are differences on several planes between Scruton's standpoint and my own. Scruton alludes to what I call the reader's empathy, but unlike me he maintains that the feelings it occasions in the reader are imagined and not real.[120] The idea that feelings in the reader may arise through application is not found in Scruton; on the whole, he is reluctant to believe that the reader's feelings are *real* not only where fantasizing is concerned but also in aesthetic contexts.

I do not think that Scruton's analysis does full justice to the often palpable actuality of the reader's or viewer's feelings. Another problem is that his explanation of the reader's feelings, like Paskins's and Charlton's, can in its present form only be applied to formally realistic literature, literature describing situations that might in principle occur in real life.

Scruton does not, of course, present any full-blown analysis of the intentionality of emotions, of what it is for an emotion to be *directed* at an object. Clearly, however, he does not require that an emotion must have a really existing object.[121] As a consequence, it becomes possible for him to say that we can in fact have feelings for fictitious characters.

Just as in connection with Lamarque's contributions, one might wish for an explication of the concept of directedness implicitly employed. Different opinions on the actual character and origin of the feelings may often underlie discussions about the reader's feelings. But when one has one's eyes opened to the hidden presuppositions of theorists like Paskins, Charlton, Walton, Lamarque, and Scruton, it becomes easy to see that divergences in the conception of an emotion – of what constitutes an emotion and its identity – are also an important cause of the disagreements about how the reader's feelings should be analysed.

8 A Poem: Gunnar Ekelöf's "But Somewhere Else"

Introduction

Like other language, literary discourse is a vehicle for the communication of thoughts, of representations. And in literature, too, feelings are associated with the communicated content in various ways. Yet, literary communication has a character of its own. I have contended that it is, basically, literature's presentationality that makes it special.

Neither literature nor other types of language are exclusively communicative, however. On the one hand, the listener or reader does not confine herself to reconstructing a communicative content – in her post-communicative processing she also adopts an attitude to the communicative content or spins it out. On the other, the text affects her not only through the communicative content conveyed but also through the emphasis and the tone of voice (in the concrete or figurative sense), the choice of words, the unuttered assumptions, and much more, and these aspects modify her impression of the things said. Such subtle, extralinguistic factors are among the features normally seen as form.

There are four main questions that I shall ask concerning form (as I did for thoughts and feelings). What is form? How is it possible for form to become an element of the literary object? What is the function or functions of form in literary contexts? And how is form associated with thought and feeling? The principal objective of the remainder of my book – the last three chapters and the concluding remarks – is to answer those questions and thus to round off the picture of literature and literary experience given above.

I have suggested earlier that there are, so far, lacunae in that picture. Criticism of it for letting important aspects of the literary texts pass undescribed was justified. In particular, the features usually called formal have been more or less left aside. This is bound to arouse scepticism, especially since those features are commonly regarded as being essential from a literary point of view. Many would say, even, that it is precisely form that lends an aesthetic character to literature, and that the aesthetic aspect of literature is the most fundamental and indispensable one.

Consequently, the final portions of my book have an important and sensitive task assigned to them. My aim is to explain the nature and role of literary form. While doing that, I must also make clear how my account of literature's formal aspects fits into the picture of literature that I have drawn so far. At the same time I should attempt to demonstrate that, after the supplementation just alluded to, my picture of literature and literary experience gives a credible overall description of its object.

For several reasons it will become necessary to carry out a much more detailed analysis of a literary text than I have done up to now. I shall begin my treatment of form in this chapter by examining a short poem. The analysis will supply me with concrete examples of formal features and formal effects, examples that I shall then use in my explication of the nature and role of literary form. The analysis also gives me an opportunity to comment for a last time on the nature of texts and the sources of their complexity.

In chapter 9, I shall formulate an answer to my four main questions concerning form in literature. I shall also indicate how the answer develops the cognitive-emotive model of some of literature's functions introduced earlier.

Naturally, my conception of what form is and how it functions has many points in common with traditional critical views. Still, the current opinions presuppose a different thought model: the now-familiar picture of the literary text as a verbal container of meaning. This gives rise to several important differences between my analysis of the form concept and the prevalent ones. After having presented my own ideas in chapters 8 and 9 I shall, in chapter 10, analyse and assess the traditional thinking about literary form. My reason for devoting a rather extensive separate discussion to the received views is that their points of departure differ so markedly from mine, and that the importance of form is so strongly emphasized in twentieth-century criticism.

With chapters 8–10 I conclude my description of how thought, feeling, and form interact in connection with literary texts and experiences of literature. In doing so, I put the finishing touch to my general account of the literary medium.

I have not taken upon myself to answer the wider question of what literature is for, but I have pointed to some possible functions of verbal art. This makes it natural to raise the question of what is usually called literature's "autonomy," and so I conclude my book with some reflections on that subject.

Gunnar Ekelöf's "'But Somewhere Else I Have Learned'"

"'But Somewhere Else I Have Learned'" ("[Men på en annan ort har jag lärt]") by the Swedish poet Gunnar Ekelöf (1907–68) is to be found in Ekelöf's 1955 collection of poems, *Strountes*. Here I quote it in Robert Bly's translation, adding a numbering of the lines:[1]

     1 But somewhere else I have learned
        the gruesomeness of hell:
        Here is the smile of hell
        here minutes and seconds exist
     5 and the bright border between sea and sky
        here the short disaster exists and the short outburst of joy
        But you, where are you, sorrow,
        which one could throw oneself into the sea to find?
        Night comes and the moon rises
    10 I open all the windows
        I know that she by my side loves me
        but is it really she

It appears obvious that "But Somewhere Else"[2] expresses a longing for an existential fulfilment that is found to be impossible in the poem's "here." Before taking a closer look at the poem's statements, however, I must make a few observations about Bly's translation. Precisely as in the case of Johnson's *Anniversaries*, it is the original version that I really wish to discuss, not the English translation. And in spite of its overall accuracy and felicitousness, Bly's translation is of course not true to the original in every respect. (Some of the divergences could not have been avoided, while others seem unnecessary.)

Bly's quotation marks around the poem's name are not in themselves a divergence, but they still deserve glossing. In this context they indicate that the poem actually lacks a title – Bly has promoted the first line, put within quotation marks, into the designation of the poem. In his marking of the lack of a title, Bly in fact respects the original more than the Swedish textual tradition does.

Nearly all the poems in *Strountes* are in fact untitled,[3] which is not without its significance. *Strountes* is multifarious in content. Poems of many different kinds have been included in the collection – some

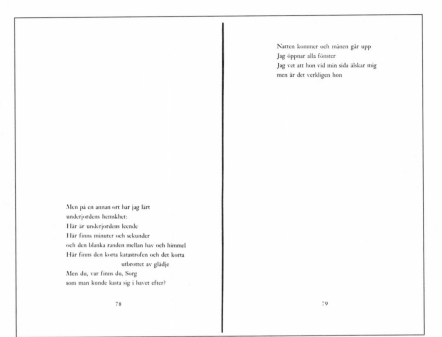

Figure 4
Gunnar Ekelöf, "But Somewhere Else" ("[Men på en annan ort]") in the
original edition of *Strountes* (*Strountes*, 1955)

similar to rough drafts and others carefully worked, some very beautiful and others more or less scurrilous. Reality's fragmentary, uncertain, and ambiguous character is a recurring theme. Full stops have
been used sparingly; in most of the poems they do not occur at all,
just as in our chosen text. In many places in *Strountes*, the full stop's
absence produces important ambiguities. The lack of titles to the
poems should be understood in the light of these and similar strategies.
In my opinion, it tends to strengthen the character of indefiniteness
which is so fundamental in the collection. In several cases – as in our
example – the poems have been skilfully made to seem like fragments,
and the fact that they are untitled becomes meaningful in that context.

In the original edition's elegant, widely spaced typography, the transition to a new poem was marked simply by typesetting its opening
just below the middle of the page so that a preceding empty space of
slightly more than half a page was created. (See figure 4.) Thus visually
the untitled poems were enclosed by an emptiness producing – as I see
it – associations with fragments disengaged from their larger, meaning-

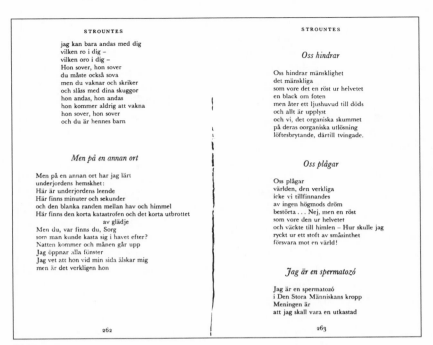

Figure 5
Gunnar Ekelöf, "But Somewhere Else" ("[Men på en annan ort]") in the
1965 and 1983 editions of *Poems (Dikter)*

bestowing context. For understandable reasons, no such expensive
layout has been chosen in later editions of Ekelöf's poems. There the
poems have been supplied with titles (normally the opening of the first
line),[4] evidently in order to make it possible to set them more closely
and still keep them apart. (See figure 5.)[5]

Certain other details in Bly's translation are less true to the original.
The word "hell" in lines 2 and 3, for instance, does not really correspond to Ekelöf's "underjorden"; "the underworld" would undoubtedly have been the closest English counterpart. I suppose Bly has
chosen the shorter "hell" to make it easier to approximate the rhythm
of the original, especially in line 2. As a result, however, Bly's translation arouses slightly different associations from the Swedish version
on this point, since "hell," unlike "the underworld," is connected with
specifically Christian beliefs.

Although Ekelöf does not make use of full stop in our poem, he
indicates where a new sentence starts: when a line opens with a capital
letter, this obviously marks the beginning of a new sentence. In two

places, Bly has neglected such new-sentence-marking capitals: lines 4 and 6 would have opened with a capital letter if Bly had followed Ekelöf's original. The changes thus introduced by Bly modify the relations between the clauses, bringing about a subtle change in the overall impression of the poem. In the original, lines 3–6 are divided into three complete sentences; they do not, as in Bly's translation, make up a single sentence. By this means, the original conveys a stronger impression that the reality "here" is disjointed, composed of separate entitities independent of one another.

I should like to point out, in this connection, that lines 10 and 11 also open new sentences in Ekelöf's original. Here, of course, the English "I," with its obligatory capital letter, is neutral to the distinction between presence and absence of a new-sentence-marking capital.

In line 5, Ekelöf's formulation "den blanka randen" has two possible meanings: "the bright border" and "the blank border." Bly has been forced to choose, and he has opted for the former alternative. That is probably justified, but no doubt it occasions a minor (inevitable) alteration of the meaning. For I think that Ekelöf's expression is to be seen as genuinely ambiguous: the meaning "the blank border" also seems to come into play in the line. The border is related to the shallow existence "here," and the word "blank"'s associations with something devoid of content, and to spaces waiting to be filled in, appear relevant in the context. (The Swedish and English words "blank" are also much alike in semantic content.)

In line 7, Bly has lowercased Ekelöf's "Sorg" ("Sorrow"). Perhaps Bly found the capital letter melodramatic, considering that the personification of sorrow has already been achieved through the apostrophe ("But you, where are you, sorrow … "). Changing the original on this point is, however, unnecessary from a linguistic point of view, and it affects some nuances of the meaning. Ekelöf's capital letter underlines Sorrow's character as a person more than the apostrophe alone can do. It thereby makes it more natural for the reader to ask herself if Sorrow is perhaps identical with the obviously desirable person who is, in the poem's last words, being spoken of as "she." It is also important that the capital letter makes the word "Sorrow" more ambiguous. Just as a person named "Faith" does not necessarily have a faith, there is no absolute need for "Sorrow" – unlike "sorrow" – to be characterized by sorrow: perhaps it is merely something or someone so called, something or someone bearing the conventional name "Sorrow."

I shall conclude these comments on Bly's English version by pointing to an important translational crux in line 8. Ekelöf's formulation "Sorg, som man kunde kasta sig i havet efter" (literally: "Sorrow, which one could throw oneself in the sea after") can in principle be construed in two ways: as meaning "Sorrow, which one could throw oneself into the sea to find" (the alternative chosen by Bly) or as meaning "Sorrow, which is such that one could throw oneself into the sea after having experienced it." As I shall attempt to demonstrate in later sections, this is an important line and one which should no doubt be seen as genuinely ambiguous. (The ambiguity is patently untranslatable, and Bly's preferred translation appears reasonable, considering that a choice has to be made.)

The Communicative Content and Expected Thematization of "But Somewhere Else"

In this section, I shall give an overall description of the Ekelöf poem's communicative content and expected thematization, such as I understand them, and then make some observations concerning the formal aspect of the poem.

The poem gives an account of the speaker-protagonist's situation. It opens with a description of the place where he[6] finds himself (lines 1–8), a place whose character is contrasted with that of "somewhere else." The later part of the poem (lines 9–12) is more narrative in nature. Lines 9 and 10 describe how night is coming; in lines 11 and 12 there is talk of a loving woman by the protagonist's side.

Already early in the poem, the speaker says that he is in the underworld. It is natural to understand the underworld, here, as being the earth, or the earthly region where we are.[7] Obviously, there are different localities in the underworld: where the speaker finds himself, he encounters its "smile," not its "gruesomeness." He is, thus, in a relatively agreeable place. Yet he lacks something: he lacks the Sorrow that one could throw oneself into the sea after. Evidently, he cannot at present make contact with this Sorrow.

The "here" in question is spoken of as a place characterized by demarcations and limitations. There are *minutes* and *seconds*, the *short* disaster and the *short* outburst of joy. Also *the bright/blank border between sea and sky* fits into the pattern: the higher and the lower do not meet but are separated by a thin but conspicuous dividing-line. The formulations suggest an unfulfilled desire for something boundless: for timelessness, for the union of heaven and earth, for limitless disaster or unbounded joy. This dissatisfaction, implicit in lines 4–6, comes to the surface in lines 7–8 in the guise of the explicitly expressed need for a Sorrow making one throw oneself into the sea.

As I already mentioned, the inquiry about Sorrow is ambiguous. Perhaps it concerns a Sorrow it is possible to encounter "here," a

Sorrow such that one can throw oneself into the sea after having experienced it (and perish?). Or else it may be a matter of a Sorrow which one throws oneself into the sea to find (perishing in the process?). In both cases, the question appears to spring from a yearning for a Sorrow which will annihilate the oppressive limitations of the speaker's life "here" and carry him over into another existence.

The ambiguity is so discernible, and the poem as a whole so well designed, that the author has probably felt the ambiguity in some degree and still refrained from removing it. It is also natural to perceive the ambiguity as enhancing the aesthetic impression. Spontaneously I see it as making the speaker's longing, the other existence, and the Sorrow alluded to appear more complex and more richly nuanced.

As I said, there is something of a dispositional divide before lines 9–12. The coming of the night brings with it a change not only in the poem's scene but also in its atmosphere. The external landscape is effaced. Something new seems about to happen: our eyes are lifted from the "underworld" to the moon. The reference to the moon underlines the possibility of change because the moon is also traditionally associated with the idea of the mutability of everything. Another association with the moon is more far-fetched, but to my mind still interesting: the moon is a celestial phenomenon affecting the sea. The moon's influence is not hemmed in by the division between sea and sky; the moon makes the higher and the lower enter into some kind of interrelationship.

Thus, boundary lines appear to be obliterated or bridged over in lines 9 and 10. And the speaker – apparently located indoors, in a room – seems to perceive this: he opens all the windows. The opening of "all" windows comes across as an act performed in order to overcome a shut-in feeling and enter into a more direct relation to the night outside, thus making oneself accessible to boundlessness. It is as if the speaker were preparing for his longed-for encounter with Sorrow and for his transformation.

The penultimate line of the poem introduces a woman who is, literally or figuratively, by the speaker's side, and it is said that he knows that she loves him. Then the poem concludes with a question which is, at least superficially, paradoxical: is she "really she"? (It would, at least on the face of it, be a contradiction in terms if she by his side were not really she.)

The question in the poem's last line is, however, formally unfinished. If the interrogative sentence were complete, it should in reason be followed by a question mark (as in line 8). Consequently, it is natural for the reader to look for an acceptable conclusion of the question, a conclusion which removes the question's paradoxical character. However, no substantial supplementation of the last sentence can claim to be supported by the text. The poem simply ends in a question without conclusion and without an exact meaning. What is clear is only that the last two lines place a female figure by the speaker's side and pose the question of her identity.

There are a few different readings of the end of the poem that merit serious consideration; I shall discuss two of them. Most natural is undoubtedly the one where "she" is taken to be an earthly woman, the speaker's wife, mistress, or such – after all, the speaker says: "I know that she by my side loves me." True, there is a difficulty with that interpretation: if she were his wife or mistress, it should be easy for the speaker to recognize her and decide whether she is "really she." The logic can be saved, however, if one assumes that "she" does not carry exactly the same meaning in line 11 and line 12. If we suppose that "she" in line 12 refers to a She with a capital S, as it were, the speaker can be construed as asking whether the woman by his side is really the one who answers his longing and his needs: " ... but is it really she who is the woman who can help me overcome all these painful limitations in my life?" According to this interpretation, the speaker (who is longing for the boundless) is still located in normal reality ("the underworld"). He has a wife or mistress by his side, and she still manages to hold him in place in his normal existence, among other things for the reason that she might, after all, prove to be the only one who can fulfil his deepest wishes.

It is, however, also possible to understand lines 11–12 in other ways. One may let one's experience be influenced by the consideration that perhaps the speaker, in fact or in his own imagination, already finds himself in that other reality for which he has been yearning. Perhaps he perceives, in that other reality, that he has a loving woman by his side, and perhaps he feels, almost without being able to believe it ("is it really she"), that she is the Sorrow which could make him throw himself into the sea, or some equivalent figure.

It is common to all the plausible interpretations of the finishing lines that I can think of that the speaker no longer knows for sure under what conditions he is living. Perhaps he unequivocally apprehends "she by my side" as his wife or his mistress, placed in ordinary reality, but is uncertain whether she does in fact afford the transcendental satisfaction he is seeking. Perhaps he conceives, instead, with some part of his self at least, the location as a transcendental reality, and the female figure – Sorrow or some equivalent being – as the final fulfiller (while he is still wondering whether he has truly understood the situation).

Before proceeding to the question of the poem's expected thematization, I should like to comment briefly on some literary devices which Ekelöf uses in the poem.

"But Somewhere Else" gives an indistinct picture of its setting. In the first part of the poem (lines 1–8), we hear talk of "the bright border between sea and sky," but otherwise the location the speaker finds himself in is not provided with any outward features at all. The poem's second part is more concrete, but even there the elements taken from reality are few, hardly individualized, and only vaguely connected with one another: the night, the moon, several windows, a woman by the speaker's side who loves him (as he knows). What is said about the reality where the action takes place is largely metaphorical or metonymical ("the underworld," "minutes," "seconds"). The sparing description of the outside world is, no doubt, motivated by the fact that the poem's principal subject is *inner* states: the speaker's experience of want and absence and limitations and his longing for existential fulfilment.

The diffuse description of the setting makes the poem evasive. Its vagueness is further accentuated by the ambiguities pointed out earlier, and also by the fragment-like aspect of the text. Not only does the poem lack title and full stops, it is also relatively short, and both its opening and its end are incomplete from a logical or linguistic point of view. The first sentence is formally marked as complete, since it starts with a capital letter; however, the earlier sentence with which the copulative conjunction "But" should link up syntactically and semantically is missing. The last sentence is obviously unfinished.

The different types of indefiniteness in the poem are balanced by rhetorical devices, especially antitheses and the repetition of words, that make the utterance more intense and sharply outlined. The fact that the poem opens with the word "But" gives the impression that what is said forms a contrast to something mentioned earlier of which the reader is not being informed. ("But" or "but" then recurs twice more in line openings, on both occasions indicating a pronounced change in the cognitive and emotional development in the poem.) The first part of the poem (lines 1–8) is wholly constructed around the opposition between the place "here" on the one hand, and on the other, first, the "somewhere else" characterized by "gruesomeness," and then the place where Sorrow is. At the end of the poem, the earthly and the transcendental poles are contrasted again ("she by my side" is set off against "she"), as are knowledge and ignorance ("I know that she by my side loves me" versus "is it really she"). As regards the repetition of words, apart from the word "But" ("but") the word "Here" also occurs three times as the first word of a line. A less observable and significant anaphora is the reiteration of "I" in lines 10 and 11. This seems a considerable amount of antithesis, contrast, and anaphora for a poem of twelve lines.

As I perceive it, the energetic, logical form increases the intensity of the utterance, making the speaker's experience stand out as more penetrating and dramatic. To me, the use of powerful form in the description of diffuse realities also creates the impression of something at once incomprehensible and coherent. Together with the crucial ambiguities in lines 7–8 and 11–12, it produces an atmosphere of distinct unreality.

According to my explanation of how experiences of literature come into existence, the reader attempts to reconstruct the intended meaning, to establish a communicative content. But thematizing and applying the content are also part of her role. I have maintained that it is justified, in that context, to speak of an expected thematization. Normally the author has no doubt implicitly counted on the reader to keep her focusings and reflections within a certain frame, to some degree anticipated by him.

It is usually easier to describe the communicative content in a relatively uncontroversial manner than to give a convincing account of the expected thematization. Where the Ekelöf poem is concerned it is also difficult to say anything exact about the content of that thematization. Some observations, however, appear to me justified.

With comparatively traditional poetry of a personal, intimate kind, it is often natural for the reader to focus on the situation in which the lyrical speaker finds himself and on the attitude to it which he adopts.[8] This applies, I think, also to the Ekelöf poem. As readers we meet a speaker experiencing his surrounding reality as, in a special way, limited and unsatisfactory. He appears to long for a kind of crisis leading to total catastrophe or boundless joy. It is probably natural for the reader to pay attention, first and foremost, to that experience of reality and to the speaker's mental strategies. She may ask herself whether she shares (or sometimes shares, or could possibly share) such an experience of reality. She may ask whether the speaker's mental strategies appear to be adequate ways of dealing with reality. Or she may simply store the experience and the strategies in her memory, as points of reference to be used, perhaps, in later situations in real life.

As I understand the Ekelöf poem, it makes a point of conveying, by various means, the picture of an existence that is strongly reminiscent of our own and is at the same time deeply frustrating in its incoherence. The poem appears not least to be intended to confront us with a yearning for the removal of the limitations inherent in our existence and for existential fulfilment. In a sense, one might even say that such a fulfilment is actualized in the poem. First the poem introduces a longing for fulfilment by associating it with an imagined, slightly personified Sorrow and with a desire resulting in the speaker's throwing himself into the sea. Then it confronts us with the speaker in a situation where he opens all the windows separating him from the moonlit night and seems to be in the course of entering a reality where some of the earlier mentioned limitations are absent. One gets the impression that it may now be possible for the speaker to transcend his circumscribed "here," to get rid of its restrictions. The poem's last line makes it natural to ask whether he is in fact just leaving the underworld. An earthly woman and another, elusive "she" are both present in the speaker's experience with approximately the same intensity, and the speaker's voice disappears in the middle of an unfinished question.

Some of the devices employed by Ekelöf erode the concretion of the things said. The external scene is described very sparingly. What is said about it is evasive because it is metaphorical or is for other reasons difficult to piece together to form a clear picture. In strategic places, ambiguities are worked up.

It is meaningful to make use of these devices. They dissolve all solid logical borderlines between our "real" world (only figuring under the spiritualizing and mythicizing appellation "the underworld" or, in Bly's translation, "hell") and a transcendent reality. If reality were described more concretely, and were given palpable inner continuity, it would appear less necessary, and less easy, to transcend it.

The poem is not meant to disintegrate into a haze, however. Its form helps to prevent that from happening. The formal patterns are, in themselves, striking, but since the crucial elements are short, simple everyday words ("But," "Here," "I"), or features such as interrogative sentences and inconspicuous ambiguities, they are nevertheless relatively discrete.

In the last line – but not until then – we are faced with a contradiction that already makes itself felt on the poem's semantic surface. Paradoxically, the speaker implicitly finds it possible that *she* (by his side) might in fact *not* be *she*. With that, the poem's fragile logical coherence is broken up – with skilful calculation, of course. The poem ends in the moment when the reality it refers to appears to be on the verge of splitting into two and the speaker seems on the way to disappearing from our underworld.

"But Somewhere Else" as a Text

In the last section, I examined Ekelöf's poem rather thoroughly. The reader will still undoubtedly have the impression that there is much more to be said about this literary work. I feel certain that that impression would remain even if I enlarged the section into a chapter, or even into a book (which would be altogether feasible). A (good) literary text is inexhaustible, as the phrase goes.

This kind of reader reaction creates a problem for me. No matter how much I enter into detail in discussing a given literary text – the communicated representations, the form, possible associations with the reader's emotions – the reader is likely to feel certain that something is missing in my account. And there is a definite risk that she will be convinced that what is missing must be the most essential part, the very heart of the mystery of literature. The fact of its absence might then be taken as a reason for finding my way of viewing literature narrow, not to say reductionist.

As I see it, such criticism would be unjust. It would rest on an insufficient understanding of what a literary text is, of the mechanisms of literary communication, and of the logic behind what is usually called the "interpretation" of literature. I shall devote three sections, forming something of an excursus, to an attempt to make it credible that my way of describing literary texts does, in principle, leave room for everything that may rationally be said about them, and that literary texts are not in themselves inexhaustible in any interesting sense. How, then, is one to explain the good and sensitive reader's fascination faced with artistically important literature, and her impression of being confronted with a secular miracle of sorts? That is a question to which I shall revert later in this chapter.

Throughout my book I have endeavoured to undermine the transportation metaphor's picture of literary communication. I have also consequently rejected the container metaphor, the picture of the text which the transportation metaphor implies. To me, the text is not a container, made out of words and with meaning as content. It is not a solid and concrete vessel with an objectively describable content. But nor is it a diffuse aggregate of indeterminate meaning always already in motion towards a new direction. I have criticized as absurd the fundamental intuitions behind the transportation metaphor, the very idea that meaning may exist somewhere other than in the author or his readers, that meaning may be found *between* them or in the space *surrounding* them.

According to my analysis, "But Somewhere Else" is not to be found outside Ekelöf and the reader of his poem except as a purely physical phenomenon, as white paper with traces of printer's ink. Ekelöf has caused certain material objects – the many interpretatively equivalent copies of the poem – to be produced because in their special visible makeup they can offer valuable experiences to an adequately equipped person. The competent reader is able to interpret the pattern of printer's ink as a sequence of characters, the characters as a sequence of sentences, and the sentences, in their special linguistic and situational context, as standing for a communicative content which she is expected to reconstruct and react to, deriving literary satisfaction in the process. (I hope that the reader of my account is in fact able, at this stage of the book, to look at the physical text and experience that this is the only outward stimulus encountering her – that she is not confronted with an enigmatic object where material reality, language, and meaning have coalesced, but that she reconstructs and reacts to textual and semantic communicative intentions in the originator, doing this on the basis of physical traces on paper and almost as a reflex action.)

The text, as it is traditionally conceived, does not correspond to any object with which I reckon in my analysis, but rather, roughly, with two such objects taken together. One is the sequence of linguistic signs: the sequence of graphemes, the sequence of words, the sequence of sentences, or however we choose to define it.[9] The other is the communicative content – the intended meaning as it appears reasonable to construe it. Both are objective phenomena. True, they are not objective in the sense that they exist independently of human consciousness – if our species were to die out, there would no longer be any linguistic sign-sequences or any communicative contents, but only their material bases: things like paper with printer's ink on it. But they are essentially objective in so far as they are apprehended in approximately the same way by all literate individuals with a command of the language in question and a basic literary understanding. So it is possible to describe the sign-sequence and the communicative content in a largely objective fashion – to state, with relative certainty, how they will be understood by a competent reader. The description of the text's sign-sequence and the description of the text's communicative content are two of the three basic components of what I shall call "descriptive textual analysis." The third and somewhat more speculative one is the description of the text's expected thematization.

It was a descriptive analysis of Ekelöf's poem that I gave in the last section. Such an analysis may, in its way, be subtle, but at the same time it has something tautologous about it: it merely registers what – as our saying goes – "is written" in the text. An interpretation of Ekelöf's poem, in the most ordinary sense of "interpretation," is in some respects less trivial: it also adds new dimensions to the experience of the poem. In my view, however, it would be a mistake to believe that the properties ascribed to texts in ordinary interpretation are, generally, objective characteristics of the text. This is a difficult point, and requires a more lengthy explanation.

The traditional way of understanding literary interpretation is, unsurprisingly, bound up with traditional thinking about texts and about meaning. It is inspired by the transportation and container metaphors. The fundamental idea is that an interpretation of a text is a statement about the text's meaning. Suppose that one sees a text as a verbal container with the meaning as its content, and an interpretation as a description of the meaning. Then one must of course, consequently, hold that the phenomenon described in a tenable interpretation is something actually present in the text. What is described in the interpretation is, thus, projected onto the text. And this is in fact something one normally does in connection with literary interpretation, no matter whether one's view of the text is New Critical, poststructuralist, or anything else.[10]

If one rejects the transportation and container metaphors, however, an entirely different light is thrown on the situation. Between the author and the reader there is, then, a physical object functioning (and intended to function) as a sign. Based on that object, the reader reconstructs a communicative content and an expected thematization. Moreover, she thematizes and applies the communicative content; what she is passing through during all this activity (occurring simultaneously in her mind) is what we call a literary experience.

It is possible to see the reader's understanding (her reconstruction of the intended meaning and/or the content of her thematization and application) as an interpretation of the text. By "interpretations," however, we are normally referring not to tacit understanding in the ordinary reader but to *explicit statements* (or the content of explicit statements) *by scholars or critics*. Such statements usually aim to place the text in an explanatory context, or to enrich the experience of the text, or both.

Let us continue to use the Ekelöf poem as our example. That text may be inserted in different explanatory contexts. One can, for example, point to experiences of Ekelöf's, or supposed mental conflicts in him, making it understandable for him to take an interest in themes like the one in the poem. Or one may refer to special events at the time he wrote, or to other literature that he read, as partial explanations for why the poem has been given precisely this content. Such moves can enrich (or, certainly, interfere with) the reader's literary experience. But one may also enrich the experience by suffusing the things said in the poem with associations – for example, by "reading" (explicating) the poem "through" (starting from) certain other literature. By arranging the light in which the poem is seen, one may create new, unexpected effects.

In the next section, I shall attempt to demonstrate how the experience of Ekelöf's poem may be modified with the help of some biographical and intertextual observations. After that, I shall try to pinpoint the difference between a descriptive textual analysis and an interpretation in the traditional sense and explain why interpretation in the traditional sense is not important for me in this book.

"But Somewhere Else":
A Possible Interpretation in Outline

The Ekelöf poem is thought to have been written in Positano, a town on the Italian west coast not far from Salerno. Ekelöf lived in Positano for a while during the journey to Italy which he undertook in 1954–5 together with his wife and a daughter of two or three.[11] The Ekelöfs rented a flat situated inside a rock on the beach. The sound of the sea reverberated in the rooms. The immediately preceding poem in *Strountes* (also untitled, but normally called "The Coast of the Sirens") makes use of this setting. In my own simple translation it reads:

> The coast of the sirens:
> In an echoing grotto flat
> the sevenfold echo
> of the Mediterranean's swell
> night after night:
> She sleeps, she sleeps
> she breathes heavily
> but you have woken up
> you have fought with shadows
> she sleeps, she sleeps
> and you are her child –
> You breathe so heavily in me
> you breathe so easily in me
> how you surge up mother
> how you surge down
> I can only breathe with you
> what rest in you
> what unrest in you –
> She sleeps, she sleeps
> you too must sleep
> but you wake up and scream
> and fight your shadows
> she breathes, she breathes
> she will never wake up
> she sleeps, she sleeps
> and you are her child[12]

The poem describes the Mediterranean as a female being, mother to the speaker. The roar of the sea is the breathing of his sleeping mother. It is as if the mother penetrated into the speaker ("You breathe so heavily in me"), and he adapts his breathing to hers ("I can only breathe with you"). It is as if he were inside her ("what rest in you / what unrest in you"), as if he were her foetus and not merely her child. Since his mother's sleep is a sleep from which she will never awaken ("she will never wake up"), a merging into the mother must result not only in a kind of liberation (for instance, from the fighting with the shadows) but also in effacement. In the poem, however, the speaker has not yet wholly realized this union with his mother ("you too must sleep / but you wake up and scream").

On crucial points, the situation is reminiscent of that in "But Somewhere Else." In both poems, the speaker appears to be on the verge of entering into an annihilating union with something outside everyday reality. In both cases, there is talk of a uniting with the sea and – explicitly or as a hint – with a female figure. Reading "But Somewhere Else" through "The Coast of the Sirens" brings out the longing for a merging with a female being that is otherwise only glimpsed in the poem. Likewise, the non-human, transcendent character of the object is exposed more clearly. In both cases, of course, the desire for a fusion has an erotic undertone. But the shadow of eroticism is also no doubt, in part, there to make graspable the need for existential fulfilment and for a merging in something greater that both poems express.

Another connection between the poems is hidden in the reference to sirens in "The Coast of the Sirens." The sirens were of course, according to Greek mythology, winged female beings who, through their beautiful, irresistible singing, enticed seafarers to come to them. The seafarers ran aground on the rocks where the sirens were sitting, and the sirens ate them. By far the best-known story of sirens is in the twelfth book of the *Odyssey* (possibly eight century BC). Ulysses and his men have to pass the sirens' place in their boat. Ulysses, curious as always, wishes to hear the sirens' singing. He lets his men tie him to the ship's mast, while he orders them to block their own ears with wax. In this way, he can listen to the song of the sirens without yielding to the temptation of throwing himself into the sea, which would be certain death. In the light of that story it is easy to see that the two Ekelöf poems allude, in different ways, to *throwing oneself into the sea in order to come into closer contact with something overpowering.*

Apart from the biographical background, and the poem's immediate context in the collection *Strountes*, I would also like to introduce Sappho – the Greek poet living ca. 600 BC – into the sphere of associations surrounding "But Somewhere Else." According to a well-known tradition, Sappho committed suicide by throwing herself into the sea from a cliff on the Greek island Leukas. The reason is said to have been unrequited love for a man, Phaon.[13] When the speaker in Ekelöf's poem brings to our minds a sorrow after which one could throw oneself into the sea, this *might* therefore trigger associations with Sappho, especially if we know that in speaking of the sea, Ekelöf must have been thinking primarily of the Mediterranean, which was also Sappho's sea.

There is one more passage in "But Somewhere Else" which *may* bring Sappho to mind. I am referring to the last four lines, particularly to the line "Night comes and the moon rises" with its laconic outlining of a nocturnal and lunar scenery frequent in Sappho's poetry. Among her lyrical poems I think especially of a well-known fragment, handed down to us via Hephaestion's *Handbook of Metrics*, which reads (in J.M. Edmonds's translation)[14]

> The Moon is gone
> And the Pleiads set,
>   Midnight is nigh;
> Time passes on
> And passes; yet
>   Alone I lie

or, in a literal translation:

> The moon has set
> and the Pleiads; it is mid-
> night; the hour passes(?);
> (but) I lie alone.

The well-educated Swedish reading public, at least, has been brought up to understand the fragment as implying that the speaker (Sappho) has arranged an amorous rendez-vous, but that the beloved has failed to appear. (Obviously, the text admits of other interpretations.) The best-known Swedish translation even says that "The hour of our appointment is past."[15]

Superficially, the final lines in Ekelöf's poem in no way describe a situation parallel to the one in the Sappho fragment. In Ekelöf, the night comes and the moon rises, and there is (in what I see as the main interpretation) a loving woman by the man's side. But the man could perhaps be said to feel alone in a deeper sense: is she by his side "really she"? Obviously, he allows for the possibility of another, more essential encounter. That the night comes and the moon rises indicates the approach of the moment that is – in the Sappho fragment as it is traditionally understood – the hour of the amorous appointment. The man opens all the windows ...

If they do in fact occur to the reader, the associations with Sappho will no doubt serve to emphasize even more the longing for fulfilment and its connections with both love and death. They also link up with the strong but in important respects frustrated need to create that finds implicit expression in many of the *Strountes* poems. In *Strountes*, there is a subtle but discernible association between the yearning for a great liberating or annihilating experience and the desire to create – as if Ekelöf were longing for an experience that (like Sappho's love experiences, according to tradition) was radical enough to put his own life at stake but also to give rise to indestructible poetry.

We do not know what role "But Somewhere Else" actually played for Ekelöf, how it functioned within his psychic economy. To me it stands out, however, as a poem satisfying multiple needs in its creator by letting him safely simulate a step into the great unknown. He vividly actualizes the idea of a person's undergoing – perhaps at the cost of his own life – a totalizing experience that obliterates the limitations now restraining him, and he describes such an experience as possible by preparing the scene for it in a fantasy. The imagining of it as a conceivable reality is already a creative act resulting in impressive poetry.

About ten years later, 28 March 1965, Ekelöf had a revolutionizing experience, provoked by an icon in the ruins of the Blachernai Palace in Istanbul portraying the Madonna with her child. The experience was the beginning of an intense, self-destructive creative period lasting, more or less, until Ekelöf's death about three years later, a period during which the poetry now regarded as his most important was produced. "But Somewhere Else" is one of many Ekelöf poems foreshadowing that later encounter.[16]

The "Inexhaustibility" of Texts: Descriptive Textual Analysis versus Interpretation

In the last section I sketched *one* possible type of interpretation of "But Somewhere Else." Among other things, I made a couple of biographical and intertextual observations and used them to relate the poem to Ekelöf's life (something that could of course have been done very differently).

The interpretation is far from unproblematic. Its general tenability can easily be questioned – for instance, the relevance of the references to Sappho may appear disputable.[17] One could even, in a New Critical or structuralist spirit, contend that biographical considerations have no proper place in the interpretation of literature. Or one could say that it makes no difference whether or not Ekelöf's situation, "The Coast of the Sirens," and Sappho's life and poems played a role in the forming of the poem. The interpretation that I suggested does in fact enrich (or, conversely: impoverish) the poem aesthetically, and this and only this makes it justified (or, conversely: inadequate). And then someone else could retort that such a view of the conditions of literary interpretation is irresponsible, and that fanciful readings with a purely aesthetical motivation are on no account to be accepted.

In the book I am now writing, however, I am not interested in the logic of interpretations-in-the-ordinary-sense, i.e., of critical or scholarly interpretations. My standpoint is – I repeat – that it is important to distinguish between, on one hand, the reading of a literary text for the sake of literary satisfaction, and on the other, the formulating of a critical or scholarly interpretation of a text. They are two different things (though the interpreting critic or scholar must of course be supposed to have read, understood, and experienced the text). And in this book I occupy myself with *the theory of literature*, not with *the principles of literary criticism or literary scholarship*. I am reflecting on the nature of literary utterance and on the mechanisms underlying the reading of literature for the sake of literary benefit. I leave aside the interpreting activities of literary critics or scholars, since they have no immediate relevance for my subject.

According to my analysis, a person reading for the sake of literary satisfaction is in principle doing two things: he is reconstructing a sign-sequence, a communicative content, and an expected thematization, and he is himself producing thematizations and applications of the communicative content. Both his reconstruction and his post-communicative processing are, naturally, acts of active re-creation or creation, not of passive registration. When reconstructing (sign-sequence, communicative content, expected thematization), he is, however, orientated towards the author and her communicative intentions. He attempts to reconstruct them, with varying success.

If he fails, the fault may lie with the author. Perhaps she has not made it easy enough, or even possible, for the reader to reconstruct her communicative intentions. The reader is not a thought-reader. The best he can attain is a reconstruction that is as reasonable as possible (given the text, and given the knowledge and experience that the author has a right to expect from her audience). And it is this optimally reasonable reconstruction of sign-sequence, communicative content, and expected thematization that a descriptive textual analysis in my sense strives to achieve.[18]

Such an analysis will necessarily be shallow in a certain sense. The reader's literary experience is in fact expected to comprise much more than a mere reconstruction of sign-sequence, communicative content, and expected thematization. His personal thematizations and applications, too, are elements of his literary experience, indeed the very elements that make it valuable to him. Without this personal content, literary experience would be not only poor but actually pointless. However, the personal content is, precisely, personal: it varies from reader to reader, and so it would be an interminable undertaking to try to describe the content of readers' thematizations and applications of a certain text. Anyway, I shall not attempt to do so. My aim in this book is to present a general analysis of literature and literary experience. It has therefore seemed reasonable to me to content myself with emphasizing the fact that literary experience *has* a personal content that lends it its relevance and attraction, and to describe some of the ways in which the experience must be thought to arise.

It should be clear from what I just said that I do not admit to having overlooked important elements of the poem in my descriptive analysis of "But Somewhere Else." First of all, there is not literally a poem, or, consequently, any elements of the poem – unless we employ the container metaphor. What is "really" (or: more literally) there is a physical object (or to be more exact: a number of pragmatically equivalent physical objects, a number of copies of the poem) functioning as a sign, and, in addition, reader processings of the visual impressions of these objects – processings anticipated, in important respects, by the object's spiritual originator, the author. In my descriptive textual analysis I account, so to speak, for the obligatory elements of a correct reading. But I make no attempt to describe the endlessly varied optional elements; I just stress that they exist and comment on their nature.

It is often said that a good literary text is inexhaustible, and I do not want to deny that. But as I formulated it, the idea obviously rests on the container metaphor: it exploits the picture of a container that cannot be emptied. Since no such container exists, talk of inexhaustibility is potentially misleading. But the idea can be reformulated in a more unobjectionable manner: it is impossible in principle to give *an exhaustive description* of what we usually call the meaning of a literary text.

Why is this impossible? Partly because meaning in literature comprises many different things (as we saw in chapter 4), and only some of these have reasonably distinct boundaries. Partly (more trivially) because no empirical phenomena at all allow of an exhaustive description.

Let me develop that double explanation. I have said that the communicative content (the intended meaning, such as the reader perceives it) can be objectively described. One cannot, however, give an *exhaustive* account of it. It is a well-established philosophical conception that no real object, not even something as relatively simple as a human hand, ever admits of exhaustive description.

Apart from the intended and the reconstructed meaning, it is also possible to discern several other factors normally referred to as "meaning." In my analysis in chapter 4, for example, I added applicatory and symptomal meaning to the list. Such kinds of meaning come into existence because the reader not only reconstructs the communicative content but also thematizes and applies it, thereby generating applicatory meaning, and because critics and scholars especially also relate texts to explanatory or elucidative contexts and so, often, come to ascribe symptomal meanings to the texts.

There is, in principle, no end to the reader's possibilities of applying a text, and it could be argued that each new reader and reading results in a new application. So the applicatory meaning of a text can be constantly enriched with new applications. Moreover, a reader's reading on a given occasion – a quantity that does, in principle, allow of objective description – cannot be described *exhaustively*, any more than other empirical phenomena can. Similar observations could be made about symptomal meaning.

This chapter has consisted of preliminaries, but of important ones. First I gave a descriptive textual analysis of Ekelöf's "But Somewhere Else." Then I explained why such an analysis is not at all an exhaustive analysis of the text. I also attempted to demonstrate, however, that what falls outside the scope of the analysis is not some unknown quintessence of literature but phenomena that are identifiable and describable, though so diversified that a thorough treatment of them is impracticable. Now that all this is done, it is possible to raise the more comprehensive question "What is form?"

9 Form in Literature

A Definition of Literary Form

It is a widely held opinion that the concept of form employed in artistic and literary contexts is unclear or vague.[1] Nevertheless one can point to several substantive ideas about artistic and literary form that are shared by practically all theorists. There is extensive agreement that form is the manner in which the aesthetic statement is made: "the *way* something is said in contrast to *what* is said."[2] Likewise, it is a common observation that form is concerned both with the artistic expression and with the content it conveys.[3] And it is hardly disputed that "form" may be used both about the completely individual form of a particular aesthetic object and about abstract patterns possibly common to, for example, a whole literary genre (like the sonnet).[4] There are certainly differences in the use of the term "form." Nevertheless, the problems with the concept of literary form are not primarily caused by uncertainty about what types of traits should be seen as formal features. Rather, those features are so disparate that it becomes difficult to perceive the logic and justification of the concept of form. In connection with Ekelöf's "But Somewhere Else," the lack of a title, the lack of rhymes, the incomplete syntax, the first-person perspective, the diffuseness of the description of reality, and the extensive use of antitheses would normally all be seen as aspects of the form. But is not this a bewilderingly heterogeneous list?

It is not necessary for my present purposes to break down our usual concept of form into tolerably unified constituents (something which would, in principle, be feasible). I shall certainly, in the course of this chapter, make distinctions in the concept. What I am really seeking, however, is a rough answer to the questions what (if anything) is common to the phenomena ordinarily called formal, what literary functions they fulfil, and how they fit into my general picture of the creating and reading of literature.

According to my analysis in this book, literature has a communicative core. From a systematic point of view, it is an absolutely fundamental fact about verbal art that the author conveys a communicative content, a complex of representations, to her readers. The reader is, however, supposed to let that material of representations initiate a literary experience – a focusing, reflecting, and applying that, among other things, will give rise to feelings in him. These aspects of the reading experience are certainly not communicated, so the creating and reading of literature can be said to *involve communication* without being *communicative through and through.*

In order to convey communicative content by linguistic means, one has to use physical signs to *represent linguistic expressions.* Different physical objects may represent the same linguistic expression. You have doubtless written your signature on many different sheets of paper in your life. The different inscriptions represent the same sequence of signs: the one forming your name.

Different linguistic expressions may *convey the same communicative content, the same (complex of) mental representation(s)* – unless one employs very strict criteria of identity. If one wishes to communicate that it is 10 p.m., for instance, one has the choice among several different, semantically more or less equivalent, expressions: "It is ten in the evening," "It is ten p.m.," and so on.

In addition, thoughts or *mental representations* of different makeup may be used to stand for the same realities, *represent the same state of affairs.* The fact that there is a white door in the corridor with a yellow knocker on it may be represented both by the thought that *there is a yellow knocker on a white door in the corridor* and by the thought that *there is a door in the corridor that is white and has a yellow knocker* (unless one imposes very strict criteria of identity on states of affairs).

In communicating one thus makes use of vehicles of meaning – physical signs, linguistic expressions, mental representations – that could have been slightly different while still fulfilling fundamentally the same communicative objectives. The visual appearance of the text may vary – different typeface, wider margins – while the text still represents the same sequence of printed characters. (Cf. the two different printings of Ekelöf's "But Somewhere Else" reproduced in the last chapter.)[5] The linguistic formulations, in their turn, may be varied at least to some extent while the communicated mental representations remain the same. And the complex of communicated mental representations can differ in shape, in some respects, without therefore representing different complex states of affairs. So one can, in a certain sense, speak of the essential and non-essential characteristics of the sign-object on each of the three levels: the physical, the expressional, and the semantic. I use "essential characteristics," in this context, to mean the representational properties, those that are, normally, central from a communicative point of view. The essential properties of the physical sign-object are those responsible for its representing a given sequence of linguistic signs. The essential properties of the linguistic sign-sequence are those responsible for its representing a given meaning. The essential properties of the meaning, of the communicative content, are those responsible for its standing for a given complex state of affairs. Such essential properties are not called formal. But all other characteristics of the physical object, the sign-sequence, and the communicative content may be conceived as formal features.

In this, I have suggested an explanation of the implicit principles according to which we classify certain traits in literature as formal. I have thereby produced a very brief, general account of what literary form is, a kind of attempted descriptive definition of literary form.

In important respects, my explanation tallies with current definitions of "form." For one thing, I too claim that form is concerned with *how* something is said, not with *what* is said. Contrary to the usual practice, however, I do not perceive form as an aspect of the text with its own positive identity. I see "form," rather, as an umbrella concept covering all properties of texts that are aesthetically relevant but non-representational (in the special sense introduced here).

Another important difference is that traditional views of literary form are based on the container metaphor's picture of the literary text. (I shall revert to this in the next chapter.) The analysis of literary form just given is, instead, compatible with my picture of the writing and understanding of literature as a conveyance of thought complexes for the reader to reconstruct and process. I have described form as certain kinds of properties of the conveyed thought complex, and also as certain types of properties of the physical sign-object and the linguistic sign-sequence used for conveying the thought complex.

If it is true that the formal features are not in fact necessary for the conveying and understanding of a communicative content, one may wonder why addressees pay any attention to form at all. The fundamental reason, I believe, is that *indirectly* non-representational traits also play a role in communicative contexts. They are often *symptomatic* in the sense that they let us know about the originator's properties or feelings or convictions (not because they *communicate* them, but because they *reveal* them). And such information is often valuable to the addressee. Say that someone answers a question from you in a hesitant manner and with some stammering. The manner and the stammering do not normally affect the verbal meaning of the utterance, so you can usually disregard them in your *communicative* processing. On the other hand, you will have every reason to take notice of them in your *post-communicative* processing, when you assess the utterance's credibility. They indicate, normally (and among other things), that the speaker herself is not certain of the correctness of her answer.

In fact, addressees do attend to many kinds of non-representational traits in connection with a physical sign-object, primarily, no doubt, because of the symptomatic value of the traits. Consequently, all sorts of features can become conspicuous to addressees. And this makes it possible for the originator to introduce, *intentionally*, special non-representational features in order to *exploit* their apparent character of symptoms. If the first and the last sentence of the text we encounter are incomplete, this is a natural indication that we have before us a fragment of a larger text. But in "But Somewhere Else," Ekelöf exploits the impression created by such incompleteness. He makes the first and last sentences incomplete, mainly, no doubt, in order to let the poem look a little like a fragment. (The aesthetic motivation for that strategy has been discussed above.) The functioning of other types of formal traits could be explained in analogous ways.

When the linguistic originator exploits non-representational features – and not merely incorporates them in her utterance unintentionally – she can do so in a manipulative or in a communicative manner. I can reprimand a child in an angry tone in spite of my not being angry, and I can do so manipulatively or communicatively. I can speak in a way that makes it sound as if I am indeed angry, with the manipulative intention that the child will interpret my tone as a genuine symptom of anger. But I can also speak in a way which reveals that I am intentionally using an angry tone and intentionally disclosing that. In the latter case, one could say that I am *communicating* that I am angry, albeit with non-linguistic means: I intentionally indicate that I feel angry, and I make my intention to indicate anger transparent. In an analogous fashion, Ekelöf *communicates* that "But Somewhere Else" is to be perceived as something of a fragment.

To sum up: there are at least two good reasons for addressees also to pay attention to the non-representational features of utterances. On the one hand, these may betray important characteristics or attitudes of the originator. On the other, the originator may have converted the features into elements used for communication, into a kind of non-conventional sign modifying the utterance's communicative content, its intended meaning.

Literary Form: Two Complications

In the last section, I gave a relatively manageable explanation of what literary form is. When reflecting on the explanation, however, one soon feels the need to make it more precise.

First, I should supplement my account of the nature of the physical sign-object's form. In connection with such an object – say, a physical copy of Ekelöf's "But Somewhere Else" – it is important to distinguish between obligatory and optional properties. The obligatory properties are those properties that a physical sign-object *must* have if it is to qualify as a copy of precisely that work. In connection with "But Somewhere Else" ("Men på en annan ort"), it is reasonably easy to specify what the obligatory properties are. They are, I would say, the property (or properties) of representing a certain specific sequence of linguistic signs, namely, the sequence of graphemes <M>, <e>, <n>, <space>, and so on.[6]

Other texts may be more complicated in this respect. Ever since antiquity there have existed poems where the arrangement of the writing or printing on the page creates a kind of picture of an object related to the poem's theme.[7] Perhaps the best-known examples, but far from the earliest ones, are the seventeenth-century funeral poems where the textual surface forms the picture of a sepulchral urn, or of the Reaper, or the like. A modern instance is Ernst Jandl's "easter week: a tower" ("karwoche: ein turm," 1985; see figure 6).[8] A correct copy of Jandl's poem is not only required to represent a specific sequence of graphemes. Another obligatory property is, obviously, that the printing must present a certain visual pattern. (Since it is difficult to know exactly how that pattern is to be specified, the only safe way of rendering the poem is to photocopy it.)

It is only the *obligatory* non-representational properties that are formal ones. It is especially important to point this out where physical sign-objects are concerned. A printed copy of Ekelöf's "But Somewhere Else" will have many optional non-representational properties. It will be set in a given typeface, occupy a specific number of square centimetres on the page, form a certain visual pattern, and so on. None of these characteristics, however, will be an element of literary form. The reason is – to put it simply – that they are not, in this case, properties *of the poem*: since they are optional, they may vary from one correct copy to another. (Cf. once again figures 4–5 in the last chapter!)

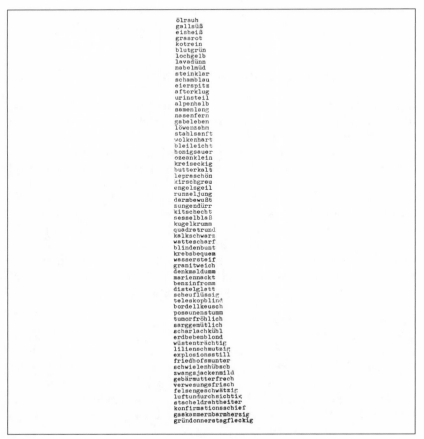

Figure 6
Ernst Jandl, "easter week: a tower" ("karwoche: ein turm," 1985)

Consequently, "But Somewhere Else" must be said to lack a *visual* literary form.

In Jandl's "easter week: a tower," on the other hand, the visual pattern is obviously, itself, part of the poem and an element of its literary form. This agrees with my newly modified definition of "literary form," for in Jandl the visual pattern must be seen as an *obligatory* non-representational[9] property of the sign-object.

It is not sufficiently precise, then, to define "literary form" as the non-representational properties of the copies of the text, of the text's sign-sequence, or of the text's communicative content. "Form" should rather be defined as the *obligatory* non-representational properties of such phenomena. (That clarification is important where the physical copies are concerned, but not really in connection with the sign-sequence or the communicative content.)

Let me now turn to another complication. One may question the reasonableness of characterizing as formal properties *all* the obligatory, non-representational qualities of the physical copies, the sign-sequence, and the communicative content. Say that we define the sequence of linguistic signs connected with "Men på en annan ort," the Swedish original of "But Somewhere Else," as a sequence of graphemes: <M>, <e>, <n>, <space>, and so on. In that case, the linguistic sign-sequence has the property of containing thirty-seven occurrences of the letter <e>, something that must obviously be an obligatory property of the sign-sequence. Nevertheless, it may seem doubtful that containing thirty-seven occurrences of the letter <e> should be seen as an element of the poem's form.

One way of dealing with that objection is to supplement the definition of "literary form" once more and say that formal properties are such obligatory, non-representational qualities of a literary text's copies, sign-sequence, or communicative content *that are significant from a literary point of view*. Then the fact that the Ekelöf poem contains exactly thirty-seven e's will not be a fact about its form, since the feature must be entirely unimportant for the literary experience of the poem.

I believe that our intuitions about literary form support this solution to some extent. What impels us to speak of literary form is probably the awareness that in texts like Ekelöf's poem qualities that are not purely linguistic or communicative also, rightly, play a role in the reader's literary experience. Presumably, it is such properties that we primarily think of as formal features.

Of course, no sharp boundary line can be drawn between what is and is not significant from a literary point of view. The fact that the Ekelöf poem contains exactly thirty-seven e's may be a clear instance of an artistically irrelevant feature, but borderline cases will never be hard to find. (One can, for instance, always discuss whether some of the less marked repetitions of sounds in a poem are to be apprehended as coincidences without artistic significance or as artistically not unimportant alliterations or assonances.) So if one adopts the solution under consideration one will, in certain cases, be unable to decide objectively whether a given trait belongs to the form of the text or not – the answer will depend on how one understands and experiences the text. But this is not necessarily a deficiency in the suggested definition of "literary form." One can just as well see it as a realistic feature of the definition, inevitable if one wishes to stay true to the basic idea behind our talk of form.

There is, however, also another, equally natural, manner of handling the definitional problem in question. If one wishes, one can consistently adhere to the contention that all obligatory, non-representational qualities are in fact to be classified as formal features. Then one has to accept the exactly thirty-seven e's as a property of the Ekelöf poem's form. But perhaps that is the right thing to do. The impression that such traits are not elements of the form may have been created simply by the circumstance that we do not, *in practice*, pay any attention to "formal" features that lack significance for the impression that the poem makes.

I believe that our normal ideas of literary form are too unclear to agree unequivocally with either alternative. I, therefore, find it unnecessary to make my descriptive definition still more precise on this point.

Form and the Cognitive-Emotive Model of Literature's Function

I have repeatedly said that the reader of literature normally reconstructs, focuses, and applies a communicative content, and that these acts have both cognitive and emotional effects, effects creating much of literature's relevance to its readers.[10] I shall now attempt to demonstrate how literary form fits into that model of the reader's processing.

According to my analysis, the author communicates a complex of thoughts, of mental representations, to the reader. The representations stand for certain states of affairs. (Ekelöf's poem is a complex of representations of the place "Here" and of things happening to the speaker in that place. Johnson's *Anniversaries* is, essentially, a complex of representations of events and incidents in the life of Gesine Cresspahl – and so forth.) The representations are put into perspective: they are made from a more or less palpable spatial, temporal, and/or evaluative point of view. (Thus the representations connected with Ekelöf's poem are marked, among other things, by a vague uneasiness at the fragmented and limited existence "here," and the representations connected with Johnson's *Anniversaries*, among other things, by a basically sympathetic attitude to Gesine Cresspahl.)

The reader reconstructs the representations and the perspectives. They form the basis of her post-communicative processing, her focusings, reflections, and applications. Faced with the communicative content, the reader implicitly asks herself questions like "Is reality like this?" and "What consequences does that have for me?" In this way, (mostly unconscious) ideas about reality and perspectives on her existence arise within her. The perspectives kept in readiness for her by the text (via its expected understanding) are, in the paradigm case, perspectives that let themselves be experienced as both tenable and emotionally satisfying (or at least bearable).

Literary form, as I have described it in this chapter, can be said to be of two principally different kinds. It is either qualities of the physical or linguistic means of expression used for communicating the representations and perspectives – *expressional form*, as I shall call it in the following. Or else it is *conceptional form*, i.e., the qualities – the non-representational properties – of the communicated thoughts, the perspectival representations, themselves. Both kinds of form are among the things reconstructed by the reader.

The reader's communicative, reconstructive processing thus involves a reconstruction of both meaning and form (expressional and conceptional). The reader builds up an impression of the complex of representations, including its formal aspects, while also being aware of the means of expression and their form. In her post-communicative processing, she has all these elements to react to.

It is on this point that a consideration of form supplements the earlier version of the cognitive-emotive model. In the post-communicative processing of the competent reader, thematizations and applications of *both* communicative content *and* form interact. In other respects, there is no need to alter the picture of the cognitive-emotive processing pattern. We can say, as before, that the reader creates or re-creates a perspective on reality with the help of the material encountering her, and that her literary experience partly consists in an affective-evaluative attitude to the elements of reality towards which it is directed. The fact that the model now also accounts for literary form only means that we are now able to provide a fuller and more adequate description of the reader's encounter with, and reaction to, the text.

With the above I have answered, broadly at least, the four questions about form raised in the introduction to the last chapter. In earlier sections, I defined literary form and also explained what it consists of, namely (artistically significant?) obligatory non-representational properties of the linguistic sign-object, of the linguistic sign-sequence, and of the communicative content. Implicitly, I have also explained how literary form comes to be a part of the literary object. Literature is based on the conveyance of communicative contents. The conveyance presupposes the use of signs (physical sign-objects, abstract sign-sequences) inevitably possessing more properties than that of representing-by-linguistic-means; at least when such "extra" properties are obligatory and are made artistically significant, they will be elements of literary form. The communicative content itself will also inevitably have other qualities apart from those of representing a complex state of affairs (global qualities, internal relations between the constituent parts of the content, and so on). Such qualities are elements of the form (at least when they are obligatory and artistically significant).

Subsequently, in this section, I have implicitly given a general clarification of the function of form. According to my explanation the form, just like the communicated thoughts, is something that the reader encounters in her reconstructive processing of the sign-object. Together with the communicated thoughts, the form constitutes the basis of her post-communicative processing, of her focusings, reflections, and applications.

Also implicitly, I have indicated how form is connected with thoughts and feelings. Literary form is the form of the communicated thoughts, or of the means of expression employed for communicating them. That is how it comes to be related to the cognitive material. And when the reader registers, and reacts to, literary form, this modifies his impression of the representations conveyed. Form may thereby affect his empathetic feelings, and the thoughts involved in his application, and consequently also the feelings associated with the latter. That is how form is related to feelings.

As I have already made clear, this is only a broad answer to my questions about form. The answer leaves many aspects of literary form unattended to and gives rise to follow-up questions of many kinds. I shall devote the rest of the chapter to three more delimited problems in connection with the functions of form. I shall be asking: What kinds of effects, more particularly, does literary form have? What kinds of mechanisms, more concretely, are responsible for the literary form's affecting us? And what is of most importance in the literary experience, form or content?

What Types of Effects Does Literary Form Have?

It is obvious that form usually plays a significant role in the reader's impression of a literary text. But what sorts of effects does the literary form have? Since features of so many different kinds may be formal properties, there is not much of a both general and substantive nature that can be said about the subject. It is possible, however, to make a few observations.

Where *the form of the expression* is concerned, formal features are actually, speaking in linguistic terms, either "prosodic" or "paralinguistic" features. Such features are usually seen as adding an attitudinal colouring and thereby modulating the statement where they occur (for example, tone of voice), or as serving to clarify the structure of the things said by a kind of punctuation (for example, pausing), or both.[11]

So it is not surprising that formal features on the physical and the sign-sequence levels have precisely that type of effect. Let me give two simple examples.

Ekelöf's "But Somewhere Else" is an unrhymed poem. (This is a formal feature on the sign-sequence level, for the lack of rhymes can be deduced from the properties of the corresponding sign-sequence.) If the poem is seen against the background of its original context of publication, that formal feature is important for the general atmosphere surrounding the poem. Rhyme had no strong position in Swedish poetry in the 1950s. In ambitious literary contexts, the use of rhyme can probably be said to have given a slightly archaizing impression, and in *Strountes* we find rhyming verse only in two demonstratively parodic poems. It is easy to understand that the use of rhyme in "But Somewhere Else" would have affected the reader's impression of the poem in an unwanted manner.

No full stop is used in the poem, and that too is a formal feature on the sign-sequence level. Since the poem marks the beginning of a new sentence by other means, it is easy to see what it would have looked like *with* full stops. (In the version below – a slight modification of Bly's translation – I also indicate the unfinished character of the last sentence by inserting three dots.)

> 1　But somewhere else I have learned
> 　　the gruesomeness of hell:
> 　　Here is the smile of hell.
> 　　Here minutes and seconds exist
> 5　and the bright border between sea and sky.
> 　　Here the short disaster exists and the short outburst of joy.
> 　　But you, where are you, sorrow,
> 　　which one could throw oneself into the sea to find?
> 　　Night comes and the moon rises.
> 10　I open all the windows.
> 　　I know that she by my side loves me
> 　　but is it really she ...

Inserting full stops makes the poem's structure clearer to the reader. The things said become more distinctly articulated, and so it is a little easier to reconstruct the poem's communicative content. In this instance, such augmented clarity appears – at least to me – an aesthetic impairment. The paucity of punctuation marks in the authentic version gives the poem a more opaque character, consonant with the elusiveness of the experience sought by the speaker. The sparing punctuation makes it more laborious for the reader to find the relevant connections.

His attempts to do so have parallels with the speaker's striving to overcome fragmentation and find connections; perhaps that helps the reader to some extent to enter into the speaker's situation. Seen in that light, the lack of full stops appears aesthetically meaningful. As regards the classification of the effect, the feature's role may no doubt be said to be at once that of modulating and that of punctuating (or rather, in this case, of *not* punctuating, of making the structure *less* evident).

The form of the thought (formal properties on the level of the communicative content) is also important for the clarity or imprecision of the things depicted or for the impression in general. Let us consider two simple examples of formal features on the level of the communicative content.

When I commented on Ekelöf's poem in the last chapter, I tried to demonstrate that it is, in various ways, calculated to make a fragmentary impression. Of course, the sign-sequence is not in itself fragmentary; the poem's fragmentary character emerges only when one reconstructs its communicative content.

If one wishes to expunge the impression of a fragment, one has to change the meaning, the communicative content, radically. (To change the form of the communicated thought, one will naturally always have to alter the verbal meaning at least to some extent.) That would make the poem clearer and change its general atmosphere – and obviously risk destroying essential qualities in it.

In the last chapter, I also pointed to the extensive use of antitheses and contrasts in Ekelöf's poem. That, too, is a formal property on the level of the communicative content. To establish an antithesis one cannot merely study the sign sequence – one has to understand the meaning of the words. And obviously one cannot remove an antithesis without at least some alteration to the linguistic meaning.

How Does the Literary Form Come to Affect Us?

I have said that the literary form affects our impression of a poem, a short story, a novel, and so on. And I have maintained that by and large this happens in the same way as when the communicated thoughts affect us: the effect is the result of focusings, reflections, applications.

The analysis implies that literary form affects us through the (normally unconscious) thoughts that it inspires in us. That is not a new idea; on the other hand, it is neither self-evident nor generally accepted. I shall say a few words about this.

The container metaphor forms the basis of traditional thinking about literary form (as of much other traditional literary theory). The literary container has a form. (The author designed the container.) The reader comes in contact with the form and is affected by it. Normally, the mechanisms behind its influence on the reader are not accounted for, but one is given the impression that the form acts as a stimulus more or less automatically releasing a response in her.

A classic example of this type of thinking is Edgar Allan Poe's essay "The Philosophy of Composition" (1846), where Poe gives a description of the principles he (allegedly) followed in composing his poem "The Raven" (1845). Poe tells us what effects he wished to produce on the reader and describes how he chose words and combinations of sounds to create precisely those results. He seems to assume that given combinations of sounds have fixed psychological effects, the same for all readers.

More interesting, but less obvious, is literary formalism's dependence on this type of thinking. According to Roman Jakobson, for example, poetry is characterized, above all, by the self-focusing nature of the poetic text. The text draws attention to its own structuring (described by Jakobson in an innovative, extremely detailed manner), which affords satisfaction to the reader (through mechanisms left unexplained).[12] Jakobson implicitly takes it for granted that the literary text is a kind of object, and that its properties admit of objective description. When describing the structure of the text, he implicitly expects all properties distinguished by his system of description to be genuine properties of the object. (Jakobson also introduces no distinction between properties that are significant and properties that are insignificant from a literary point of view; he appears to take all textual properties that his system of description allows us to discern as significant.) One gains the impression that the reader is thought to perceive the properties described unconsciously and to be affected by them. Jakobson does not discuss how this influence operates; therefore, the effects appear to be conceived as automatic.

In reality, the situation is undoubtedly far more complex. I.A. Richards had already found, when examining actual reader reactions to given poems in *Practical Criticism* (1929), that readers vary not only in their ability to apprehend form but also in their reactions to the formal features. For that reason, among others, Richards regarded such things as artistically significant acoustic features of a poem not as objective properties of the text but as projections of the reader's impression onto the objective sound material. And he spoke of the reader's impression as if it were the result of a cognitive and emotional processing rather than an automatic response: "the rhythm which we admire, which we seem to detect actually *in* the sounds, and which we seem to respond to, is something which we only *ascribe* to them and is, actually, a rhythm of the mental activity through which we apprehend not only the sound of the words but their sense and feeling. The mysterious glory which seems to inhere in the sound of certain lines is a projection of the thought and emotion they evoke, and the peculiar satisfaction they seem to give *to the ear* is a reflection of the adjustment *of our feelings* which has been momentarily achieved."[13]

Today, when we have the intellectual framework of cognitive psychology for support, it should seem a natural idea that, principally, cognitive processing mediates between the registering of a linguistic sign-sequence and the experience of form.[14] Reuven Tsur's detailed study of subtle formal effects in his *Towards a Theory of Cognitive Poetics* (1992), for instance, builds throughout on the idea of "cognitive processes underlying the response."[15] Tsur's work could be seen as a most noteworthy development of the perspective found in the passage quoted from Richards.

What Is More Important:
Form or Communicated Thought?

The reader reconstructs and reacts to the communicated complex of thoughts and to the literary form. Both are parts of the basis of her literary experience, and so, of course, they must be suitably adjusted to one another. The form should, in Richards's words, work in "close cooperation" with the meaning, "modifying it and being modified by it."[16]

Here it may seem natural to ask, how important is the form for the experience of a literary text, and how important is the communicative content? When one reflects on that question, it is even more necessary to distinguish between expressional and conceptional form.

I myself would say that the communicative content, the communicated complex of thoughts, normally plays a far bigger and more fundamental role for the literary experience than does expressional form (visual, acoustic, rhythmic, and other such effects). It is not, however, difficult to find instances of other assessments. "In ordinary speech," says psychoanalyst Gilbert Rose in a well-known treatment of aesthetic form, "sense comes first and sound is subordinated. In the case of a poem, meaning per se is its least important element and paraphrasing it for 'meaning' inevitably destroys the poem."[17] Moreover, it varies from text to text, and to some extent also from reader to reader, how much importance it appears natural to attach to expressional form and communicative content respectively (expressional form normally plays a bigger role in poetry than in prose).

So much for expressional form. As regards conceptional form, I have analysed it as an aspect of the communicated thought complex. While expressional form, as I see it, mainly helps to create cohesion and atmosphere, conceptional form constitutes the very perspective in which we mentally view the state of affairs described.

Since conceptional form is itself an aspect of the communicative content, it would be senseless to ask "How important are the respective roles of conceptional form and communicative content for the experience of literature?" It is meaningful, however, to pose a slightly different question: "How important a role do the communicated thoughts play, in their concrete shape, and how important a role is played by the state of affairs described?"

In that connection, I would like to emphasize strongly the importance of the concrete conceptional form of the thought. In Ekelöf's poem, the naked state of affairs is that a man, with a loving woman by his side, finds himself in a place affording pleasant but limited experiences, and that he opens all the windows when the night comes and the moon rises. That complex state of affairs is not in itself especially efficient as a releaser of impressions and experiences. Only the special perspectives introduced by the conceptional form, by the communicated thoughts *in their wholly specific shape*, turn the description into a productive starting point for a literary experience.

10 Traditional Ideas about Literary Form

The Container Metaphor and the Talk of Literary Form

In the last chapter I said that what we call literary form is, in reality, the (artistically significant?) obligatory non-representational properties of the physical sign-object, of the linguistic sign-sequence, and of the communicative content. I also explained how form enters into the literary process and how form is related to thought and feeling. In addition, I gave an analysis, in general terms, of the literary function of form.

The features I discussed are in fact normally spoken of as formal. In several other respects, however, my view of literary form diverges from current opinion. In this chapter, I shall present for discussion some crucial points in the traditional outlook on literary form and its purpose. My principal aim is to clarify and defend the analysis of literary form propounded in the last chapter.

The thinking about literary form often takes philosophical concepts of form as its point of departure.[1] Here, however, I shall leave the concept's philosophical content aside. Behind the philosophical and critical concepts of form lies the more mundane concept. In my opinion, it is just that concept which is the natural starting point if one wishes to describe and explain the traditional thinking about literary form.

We can say of all physical objects that they possess some form or other. What we are referring to, then, is the external shape defined by the object's contours. (For some forms we have standard linguistic designations: "circular," "cubical," and so on.[2] When characterizing more irregular forms, we create descriptions from case to case.) The basic reference of our everyday concept of form is, as I see it, an object's form in this simple sense, what I shall call *physical form*.[3]

A literary text, however, is not a physical object, and so it has no physical form.[4] Literary texts possess form in a metaphorical sense, not in an altogether literal one.[5]

In fact, it is quite common to use the everyday concept of form in a transferred sense. We may speak not only of the form of a literary text, but also of forms of social intercourse or of the form of a logical deduction. Behind this lies the well-known human propensity for thinking about difficult and indistinct phenomena using the analogy of tractable and familiar ones. In this case, it makes us talk of abstract entities – literary texts, social intercourse, logical deductions – as if they were concrete objects: physical things with a physical form.[6]

In common parlance, thus, we speak of the literary text as if it were an object (analogous to a physical object) possessing a form (analogous to a physical form). The reflection of this usage in aesthetic theory is the view of form explicitly advocated by Theodore Meyer Greene in *The Arts and the Art of Criticism* (1940): "Every work of art exists in some medium, possesses some form, and, if it has any artistic merit whatever, has some expressed content. ... The 'matter' of a work of art is that in it which has been expressively organized. The 'form' of a work of art is the expressive organization of its matter. The 'content' of a work of art is that which finds artistic expression through such formal organization of its matter."[7]

The work of art, then, according to Greene, is an object that exists in a certain medium. (As regards the literary text, it is a *verbal* object; it is *made of language, of words*.)[8] The artistic object has been given a certain form; in addition, the object has a content. Obviously the container metaphor lies behind these ideas: the conscious or unconscious fiction that meaning can be deposited and transported in, for instance, a verbal container.[9]

It follows from the transportation and container metaphors, and from the possibility of transferring the form concept from concrete to abstract phenomena, that the literary work can be said to have a form. This is also reflected in Greene's analysis. However, he ignores the fact that the systems of metaphors employed make it possible to ascribe a form to the content as well. The meaning is to be conceived as (or: analogous to) a physical substance enclosed in a material container. But a physical substance always has some form or other. Hence it must be possible to say that the aesthetic content possesses a form.

Such a mode of expression is in fact in common use. According to ordinary critical parlance based on the transportation and container metaphors, Ekelöf's "But Somewhere Else" is written in the first-person form. And that is not a fact pertaining to the linguistic expressions – the first-person form is an aspect of conceptional form, of the form of the content.[10] Some other relatively well known ideas about literary form also reflect the circumstance that both the linguistic container (the verbal expression) and its content (the thought complex, the meaning) possess a form. The difference between container and content form is, for example, no doubt of fundamental importance for the distinction between "outer" and "inner" form common in the German tradition.[11] And when Louis Hjelmslev distinguished between "form" and "substance" in connection with both the linguistic expression and the linguistic content – a practice that later influenced narratology – that too indirectly reflected the fact that both container and content are traditionally conceived as having a form.[12]

Greene's analysis illustrates the fundamental structure of traditional ideas about literary form. If one starts from the transportation and container metaphors and proceeds consistently, one inevitably arrives at an analysis like Greene's (supplemented with the idea of the form of the content, of conceptional form).

Is there anything wrong with these traditional ideas, and if so, what?

Let me say, first, that I find the concept "form" unobjectionable in itself. It can be applied in a literal sense to aspects of physical objects; there is certainly nothing wrong with that. It can also be used metaphorically about abstract phenomena in many different contexts: about forms of social intercourse, about the form of a logical deduction, and so forth. On the whole, such metaphorical equating of abstract and concrete entities probably does more good than harm.

But metaphors do not provide the most correct picture of reality that we are capable of creating. Replacing a theory formulated in metaphorical terms with a more literal account is therefore a theoretical improvement.

The traditional ideas about literary form are founded in metaphor: they build on the transportation and container metaphors. Literary form is conceived, on one hand, as the form of the container presupposed by the container metaphor, and on the other, as the form of that container's content. We know, however, that containers like these cannot exist. There can be no objects that are at once physical (and hence possible to read), made up of words (which are, in actual fact, abstract entities), and containing meaning (another abstract phenomenon). The very idea of such a physical-abstract mixture is illogical.

Moreover, the picture of linguistic communication implied by the transportation and container metaphors is also hopelessly misleading in other important respects. For instance, the meaning of a text is basically thought of as *one*, homogeneous object – that which is encased in the container. Interpretation is conceptualized, ultimately, as *one*, homogeneous activity: that of retrieving the container's content. The model assigns no meaning-shaping role to the addressee: her business seems to be, simply, to recover a prefabricated meaning. This is only one example; there are many others.

I can see, therefore, two weighty reasons for accepting the basic analysis of "literary form" that I put forward in the last chapter, and for rejecting traditional ideas about literary form. Unlike the traditional picture, my analysis is logically consistent: I do not rely on objects possessing logically incompatible properties. And in contrast to the traditional ideas, my analysis can be incorporated into a modern and reasonable overall picture of linguistic communication.

The Traditional Understanding of the Concept of Literary Form

The concept of literary form has the reputation of being extraordinarily problematical. "It would be easy," says René Wellek, "to collect hundreds of definitions of 'form' and 'structure' from contemporary critics and aestheticians and to show that they contradict each other so radically and basically that it may be best to abandon the terms."[13] In the light of this, one may wonder whether I did not grossly oversimplify the situation when outlining a basic structure in the traditional thinking about literary form.

"Form" may possess a marked multiplicity of meaning. But the concept is not, in my opinion, impenetrable or unstructured. Basically, form is one of two things. Either it is physical form: the shape defined by the contours of a physical object. (In a figurative sense, form is also the analogue of physical form in an abstract entity: the structuring of the "matter" met with in the abstract "object.") Or else, "form" denotes the forming principle responsible for the emergence of physical form, or of abstract form, as it did as early as in Plato and Aristotle.[14] (This second use of the term, which I have neglected in the foregoing, has played, and still plays, a considerable role in criticism. It is conspicuous in connection with concepts like "organic form" and "inner form," but it also turns up in the discussion in other contexts.)[15]

Other, more specialized meanings of "form" can be seen as variants of these two main types.[16]

There is certainly a genuine multiplicity in connection with the concept of form; the two main meanings do indeed have many ramifications. In addition, however, the fact that the concept of form has so universal an application creates a somewhat unjustified impression of polysemy. A form may be ascribed to practically everything that can be thought or spoken of, whether abstract or concrete. No wonder, then, that form appears to be something multifarious and evasive.

Where artistic and literary form is concerned, the situation is further complicated by the fact that traditional aesthetic thinking about form combines two different systems of metaphors and two distinctions. Properly speaking, form contrasts with matter (or materials). Each physical object is, of necessity, made up of some material or other and has some form. Through metaphorical analogy, this is true also of every abstract object. When seen in the light of the transportation and container metaphors, however, artistic and literary works possess not only matter and form but also a content. So the aesthetician has three interrelated concepts to consider ("form," "matter," "content"), not just two ("form," "matter").

Some theorists (like Greene) manage to keep this complicated model together. They appear, more or less clearly, to conceive of the work as a container, composed of a special material, supplied with a definite form, and enclosing a determinate content. For most theorists, however, it seems, rather, as if we are concerned with a double model: with (at least) both a "form"/"matter" and a "form"/"content" distinction.[17] They normally imagine that form as opposed to matter must be something different from form as opposed to content. The natural opposite of the content appears to be the container enveloping it. And so they are led to identify literary form with the verbal container encasing the communicative content.

That identification is quite common. Wladyslaw Tatarkiewicz, for example, writes: "In verbal art, form and content were separated because only in this art do they form two different, clearly divided, and very dissimilar strata, viz., words and things (*verba* and *res*). Here the form is linguistic, the content material. The reader is presented directly only with words by means of which he may indirectly represent things."[18]

It is not true that words are "presented directly" – in contrast to the printer's ink and the white paper, words are abstractions. Moreover, Tatarkiewicz confuses the *subject-matter* of verbal compositions with their *contents* – the contents (or meanings) are of course not material in nature, not "things." But this is of little consequence in my present context. What I want to point out is that Tatarkiewicz identifies the form with the linguistic expression, while he lets the things meant constitute the content. (Just like Greene, Tatarkiewicz ignores the fact that we normally also ascribe a form to the content.)

The way of thinking represented by Tatarkiewicz is undoubtedly prevalent among literary scholars and critics. As I have just indicated, I see it as based on a misunderstanding of the underlying metaphors. It builds on the container metaphor and exhibits the inevitable weaknesses. But it is problematic in other ways as well. Since its notion of form is, in reality, a conflation of the concepts "form" and "matter," it is beset with inner tensions that are difficult to overcome. Nor does the model agree with everyday language based on the container metaphor. In common parlance, both the linguistic expression and its content are in fact spoken of as if they each possessed a form and a material substance.

Standard Criticism of the Form/Content Distinction

René Wellek has seen the latter problem and delivered well-known criticism of the idea that a literary text consists partly of form (linguistic expressions) and partly of content. He starts precisely by demonstrating that both the linguistic expressions and their contents are usually spoken of as if they comprised both a form and a material substance.

> If we understand by content the ideas and emotions conveyed in a work of literature, the form would include all linguistic elements by which contents are expressed. But if we examine this distinction more closely, we see that content implies some elements of form: e.g. the events told in a novel are parts of the content, while the way in which they are arranged into a "plot" is part of the form. Dissociated from this way of arrangement they have no artistic effect whatsoever. The common remedy proposed and widely used by Germans, i.e. the introduction of the term "inner form," which originally dates back to Plotinus and Shaftesbury, is merely complicating matters, as the boundary line between inner and outer form remains completely obscure. It must simply be admitted that the manner in which events are arranged in a plot is part of the form. Things become even more disastrous for the traditional concepts when we realize that even in the language, commonly considered part of the form, it is necessary to distinguish between words in themselves, aesthetically indifferent, and the manner in which individual words make up units of sound and meaning, aesthetically effective.[19]

Though Wellek has a point here, it consists, in reality, only in the indication of the troublesome inner tensions in Tatarkiewicz-like conceptions of literary form. Wellek's criticism is not relevant in connection with models like Greene's which respect the genuine implications of the container metaphor in thinking about literary form (and therefore accept as unproblematical the duality that worries Wellek). Least of all does Wellek's criticism prove that the traditional concepts "form" and "content" are deficient in themselves, i.e., impossible to define in a consistent and productive manner.

Wellek is not aware, however, of the limited scope of his observations. On the contrary, he takes them as a justification for stating that we had better stop employing the concepts "form" and "content" altogether. And he suggests that we should, instead, introduce a different pair of terms: "materials" and "structure." In the words of Wellek, "It would be better to rechristen all the aesthetically indifferent elements 'materials,' while the manner in which they acquire aesthetic efficacy may be called 'structure.' This distinction is by no means a simple renaming of the old pair, content and form. It cuts right across the old boundary lines. 'Materials' include elements formerly considered part of the content, and parts formerly considered formal. 'Structure' is a concept including both content and form so far as they are organized for aesthetic purposes. The work of art is, then, considered as a whole system of signs, or structure of signs, serving a specific aesthetic purpose."[20]

Wellek's distinction is, in fact, simply a distinction between form ("structure") and matter ("materials").[21] The literary object (comprising both container and content) is supposed to be made up of different sorts of materials and to have a certain form. Only the form is perceived as being aesthetically relevant; the materials are said to be "aesthetically indifferent."

As we can see, Wellek wishes to eliminate the concept of literary form, to replace it with other categories. In principle, I have no objections to that; my own analysis of the term in the last chapter also resulted in a considerably altered conception of form. I am, however, critical of Wellek's (still not obsolete)[22] standpoint (and not only of his arguments for it). My most important reservation concerns Wellek's markedly formalistic attitude. Of the three interrelated concepts "matter"–"form"–"content," Wellek in fact retains "matter" and "form," seeing only form as aesthetically significant. Wellek's terminology is thus specially designed to suit an aesthetic standpoint that we would, in my opinion, be justified in calling extreme.

Moreover, Wellek casts doubt on the value of the distinction between "outer" and "inner" form. Wrongly, to my mind, he tends to see it as impossible to determine. As a result, Wellek's analysis comes to neglect the difference in literary function between expressional form (contributing to the articulation of communicative content, and also interacting with it and putting it in a special light) and conceptional form (being a highly important aspect of the communicative content itself).

Wellek's criticism of the form-content dichotomy can be said to amount to the contention that there is no meaningful way of drawing the distinction. For my part, I claimed that Wellek merely points to weaknesses in the most usual conception of literary form and literary content, the one that is here called the Tatarkiewicz model. Wellek's objections affect neither the Greene model (otherwise certainly not immune to criticism) nor the concepts of form and content that I myself constructed in the last chapter. I also took the opportunity to make objections to Wellek's counterdististinction, that between materials and structure.

Wellek has been a particularly prominent critic of the concept of form. There is, however, a widespread feeling among theorists of literature and the arts that the distinction between form and content is suspect, and as a consequence so too are the concepts "form" and "content." It is often said, and generally believed, that form and content are, properly speaking, inseparable. In "Concepts of Form and Structure in Twentieth-Century Criticism" (1958), for instance, Wellek speaks of "the inseparability and reciprocity of form and content" and takes it as evidencing the claim that "the old distinction between form and content is untenable." He adduces, approvingly, a quotation from Harold Osborne where it is said that form without content would be sound without meaning, and that content without form is a notion devoid of substance, "for when it is expressed in different language it is something different that is being expressed."[23]

Precisely the literary text's supposed lack of paraphrasability is usually in the forefront when it is argued that form and content are inseparable. John Peck and Martin Coyle write: "Strictly speaking, form and content are inseparable: there is no paraphrasable content in a text which we can separate from the way in which it is presented."[24]

In my opinion, however, it is an unclear and somewhat misleading idea that form and content are inseparable. There is some truth in it, but that truth could be formulated in better ways.

In fact, it is easy to see that the thesis "Form and content are inseparable" is far from unequivocal. "Form," "content," and "inseparable" can have several meanings. I shall point to some particularly important imprecisions involved.

First: the concept of form is in fact applied to several different entities entering into the literary process. Reasonably, their respective "forms" – the "form" of the linguistic expression, the "form" of the communicative content, and so on – play different roles in the process. It appears well advised, then, to keep at least expressional form and conceptional form apart.

Second: it is not at all clear what the word "content" refers to. What I call "meaning" or "communicative content" may seem to be the most natural candidate. Sometimes, however, theorists rather seem to have *the content of the reader's literary experience* in view.

Third: what is entailed in the inseparableness of form and content? This question requires a more extensive discussion.

One possibility seems to be to understand the word literally: literary form cannot exist without literary content, nor literary content without form. That idea is debatable, but in my present context there is no need to take up space with a close examination of its tenability. Even if form and content were in fact inseparable in the sense indicated, that would not make the form/content distinction unjustified. Form and matter are clearly inseparable in the required way: form is always the form *of* something, and everything that exists must have *some* form. But this hardly makes the form/matter distinction suspect. And I cannot see why a corresponding inseparability of literary form and literary content would make the literary form/content distinction questionable from a theoretical point of view.

So what do Osborne, Wellek, Peck, and Coyle mean by saying that form and content are "inseparable"? I believe that their basic idea could be rendered thus: "It is true that one can, analytically, distinguish between form and content, but from an aesthetic point of view such a distinction is pointless." Then the reasons for finding the distinction aesthetically pointless may vary.

Let us look at Osborne's criticism of the form/content distinction, the criticism that Wellek quoted with approval in 1958. Osborne writes: "The form of a poem, the prosodic structure, the rhythmic interplay, the characteristic idiom, are nothing any more when abstracted from the content of meaning; for language is not language but noise except in so far as it expresses meaning. So, too, the content without the form is an unreal abstraction without concrete existence, for when it is expressed in different language it is something different that is being expressed. The poem must be perceived as a whole to be perceived at all. There can be no conflict between form and content ... for neither has existence without the other and abstraction is murder to both."[25]

At least three arguments can be discerned in the Osborne passage. One is that form and content are inseparable, that they must always be found together. (Cf. "the content without the form is an unreal abstraction without concrete existence"; "The poem must be perceived as a whole to be perceived at all"; "There can be no conflict between form and content ... for neither has existence without the other.") I find that argument irrelevant. As I pointed out above, apropos of the form/matter distinction, such inseparability in no way shows that the underlying distinction is pointless. Precisely the same things could be said about a spot of yellow paint: "The paint spot without the form is an unreal abstraction without concrete existence"; "The paint spot must be perceived as a whole to be perceived at all"; "There can be no conflict between the form and the paint ... for neither has existence without the other." And correct or not, such observations clearly do not prove that the distinction between form and matter, between the paint spot's contours and the paint making up the spot, is pointless.

But Osborne has more arguments. In speaking of expressional form ("the prosodic structure") he says that it obtains as "nothing," just "noise," if imagined separate from its meaning-conveying function (i.e., from its representational aspect). I find that statement exaggerated. True, sound structures and such may be elements of expressional form as I define it. And seeing them as parts of expressional form is certainly to focus on their non-semantic aspect, to perceive them as sound. But in my opinion, Osborne is wrong in describing them, in their purely acoustic aspect, as "noise." His idea seems to be that the non-semantic properties of the linguistic expression, the ones supposed by him to constitute form tout court, are in actual fact without positive value from an aesthetic point of view. As I tried to show in the last chapter, however, the non-representational properties of the linguistic expression – phonetic and others – can add an important dimension to the reader's impression of a text. They are not necessarily devoid of aesthetic significance; Osborne's objection appears unjustified.

A third argument of Osborne's is that it is impossible to imagine the content apart from its actual form, for "when it is expressed in different language it is something different that is being expressed." His idea appears to be that the literary text cannot be paraphrased. If the exact linguistic expression is changed, the result will be a different communicative content.

The argument, as I understand it, says that an alteration of expressional form inevitably leads to a change in communicative content. And from this Osborne draws, I think, the conclusion that the distinction between form and content is mistaken in the sense of being aesthetically pointless. But I cannot see that the conclusion follows from the premise. The communicative content, with its quite individual character, is in all cases an aesthetically relevant phenomenon. And in examining or discussing it we examine or discuss something different from either expressional or conceptual form. So in our thinking about literature we will obviously always need the concept "communicative content," and the distinction between form and (communicative) content, or some other conceptual tools capable of being used for the same purpose.

Form, Content, and Paraphrasability

The last section was a critique of standard objections to the form/content distinction. Above all, I endeavoured to refute the arguments of perhaps the most notable opponent of the distinction, René Wellek.[26] As for myself, I cannot find that the criticism from Wellek, Osborne, and others has any real justification. The talk of "form" and "content" is no doubt unsatisfactory on many counts – not least because of its debts to the container metaphor – but it *can* be given a reasonable meaning. And the terms conceptualize important factors in connection with literary communication, so we cannot very well rid ourselves of them without adequate replacements. (Something that Wellek clearly saw.)

In my opinion most criticism of the form/content distinction overshoots the mark. But having said that, I wish to add that it is easy to perceive an important and commendable motive behind the criticism: a strong desire to emphasize that literature must not be understood reductively as a communication of assertions, that an unreservedly cognitivist view of literature is untenable.

There is one popular conception of literature – cf. Searle's ideas, discussed in chapter 5 – according to which the purpose of a literary text is to make some significant statement about reality. If one entertains that idea, one naturally sees it as a central task of literary analysis to discern and evaluate the message conveyed by the text. Practically all professional students of literature, however, including myself, consider that type of literary aesthetics indefensible. The usual way of dismissing theories of this kind is to say something along the lines of: "Form and content are inseparable. The content of the text can only be expressed by means of the very words actually used in the text. In attempting to paraphrase a literary text, to formulate its 'message' using other verbal means, one in reality distorts the text's content." This idea can be found in Greene,[27] and it acquires its classic formulation in Cleanth Brooks's essay "The Heresy of Paraphrase" (1947). Since then it has become ubiquitous; here, we have encountered it in Osborne and in Peck and Coyle.

In principle, I agree that one cannot reformulate a literary text without distorting its content. But it is important, I believe, to ask oneself *in what sense* this is true, and *for what reason* literary texts do not, in the final analysis, allow themselves to be paraphrased.

Let me first point out that in reality minor changes in a literary text do *not necessarily* affect its meaning. In chapter 9, I played with the idea of Ekelöf having put full stops (and three finishing dots) into "But Somewhere Else":

> 1   But somewhere else I have learned
>   the gruesomeness of hell:
>   Here is the smile of hell.
>   Here minutes and seconds exist
> 5   and the bright border between sea and sky.
>   Here the short disaster exists and the short outburst of joy.
>   But you, where are you, sorrow,
>   which one could throw oneself into the sea to find?
>   Night comes and the moon rises.
> 10   I open all the windows.
>   I know that she by my side loves me
>   but is it really she ...

That would have changed some linguistic details but not, as far as I can see, the poem's verbal meaning, its *communicative* content. So one *may* in fact alter the (expressional) form without automatically modifying the (communicative) content.

In my earlier analysis of this alternative version of the poem I pointed out that the impression would nevertheless be influenced in an aesthetically significant mannner. (I maintained that the introduction of full stops added precision, and that it thereby dispersed some of the poem's aesthetically important opacity.) So the change in expressional form here does, in a certain sense, involve an alteration of the "content." Not of the *communicative content*, however, but of *the content of the (competent) reader's experience of the poem*.

The thesis that form and content interact is actually often underpinned with references to the content of the literary experience, not to the communicative content. Brooks says, in one of the most crucial passages of his article about paraphrasability, that we cannot "reproduce the effect of the total context in a condensed prose statement."[28] The "effect" Brooks is referring to is not what I call "communicative meaning" but precisely the content of the reading experience, the effect on the reader. According to Brooks, in changing the linguistic expression we alter either the communicative content or, at least, the content of the literary experience. In Brooks's opinion, an extensive paraphrase of a poem could approximate the poem's verbal import but not such things as its "tension" and "dramatic force."[29]

Here, I think, we are at the heart of the paraphrasability problem. In altering a literary text, even in such subtle respects as that of expressional form, we run the risk of influencing the literary experience.[30] This is due to the presentationality of the literary text. The text (the linguistic expression together with the communicative content indicated by it) is created in order to be experienced and to give rise to associations. No text that in *any* respect differs from (the authentic version of) Ekelöf's "But Somewhere Else" can be *completely equivalent as a starting point for associations.* No other text can be reasonably expected to release exactly the same associations in a reader. If formulations in the poem are altered, the point of departure for the reader's associations will be different. It follows from this that a literary text does not allow of "translation" into an even marginally different sign-sequence without potential consequences for the text's artistic effectiveness.[31]

I wholly concur in the censure that Brooks and others have passed on cognitivist reductionism in the literary field. But in my opinion that criticism affects neither the concept "form," nor the concept "content," nor the distinction between them. It is true that the cognitivist reductionist operates with the concept of content and with a distinction between form and content. But the notions of form and content themselves should not be blamed for his lack of understanding of the concepts and their roles.

Form and Aesthetic Enjoyment

It is not only conceptions of what form is, and of the form/content distinction, that make up the traditional ideas about literary form. The tradition also comprises several more or less distinct notions of the function of literary form.

In the last chapter, I argued that literary form modifies the communicative content or, at least, the reader's impression of the literary text. So far, my convictions largely conform with the traditional view. In other respects, the agreement may seem less. Above all, I should like to comment on the relation between my standpoint and two rather specific and well-known ideas about literary form. One is the idea that the essential function of literary form (apart from its constituting and organizing role) is to afford aesthetic enjoyment. The other is the notion, inspired by psychoanalysis, that literary form (apart from its constituting and organizing role) is essentially a defence mechanism or a testimony of control. I shall devote a separate section to each of these two ideas.

Aesthetic brilliance is not infrequently perceived as the principal merit of a literary text, and literary form as being decisive for the aesthetic impression. This has been the case throughout the twentieth century, and remains so.[32] Thus in this chapter we have been presented with Wellek's insistence that only the structure of a literary text is aesthetically relevant. A contemporary exponent of this type of idea is Reuven Tsur. According to him, the poetic text offers its reader "aesthetically significant structures of aesthetically neutral materials."[33] The affinity to Jakobson's structuralism and to Wellek's analysis in terms of materials and structure is clear (and Tsur in no way conceals this).

In Tsur's version of the theory, poetry manipulates the normal functioning of our cognitive processes, which results, most importantly, in a heightened degree of awareness in us. Poetry forces us to experience the world in an unfamiliar manner; our habitual perspective on reality is suspended. We come to see things with the freshness of a first encounter. On this point, Tsur concurs with the early-twentieth-century movement known as Russian formalism; he quotes, with approbation, Viktor Šklovskij's famous statement in "Art as Technique" ("Iskusstvo kak priem," 1916): "Habituation devours works, cloth[e]s, furniture, one's wife, and the fear of war. 'If the whole complex lives of many people go on unconsciously, then such lives are as if they had never been.' And art exists that one may recover the sensation of life; it exists to make one feel things, to make the stone *stony*. The purpose of art is to impart the sensation of things as they are perceived and not as they are known. The technique of art is to make the object 'unfamiliar,' to make forms difficult, to increase the difficulty and length of perception because the process of perception is an aesthetic end in itself and must be prolonged."[34]

Tsur's idea, then, is that literary form restructures our mode of cognitive processing, thereby liberating us from the indifference and routine of habitual perception and enabling us to experience things aesthetically. This idea of the aesthetic role of form is often encountered in literary contexts. It is far from being the only one,[35] but it is the standpoint that I shall use as an example.

At first sight, Tsur's view of the function of poetry (or literature)[36] differs sharply from the cognitive-emotive model introduced here. I do not believe, however, that aesthetic-formalist theories like this one are incompatible with the model. I rather regard them as actualizations of one of the many possibilities it keeps open.

I want to seize this opportunity to emphasize that my theory of literature and literary experience in no way implies a contesting of the existence or importance of what is commonly called aesthetic experience. I do not for a moment wish to deny that we, as readers of high-quality literature, have the impression of encountering a text – a separate, autonomous object – possessing an inexplicable fascination that, so we feel, could not very well have been produced by other means. As Eliot has it: "The effect of a work of art upon the person who enjoys it is an experience different in kind from any experience not of art."[37]

To content oneself with saying this, however, would be to see literary experience in a one-sidedly phenomenological perspective. It would be like confining oneself, concerning the rainbow as a natural phenomenon, to the observation that we do in fact sometimes perceive rainbows and that seeing a rainbow is a very special experience (of which perceptive descriptions "from within" can be given). What physical and psychological processes underlie the visual experience of a rainbow is of course also an interesting question. And correspondingly one may inquire into the processes behind aesthetic experiences. To do so is not to deny the existence of the experience, but to approach the phenomenon from the outside as it were. It is to ask not what it is like to have the experience, but what mechanisms make the experience possible. In my exposition in this book, I have been looking at literary experience both from within and from without. The cognitive-emotive model, however, is unequivocally formulated from the external point of view. The model offers an external perspective on the reaction that phenomenologically, to the reader herself, manifests itself as an aesthetic experience.

I by no means deny that we are confronted with distinctive and aesthetically fascinating structures when experiencing literary texts. But in my eyes, that fact itself raises several questions. In Richard Eldridge's words: "Some explanation is required of why human beings either do or ought to take an interest in unique organizations of complexities."[38]

In principle, two types of explanation are possible. One option is to maintain that people by nature gain pleasure from the experience of literary structures, that there is, so to speak, an innate biological mechanism that explains why the experience of aesthetic form is enjoyable to us. I myself, however, find it difficult to believe that in our biological equipment there is something as specialized as a specifically aesthetic drive or need. In this book I have assumed, instead, that literature caters, in some more or less complex way, to human needs familiar from other contexts in life. And I have imagined that cognitive processing on the reader's part normally intervenes between the communicative content and the satisfaction of the need. If the problems are seen in this perspective, further questions arise: What human needs may literature cater to? How is it possible for literature to satisfy those needs? And what does the reader do in her mediating cognitive processing? It is on this point that the cognitive-emotive model finds its place in my account, as does the discussion of the reader's focusings, reflections, and applications.

Aesthetic formalists often attempt to satify the need for explanations pointed out by Eldridge. Thus Tsur, assisted by Šklovskij, offers us the explanation that the aesthetic structures disautomatize perception. But of course that explanation, too, raises new questions. Even supposing that the explanation is true as far as it goes, we may ask: "Why do we find it valuable to 'recover the sensation of life,' to feel things, to experience the stoniness of the stone?"

Again, one possible answer is that owing to our biological constitution such types of experience do simply automatically release a sense of pleasure. I would, however, here as elsewhere, be more inclined to look for mediating cognitive processing. Experiencing things in an unusual way[39] may perhaps be satisfying because it reveals reality as full of new and interesting possibilities for the beholder. Think of the little child living in a world whose properties are largely unknown to it. The child devotes close attention to things that to us are trivial, testing them with hands and mouth in its search for their possible usefulness in satisfying some of the child's needs. A disautomatized seeing, a seeing where reality has regained something of its so to speak childish newness, is perhaps, among other things, a frame of mind where the world is (unconsciously) perceived as an exciting and potentially accommodating place full of as yet unexperienced possibilities for fulfilment. It would be possible to attempt to explain the undeniable fascination of "disautomatized" aesthetic perception along these or similar lines.

The suggested explanation is of course in itself speculative, and it does not matter much whether it is tenable or not. My reason for sketching it was merely to demonstrate that the cognitive-emotive model also has, in principle, the power to incorporate ideas such as Šklovskij's and Tsur's. Even an experience of pleasurable disautomatization could in principle be explained using the approach represented by the model.

Form and Mental Control

An external perspective on aesthetic experience is also provided by literary theory orientated towards psychoanalysis.[40]

It was Freud himself who first presented, in "Creative Writers and Day-Dreaming," a hypothesis about literary form based on psycho-analysis. Freud took it for granted that literary form could afford pleasure. He supposed that this benefit, in its turn, made the text attractive to the reader and enticed him into engaging in, and taking over, the fantasy offered him by the author. Form was therefore thought to give an "incentive bonus," a *fore-pleasure*."[41]

Freud's idea lives on, but later psychoanalytical theorists have also thought along other lines. Like Freud, however, they have mostly seen aesthetic form as a kind of ancillary phenomenon in the experience of art and literature. The essential thing is the fantasy content conveyed; form has an important but subordinate function.

Lesser, for example, distinguishes between three functions of literary form: "to give pleasure; to avoid or relieve guilt and anxiety; and to facilitate perception – to silhouette the material with the desired degree of clarity."[42] Thus Lesser sees clearly that form (presumably, concep-tional form) has a rational, organizing function. But he also regards form as a literary means of alleviating the reader's uneasiness about the fantasy material introduced. A well-poised form conveys the impression of order and control, the feeling that the perilous fantasy material has been brought under control and may be enjoyed without risk.[43] As Brian Rosebury far later formulated the same idea: "the aesthetic wholeness of art, its realised structures, offer a paradigm of control over desire."[44]

Holland has followed in Lesser's footsteps, but more resolutely maintained that form functions as a defence mechanism.[45] According to Holland, one of its many means of mitigation consists in making it possible to shift the reader's attention, to some extent, from the fantasy material to the form.[46] Similar views have been presented by Kofman.[47]

Such observations, too, are in principle easy to combine with my own analysis of the function of literary form. In fact, I already made use of related ideas ("The Problem of Tragic Pleasure," chapter 7). The author's control of the material – of language, of dispositional problems, of intellectual and emotional complications – is among the things that the reader may focus, reflect on, and apply. Consequently, form can give an effective impression of our ability to be master of our existence. A reader may concentrate on the power of combination and amalgamation demonstrated in the text, and perhaps, with satis-faction, experience a similar creative versatility as also being possible in her own relations with the world.[48]

Naturally, the literary text (the sign-sequence and the communicative content) is often formed with extraordinary skill and precision – Ekelöf's "But Somewhere Else" is a good example. In such cases, the text may appear as an almost superhuman creation through the masterly, many-layered control of sound and language and conflicting intellectual and emotional possibilities that it shows. At the same time, it is easy to identify it as the product of a human intellect.

In aesthetics orientated towards psychoanalysis, one encounters the related idea that the work of art gives the viewer an idealized picture of her own mind. Gilbert Rose has formulated it in the following manner: "In aesthetic form, the refined sensibility comes to appreciate an ideal standard of ego functioning: several ego activities operating harmoniously together, in a relatively autonomous and conflict-free manner. ... In the art work, the tension of irreconcilable inner forces is rendered dynamic and changing, on the one hand, yet resiliently contained, on the other. What is objectified in aesthetic form is a perceptual model of the smooth orchestration of the dual aspects of time, place, and person, in the light of reality and the self. As this is an *idealized* representation of the working of one's own mind, it has the effect of replenishing secondary narcissism and enhancing self-esteem."[49]

When Rosebury maintains that literary structures can "offer a paradigm of control over desire," or when Rose says that they may make one "appreciate an ideal standard of ego functioning," they must, in reason, tacitly assume that this is done via (unconscious) cognitive processing in the reader. The reader must be supposed to apprehend the content of the text, consider the perfection of the form, and perceive the possibility that her own mind can work equally well. So the perspective on the functions of literary form outlined in the last chapter can also accommodate these observations inspired by psychoanalysis.

In my view, then, literary form – expressional form, conceptional form – is among the things that the reader can focus, reflect on, and apply in order to modify her perspective on her own existence. This is obviously an idea with a wide range of possible applications. As we saw, my analysis can integrate notions as superficially varied as the idea that the function of form is to afford aesthetic enjoyment and that form enhances our self-esteem by presenting an idealized picture of the workings of our minds.

My characterization of the functions of literary form, presented in the last chapter and defended in the present one, has been formulated in rather general terms. De facto, however, the concept of form covers many types of phenomena, and these appear to have somewhat different effects. For that reason it is, I believe, hardly possible to find precise and unequivocal answers to the question of what literary form brings to the text and to the experience of literature. What I have attempted to do in chapters 9 and 10 is to point to the basic mechanisms underlying the operations of literary form and to some prominent functions of form.

Concluding Remarks:
On the Nature of Literature's
Autonomy

Introduction

In this book, I have presented a general theory of literature and literary experience comprising several components.

Its foundation is a pragmatics-based analysis of how linguistic communication operates. I contend that the originator forms a communicative intention and supplies her addressee with material indications (in the form of sound or writing) of what her communicative intention is. The addressee attempts to understand what the originator's communicative intention amounts to; in addition, he reacts to the things understood.

To that analysis of linguistic communication I have added an account of how literary communication differs from linguistic communication in general. I see the distinguishing character of literature in its presentationality, i.e., in the fact that the communicative content is implicitly meant to give rise to associations, not to inform or to convey directives.

In all essentials, these two components of the theory were already present in my earlier book *A Theory of Literary Discourse*. Here, I have supplemented them principally with an analysis of how cognitive, emotive, and formal elements interact in the reader's processing of the communicative content. I have supported my argument with explanations of concepts such as "thought," "emotion," "form," and so on, and with enquiries into the intellectual, emotional, and formal aspects of literature.

In my description of literary communication, I have systematically avoided basing my reasoning on the figurative language commonly used, i.e., on the transportation and container metaphors in their various guises. In many respects, my account has become a criticism of traditional ideas about literary communication and about the interaction of cognitive, emotional, and formal elements in verbal art. I have devoted a good deal of space to the clarification of the relationship between my analyses and more established ways of thinking.

In these respects, my work is finished. I would, however, like to conclude the book with an attempt to forestall a kind of criticism of my theory that lies near at hand. What I have in mind is the objection that the theory is reductionistic, that it disregards the autonomy of literature.

It is true that I have not undertaken to provide a real answer to the question of what gives literature its value, and that I have emphasized the fact that the reader's profit may be of many different kinds. But I have nevertheless repeatedly stressed that literature can have a cognitive-emotive value consisting in helping the reader to modify his perspective on life. One may ask: does not that idea unjustly involve literature in hopeless competition with such things as science and the immediate experience of reality?

In the light of the traditions of literary criticism and theory, such an objection is easy to understand. I cannot find it justified, however. The accusation of reductionism appears to me to be difficult to uphold if one reflects more closely on the problems at issue.

In my concluding remarks I shall first describe how the theory in this book is related to what might be called "the autonomy doctrine." Then I shall demonstrate that it is possible to reject the idea of literature having a purpose in itself without, for that reason, being forced to place oneself in a reductionistic position. Lastly, I shall compare my attitude to literature's autonomy and value problems with that of some other contemporary theorists.

On the Previous History of the Autonomy Doctrine

Being autonomous is, roughly, to be independent or self-governed. "Autonomous" goes back to the Greek word *autonomos* ("living according to its own laws"), a word formed, in its turn, from the words *autos* ("-self") and *nomos* ("law"). The terms "autonomous" and "autonomy" are used in several domains; their exact meaning varies. Even if one keeps to the literary field, the words have a small spectrum of interrelated meanings. Few ambitious attempts have been made to clarify the import of "autonomy" as employed in connection with literature and the other arts.[1] And I know of no real historical account of the use of the term in aesthetic contexts.[2]

It was in the eighteenth century that a clear idea of what we would nowadays call the autonomy of the aesthetic sphere came into existence. The century's most influential analysis of the distinctive nature of the aesthetic is found in Kant's third critique. As far as I understand, however, the emergence of the word "autonomy" as a technical aesthetic and literary term is a twentieth-century phenomenon connected with Russian formalism and its continuation, Prague structuralism.[3] Roman Jakobson's idea about the poetic function of language – i.e., about self-focusing language – as being dominant within poetry (or within literature as a whole?), an idea best known from his much later article "Linguistics and Poetics" (1960),[4] was in fact already launched early in the 1920s. It appears to have given rise, at that time, to the view that literary structures possess autonomous value, which was obviously taken to mean intrinsic value.[5]

Prague structuralism appears to have modified the radical view of literature's autonomy propounded by Russian formalism. Perhaps one could say that the idea of the *intrinsic value* of literary linguistic structures was largely transformed into an insistence on their *unique character*. According to Victor Erlich, Jakobson, among others, then came to see art as "a distinct mode of human endeavor, not wholly explicable in terms of other spheres of experience, yet closely related to them."[6] The same attitude is found in Jan Mukařovský's writings from the mid-1930s. In Mukařovský, however, the concept "autonomous sign" can be said to acquire the status of a technical term. For that reason among others, Mukařovský's aesthetics forms a natural starting point for an introduction to the autonomy doctrine such as I understand it.

One of Mukařovský's main ideas is that Saussure's linguistics also provides a model for the understanding of aesthetic phenomena. It must be possible to analyse the arts' production of signs within the framework of a general theory of signs, a "semiology" like the one heralded by Saussure. Not least in the essay "Art as a Semiological Fact" ("L'Art comme fait sémiologique," 1934, 1936), Mukařovský offers an account of the special semiological character of the arts.

Mukařovský wishes to regard an art work as a sign. In his thinking about signs he adopts the traditional idea (presented above)[7] according to which a sign is a phenomenon standing for something outside itself that constitutes its meaning. Mukařovský asks what, then, a work of art designates. He finds that an art work lacks really specific reference: its reference is "not distinctly determined."[8] This is a consequence of the fact that the work does not have a "communicative" function, as he calls it, but must be seen as "an *autonomous* sign."[9] There is, however, according to Mukařovský, an "indeterminate reality" to which the work of art refers, namely "the total context of what are called social phenomena: e.g., philosophy, politics, religion, economy, etc."[10]

Mukařovský does not deny that a work of art may *also* convey a content in the usual, communicative fashion. "Besides its function as an autonomous sign, the work of art also has another function: that of being a *communicative* sign," he affirms. "Thus the poetic work functions not only as a work of art, but also, and at the same time, as an utterance [*parole*] expressing a state of mind, a thought, an emotion, etc. ... Hence the work of art has a double semiotic function, an autonomous and a communicative one, of which the second is above all reserved for the arts which have a subject [*sujet*]. In the development of those arts, one can also see how the dialectical antinomy of the autonomous sign's function and the communicative sign's function makes itself felt more or less markedly."[11]

For Mukařovský, however, it is the art work's character as an autonomous sign that gives it an aesthetic dimension and makes it impossible to reduce art to statements. One cannot, so to speak, gather information about reality from a work of art in a straightforward manner. One always has to take into consideration that art's reference to society is indirect and implicit: "It follows from the semiological character of art that a work of art must not be used as an historical or sociological document without a preceding assessment of its documentary value, i.e., of the nature of its connection with the given context of social phenomena."[12]

In a somewhat later essay, "Poetic Designation and the Aesthetic Function of Language" ("La Dénomination poétique et la fonction esthétique de la langue," 1936, 1938), Mukařovský introduces "the aesthetic function of language" as the name of the function belonging to autonomous literary signs. Connecting on to Karl Bühler's analysis of the functions of language – then absolutely new – Mukařovský says that communicative utterance has an expressive, a representative, or an appellant function.[13] These functions are to some extent present in literary language as well, but there a shift in main focus has taken place. In the literary work an aesthetic function prevails, based on the work's character as an autonomous sign.[14]

Mukařovský conceives that language's reference to reality is weakened when language has an aesthetic function, and that the interest is then concentrated, instead, on "the sign itself."[15] (That idea was in all probability influenced by Jakobson.) But Mukařovský still insists that the literary work has something to say about reality, albeit in an indirect manner: "The weakening of the immediate relation of poetic designation to reality is counterbalanced by the fact that a poetic work as a global designation enters into relation with the *total* set of the existential experiences of the subject, be he the creative or the perceiving subject."[16]

This is a key element in Mukařovský's theory. His idea about the autonomy of art amounts to the contention that *artistic signs have a markedly distinctive character*, not that *the values of art are independent of all other values in life*. There is a good formulation of Mukařovský's standpoint in a third, larger exposition from the 1930s, "Aesthetic Function, Norm, and Aesthetic Value as Social Facts" (*Estetická funkce, norma a hodnota jako sociální fakty*, 1936).

> The dominance of aesthetic value over all other values finding expression in art is consequently something other than just an outward dominance. The influence of aesthetic value does not consist in its absorbing the other values or pushing them aside. It is true that it detaches each of these values from its immediate connection with the corresponding existential value. But in return it takes the whole complex of values that, as a dynamic unity, forms part of the art work and connects it with the global system constituted by the values that are the driving forces behind the life practice of the collective receiving the art work. ... In this perspective, the autonomy of the work of art, and the dominance in it of aesthetic value and the aesthetic function, do not at all appear as something which suspends the relationship between the art work and natural and social reality, but on the contrary as the force giving it life.[17]

To sum up: Mukařovský emphatically maintains that the artistic or literary work does not, ultimately, possess an expressive, representative, or appellant function. Instead, the work is "autonomous." With an autonomous work, the receiver's immediate attention is directed towards the work itself. Indirectly, however, the autonomous work is intimately connected with his existential and social world.

On the Content and Validity of the Autonomy Doctrine

I do not know to what extent it is due precisely to Mukařovský's influence that the concept of autonomy – under that designation – secured a place in aesthetics and literary theory. But in all events his theory forms an excellent starting point for an understanding of the different meanings or semantic tendencies that the term "autonomy" exhibits in those disciplines today.

The standard purpose of a linguistic expression is to convey meaning. Normally, it is the meaning conveyed that is essential, while the signs used for transmitting it are of no independent interest. The main idea behind Mukařovský's Jakobson-like analysis is that the situation is different in connection with art and literature. The artistic or literary sign does not simply let itself be reduced to a carrier of conventional meaning. It is "autonomous"; where art and literature are concerned, the immediate interest is directed towards the sign itself. This basic idea can be faceted in various ways so that different aspects of the notion of literature's autonomy are brought out.

One aspect of this idea of autonomy – or perhaps, rather, a tacit assumption underlying it – is the conception that the literary composition, the text or work, constitutes a separate, independent phenomenon. Evidently Mukařovský's analysis presupposes that the literary "sign" has, in some sense, a genuine *existence*. Without a distinguishable, substantial, and independent literary sign on which attention can be focused, the foundation of his theory must collapse. So from one point of view, Mukařovský's ideas about autonomy – and most of the conceptions of autonomy that will be referred to briefly in the following – can be seen as *ideas of the genuine existence of texts*.

At the same time, Mukařovský's theory stresses that art works do not allow themselves to be reduced to carriers of meaning. That must imply, among other things, that they cannot be reduced to conveyers of assertions. This is the idea that *the conveyance of assertions is not essential to literature*, which is another of the most prominent aspects of the autonomy doctrine. It is, for example, mainly the conviction that a literary work does not admit of being construed as an assertion that makes Northrop Frye describe the work as an *autonomous* verbal structure:

> In all literary verbal structures the final direction of meaning is inward. In literature the standards of outward meaning are secondary, for literary works do not pretend to describe or assert, and hence are not true, not false. … In literature, questions of fact or truth are subordinated to the primary literary aim of producing a structure of words for its own sake, and the sign-values of symbols are subordinated to their importance as a structure of interconnected motifs. Wherever we have an autonomous verbal structure of this kind, we have literature. Wherever this autonomous structure is lacking, we have language, words used instrumentally to help human consciousness do or understand something else.[18]

According to Mukařovský, the basically autonomous, non-communicative character of the literary sign also implies that *expressing the author's inner states is not essential to the text*. Consequently, the text does not allow itself to be reduced to a carrier of the author's intentions either. This is a third well-known aspect of the autonomy doctrine, sometimes developed into a rather extravagant position. Martin Esslin once wrote: "Great works of art have an autonomous existence, independent of the intention and personality of their creators and independent also of the circumstances of the time of their creation."[19]

If the artistic or literary work does not have its meaning wholly or partly determined by the intentions of its author, it becomes possible for that meaning to shift with time to a varying degree. "We have to think of the work of art as in some measure autonomous, as unconstrained by its history,"[20] says Anthony Savile in a critical examination of this notion. If one attaches importance to this aspect of autonomy thinking, one will be prone to ascribe a potentially inexhaustible meaning to the literary text.

A fourth aspect of the idea about the autonomy of art and literature is perhaps the most important of all. This is *the idea that art and literature possess a value of a wholly unique kind* irreducible to values met with in other connections. (As we saw, it was underlined in Mukařovský's analysis that a specifically aesthetic value is the dominant value in art.)

This idea often occurs in a radical form, as a notion about the *purposelessness* of art, and the conception of the autonomy of art is often explained, simply, as the idea that art is purposeless. András Horn, for example, employs these two terms almost synonymously in speaking of "art's autonomy, its purposelessness."[21] And Sally Markowitz comprehends the idea of "an autonomous aesthetic realm" as the idea of "a dimension of vision and meaning that cannot be reduced to the merely moral, political, religious ... "[22]

Thus I have indicated four elements of the autonomy doctrine: the conviction that the art work is a genuine object, that it is essentially non-assertoric and non-intentionalist in character, and the belief in its specifically aesthetic nature or even in its purposelessness. As I understand the matter, it is normally one (or several) of these ideas that is finding expression when literature is said to be "autonomous."

In my opinion, the ideas concerning literature's autonomy just accounted for are entirely correct on many points. In certain respects, however, they rely on untenable conceptions of signs and communication, or on a muddled use of concepts such as "purposelessness" or "intrinsic value." Thus I see the theory of literature and literary experience presented in this book as partly compatible and partly inconsistent with the autonomy doctrine.

In my analysis of linguistic and literary communication, I have criticized the transportation and container metaphors and refrained from relying on them. As a result, there is no room in my conceptual apparatus for the concept of a work or text if it is understood in the traditional way as inspired by the container metaphor.

In dissociating myself from the idea that a text is a genuine object, I reject *one* crucial element of the autonomy doctrine. It is precisely the work or text that is imagined to constitute the autonomous aesthetic object. (In this respect, my thinking diverges considerably from that of Mukařovský, who is, naturally, much indebted to older ways of looking at communication.)[23]

Instead of allowing for texts, I presuppose the existence of phenomena such as material sign-objects, linguistic expressions, intended meanings, and reconstructed meanings. Though these entities do indeed figure as authentic objects in my theory,[24] that hardly amounts to saying that I espouse the opinion that there are separate, genuine, literary artefacts.

According to my general analysis of how linguistic communication works, the addressee attempts to identify (and react to) the content communicated to him by means of the linguistic sign-object. As a consequence, the author's communicative intentions play an important role in my analysis of communication. I do not, however, identify meaning with intended meaning. Understanding the author's verbal meaning is, as I see it, an important but still subordinate aim for the reader. To me, the meaning of a literary work is partly created by author intentions and partly not.

Even if I see a good deal of what is generally called "meaning" as being determined by the reader, I cannot, therefore, unreservedly describe literature as autonomous with respect to author intentions. I cannot agree with Esslin that the meaning ("existence") of literary works is simply "independent of the intention ... of their creators."

As regards the difference between literature and other kinds of linguistic compositions, the concept of presentationality is at the heart of my analysis: according to my theory, literary discourse is almost without exception presentational. By my definitions, then, the informational, assertoric function of language cannot be the dominant one in a piece of presentational discourse. Consequently, I share the opinion that the literary work has a non-assertoric character. (I regard it as possible for a literary text to convey assertions, in a certain sense at least, but I do not see the conveyance of assertions as one of its necessary or principally significant elements.) So we have here, at least, *one* important part of the autonomy doctrine that I fully accept.

One question remains: Is my theory consistent with the idea that literature is purposeless or, at least, has a specifically aesthetic character? I have maintained that the reader (mostly unconsciously) applies the things read to his own situation. He pays special attention to some aspects of what he reads, he implicitly reflects on such things as whether similar states of affairs can be found in the real world, and he registers some of the consequences for himself of the ensuing picture of reality. In that manner literature may, among other things, function as an aid to the reader in his orientation in reality.

I do not, for that reason, disavow that an aesthetic experience arises in a person reading, for instance, Ekelöf's "But Somewhere Else" in an adequate way. (I touched on this matter in the last chapter.)[25] Nor do I deny that aesthetic considerations are different from theoretical, moral, or pragmatic ones. Aesthetic excellence is different from truth, moral goodness, usefulness, and so on; aesthetic value cannot be identified with, or reduced to, any other type of value. In that sense I subscribe to the opinion that literature has a clearly distinctive character, aesthetic in nature. I even embrace the idea of the purposelessness of literature – to the extent that its only implication is that literature has no non-aesthetic purpose.

What complicates matters is that I hold – much like Mukařovský – that on the whole our aesthetic experiences support more general interests in our lives. The aesthetic experience that literature affords may, for example, in my opinion, be an instrument for our orientation in reality. And literature would not be of interest to us if it did not – in that or in other, related ways – help us to manage our lives. So I do not believe in the autonomy or purposelessness of literature if it is taken to imply that literature lacks instrumental value, that the experience of literature has a value strictly in itself. I think that supplying profits of kinds well known from non-aesthetic contexts does, in fact, form part of literature's normal functions.

As I see it, then, verbal art has something unique, something specific to literature, to give us, but its value can nevertheless normally be regarded as being non-intrinsic. I shall devote the last three sections of the book to clarifying and defending that standpoint.

On the Instrumentality and Irreducibility of Literature

When theorists speak of the autonomy of literature, the idea of literature's purposelessness and the idea of its distinctive value tend to merge. This makes it seem that one cannot deny that literature lacks a purpose without at the same time depriving literature of its distinctive character and reducing it to something else, such as morality, science, or religion.[26]

In reality there is no essential connection between the idea that literature possesses a distinctive, unique value and the idea of its purposelessness, its non-instrumentality. I myself wholeheartedly concur with the view that literature's value is special and cannot be identified with any other. But I have important reservations about (most versions of) the idea of literature's purposelessness, its intrinsic value, its non-instrumental character.

We all believe that literature has something to give to people, that it helps us actualize something that is valuable to us. But we can conceive of that contribution in two ways. We may either think that our need for aesthetic experiences is so basic that it cannot be said to be a special instance of some other, more fundamental, human need. Or we may, on the contrary, believe that aesthetic experiences help to satisfy more fundamental needs of one kind or another and that this explains their attraction.

I myself belong to the latter camp. I find it difficult to imagine a reasonable overall analysis of the structure of human motivation where the need for aesthetic experiences is introduced as being as fundamental to our species as our physiological needs for food or rest or our immaterial needs for things like safety and love. This, of course, touches on comprehensive and complex anthropological issues that I cannot really address. So the observation is not meant as a refutation of the idea that the reading of literature is an end in itself, but merely as an indication of my doubts and of the reasons for them. I shall concentrate, instead, on trying to solve a problem that presents itself to those who, like myself, do *not* see literature as purposeless.

I have just said that I cannot find the notion of literature's purpose-lessness anthropologically credible. But if one holds instead that the reading of literature helps us to satisfy more fundamental needs than that for aesthetic experiences itself, one encounters other difficulties, for then one undeniably ascribes a kind of instrumentality to the reading of literature. It may appear that one's position has to be reductionistic, that it must involve a disregard of important dimensions of verbal art and a reduction of literature and literary experiences to a means, in principle replaceable, to non-aesthetic ends. My stand-point, however, is that the value of literature may be called instrumental if one chooses, but that literature and literary experiences cannot because of that be reduced to anything else. I shall attempt to develop and defend this thesis.

I would like to point out, first of all, that it is one thing to be the means to an end and another to be replaceable. The bicycle, for example, is a means of conveyance whose value is, basically, certainly instrumental in nature. But that does not mean that bicycles could without some loss be replaced with other, in some respects more effective, means of transport – cars, planes, and so on. The bicycle has special characteristics, and consequently special advantages (and, naturally, special drawbacks too). For that reason it has, so to speak, its special niche, humble though it may be, among our means of conveyance and hence among the things that make our lives easier. An analogous point could be made about literature.

Since I keep saying that literature and literary experience afford values met with in other contexts as well, one may ask: What values? Personally, I find it natural to perceive literature as facilitating my intellectual and emotional orientation, as being one of the things that help me to satisfy my need for perspective and for emotional adaptation to the facts of life. I do not wish to generalize that observation and present it as a truth about what literature's value consists in. But let us say, for the sake of argument, that literature does in fact help us with our intellectual and emotional orientation. That does not mean that literature could be replaced by, for instance, science or religion. True, science and religion offer different kinds of information or guidance, intellectual or emotional. But literature certainly differs from scientific or religious discourse in many respects. It thus stands to reason that it also has special advantages (and special disadvantages) as a means of orientation in the world. And in that case, its role can hardly be taken over without loss by science, religion, personal experience, or whatever replacement we may choose to suggest. It appears more natural to think of science, religion, literature, and personal experience as different means of orientation in reality, each with its own unique character and unique range of possibilities.

Such a view of literature's role in our lives integrates verbal art into a more comprehensive whole of human activities. It makes it possible to hold to the idea that literature is something distinctive and irreplaceable. At the same time, it steers clear of the idea that the experience of literature possesses intrinsic value in a strict sense, that it is literally purposeless.[27]

I hope to have demonstrated clearly enough that literature can in principle be conceived of as having a distinctive character, and as being irreplaceable, even if literature is taken to function as the means to an end. It is evidently possible, then, to ascribe a kind of instrumentality to literature without for that reason landing in reductionism. But on the other hand, this certainly does not prove that literature *is* in fact instrumental in nature.

It may even appear unreasonable to think that literature – as opposed to isolated novels with a purpose – could have an instrumental character. We do not *use* a literary work in the sense in which we *use* a tool or a bicycle. When employing a screwdriver, we have first identified a task – the turning of a certain screw – and we make use of the screwdriver to perform the task. When reading a literary work we are in no analogous situation. We are, rather, reading the text with an open mind, only in order to understand and experience it. Where is the instrumentality in that?

I do not deny the difference indicated; it is altogether real. But I cannot find that it concerns instrumentality.

I can see two major differences between the screwdriver case and the literary case. First, we *consciously* use the screwdriver as an instrument, but we use literature *unconsciously*. Our post-communicative processing of what we read – the processing that I regard as potentially forming part of our endeavours to orientate ourselves in the world – is, in Frijda's words, "neither deliberate nor a conscious process." It is natural for our conscious minds to apprehend our reading and experiencing as purposeless, as an occupation with the text for its own sake. Seen from the outside, however, the reading normally appears – at least to me – as an occupation with the problems of life, as a kind of continuous assessment of possible attitudes to reality.

Another difference between the two cases is the following. When using the screwdriver we have a *preconceived* idea of what we intend to achieve. But as readers of literature we do not normally have any real prior conception, conscious or unconscious, of what the text will have to afford. We are entitled to expect that it will have *something* to offer; otherwise, it would lack a raison d'être. But we do not know *what* – any more than we know, in ordinary life, what experiences await us around the next street corner.

As users of a screwdriver we are, thus, to put it simply, *consciously* employing a tool in order to achieve *a result basically planned in advance*. As readers of literature we are, I think, *unconsciously* employing the text as a means of adjusting our perspective on life, *without prior knowledge* of what, if any, more exact benefit we will be able to derive from our reading. In themselves, these are great and significant differences. But they do not remove the character of instrumentality present in the reading of literature. That reading can still be, among other things, a particular means of orientation with special merits and drawbacks, not a purposeless activity in the strict sense.

Horn on the Autonomy of Literature

Here in my concluding remarks I have attempted to show how the theory in my book is related to current ideas about literature's autonomy. Where my analysis departs from the autonomy doctrine, I have tried to justify my divergent standpoint.

I have in particular discussed the question of the purposelessness of literature. In that connection, I have emphasized that ascribing instrumentality to literature is not necessarily a manifestation of reductionism.

It is possible to conceive of literature as a means to an end *and* as being impossible to replace by other, equally good or valuable means.

In conclusion, I would like to defend myself against the imagined accusation of reductionism in yet another way. I want to show that theorists embracing the idea of literature's autonomy may in practice very well mean – just like myself – that literature caters for non-aesthetic needs in its own special, irreplaceable manner. To that end I shall, in this section and the next, comment on two relatively recent and ambitious explanations of what literature's value consists in: András Horn's in his *Foundations of Literary Aesthetics* (*Grundlagen der Literaturästhetik*, 1993) and Peter Lamarque and Stein Haugom Olsen's in their *Truth, Fiction, and Literature* (1994).

In his wide-ranging and well-informed book inspired both by German and by British/American traditions, Horn describes it as the central function of art and literature to supply us with satisfactory aesthetic experiences: aesthetic value is the cardinal point in literature.[28] Horn understands the aesthetic comparatively broadly, however. According to him, it is not only literature's form that affords aesthetic satisfaction, but also aspects of its communicative content: not only the aesthetic radiance and the purposelessness of the literary work, but also the picture of reality and the inner human states made visible through the aesthetic expression (123–277).

Moreover, Horn does not treat aesthetic enjoyment as a fundamental, inexplicable fact: he asks *why* the aesthetic gives us pleasure. His answer takes an argument about human nature and the essence of liberty as its point of departure.

Horn starts from a Hegelian definition of liberty according to which freedom consists in being in oneself when being in otherness ("in seinem Andern bei sich selbst zu sein"). That is to say, approximately: freedom is to be one with that which is apparently other or different; for example, with nature. Horn regards Hegel's identification of spirit and nature as untenable, however, and therefore speaks of freedom, instead, as a "being-in-that-which-is-one's-*own*" (400).

The phenomena met with in literary experience – the form, the content – are not literally free. We are confronted with a *seeming* freedom – where the content is concerned, with a "*a seeming being-in-that-which-is-one's-own in the sensuous-significant other.*" When the content is made visible in the form in a successful literary creation, there is nothing in the form that is not determined by the content. For that reason, content is, seemingly, in that which is its own when it is in the outward, signifying form (402). With analogous arguments Horn also points to possible manifestations of (seeming) freedom in other varieties of the aesthetic. This (seeming) freedom in the aesthetic object is, further, conceived as liberating the viewer or reader. According to Horn, the aesthetic "through its own freedom makes possible and effects freedom in the recipient" (419).

The aesthetic freedom characterizing art is thus supposed to provide people with a sense of freedom. (Horn does not explain the mechanisms responsible for this effect.) According to Horn, who is here paraphrasing Hegel, art and literature cater to a need for freedom that cannot be satisfied by other means: "Precisely because man's sensual freedom cannot be completely realized in his objective existence, and his need of freedom must therefore remain unsatisfied in the sphere of nature, man creates an artificial world in order to be able to take delight in himself, there, in his full and unrestricted freedom"(411).

There is of course much to discuss in Horn's analysis. One may, for example, call into question his idea about the nature of freedom, and also the notion that a happy relation between content and form arouses precisely an experience of freedom in the recipient when apprehended adequately.

I myself would also like to object that Horn leaves wholly unexplained how purely imagined liberty can provide genuine satisfaction of the need for freedom. His theory would have to be supplemented with an explanation of the operative mechanisms connecting seeming freedom in art, ideas about freedom arising in the recipient, and positive psychological effects – an explanation such as my references to thematization and application. Lastly, I regard Horn's idea about what gives literary works their value as being much too specific. It is easy to integrate with my analysis: nothing hinders the reader from focusing on an experienced quality of freedom in the communicative content and from letting this give rise to pleasurable ideas about his own possibilities of being free. But I would see that type of response to literature as only one among many reasonable alternatives.

I find it interesting to reflect on Horn's explanation of the value of literature and to compare it with the analyses that I have outlined. But what is relvant for me, here, is primarily Horn's way of handling the question of literature's autonomy.

If I understand Horn correctly, he implicitly commits himself to the opinion that literature is autonomous. In any case, he evidently assumes that art and literature have had an autonomous status at least from the nineteenth century onwards (88–90). As I mentioned earlier, he treats autonomy and purposelessness as equivalents (88), and he regards aesthetic value as being constitutive of verbal art.

Nevertheless, Horn can be said to understand literature as a non-replaceable means to an end and to ascribe intrinsic value only to that end. He describes art and literature as offering an experience of freedom that cannot be produced equally well by any other means. He seems to conceive of art and literature as satisfying a constitutive, spiritual, human need: that of freedom. In reality, then, Horn ascribes – just like myself – an aesthetic character, but also a kind of instrumentality, to literature. Thus his Hegelian version of the autonomy doctrine appears to be, in principle, about as much or as little reductionistic as my own standpoint.

Lamarque and Olsen on Literature's Autonomy

Lamarque and Olsen strongly emphasize that they see literature as autonomous. They write: "Ours is a non-reductionist account, it (unfashionably) acknowledges the autonomy of literature and literary criticism; it does not seek to reduce the study of literature to rhetoric, *belles-lettres*, philology, ethics, civic studies, or whatever. ... Literature does not need to be justified as a source of moral precepts or an adjunct to philosophy or the social sciences. It is its own justification, providing its own rewards."[29]

Thus Lamarque and Olsen unequivocally declare that literature has a distinctive character. Their talk of literature as "its own justification" tends to give the impression that the two theorists also embrace some variant of the idea of the purposelessness of literature. At the same time, however, Lamarque and Olsen provide an explanation of what makes literature valuable, an explanation that – though indeterminate in some respects – appears to supply literature with instrumentality of a kind.[30]

The idea that a literary practice exists is quite as essential to Lamarque and Olsen's literary aesthetics as it is to mine.[31] Unlike myself, however, the two authors maintain that the value of the individual literary work has to be explained by making it clear why the literary practice itself is valuable (442, 444). Their answer to the latter question amounts to the contention that the literary practice forms an integral part of our culture where it is – together with philosophy, religion, and so on – "one of the practices that define what we hold to be important and valuable" (455–6). Perhaps Lamarque and Olsen would be willing to say that the literary practice is part of a comprehensive system by whose aid we orientate ourselves in reality.

More specifically, Lamarque and Olsen consider that a literary work always has a *theme*. Or, rather: when the reader reads the work in accordance with the rules of the literary practice, she construes it as the carrier of a theme (266). The theme is that which the work is, principally, about, and a work of high quality has a theme of great human interest (e.g., 285, 402; chap. 16, passim). When reading in compliance with the rules of the game we are, according to Lamarque and Olsen, in the first place elaborating an *appreciation* of the text. That in its turn is thought to consist in identifying the theme and making it clear to oneself how it has been developed and interpreted in the work (402, 408–9).

"Perennial" themes are considered to be of special value as subjects of literary works (405–11). Such themes are, above all, certain philosophical topics such as freedom, determinism, or responsibility, but also some subjects with a primarily religious background such as purity, divine order, or forgiveness (406–7). The appreciation of literary works gives the import of the corresponding concepts a concretion for us that cannot be achieved in other contexts. In Lamarque and Olsen's opinion, it is a major purpose of a literary work to "develop in depth, through subject and form, a theme which is in some sense central to human concerns and which can therefore be recognized as of more or less universal interest" (450). Since the relevant thematic concepts cannot present themselves as fully in everyday life as in literature, verbal art has "developed into a special kind of cognition that has come to constitute, in part, the themes that have been central in the culture" (452). To take a concrete example, Arnold Bennett's *Anna of the Five Towns* (1902): "*Anna of the Five Towns* organizes a described universe in such a way that the reader who applies concepts like 'freedom of the will,' 'determinism,' 'victim of external forces beyond human control' in the appreciation of that work will come to see how, in that universe, human beings are controlled by external forces. There is no similar order in the real world that will make these concepts meaningful in this way. Daily life does not offer the sort of visible connections that the artistic narrative defines. These connections emerge in the artistic presentation of the subject" (454).

Just like Horn's theory, this analysis may, in itself, be integrated into my model. I can well imagine a reader who focuses on the limitations of Anna's freedom, uses them to reflect on the possibilities of freedom, and applies her reflections to her own situation by letting them affect her cognitive and emotional experience of her situation in life. But, like Horn's analysis, that of Lamarque and Olsen appears to me to be too specific. It assumes the existence of *one* relatively sharply demarcated type of relevant profit to be derived from imaginative literature, while I reckon with *several* types.

I can also think of other objections. While Lamarque and Olsen pay attention to the reader's focusing, they merely touch on what I call non-self-orientated associating, and application in my sense is not mentioned at all. Consequently, Lamarque and Olsen certainly regard the reader of a work like *Anna of the Five Towns* as concentrated on understanding the novel's representation of, for instance, the possibilities of freedom. But they do not really explain why an understanding of that aspect of the novel should be valuable to the reader.[32]

Just as in connection with Horn, however, what I particularly wish to direct attention to is the fact that, in the authors' view of literature, verbal art is characterized by both autonomy and instrumentality. Lamarque and Olsen state most emphatically that literature is autonomous. But at the same time they see the value of verbal art, ultimately, in the fact that literary works "can contribute to the development and understanding of the deepest, most revered of a culture's conceptions" (22). In reality, then, Lamarque and Olsen's view of autonomy seems to involve, just like my cognitive-emotive model, the ascription of both an aesthetic aspect and a kind of instrumentality to literature. If my cognitive-emotive model were reductionistic, it would be difficult to see why Lamarque and Olsen's version of the autonomy doctrine should not also be thus characterized.

That said, however, I would like to add that there are many ways of developing the idea that literature is both irreducible and instrumental. We can imagine a scale ranging from a limited instrumentality close to absolute purposelessness to instrumentality of a more and more substantial nature. On such a scale, my ideas about literary experience and its value would no doubt have to be placed further from purposelessness than those of Horn or of Lamarque and Olsen.

Notes

Introduction

1 The analysis develops and revises Nicholas Wolterstorff's account of the pragmatic mode of fictional discourse in his *Works and Worlds of Art* (1980); *presenting* is a key notion in Wolterstorff's version too. My conceptions of literature's distinctive communicative character are presented in far more detail in chaps. 3–4 below.

2 I assume, here, the existence of an outer world independent of our ideas of it. I do not maintain that we can, so to speak, step out of our ideas and our language and see and describe reality as it is. I contend, however, that our ideas are, ultimately, put to the test by reality. They may prove to lack real background. For instance, actions founded on our beliefs about reality may fail.

3 It would be too demanding, and in this context carry us too far, to attempt to explain how my standpoint relates to contemporary philosophical views of knowledge, reality, and objectivity. However, where objectivism versus relativism is concerned, or the possibilities of a rational, scholarly exchange of views, my opinions are influenced by, above all, Richard J. Bernstein's *Beyond Objectivism and Relativism* (1983) and Göran Hermerén's *Art, Reason, and Tradition* (1991).

4 See esp. chaps. 3 and 5 in *A Theory of Literature Discourse* (1990).

5 Reddy, "The Conduit Metaphor," esp. 286–92 and 311–24. For further discussion of metaphors for language see, e.g., Sweetser, "English Metaphors for Language."

   Reddy's analysis, first presented in 1979, figures in such contexts as a respected classic (see, e.g., Sweetser, 713). It is true that Joe Grady has recently proposed a new analysis of the relevant metaphorical modes of expression, but in my opinion he simply overlooks their illogicality, which is my main concern here ("The 'Conduit Metaphor' Revisited," esp. 211–12).

6 Reddy, "The Conduit Metaphor," esp. 297–9 and 302–6.

7 A literary work is normally thought of as some sort of really existing object whose exact ontological status is difficult to determine. Examples of this are given in chap. 4. There have, however, long been theorists, especially some philosophers, who have denied, on somewhat different grounds, that names of literary works have homogeneous denotations. They have tended to see such names as a kind of shorthand expressions with context-dependent reference. See, e.g., Rudner, "The Ontological Status of the Esthetic Object," and Tilghman, "The Literary Work." I have argued in favour of a kindred view in, among other publications, "Ontology of Literary Works" and *Theory of Literary Discourse*, 141–7. I return to the subject in chap. 4 below.

8 Cf., e.g., Barthes, "De l'œuvre au texte."

9 Naylor, *Mama Day*, 3.

10 The idea of linguistic and literary communication underlying these remarks is developed out of philosophical and linguistic pragmatics. I build especially on Paul Grice's philosophy of language from "Meaning" (1957) onwards, now collected in Grice, *Studies in the Way of Words*.

11 This is sometimes seen as the most fundamental truth about literary interpretation, the very key to an understanding of it. See, e.g., Rorty, "The Pragmatist's Progress."

12 I think especially of Jonathan Culler's description of literary competence in his *Structuralist Poetics*, esp. chap. 6, and of Stein Haugom Olsen's analyses of literary practice, most recently in Lamarque and Olsen, *Truth, Fiction, and Literature*, esp. chap. 10.

13 In *Theory of Literary Discourse*, 93–4, I have suggested an approach to that type of problem.

Chapter One

1 Maslow, *Motivation and Personality*, 15–22.

2 See, e.g., Roediger et al., *Psychology*, 438–44. From now on I cite no authorities when mentioning well-established psychological facts.

3 Frijda, *The Emotions*, 370.

4 Gulz, *The Planning of Action*, 39.

5 For more realistic and complicated models of the processing structures, so-called "architectures," see, e.g., Newell, Rosenbloom, and Laird, "Symbolic Architectures for Cognition," esp. 109–11. Note, however,

that the article in question, which focuses on "the fixed system of mechanisms that underlies and produces cognitive behaviour," has an exclusively cognitive orientation. Cf. also, e.g., Stillings et al., *Cognitive Science*, chap. 2, esp. 16–19.

6 See, e.g., the considerations in Eysenck and Keane, *Cognitive Psychology*, 62.

7 The figure after Gulz, *The Planning of Action*, 72 (with some simplifications). Gulz's model, in its turn, follows (with modifications) W.T. Powers's *Behavior: The Control of Perception* (1973). The models of the mechanisms of visual perception that are now the centre of attraction (mostly further developments of David Marr's) are far more confined and at the same time far more precise; cf., e.g., Eysenck and Keane, *Cognitive Psychology*, chap. 2. It would also be normal to assume that information exchange between parallel processing systems is involved, rather than simple feedback mechanisms; see, e.g., Edelman, *The Remembered Present*, Chap. 4.

8 R.W. Thatcher and E.R. John, *Foundations of Cognitive Processes* (1977), 294, quoted from Dennett, "Consciousness," 162.

9 Roediger et al., *Psychology*, 160.

10 Cf. Rorty, *Philosophy and the Mirror of Nature*, 205 and 243. See also Edelman, *The Remembered Present*, 212–13, and the literature cited there.

11 It has been disputed whether mental representations should be thought of as analogous representations (like pictures) or non-analogous representations (like propositions). See, e.g., Tye, *The Imagery Debate* and Keane, "Propositional Representations," 294–5. Edelman holds that we have reason to believe that both representational techniques are used by the brain (Edelman, *The Remembered Present*, 195–6).

12 In reckoning with intentional states consisting of mental representations supplied with psychological modes I follow, primarily, Searle, *Intentionality*, 6. My terminology is not, however, identical with Searle's; among other things, Searle does not speak of mental representations but of the "propositional," "representative," or "intentional" content of an intentional state.

13 Peacocke, *Sense and Content*, 8 ("all experiences have nonrepresentational properties") and 12–16 (the examples; for the term "sensational property," see, e.g., 14).

14 A description of a visual experience can, moreover, obviously never be phenomenologically equivalent to the visual experience itself – the very visuality of the visual experience already prevents that. The differences between visual and verbal media also have a number of other special consequences; see, e.g., Walton, *Mimesis as Make-Believe*, 306–9.

15 See Lazarus, "Emotions and Adaptation." Cf. Heckhausen, "Intervening Cognitions in Motivation."

16 In psychology and the philosophy of mind, "emotion" normally refers to a larger-scale state usually involving feelings. Cf., e.g., Frijda, *The Emotions*, 251–2 and William Lyons, *Emotion*, 2–16 and chap. 8.

17 Cf., e.g., Blocker, *Philosophy of Art*, 113–14 and Greenspan, *Emotions and Reasons*, 22–3.

18 Naturally, this explanation concerns current emotional experiences only (like my fear just now of a certain wasp) and not long-standing emotional dispositions (like my enduring fear of wasps). The explanation of emotional experiences forms the obvious starting point, however, for an explanation of emotional dispositions. Cf. William Lyons, *Emotion*, esp. 56–7.

19 Frijda, *The Emotions*. "Frijda's type of theory now has rather general agreement," says Keith Oatley ("Emotion," 130).

20 Frijda, *The Emotions*, 453–63.

21 Ibid., 5, 71, 257, et passim. Following Frijda, Oatley also sees "readiness for action" as "the core of an emotion." Oatley, *Best Laid Schemes*, 19–20.

22 Lyons, *Emotion*, 58 (the emotion is "a bodily state caused by ... an evaluative attitude").

23 Greenspan, *Emotions and Reasons*, 4 and 14 respectively.

24 Levinson, "Emotion," 21.

25 Currie, *The Nature of Fiction*, 192; my italics.

26 According to Carroll, an emotion is "made up of at least two components: a cognitive component, such as a belief ... and a feeling component ... where, additionally, the feeling state has been caused by the relevant cognitive state" ("Art, Narrative, and Emotion," 196).

Chapter Two

1 I base my opinion partly on my personal impression of the collection, partly on its foreword. Cf. Smith and Hodell, "Förord," esp. [7].

2 Axelsson, "Ljusets frihet," 148–9. I remind the reader again that all translations are my own, unless otherwise indicated.

3 Ibid., 149. For the quotations in the rest of this section see ibid., 150–1.

4 Updike, "Pygmalion," 73–5.

5 Ovid, *Metamorphoses*, 233–4.

6 See Frenzel, *Stoffe der Weltliteratur*, 627–30. According to Frenzel (628), the association with art and artistry first appears in the eighteenth century.

7 What is new here is the negative evaluation, not the use of the myth to symbolize a man's educating of a woman. Cf. ibid., 629–30.

8 Shaw, *Pygmalion*, 66.

9 Notions of this kind are widespread, even if my own standpoint is distinctive in some respects. My contentions in this section are particularly

closely akin to ideas in chap. 6 of Novitz's *Knowledge, Fiction, and Imagination*, in Lamarque and Olsen's *Truth, Fiction, and Literature*, and in Stecker's *Artworks*, chap. 13. They are, however, also closely related to Charles Altieri's applications to literary form of Nelson Goodman's analyses of exemplification – see Altieri's *Painterly Abstraction* – and to Altieri's conceptions of literature as "performance" (*Act and Quality*, esp. 174). In addition, my position links up with Freudian literary-theoretical traditions, esp. Lesser's *Fiction and the Unconscious* and Holland's *Dynamics of Literary Response*. My views on those and other similar accounts will be made clearer in chaps. 5–7 and chap. 9.

10 Cf. Axelsson, "Ljusets frihet," 150.

11 Winnicott, *Playing and Reality*, 52.

12 Frijda, *The Emotions*, 325.

13 In *Theory of Literary Discourse*, 195–9, I used this idea for providing a hypothetical sketch of how literary compositions may have evolved from non-literary language. Cf. Kendall Walton's conception of artistic representations as "artificial prompters" (*Mimesis as Make-Believe*, 22).

14 Graesser, Singer, and Trabasso, "Constructing Inferences," 372. Mostly, however, students of the psychology of reading are evasive where the overarching, work-world-relating structures of literary reading are concerned. See, e.g., Zwaan's cautious formulations in his *Aspects of Literary Comprehension*, 152–3 and 164–9.

15 Gerrig, *Experiencing Narrative Worlds*, chap. 6.

16 Ibid., 225–7.

17 Gerrig suggests another explanation of the Yale/Princeton effect (ibid., 226).

18 Frijda's so-called "Law of Concern" ("The Laws of Emotion," 351).

19 Lyons, *Emotion*, 35.

20 Many other explanations of this phenomenon have been suggested. I revert to the subject in chap. 7.

21 Santayana, *The Sense of Beauty*, 120.

22 The same thing occurs in speech: we experience heard words, sentences, meanings, and emotional values as if they were physically present in the sounds perceived. Undoubtedly, it is not least this experience of the embodied expressivity of writing and speech that makes it natural for us to use transportation and container metaphors when talking of linguistic communication. Phenomenologically, a speech or a piece of writing actually stands out as exposing, in itself, a text (words, sentences, etc.) and a meaning.

This also goes to show that embodied expressivity is not an exclusively aesthetic phenomenon. That is one of the reasons why I would not myself use Santayana's analysis as an analysis of the mechanisms underlying the experience of beauty or aesthetic expression (but merely as one of the building blocks for such an analysis). Cf. John Hospers's discussion of Santayana's theory of aesthetic expression (*Meaning and Truth*, 67–72).

23 By "Updike's 'Pygmalion'" I mean here, approximately, "the complex of representations constituting the communicative content of Updike's 'Pygmalion.'" Thus, my observations do not presuppose the existence of *works* in the traditional sense, i.e., verbal containers of meaning. (The reference to Updike's "Pygmalion" in the analysis above is relatively easy to eliminate, as I shall demonstrate in chap. 4.)

24 *Poetics* 1451b5–8. I quote Stephen Halliwell's translation (Aristotle, *Poetics*, 59).

25 Aristotle gives another explanation: poetry is about the probable (and hence generally applicable), while history is about the true (and hence particular). *Poetics* 1451a36–1451b5.

26 Kant, *The Critique of Judgement*, 175–6.

27 Hegel, *Aesthetics*, 1:111.
  Concerning the connections between Kant's view of aesthetic ideas and Hegel's aesthetics, cf. Crowther, *Art and Embodiment*, 79–80.

28 Hegel, *Aesthetics*, 1:101.

29 Included in Wimsatt, *The Verbal Icon*. A recent treatment of the subject, relating to Wimsatt's, is Knapp's in his *Literary Interest*, chap. 3.

30 Timofeev, *Osnovy teorii literatury*, 48.

31 In *Art and Embodiment*, e.g., Crowther, apostrophizing Hegel, sees art as "a mode of understanding which is half-way between the concrete particularity of material phenomena, and the abstract generality of pure thought" (5). Crowther's "ecological" aesthetics focuses on art's sensual testifying to our bodily nature and our intertwining with the world.

32 For this type of criticism of cognitivist aesthetics, see, e.g., Stolnitz's "On the Cognitive Triviality of Art." Different types of defence of literature's cognitive value are more common, though. See, e.g., Novitz, *Knowledge, Fiction, and Imagination*, chap. 6; Knapp, *Literary Interest*, chap. 4; and Lamarque and Olsen, *Truth, Fiction, and Literature*, chap. 17.

33 Cf., e.g., Lesser's assumption that fiction releases trains of association related to the self ("analogizing") especially "because of the extreme connotativeness of its episodic language" (*Fiction and the Unconscious*, 242).

34 Mandler, *Mind and Body*, 296.

35 The concept "functional pleasure" was first introduced by Charlotte Bühler in her book *Kindheit und Jugend* (1931). For a modern discussion of the concept see, e.g., Frijda, *The Emotions*, 365–6.

36 Mandler relies partially on this mechanism in explaining our experience of art. See, e.g., *Mind and Body*, 296.

Functional pleasure, and pleasure caused by the right degree of complexity, must reasonably be just as likely in connection with non-literary compositions. Hence an additional explanation seems to be required if these pleasure mechanisms are to be conceived as especially important precisely in literary contexts.

37 For a defence of a similar position concerning fear, see Morreall, "Fear without Belief," esp. 360–2 and 366.

38 See, e.g., Freud, "Creative Writers and Day-Dreaming," 137–41; Kofman, *The Childhood of Art*, 117, 122, 134, et passim; Schönau, *Einführung*, 45, 52, 72, et passim.

39 This idea can be glimpsed in many studies in the psychoanalytical tradition. It is applied explicitly and consciously by Lesser (*Fiction and the Unconscious*, esp. 200–4).

40 The games-of-make-believe theory, which has had considerable impact, was launched by Kendall Walton. Its most complete version is presented in Walton's *Mimesis as Make-Believe*, chap. 1. The curiosity theory is associated above all with Noël Carroll's analyses of horror in film and literature. See, e.g., *The Philosophy of Horror*, esp. 184.

41 Tsur, *Toward a Theory of Cognitive Poetics*; see esp. 3–7. Tsur relates his standpoint to the Russian formalist idea of art as a disautomatization of our experience of reality (esp. 4).

42 My reservations concern, above all, Walton's games-of-make-believe theory and the psychoanalytical theory of sublimation (putatively explaining how it is possible for fantasies to afford satisfaction). My objections to Walton's theory are presented concisely in chap. 3. As regards the idea of wish-fulfilling fantasies I shall confine myself, in this context, to pointing out that fantasies do *not* by themselves fulfil wishes. (This is easiest to see where unsatisfied physiological needs are concerned. Hunger fantasies, e.g., do not fulfil the hungry person's desire for food, even in part.)

The internal problems of the theory of sublimation are not unknown (cf. Schönau, *Einführung*, 9). For representative criticism of Freudian catharsis theory see, e.g., Frijda, *The Emotions*, 445.

43 Where form-orientated reactions are concerned, this will be demonstrated only in chaps. 8–10.

Chapter Three

1 For a fuller presentation of my standpoint, see *Theory of Literary Discourse*, esp. chaps. 2–5, chapters entering deeper into many of the subjects discussed below. (On especially important points in the following, specific direct references to the earlier book will be given.)

2 See Reddy, "The Conduit Metaphor," esp. 286–7. Cf., e.g., Harris, *The Language Myth*, esp. 11.

3 My smile should be imagined, here, not as an involuntary reaction but as being evidently intentional and evidently sincere.

4 This description of how meaning is conveyed concurs with the Gricean tradition. As I have already pointed out, H.P. Grice developed and applied an intention-based analysis of meaning and communication in a series of articles, of which "Meaning" (1957) and "Logic and Conversation" (1975) are the best known. These and other relevant contributions by Grice can now be found in Grice's *Studies in the Way of Words*.

Analyses of the Gricean type may be said to be predominant, nowadays, where the meaning of actual utterances is concerned. Analyses within the Gricean tradition differ among themselves, however, the version in my text being, in its particulars, my own variant.

5 Since we are to suppose that my smile is sincere (cf. note 3 above). Insincerity in communication will be commented upon later in this section.

6 In talking of human communication I am, both now and later, referring to communication governed by intentions. That is to say that I do not, unlike many semioticians, use the wider concept according to which communication presupposes simply "the passage of a signal ... from a source ... to a destination." I quote Eco, *A Theory of Semiotics*, 8.

7 The description of the intention could be made much more precise and specific; cf. my next note.

The infinite regress glimpsed behind the three dots in the description of the intention is a much-discussed crux in Gricean meaning analysis. See esp. Schiffer, *Meaning*, and Grice, "Meaning Revisited," in *Studies in the Way of Words*.

8 I could also have communicated my joy in seeing you by saying, e.g., "How nice to see you!" Reflecting upon the difference in import between that utterance and the warm smile gives some indication of the subtlety of the smile's intended meaning.

9 For analyses of what is here called "mutual knowledge" (also known as "common knowledge," "*mutual knowledge," and "mutual manifestness"), see esp. Lewis, *Convention*, 52–60; Schiffer, *Meaning*, 30–42; Sperber and Wilson, *Relevance*, 15–21 and 38–46. Since our mutual "knowledge" may well be mistaken, it would, strictly speaking, be more adequate to talk of mutual assumptions.

10 I do not even feel committed to the actual existence of intentions – as pointed out in chap. 1, I wish to leave undecided the question of the possibility of the future elimination of mentalistic expressions.

11 I disregard, here, a possible complication: it *may* be the case that I actually *want* you to perceive my friendliness as feigned.

12 Cf. Frijda's statement, quoted earlier, that we evaluate the significance of events in our surroundings involuntarily and unconsciously.

13 This should not be conceived of as a remarkable creative achievement. Undoubtedly, we all daily let fall many remarks that have never before been made by anyone in exactly the same words. In the text, however, I am thinking especially of simple non-verbal communicative acts. My aim is to suggest how it is possible to build a system of communicative conventions starting from scratch.

14 Strawson, *Logico-Linguistic Papers*, 174–5. The lecture in question ("Meaning and Truth") was originally given in 1969.

15 I do not wish to imply that the first human communication was in fact gestic or mimic, although some argue that it was – see, e.g., Armstrong, Stokoe, and Wilcox, *Gesture*, 18–19 and 223–9. The majority opinion, however, which I share, is that vocal communication must be primordial. See, e.g., Bickerton, *Language and Species*, esp. 142, and Ploog, "Evolution of Vocal Communication," esp. 6–7 and 25.

16 In connection with the following hypothetical sketch of the development, cf. my *Theory of Literary Discourse*, 54–5, and the literature cited there.

17 Especially well known is Paul Ricœur's idea that writing in general entails a "distanciation" suspending the connection between sign-sequence and originator, thereby making meaning independent of the originator's intentions. Se esp. *Interpretation Theory*. For objections to Ricœur's analysis see, e.g., Wolterstorff, "Are Texts Autonomous?" and my *Theory of Literary Discourse*, 94–8.

18 *Sunday Times*, 12 August 1990, 20.

19 They have been dealt with in my *Theory of Literary Discourse*, the two complications mentioned in the text esp. in 52–60 and 90–4 respectively.

20 Cf. John Searle and Daniel Vanderveken's observation that linguistic utterances almost always express psychological states. (More exactly, that illocutionary acts with a propositional content always express psychological states corresponding to that content.) See Searle and Vanderveken, *Foundations of Illocutionary Logic*, 18.

   Written compositions cannot always literally be said to convey intentional states; nor, strictly speaking, can the newspaper notice in question. For the additional explanations required, see my *Theory of Literary Discourse*, 86–91.

21 From a structural point of view, communicated intentional content and communicated purpose by and large correspond to what is called, in speech act theory, the propositional content and the illocutionary force. My interpretation of "propositional content" and "illocutionary force," and my explanation of the relevant phenomena, cannot, however, be said to be altogether compatible with those of speech act theory.

22 As far as I can see, presentational discourse represents a modification of informational or directive discourse. The aim of conveying a conviction or a desire disappears or is decisively weakened (since the manifest content of the utterance is not believed or wished by the originator, or since the content's basis in reality is relatively unimportant in the circumstances), while the expectation that the content, or the act of communicating the content, will prove cognitively or emotionally rewarding to the addressee – a universal expectation in connection with communication – remains in force. Cf. my *Theory of Literary Discourse*, 195–200.

23 Wolterstorff, *Works and Worlds of Art*, 233.

24 I evaluate Wolterstorff's idea of the fictional stance in my *Theory of Literary Discourse*, esp. 30–4 and 137–9.

25 So far I agree with Gadamer's statement that "understanding always involves something like the application of the text to be understood to the present situation of the interpreter" (*Truth and Method*, 274). Gadamer's theory of application has other problematic aspects, though. I shall comment briefly on this subject in chap. 6.

26 Since my description of presentational discourse is intended to provide, at the same time, a description of literary communication, one may find it disquieting that the account given completely ignores literary *form*. However, I remind the reader once again that formal and, in the traditional sense, aesthetic aspects of literature will be discussed only much later in my exposition (chaps. 8–10).

27 On the history of the concept of literature see, e.g., Escarpit, "Définition du terme 'littérature'"; Markiewicz, "The Limits of Literature"; Wellek, "What Is Literature?"

28 See on this point esp. statements from scholars in the area or the classificatory principles of major library classification systems, e.g.: Wellek and Warren, *Theory of Literature*, 20–6; Shusterman, *Object of Literary Criticism*, 36–7; Dewey, *Dewey Decimal Classification*, 1:391; Immroth, *Library of Congress Classification*, 224–5.

29 My view of that matter is presented at full length in *Theory of Literary Discourse*, chap. 7.

30 Currie's basic view of fictionality became known through his article "What Is Fiction?" In my discussion of Currie in this section, however, only *The Nature of Fiction* is taken into consideration. References to this book are given in parentheses in the text.

31 Currie's own term is "fictive" communication and "fictive" utterance, but I prefer the adjective "fictional." As utterances, "The Freedom of Light" and "Pygmalion" are just as real as the notice about John Sykes and the British Army's recruitment advertisement. What is fictive, made up, are the persons, events, etc. forming part of the content of the stories.

32 This is Currie's most simple, least technical formulation of his basic idea. It is developed in more detail in *The Nature of Fiction*, 31–4.

33 Lamarque and Olsen, *Truth, Fiction, and Literature*, esp. 43–6.

34 By a "fictional" composition I mean a composition which not only contains minor fictional elements but whose persons, events, etc. are largely invented.

35 For my standpoint on the characteristics of fictional discourse, see *Theory of Literary Discourse*, esp. 31.

36 Currie's analysis is influenced by Walton's theory of the intercourse with fiction as an activity of making-believe, a theory touched upon in the last chapter. On the relationships between Currie's and Walton's accounts, see Currie, *The Nature of Fiction*, xi–xii, 18–19, et passim.

37 See Lamarque and Olsen, *Truth, Fiction, and Literature*, esp. 45–6. It does not seem necessary, here, to discuss the relationships between Currie's theory and the Lamarque/Olsen analysis in detail.

38 See the section "Walton, Lamarque, and Scruton on Feelings for Fictitious Characters" in chap. 7 below. (The difference between the analyses naturally leads to different understandings of the reader's emotional reactions.)

39 Essentially the same argument has been put forward by other theorists as well. I develop the argument, referring also to contributions by others, in my arcticle "On Walton's and Currie's Analyses," esp. 85–7. Note that Currie's reply in his *Image and Mind*, 161, concerns another objection of mine (which he misunderstands).

40 My article "On Walton's and Currie's Analyses" contains a sustained and somewhat more extensive criticism of the games-of-make-believe theory.

41 I quote from Lowell, *Selected Poems*, 43–4.

42 Cf. Williamson, *Pity the Monsters*, 65.

43 As it undoubtedly does in other *Life Studies* poems as well. See, e.g., "Waking in the Blue," set in a mental hospital (*Selected Poems*, 47–8).

44 Mazzaro, *Robert Lowell*, 113.

45 It is interesting to compare the colours in "Father's Bedroom" with those in the portrayal of Uncle Devereux at the end of "My Last Afternoon with Uncle Devereux Winslow (1922: The Stone Porch of My Grandfather's Summer House)," a passage in *Life Studies* where death and the colours blue and white play a principal part (Lowell, *Selected Poems*, 36).

46 Mazzaro, *Robert Lowell*, 113.

Chapter Four

1 The result being *reconstructed meaning*, i.e., the addressee's more or less successful reconstruction of the intended meaning. This important factor

of meaning, often figuring in discussions of meaning, has sometimes also been identified with *meaning* itself. The concept "reconstructed meaning" should be kept apart from the wider concept "applicatory meaning" dealt with below.

2 One may of course try to combine intended, conventional, and applicatory meaning in different ways in order to form a more complex entity, possible to identify with meaning *tout court*. In my opinion, however, the attempts in that vein made to date are not worthy of imitation; I shall comment on some of them in the next section.

3 At least in some contexts, even elements appearing symptomatically are generally spoken of as the meaning or part of the meaning. When underlying psychic formations are laid bare in a psychoanalytical interpretation, these are often referred to as the text's meaning. For example, "Resistance to the 'application' of psychoanalysis to art and the denial that accompanies the unveiling of *the works' meaning* stem from the aversion men feel toward their own *infantile incestuous desires*, which have subsequently been completely repressed" (Kofman, *The Childhood of Art*, 99; my italics).

4 Leibowitz, "Robert Lowell," 217.

5 Hamilton, *Robert Lowell*, 260.

6 A fairly extensive account of how I regard the more important current alternatives is given in my *Theory of Literary Discourse*, chap. 5.

7 This idea has already been expressed by Saussure and was long espoused even in frontline research. See, e.g., Saussure, *Course in General Linguistics*, 11–12; Chafe, *Meaning and the Structure of Language*, 15–16; Katz, *Semantic Theory*, 24.

8 Beardsley, *Aesthetics*, 25.

9 See, e.g., Hirsch, *Validity in Interpretation*, 46–7.

10 See, e.g., Culler, *Structuralist Poetics*, 19 (where meaning in poetry is described as "an empty but circumscribed space") and Davies, *Definitions of Art*, 194 (where Davies allots a meaning-determining function to artistic conventions, but also speaks in the plural of the "interpretations that can be put on the work in the light of the conventions that are applicable to it").

11 The important distinction between linguistic formulations and language in use is made in different terms by different theorists. A small selection from current terminologies is presented in Wendell V. Harris, *Interpretive Acts*, 26–8.

12 To the best of my knowledge, William Tolhurst was the first to propound that thesis with a full awareness of its theoretical implications. See Tolhurst, "What a Text Is," esp. 5–9.

13 I foresee the objection that the conventional meaning of the utterance should be analysed differently – e.g., as "Someone pragmatically salient

313 Notes to pages 87–90

called 'Charlie' is ill." But more sophisticated descriptions of conventional meaning will not save conventionalism. In this case the suggested improvement is merely cosmetic, since what the addressees in the text are after is certainly intended reference, not pragmatic salience in itself (for which reason fresh counterexamples could easily be constructed). The importance of pragmatic salience no doubt lies in its providing a clue to intended reference.

14 Bartsch, *Norms of Language*, 212.

15 The arguments usually brought forward are inspired by, or related to, Ricœur's theory of distanciation (briefly commented upon in chap. 3 above, note 17).

16 The importance of that fact has been skilfully pointed out by Stephen C. Levinson. See his *Pragmatics*, 26 and 112–13.

17 The problems surrounding irony are often brought forward by those wishing to prove the inadequacy of conventionalism even in literary contexts and the necessity of taking authorial intentions into account. See, e.g., Tolhurst, "What a Text Is," 6–9 and Juhl, *Interpretation*, esp. 121–4.

18 In my opinion, that is how Wolfgang Iser's standpoint in *The Act of Reading* should be understood. See, e.g., Iser's preface to the second edition (*Der Akt des Lesens*, i).

19 Fish, *Is There a Text in This Class*, 322.

20 Juhl, *Interpretation*, esp. 47 and 67–8.

21 To be sure, Juhl has drawn no such consequences from his theory. In *Interpretation* he evades the problem by not discussing cases where it is impossible to recover the intended meaning.

22 Hirsch, *Validity in Interpretation*, 31.

23 Some other theories of meaning and interpretation operate with a more or less similar, complex picture of the process of communication. Especially closely related to my own analysis are those of Tolhurst ("What a Text Is"), Wendell V. Harris (*Interpretive Acts*), Currie (*The Nature of Fiction*), and Jerrold Levinson ("Intention and Interpretation in Literature"). Space does not permit me to comment on them here. Part of my view of Currie's standpoint on meaning and interpretation was, however, presented in my article "Walton's and Currie's Analyses."

24 Cf. Reddy, "The Conduit Metaphor," esp. 287–90, and the section "On the Transportation and Container Metaphors" in the Introduction above.

25 In my view, "work" is in fact a better designation than "text" for the literary verbal composition, "text" being more polysemous. Unlike "work," "text" may also be used to refer, among other things, to the physical text (e.g., the patterns of printer's ink in a book) or the sign-sequence (e.g., the sequence of words or graphemes exploited). Unfortunately, however, if one uses the term "work" one tends to give the impression of being behind the times. (Though the two words denote the

same phenomenon, public scholarly consciousness connects them with somewhat different understandings of the nature of a verbal composition, "work" provoking associations with something more stable and author-dominated and "text" making one think of a more contradictory and independent entity.)

26 Pollard, "Literature and Representation," 167.

27 The formulations are taken from Leibowitz, "Robert Lowell," 217.

28 For example, Nelson Goodman says, substantiating his statement in the most convincing manner: "Plainly, having the same shape, size, etc., is neither necessary nor sufficient for two marks to belong to the same letter" (*Languages of Art*, 137–9; I quote from 137).

29 Odenstedt, "The Meldorf Inscription," esp. 77–8.

30 Hamilton, *Robert Lowell*, 269.

31 With the reservation that the alternative approach is often unable to duplicate the polysemy of folk-theory formulations.

32 The expression has been chosen for practical reasons only, and no text concept is smuggled in by the back door. The designation is simply a proper name denoting a definite, particular physical object. In principle, any name would do the job.

33 My most extensive treatment of the subject, unfortunately, is a book in Swedish, *Verkbegreppet*. All that is said about the concept of a text here has been dealt with more profoundly and on a broader scale in that book, esp. in its chaps. 5–7. My present two sections on the concept of a text transcend the former account only in so far as some more recent theoretical contributions are also mentioned.

My previous discussions in English of the concept of a text are the article "Ontology of Literary Works" and *Theory of Literary Discourse*, 141–7.

34 As Reddy has pointed out, these ontological problems concern not only literary texts but all objects supposed to be intentionally produced signs – hence also the presumed denotata of designations like "word," "phrase," or "sentence" ("The Conduit Metaphor," 301), or, for that matter, the denotata of words like "memo," "letter," or "book."

35 Aldrich, *Philosophy of Art*, 32.

36 Sclafani, "The Logical Primitiveness," 26.

37 Ibid., 27.

38 Aldrich, *Philosophy of Art*, 33.

39 "Paradoxical in its mode of existence, a literary work is both one and many" (Armstrong, *Conflicting Readings*, 43).

40 The Type Theory was foreshadowed in Stevenson's "What Is a Poem" (1957) and propounded in a fully developed form in Margolis's "The Identity of a Work" (1959). From the 1960s onwards it has become very

popular. Some of the important contributions from various decades advocating it in different forms are Wollheim's *Art and Its Objects* (1968), Wolterstorff's "Toward an Ontology of Art Works" (1975), Currie's *An Ontology of Art* (1989), and Jerrold Levinson's "Work of Visual Art" (1996).

41 Recently, however, Christopher Hutton has surveyed extant thinking about the type/token distinction, pointing to some good reasons for doubting the value of the distinction (*Abstraction and Instance*).

42 It has in fact been common to identify types and similar constructs with sets. See, e.g., Stevenson, "What Is a Poem," 330; Quine, "Ontological Relativity," 196; Smith, "On Generics," 29.

43 I am thinking, above all, of Wollheim's *Art and Its Objects* and of Wolterstorff's "Toward an Ontology of Art Works." To my mind, none of the attempts is entirely fortunate; see my *Verkbegreppet*, 150–64.

44 Margolis's views have been set out, in somewhat differing versions, in a large number of contributions; see also, e.g., his "Ontological Peculiarity" and his "Ontology of Art." Margolis leaves unexplained how it is possible for a meaning to be embodied in physical objects, nor does he specify what more precise relations he imagines to exist between tokens of the same type.

45 Rudner, "The Ontological Status of the Esthetic Object," 385.

46 See Bachrach, "Type and Token."

47 See my *Theory of Literary Discourse*, 139–44.

48 Considerations like these made the Swedish scholar Gunnar Hansson into an early and consistent advocate of the idea that the text as usually conceived is a chimera. See, e.g., *Författaren dikten läsaren*, 115.

49 The idea that meaning is a kind of thought in the head of the user of language is old and deeply rooted – see, e.g., Lyons, "Bedeutungstheorien," 11–12. The idea is by no means obsolete – see, e.g., Searle, *Intentionality*, esp. chap. 8, "Are Meanings in the Head?" My own description of the process of communication also implies, of course, that at least some of the most important varieties of what we call "meaning" are mental phenomena (viz., intended meaning, reconstructed meaning, and applicatory meaning).

Meaning (in the word's different senses) being the crucial factor where literary texts are concerned, it is not surprising that older theories about how literary texts exist have sometimes identified literary texts with mentally existing meanings. See, e.g., Collingwood, *The Principles of Art*. More recent theories may also come close to such an understanding, though formulating it in a more sophisticated fashion. See, e.g., Haapala, *What Is a Work?*, esp. 208–9.

50 Cf. Roman Ingarden's arguments against the idea that a literary work is a mental phenomenon (*The Literary Work of Art*, esp. par. 4).

Chapter Five

1 "Thought" has no precise established import either in everyday language or in psychology or philosophy. I consider, however, that my definition falls within the concept's normal scope.

   When the notion of a thought is at its widest, every "product of mental action or effort" can be called a thought. (Cf. the headword "thought," 1.c., in Simpson and Weiner, eds., *Oxford English Dictionary*, 17:983.) This seems to be a definition which, unlike mine, does not in principle exclude emotions from being thoughts. Often however, esp. in philosophical contexts, a thought concept narrower than mine is employed. In that usage, perceptions are not characterized as thoughts, sometimes not even fantasies and the like. (See, e.g., Butchvarov, "Thought," 897–8. Cf. Peacocke, *Thoughts*, chap. 1.)

2 Cf. the description of the structure of intended meanings in my *Theory of Literary Discourse*, esp. 135–7. (What is here called a "mental representation" is there referred to as "intentional content.")

3 There are well-known exceptions – e.g., greetings like "Hello!" – but these exceptions are fairly marginal.

4 I have explained my view of their status much more thoroughly in another context, apropos Hugo Ball's poem "Karawane." See *Theory of Literary Discourse*, 243–9, esp. 248, note 64.

5 Johnson, *Jahrestage*. When possible I quote the English translation (*Anniversaries*), a version of the novel abridged in accordance with Johnson's instructions. When the translation departs significantly from the German original this will be indicated.

6 It is true that the first dated one-day-section of the novel concerns 21 August 1967 (cf. the description below of the novel's structure). The events in the undated introductory section should, however, in reason be imagined as taking place on the day before (considering, e.g., the expression "Next morning"; *Anniversaries*, 1:4).

7 This is emphasized by the fact that a special reference book indexing the novel's persons and locations has been published: Michaelis, *Kleines Adressbuch*.

8 My remarks about Johnson's book concern the novel in its entirety, as it presents itself in the unabridged German edition. They are not always correct for the English translation – in that version, e.g., several of the original one-day sections have simply been excluded.

9 A well-known passage is Johnson, *Anniversaries*, 2:590 (cf. *Jahrestage*, 4:1822).

10 See, e.g., Johnson, *Anniversaries*, 1:7 (quoted below).

11 There is a "contract" between Uwe Johnson and Gesine described esp. in Johnson, *Jahrestage*, 4:1426–8. (The one-day section in question is

not included in the English translation.) See also the other loci indexed by Michaelis under the headword "Uwe Johnson & Gesine Cresspahl" (*Kleines Adressbuch*, 135–7).

12 Johnson has, himself, commented on the ambiguity. See "Einführung in die *Jahrestage*," esp. 15 and 24.

13 Johnson, *Anniversaries*, 1:5–8.

14 Johnson himself also grew up in Mecklenburg, and that province plays an important part in his writings. See, e.g., Fahlke, "Heimat als geistige Landschaft," 166–81.

15 Something which is, in fact, sometimes done by force of considerations of the type just sketched. See, e.g., Stolnitz, "On the Cognitive Triviality of Art."

16 Cf. the views expressed in Lamarque and Olsen, *Truth, Fiction, and Literature*, e.g., 1–5, views which I share in all essentials. My remarks about literature's cognitive significance in the following normally parallel observations in Lamarque and Olsen's book (and in the analytical tradition to which we all belong). Cf. esp. Lamarque and Olsen, *Truth, Fiction, and Literature*, chap. 15, and the literature cited there.

17 Schumach, "New York City," 865–79.

18 See Hospers, *Meaning and Truth*, 233–8, esp. 237.

19 Perhaps he is in fact, in some special cases, asserting. Cf. the section "Statements in Literature: John Searle's Analysis" below.

20 I would like to emphasize that I do indeed see this formulation as metaphorical. Unlike Kendall Walton and many others, I do not believe that in reading literature we have to imagine coming into actual contact with the make-believe world. Cf. my previous discussion of Walton's and Currie's analyses of fictional discourse in terms of make-believe (in the section "Fictional Utterances" in chap. 3 above).

21 In my view, the phenomenon usually called "concrete universality" has its root in this fact. Cf. the section "Literature's Concrete Universality" in chap. 2 above.

22 This is, and has long been, the common way of understanding the question about literature and truth within analytical aesthetics. Cf., e.g., Cebik, *Fictional Narrative and Truth*, 98 and Lamarque and Olsen, *Truth, Fiction, and Literature*, 5–11. McCormick, *Fictions, Philosophies, and the Problems of Poetics*, 82–9, describes in an instructive manner fundamental differences between what he calls an "analytic" and a "hermeneutic" perspective concerning literature and truth.

23 Cf. Hospers's survey of other meanings of "truth" ("sincerity," "acceptability," "value for mankind," etc.) (*Meaning and Truth*, 141–4).

24 "Truth" in those two wider senses is dealt with primarily in chap. 6 (on thematization) and in chap. 7 (on the affective dimension of literature) respectively.

25 Cf. Lamarque and Olsen, *Truth, Fiction, and Literature*, esp. 7–8 and 10.

26 Cf., e.g., Cebik, *Fictional Narrative and Truth*, 44 and the literature cited there.

27 Brian Rosebury, e.g., contends that fiction never contains truths. See his *Art and Desire*, 34.

28 See esp. Searle, *Expression and Meaning*, 12–13. "The point or purpose of the members of the assertive class," says Searle, "is to commit the speaker (in varying degrees) to something's being the case, to the truth of the expressed proposition" (ibid., 12). Or: "The point of statements and descriptions is to tell people how things are" (Searle and Vanderveken, *Foundations of Illocutionary Logic*, 13). Cf. Searle, *Speech Acts*, 29 and 66, and also Searle and Vanderveken, *Foundations of Illocutionary Logic*, 183.

29 Searle simply introduces the term "point" as a rough synonym for "purpose": "The point or purpose of a type of illocution I shall call its *illocutionary point*" (*Expression and Meaning*, 3; cf. Searle and Vanderveken, *Foundations of Illocutionary Logic*, 13). According to Searle's theory there is a kind of conceptual symbiosis between type of illocutionary point and type of illocutionary act: "In general we can say that the illocutionary point of a type of illocutionary act is that purpose which is essential to its being an act of that type" (Searle and Vanderveken, *Foundations of Illocutionary Logic*, 14).

30 Cf. *Theory of Literary Discourse*, 22–6, and the literature cited there (23, note 23).

31 Searle, *Expression and Meaning*, 73–4.

32 What is problematic in this context is not of course the fact that the opening sentence of *Anna Karenina* is so imprecise that it must be difficult to determine whether its content corresponds to reality or not. (What are the criteria of a happy family? Of an unhappy family? And how are we to decide whether two families differ in their ways of being unhappy?) It is easy enough to provide examples from everyday life of utterances just as imprecise that still reasonably qualify as statements.

33 There is a distinction – seldom observed, but to my mind highly important – between the kind of meaning appertaining to whole utterances and the kind of meaning appertaining to parts of utterances. Cf. Schiffer, *Meaning*, esp. 4–5. Schiffer discusses utterance wholes of a very simple nature: one-sentence utterances and the like. But utterances of sentences etc. may naturally be parts of larger utterance wholes.

34 Actually, I prefer David Magarshack's translation: "All happy families are like one another; each unhappy family is unhappy in its own way" (Tolstoy, *Anna Karenina*, 17).

35 It is not uncommon for a novel, especially a nineteenth-century novel, to open with a formulation seemingly purporting to convey a general truth.

Think of Jane Austen's *Pride and Prejudice* (1813), beginning with the remark "It is a truth universally acknowledged, that a single man in possession of a good fortune, must be in want of a wife," or of the first sentence in *La Dame aux Camélias* by Alexandre Dumas fils (*La Dame aus Camélias*, 1848): "It is my considered view that no one can invent fictional characters without first having made a lengthy study of people, just as it is impossible for anyone to speak a language that has not been properly mastered" (Austen, *Pride and Prejudice*, 51; Dumas *fils*, *La Dame aux Camélias*, 1). Those openings too have certainly been chosen with a view to thematic effects and could be analysed along similar lines to the Tolstoj example.

36 Grambow, "Johnson, Uwe," 122.

37 Johnson, *Anniversaries*, 2:501–2.

38 I can certainly see problems with the concept, problems related to the concept "point" and the basic characteristics of Searle's speech act theory. I shall, however, leave those underlying problems aside in this context.

39 The concept "statement" is at present hardly determinate enough to allow us to say that Searle's strong definition covers the normal way of understanding the concept, the weaker interpretation being atypical. It is my impression, however, that pragmatics has created a tendency to sharpen the traditional, indistinct concept of a statement along the lines exemplified by Searle's analysis. Nowadays, statements are often said to be "*primarily* used to convey information," "used *primarily* to convey information" (Quirk et al., *Comprehensive Grammar of the English Language*, 803; Crystal, *Dictionary of Linguistics*, 325; my italics.)

40 Austin, *How to Do Things with Words*, 104. Austin appears to be thinking primarily of statements in poetry.

41 Concerning the concept of an indirect speech act, see esp. the article "Indirect Speech Acts" in Searle's *Expression and Meaning*.

42 Larkin, *Collected Poems*, 195. The editor gives "August? 1972" as a date for the text (ibid.).

43 It follows from the analysis of literary communication in chaps. 3–4 above that what is said in a literary text should, formally, be understood as said by the author, unless another speaker is indicated. I am well aware that this approach is controversial, but it plays too insignificant a role in the present context to need an extended defence here. For a sustained argument in its favour see, e.g., Wolterstorff, *Works and Worlds of Art*, 163–79 and my *Theory of Literary Discourse*, 104–13.

44 It is true that the two diverging meanings coalesce to a certain extent: according to Larkin's formulations in the poem, what is left of his life is, in reality, only death.

45 The word "climbers" is ambiguous here, referring, explicitly, to mountaineers while connoting, at the same time, careerists (thereby

strengthening the connection between the opinion that the view is fine from fifty and opportune falseness).

46 Cf. the preceding note.

47 It is no doubt effects of this kind that motivate the widespread opinion that literature's form and content cannot be separated, that poetry cannot be paraphrased, etc. I discuss such ideas in some detail later on, esp. in chaps. 8–10.

48 Searle, *Expression and Meaning*, 74.

49 English-speaking literary aesthetics settled accounts with the standpoint in question in the 1940s. Its best known adversary is surely Cleanth Brooks – see esp. his famous essay "The Heresy of Paraphrase." Brooks adduces several good arguments against the standpoint; the arguments that I use in the text are, however, different.

50 Implicit assertions via fictions are indeed possible, and perhaps also implicit assertions conveyed by fictional compositions taken as wholes. Concerning the possibility of literary works with an informational communicative function, see my discussion in *Theory of Literary Discourse*, 243–9.

51 I assume, here, that Searle is referring to *literature* in speaking of a "work of fiction" in the quoted passage. In some kinds of non-literary fictions – e.g., in commercial advertising – cases where it would be reasonable to say that the discourse as a whole conveys an assertion (or an exhortation) are no doubt more frequent. Cf. *Theory of Literary Discourse*, 200–4.

52 It is no doubt considerations similar to the ones just presented that have made some theorists such as Brian Rosebury maintain that fiction is by its very nature incapable of conveying assertions. In Rosebury's case the standpoint is motivated by the idea that the conventions surrounding literary fiction, "the fictional convention," prevent the making of genuine assertions (*Art and Desire*, 32–3; I quote from 32). His idea is formulated somewhat sweepingly and apodictically, but what has been said in this chapter lends it some, conditional, support.

53 About the contemporary reception of *Life Studies*, see Hamilton, *Robert Lowell*, 268–73. Procopiow, *Robert Lowell*, 248–51, gives a temporally more extended account of how the collection's tendency towards personal confession has been assessed.

54 It does, however, convey certain statements that can possibly be regarded as etiolated assertions – which motivates my reservation "on the whole." Cf. the end of this section and the section "Statements in Literature: John Searle's Analysis" above.

55 Johnson, *Anniversaries*, 1:10.

56 Johnson's novel is told from a position close to Gesine's (cf. the sources referred to in note 11 above). In this particular passage the opening "Yesterday" helps to indicate that the things depicted are seen from

Gesine's incidental temporal viewpoint, that of 23 August 1967. It is, moreover, made evident by various means ("front page," etc.) that the information goes back to the contents of a newspaper, and the novel has already found time to introduce the *New York Times* as Gesine's favourite paper.

57 X "expresses" Y in this sense if and only if (1) Y is an intentional state, (2) Y was a cause of the production of X, and (3) the existence of Y can be inferred from X. From the passage in *Anniversaries* (X) one can reasonably infer Johnson's conviction (Y), which is an intentional state and presumably a contributory cause of the production of the passage with its present content.

Johnson's communicative intention is expressed in this sense, but there are also intentional states – e.g., convictions like the one discussed – that have found expression without being communicated – *expressed but non-communicated thoughts*.

This concept of expression is close to Alan Tormey's; see *The Concept of Expression*, esp. 43.

58 Johnson worked with newspaper cuttings pasted onto sheets of paper (cuttings now in the Uwe Johnson Archive in Frankfurt am Main). One might think, therefore, that the facts should have been obvious to him, and that divergences from the facts have to be intentional. So they undoubtedly are in many cases, but some of the deviations may well be caused by misunderstandings or misinterpretations. For one thing, it was not possible for Johnson to reconstruct, solely from his cuttings, the larger context in the newspaper of which the articles, pictures, and notices originally formed parts.

59 Johnson, *Anniversaries*, 1:11–12.

60 Hospers, *Meaning and Truth in the Arts*, 74.

61 Hospers, "Implied Truths in Literature," 201.

62 See, e.g., John Lyons's treatment of the referential theory of meaning in his article "Bedeutungstheorien," 8–11, esp. 9. Cf. also Wittgenstein's famous criticism of the theory of linguistic designations as names in his *Philosophische Untersuchungen*, esp. par. 1–11 (*Philosophical Investigations*, 2^e–6^e).

63 Consider esp. Hospers's basic definition of the reference relation underlying meaning: "Whenever one item in our experience stands for another, the first item is said to *represent* the other, or to be a *symbol* of the other, while the thing symbolized or represented is called the *referent* of the symbol" (*Meaning and Truth*, 29; cf. also, e.g., ibid., 123, where the referent is spoken of as "things" or "a situation").

64 See esp. ibid., 158–9, where Hospers among other things talks of words as "symbols by which propositions can be mediated" (159). Naturally, there are weaknesses in such "ideational" theories of meaning as well; cf., e.g., Lyons, "Bedeutungstheorien," 11–13.

65 Cf., e.g., Margaret Macdonald's treatment of the problem in "The Language of Fiction," esp. 184–7, and the literature cited by her. See also Cebik's description of the discussion (*Fictional Narrative and Truth*, 98).

66 The very concept of a fictional sentence is already infelicitous (and by and large abandoned in modern literary theory). The notion presupposes that a *sentence* either does or does not bear the stamp of fiction. But as our example demonstrates ("Yesterday the Air Force flew 132 missions over North Vietnam"), sentences may certainly be used fictionally in some contexts and non-fictionally in others. Fictionality and non-fictionality pertain to utterances, not sentences.

67 Hospers, "Implied Truths," 213: "an important sense of truth in literature, and one which it seems to me that many critics who have made claims for truth in literature have had in mind without being fully aware of it."

68 Ibid., 210.

69 Ibid., 213.

70 Ibid., 212. In the quotation, Hospers also seems to express the idea that correct interpretations of one and the same work may very well contradict each other. That is a view which is nowadays held by many; see, e.g., Robert Stecker's criticism of the standpoint in "Incompatible Interpretations" and in *Artworks*, chap. 7, and the literature cited there. Like Stecker, I find the view untenable.

71 Mellor, "On Literary Truth," esp. 159–60.

72 Ibid., 166–7.

73 An idea similar in this respect is advocated in the latest more comprehensive treatment of the problem, that of Lamarque and Olsen. There the authors, like myself, start from the view of literature reading as a practice. Unlike me, however, they conceive of the rules of the practice as being so precise that quite determinate propositions are established and ascribed to the work in the course of the correct reading of it. At least that is how I understand their idea (e.g., 327–8) that a reading of fiction in accordance with the rules establishes "general propositions" (whose truth-value is not, however, seen by Lamarque and Olsen as their most essential property from a literary point of view).

74 Cebik, *Fictional Narrative and Truth*, 130–1.

75 Ibid., 102–5 and chap. 8.

76 About presuppositions in general see, e.g., John Lyons's treatment of conversational implicatures and presuppositions in his *Semantics*, 2:592–606. Cebik's supposed derivations are more or less debatable in themselves, and he seems to have largely overlooked the pragmatic dimension of language. What silent presuppositions one makes in uttering a certain sentence may in fact vary from case to case. Especially, we are not entitled to assume that presuppositions normally made in everyday situations will automatically be present in literary contexts as well.

77 Cebik, *Fictional Narrative and Truth*, 116.
78 See, e.g., ibid., 210–11.
79 McCormick, *Fictions, Philosophies, and the Problems of Poetics*, 121.
80 See, e.g., Lotman, *Die Struktur literarischer Texte*, 35. Cf. Ann Shukman, *Literature and Semiotics*, esp. 14 and 123–4.
81 Cf. Goodman, *Languages of Art*, 53.
82 "A form of exemplification that is particularly important in the arts is expression. Thus a painting is said to express terror, a poem to express sadness, a trio to express bliss" (Catherine Z. Elgin, *With Reference to Reference*, 82).
83 Ibid., 79–80.
84 An awareness of that fact is not always to be found among theorists inspired by Goodman. A few pages later Elgin writes of works of art: "Each work determines which of the labels it instantiates are relevant to its own interpretation. It does so by singling them out, serving as a sample of them, referring to them" (ibid., 86). But works of art are not living agents performing acts all by themselves, so in the final analysis it cannot be they who determine, single out, refer.

Chapter Six

1 See the section "The Reading of Literature: A Cognitive-Affective Processing Pattern" in chap. 2.
2 "Intentions, purposes over and above the telling of the story, Johnson has ... always denied" (Bengel, "Johnsons *Jahrestage*," 318).
3 Johnson, "Vorschläge," 402–3. For the dating of the text and other background information, see Bernd Neumann's exhaustive Johnson biography, *Uwe Johnson*, 671–2. Johnson's article has been reprinted in Gerlach and Richter, eds., *Uwe Johnson*.
4 Durzak, *Gespräche über den Roman*, 430–1. Durzak informs us (ibid., 529) that the interviews in his book were conducted between spring 1973 and spring 1975.
5 True, in the quotations from Johnson the reader's post-communicative processing stands out as entirely unrestrained by rules or norms. Later in this chapter I shall introduce a phenomenon which I call "expected understanding" and to which I assign an important role in the post-communicative processing of the addressee. This idea of an expected understanding is not found in the Johnson quotations.
6 I call the representations that the reader associatively connects with the communicated ones "secondary." (They are secondary in relation to the *communicated* representations constituting the starting point of the reader associations.)
7 See, e.g., Träger, ed., *Wörterbuch der Literaturwissenschaft*, 517 or Baldick, *Concise Oxford Dictionary of Critical Terms*, 225. The concept of

a theme is also used to denote frequently recurring literary motifs. Within the formalist and structuralist traditions there are yet other employments of the term, usages which I disregard here.

8 See Gadamer, *Truth and Method*, esp. 274–8. I comment on Gadamer's concept of application in the next section.

9 It is also my opinion that focusing, non-self-orientated associating, and application do in principle (variously structured) occur in the addressee's post-communicative processing of texts of all types – hence also of poems, jokes, specialist books, summonses, and so on.

10 Cf., e.g., statements such as the following (from Derrida): "Meaning is determined by a system of forces which is not personal. It does not depend on the subjective identity but on the field of different forces, the conflict of forces, which produce interpretations" (Kearns and Newton, "Interview with Jacques Derrida," 22. I quote from Holland, *The Critical I*, 156).

11 Lesser, *Fiction and the Unconscious*, 200.

12 It is worth noting, however, that Lesser does, in passing, point to the possibility that the reader's satisfaction may be occasioned by her acquiring of new perspectives on reality: "At times at least, it has been suggested, the reading of fiction may help the ego in dealing with its own problems, calling attention to considerations and ways of resolving conflicts the ego may have overlooked" (ibid., 101).

13 Gadamer, *Truth and Method*, 163.

14 Cf. ibid., 275–6 and 297.

15 Ibid., 274.

16 Nussbaum, *Love's Knowledge*, 257.

17 Ibid., 166. Cf. kindred formulations on 44, 47, 252–3, et passim.

18 See my *Theory of Literary Discourse*, esp. 41–4.

19 Neumann, "Heimweh," 279. Later, Neumann has tended to foreground the self-analysis that Johnson carries out in *Anniversaries*. See esp. Neumann, *Uwe Johnson*, 605.

20 The difference between the German and American reception of *Anniversaries* has been emphasized by Ulrich Fries, who sees it primarily in the Germans' interest in the political dimension and the Americans' preoccupation with the book's narrative technique. (*Uwe Johnsons "Jahrestage,"* 179; cf. ibid., 13–15).

21 Bengel, "Johnsons *Jahrestage*," 304. The same aspects of *Anniversaries* are treated as central also, e.g., by Hans Scholz and Günther Schloz. See Scholz, "Mutmassungen über Uwe," and Schloz's review of *Jahrestage 4*.

22 Bengel, "Johnsons *Jahrestage*," 320.

23 Neumann, *Utopie und Mimesis*, 297–8.

24 Ibid., 302.

25 Fries, *Uwe Johnsons "Jahrestage,"* 17.

26 Ibid., 149, 154, 178.

27 Johnson, *Anniversaries*, 2:589–90.

28 Neumann believes that the encounter takes place on the Danish island of Bornholm in the Baltic (*Uwe Johnson*, 5 and 676–7). However, several indications in the text make it clear that the scene is set on Sjaelland, not far from Copenhagen.

29 Johnson, *Anniversaries*, 2:644.

30 Many have commented on the ending of *Anniversaries*. The themes of breaking up and of death met with in the finishing passages ("even the incidental contact with the water acquires the character of a crossing of boundaries") have been stressed in an explicit and detailed manner especially by Ingeborg Gerlach ("Aus der Sicht des vierten Bandes," esp. 258–60; the quotation comes from 260. Cf. also Neumann, *Uwe Johnson*, 842–3).

31 The content of the concept of identification will not be discussed until the next chapter.

32 The close relationship between Gesine on the one hand, and Uwe Johnson and his wife Elisabeth on the other, has been emphasized by Neumann. See, most recently, *Uwe Johnson*, 176, 298, 830, and (esp.) 624–5. Johnson himself energetically denied any autobiographical connections between himself and Gesine, but with extremely superficial arguments: Gesine is a woman while he is a man, she was born in 1933 and he in 1934, etc. See Johnson, *Begleitumstände*, 441–4.

33 Moeller, "Uwe Johnson."

34 Riordan, *The Ethics of Narration*, 215–17; the quotations come from 216 and 217 respectively.

35 Becker, "Eine Bitte," 191.

36 Baumgart, "Bibliothek – zum Lesen empfohlen." I quote – with the archive's kind permission – from a typewritten manuscript in the Uwe Johnson-Archiv, Frankfurt am Main, here p. 5.

37 Ibid., 3.

38 Ibid., 7.

39 Ibid., 10.

40 Cf. my *Theory of Literary Discourse*, 69 and 246.

41 Freud, *Jokes*, 55.

42 One can certainly call the reasonableness of this analysis into question. Above all, it may sound unnatural to say that being put forward as being funny is part of the intended meaning of a joke. But I should like to make three observations in that connection. First: the modes of expression of everyday language need not bind us when we forge a theoretical analysis. Second: we find ourselves, here, in a zone of transition between things communicated and non-communicated, a zone where all fixings of well-defined boundaries must be arbitrary to a considerable

extent. And third, and most important: what I am after is not the drawing of exact limits. My aim, at this point, is to make it credible that there are expectations concerning the addressee's processing *transcending* the mere expectation of an understanding and application of the communicated content. It is these extra expectations that have to do with expected understanding in my sense.

43 This is an observation that has, with justice, played a considerable role – one might say a key role – in modern philosophy of language. See, e.g., Furberg, *Saying and Meaning*, esp. 93–4; Grice, "Logic and Conversation," esp. 45–6; Sperber and Wilson, *Relevance*, esp. 47–8 and 50.

44 Cf. Freud, *Jokes*, 55–8.

45 In discussing expected understanding, I am thinking about the reading of texts from the reader's own time and culture. A reading of the *Odyssey* (probably eighth century BC) may certainly be competent even if it is not able to identify the expected understanding correctly. If one wishes to take into consideration also the reading of literature from other times and cultures, the bases of the argument have to be made broader. In this context, I have wanted to avoid complications of the sort indicated.

46 Even if one is, like Olsen, a meta-conventionalist regarding the practice of reading as being governed by highly precise rules, one must apprehend identifications of themes as objectively correct or erroneous. Cf. Olsen, *End of Literary Theory*, 16 and Skilleås's remarks about that passage ("Anachronistic Themes," 129). Cf. also Lamarque and Olsen, *Truth, Fiction, and Literature*, chap. 16, and my chap. 5 above, note 73.

47 Beardsley, *Aesthetics*, 2nd ed., 403. On the other hand, Beardsley (ibid., 423) sees the reader as being creative in other ways than through focusing: she may, e.g., contemplate statements made by the work or assess their tenability (a special case of what I call "non-self-orientated associating").

48 Ibid., li.

49 That Juhl sees themes as existing in the work itself becomes clear in, e.g., his criticism of Jauss's interpretation of Goethe's *Iphigenie auf Tauris* (Juhl, *Interpretation*, 226–8). Like Beardsley, Juhl perceives the reader as being creative in other respects than that of focusing (ibid., 233–4).

50 The author's statements are certainly not decisive. They do not in principle prevent us from arguing that Johnson, without clearly realizing it himself, wants to have his novel understood in a special, determinate fashion. My point is, rather, that it should be obvious by now – from all that I have said about the novel, and about possible ways of understanding it, and about the intentions disclosed by Johnson – that an argument along such lines will in fact have little chance of seeming plausible. (As I made clear, though, I believe that Johnson overlooks the fact that

he has, after all, certain approximate expectations concerning the general drift of the reader's post-communicative processing.)

51 Consider, e.g., Jonathan Culler's well-known description of conventions employed in the reading of literature (*Structuralist Poetics*, 115).

52 In the same vein – and with interesting examples – William Lyons has recently defended the viewer's freedom to let historical and art-historical knowledge affect his experience of an art work. See Lyons, "On Looking into Titian's *Assumption*," esp. 149–50.

53 Parsons, *How We Understand Art*, 20.

54 Ibid., 25. Parsons emphasizes other characteristics as well in the responses of the most advanced viewers, e.g., "an alert awareness of the character of one's own experience, a questioning of the influences upon it, a wondering whether one really sees what one thinks one sees" (ibid.). Obviously, these informants are well aware of the complexities involved in creating, viewing, and assessing art, and they let this come to the fore in their remarks. It appears unfortunate to me, even misleading, when Parsons describes this way of viewing art as centred on "autonomy" (ibid.).

55 See, e.g., *Theory of Literary Discourse*, 40.

56 Hye, *Uwe Johnsons Jahrestage*. Hye's book was written before the publication of the last volume of Johnson's novel, which one should bear in mind when evaluating her contribution. For critical remarks on Hye's interpretation, see Fries, *Uwe Johnsons "Jahrestage,"* 13–14, and the literature cited there. "Nowhere is Hye commended for her work, at least not in the German secondary literature," says Fries (14, note 16).

57 Hye, *Uwe Johnsons Jahrestage*, 17 and 56 respectively. Hye's interpretation does not completely lack foundation. By various means, Johnson makes sure that his readers come to associate the treatment of black Americans with the treatment of Jews in the Third Reich, and the violent history of twentieth-century Germany to the war in Vietnam. Hye is also right in maintaining that literal repetition plays a not insignificant role in the novel. Its very title, *Anniversaries*, is indeed concerned with repetition, as is its opening scene (not quoted by me), where the waves of the Atlantic – in Johnson's text explicitly contrasted with those of the Baltic – are seen rolling in towards the New Jersey coast. In Hye's interpretation, these waves become "an emblem of the eternally recurrent" (*Uwe Johnsons Jahrestage*, 17).

58 Baumgart, "Bibliothek – zum Lesen empfohlen," 5.

59 I am aware of the fact that Hye's interpretation, and the rejection of it, form part of the *critical* or *scholarly* language game. A relativist could argue, therefore, that Hye's interpretation is in fact acceptable in the *literary* language game. As will become clear in the following, I do not believe that this is correct. It is, however, already difficult, for

theoretical reasons, to produce credible assessments of the acceptability of ordinary readers' thematizations.

60 Cf. Rorty, "The Pragmatist's Progress," 103.

61 Ibid., 105–6. Note that Rorty implicitly refers to what I call focusing and non-self-orientated associating when he talks of reading "in the light of" other phenomena and of "seeing what happens," and that he presupposes a reader application when speaking of the result of reading as potentially "exciting and convincing."

62 For further examples of varieties of pragmatism in the theory of interpretation, see Shusterman, *Pragmatist Aesthetics*, chap. 4. Cf. Robert Stecker's criticism of Shusterman, Rorty, and Fish in his *Artworks*, chap. 11.

63 Holland, *The Critical I*, esp. 49–50, 57, and 100–1.

64 The formulation is borrowed from Palmer, *Literature and Moral Understanding*, 159.

65 See esp. Holland, *Five Readers Reading*, 13–14.

66 Margolis, *Art and Philosophy*, chaps. 3 and 4.

67 Cf., e.g., ibid., 111–12.

68 Ibid., 151.

69 Ibid., 155.

70 Barnes, *On Interpretation*, is another well-known work defending the thesis that "critical practice *both* tolerates a plurality of sometimes incompatible interpretations of artworks *and* nevertheless allows that confrontation and significant defeat may take place between critics" (1). Barnes's book (chap. 5) contains a critical examination of Margolis's theory.
   Here, I bypass Barnes's actual discussion, more orientated towards the logical structure of the argumentation than towards aesthetics.

71 Torsten Pettersson attempts to develop Margolis's theory further in his *Literary Interpretation*. The thrust of Pettersson's argument is that interpreting consists in the extracting of implications from the work's verbal meaning (chap. 5, esp. 86–7); it is a fundamental idea of Pettersson's that "acceptable interpretations ... may be divergent to the point of incompatibility" (107–8). The vagueness of Pettersson's concept of implication renders his theory relatively empty (cf. the problems in connection with implication touched upon in the last chapter apropos Hospers, Mellor, and Cebik).

72 Cebik, *Fictional Narrative and Truth*, 232.

73 A pragmatist or a theorist orientated towards reader response would not, normally, disown the cognitive importance of literature but see it exclusively in precisely the fact that literature may function as a cognitive impetus. An instructive treatment of literature's cognitive value along such lines is found in Prado's *Making Believe*, e.g., 104, 108, and 151.

74 Apart from the books by Novitz and by Lamarque and Olsen mentioned below, this goes for several of the works that I have cited here earlier, especially for those by Cebik, Prado, and McCormick.

75 Novitz, *Knowledge, Fiction, and Imagination*, chap. 6; Lamarque and Olsen, *Truth, Fiction, and Literature*, esp. chaps. 15–17.

76 Esp. in "Concluding Remarks: On the Nature of Literature's Autonomy."

77 Novitz, *Knowledge, Fiction, and Imagination*, 118.

78 Ibid., 142.

79 Ibid., 131–2.

80 Since Novitz does not clearly perceive the role of expressed, non-communicated thoughts, he does not observe that a fictional text "in itself" may sometimes provide the reader with some evidence for an assumption about reality *without the author's putting forward any genuine statement*. Cf. ibid., 132.

81 Ibid., 137.

82 Ibid., 120.

83 Johnson, *Anniversaries*, 1:9.

84 Cf. Novitz, *Knowledge, Fiction, and Imagination*, esp. 120, 134–5, and 140–1.

85 Ibid., 137.

86 In principle literature must, of course, have the capacity to incite all conceivable types of ideas about reality.

87 Cf. Churchland, *Matter and Consciousness*, 178–9. My observations about literature's possible role in the forming of distinctions and concepts, and about the cognitive value associated with this, are highly influenced by analogous remarks by Churchland.

88 Hospers, *Meaning and Truth*, 178.

89 See. e.g., Goodman, *Languages of Art*, 233, 238, and 260 (exemplification, expression, and aesthetic value) and 258–9 and 262 respectively (the role of the cognitive aspect of art and literature and its relations to emotions and form). One problem with Hospers's and Goodman's formulations is their pronouncedly objectivistic character: meaning is associated with the works themselves so directly that it seems difficult to defend today.

90 For thinking along such lines see, e.g., Stolnitz, "Cognitive Triviality of Art."

91 Cf. McCormick's contrasting of an analytical and a hermeneutical approach to literature and truth (*Fictions, Philosophies, and the Problems of Poetics*, 82–9).

92 It is, at bottom, this simple fact that explains why literature does not allow itself to be paraphrased as relatively successfully as non-fiction.

93 Evidently, concrete phenomena are closer to us than more abstract ones, forming the soil from which abstraction grows (as Piaget, among others, has maintained).

94 Lesser, *Fiction and the Unconscious*, 242.

95 Philip Davis, *The Experience of Reading*, 44.

96 In its general drift, this argument agrees with several accounts of literature's cognitive importance from recent years. I find especially interesting Nussbaum, *Love's Knowledge*, Palmer, *Literature and Moral Understanding*, chap. 8, and Lamarque and Olsen, *Truth, Fiction, and Literature*, chaps. 16–17. My description of the underlying cognitive mechanisms is not, however, identical with theirs.

Chapter Seven

1 Some emotional responses are no doubt conditioned by genetic factors; cf., e.g., Morreall, "Fear without Belief."

2 Bosanquet, *Three Lectures on Aesthetic*, 74.

3 Cf. Blocker, *Philosophy of Art*, 100–1 and the literature cited there. Blocker himself is of a different opinion; I discuss his view below, in the section "The Ideas of Objective Correlatives and Embodied Emotions."

4 See esp. note 11 below.

5 Lyons, *Emotion*, 59.

6 Nevertheless they *can* acquire some significance for experiences of the poem. There may, e.g., be readers who are well acquainted with Lowell's biography and cannot, or will not, prevent their knowledge of Lowell and his real feelings from affecting their experiences of the poem. (Their thematizations and applications of the poem may of course still be acceptable according to my analysis.)

7 Cf. Alan Williamson's observation that Lowell's "use of fact" in the poems about his father's death "gives us the real, numbed pain of the life surrounding a death in a way that no traditional elegiac stance ever could" (*Pity the Monsters*, 65).

8 Leibowitz, "Robert Lowell," 217, my emphasis. It may be inferred from the context that the characterization is meant to be applicable to "Father's Bedroom" too, in spite of the fact that the example actually adduced by Leibowitz is taken from another poem.

9 One might think that the same could be said of communicated thoughts. Notice, however, that one cannot communicate a thought without entertaining it, without "having" it in some sense. True, it is possible to communicate a thought without believing in its correctness, but this nevertheless requires that the thought is somehow brought into existence in one's mind.

10 According to the majority view – which is certainly not uncontested – the question of whether an author is sincere in his literary writings is aesthetically irrelevant or simply meaningless. Cf., e.g., Wayne Booth's dismissal of "pointless and unverifiable talk about such qualities as 'sincerity' or 'seriousness' in the author"; (*The Rhetoric of Fiction*, 75).

I myself would like to take up an intermediate position and say that the author's real feelings (or the reader's impression of the author's real feelings) may indeed have *some* relevance for the reading experience. For, first, knowledge of the author's real feelings may affect the biographically well informed reader (cf. note 6 above). And second, the feelings that are (actually or seemingly) expressed but not communicated may be in harmony with, or clash with, the communicated feelings, which may result in positive or negative aesthetic effects.

11 If one calls Lowell's poem "sad," it is thus not necessarily a question of a projection onto the poem of *the feelings actually arising in the reader.* It may just as well be a projection onto the poem of *the communicated feelings.* In general, I think, it is the feelings that we understand as being communicated or expressed through the art object that we project onto it.

12 The distinction between feelings expressed (here: communicated) and feelings described is well known. See, e.g., Collingwood, *The Principles of Art,* 111–12.

13 Axelsson, "Ljusets frihet," 144.

14 Ibid., 145.

15 Cf. Morreall, "Fear without Belief," 359–66, esp. 363–4 and 366.

16 Cf., e.g., Matravers, *Art and Emotion,* 74 and 76.

17 Gilbert and Kuhn, *A History of Aesthetics,* 537.

18 Lesser, *Fiction and the Unconscious,* 200; Nussbaum, *Love's Knowledge,* 166.

19 In my opinion, the idea of "participation" has been interpreted too literally by Kendall Walton when he holds that we make-believedly enter fictive worlds when experiencing works in the representational arts. (I comment briefly on Walton's views in the last section of this chapter.) I would also say, e.g., that Novitz's and Feagin's interesting analyses of readers' emotional involvement claim too much: Novitz, *Knowledge, Fiction and Imagination,* 75–9; Feagin, *Reading with Feeling,* chap. 4.

20 See esp. Feagin, *Reading with Feeling,* 112.

21 Currie, "The Paradox of Caring," 69.

22 In a similar vein, Alex Neill (who is sympathetic to Feagin's general account of simulation) has recently contended that "we shall need to appeal to more than simulation to explain our empathetic responses to fiction" (Neill, review of Feagin, 71).

23 Walton, "Spelunking, Simulation, and Slime," esp. 40–3. It is true that Walton, too, in effect understands reactions to fictive characters as reactions to characters who, in our make-believe, do actually exist.

24 See, e.g., Brenner, *Elementary Textbook of Psychoanalysis,* 44–9 or Wolman, *Dictionary of Behavioral Science,* 171.

25 Freud, "Psychopathic Characters on the Stage," 121–2. The quotation comes from 122 (with Freud's own emphasis).

26 See the discussion of identification in Holland, *Dynamics of Literary Response*, esp. 277–80.

27 Schönau, *Einführung in die psychoanalytische Literaturwissenschaft*, 57–61, gives a well-informed survey of the literary applications of the concept of identification, observed from the vantage point of psycho-analytical literary criticism. Cf. also Kofman, *The Childhood of Art*, 114–19. A discussion of the concept dissociated from Freudianism is found in Carroll, *The Philosophy of Horror*, 88–96.

28 See, e.g., Nussbaum, *Love's Knowledge*, 162; cf. also 252–3.

29 Novitz, e.g., speaks of our "emotional involvement" in the fictive events as if it were more or less identical with our tendency "to identify emotionally with its central characters" (*Knowledge, Fiction and Imagination*, 78 and 79 respectively).

30 Carroll, "Art, Narrative, and Emotion," 200.

31 Carroll does propose such a "general mechanism or structure" (ibid., 201–7), but I shall refrain from discussing it here.

32 As Schönau rightly emphasizes (*Einführung in die psychoanalytische Literaturwissenschaft*, 58).

33 Van Dijk and Kintsch, *Strategies of Discourse Comprehension*, 322–3 and chap. 10.

34 Just and Carpenter, *The Psychology of Reading*, 224, my emphasis. Cf., e.g., van den Broek, "The Causal Inference Maker," 441, or Garrod and Sanford, "Referential Processes in Reading," 465.

35 Cf., e.g., van Dijk and Kintsch, *Strategies of Discourse Comprehension*, 15–16 or Just and Carpenter, *The Psychology of Reading*, 250.

36 And certainly to many important and subtle *cognitive* effects as well. Observations analogous to those made here would have been possible also in chaps. 6 and 7.

  Cf. also Susan Feagin's ideas about how temporal factors contribute to the constitution of the affective aspect of aesthetic experiences (*Reading with Feeling*, chap. 10).

37 Carroll, *The Philosophy of Horror*, 137.

38 Especially in the section entitled "The Problem of Tragic Pleasure."

39 It is not unnatural to think that the Jackal panders to submerged aggressive wishes in the reader, while at the same time the novel places the ultimately victorious Lebel at her disposal as an object of ego identification (while the eminent General de Gaulle, figuring in the background, is apt to be associated with the superego).

40 The role of feelings as an instrument of evaluation has been skilfully emphasized by Nussbaum. See esp. her brilliant remarks about the passage in Proust's *Remembrance of Things Past* (*A la recherche du temps perdu*, 1913–27) where the fictive narrator finds himself deserted by his girlfriend Albertine; Nussbaum demonstrates, in that context, how only

our emotional reactions can give us the necessary "sense of proportion, of depth and importance" when it comes to comparing the relative significance to us of our various interests. (Nussbaum, *Love's Knowledge*, 261 and 263–4; the quotation comes from 264. The Proust passage in question comprises the end of *The Captive* and the opening of *The Sweet Cheat Gone*.)

41 Lyons, *Emotion*, 58; Greenspan, *Emotions and Reasons*, 14.

42 Cf. Greenspan's quite opposite opinion: "Emotions serve as rewards or punishments ... by 'registering' evaluations in positive or negative affect" (*Emotions and Reasons*, 80).

43 Ibid., 4.

44 Cf. Noël Carroll, "Art, Narrative, and Emotion," 195 ("Bodily feelings ... are not directed at anything. They are physical states") and Matravers, *Art and Emotion*, 18, speaking directly of Greenspan ("As affective states do not have ... propositional contents, their object-directedness would be a mystery").

45 Greenspan could say, here: Consider the very fact *that you risk being stung by the wasp* as the proposition! Possibly, Greenspan's analysis is to be understood along such lines. But my objection still remains: it is true that (the perception reflected in) the proposition releases the feelings but, as I see it, the proposition is not in itself evaluative. On the contrary, it is its emotional *effect* that, basically, *constitutes* the evaluation of the situation.

46 Lotze, *Geschichte der Ästhetik in Deutschland*, 259.

47 Tolstoy, *What Is Art?*, 39–40.

48 Richards, *Principles of Literary Criticism*, 267.

49 For an assessment of this type of aesthetics in general terms see, e.g., Blocker, *Philosophy of Art*, chap. 3 or Sheppard, *Aesthetics*, chap. 3.

50 *Poetics* 1453b11–12. As before, I am using Stephen Halliwell's translation (Aristotle, *Poetics*, 75).

51 Cf. *Poetics* 1448b. Elizabeth Belfiore has recently described Aristotle's basic view of tragic pleasure as follows: "This pleasure is the pleasure of contemplating, for its own sake, the relationship betwen imitation and objects imitated – the terrible and pitiable perceptible objects ... – and of coming in this way to understand the human condition. Katharsis as well as the pleasure of contemplation is the end of tragedy, for understanding produces a katharsis of emotional extremes that results in an emotional mean state. As a natural result of contemplation, or, rather, as an integral part of it, katharsis is a part of the 'pleasure that comes from pity and fear.'" (*Tragic Pleasures*, 348).

52 Hume, "Of Tragedy," 3:261–2. Hume's essay is still much discussed; see, e.g., Robert J. Yanal's and Alex Neill's exchange of views in *Journal of Aesthetics and Art Criticism* 49 (1991) and 50 (1992) and the literature cited there.

53 For two proposals from the 1990s see, e.g., Carroll, *The Philosophy of Horror*, chap. 4, esp. 184 and Kuhns, *Tragedy*, chap. 3, esp. 65–6, 67, and 69.

54 Hume, "Of Tragedy," 3:258.

55 Jerrold Levinson has presented a differently structured and more finely differentiated classification of proposed solutions to the paradox of tragedy ("Emotion," 29–30). In his terminology, my standpoint would be called an "organicist" explanation and Hume's a "conversionary" one.

56 See Carroll, *The Philosophy of Horror*, 191 and the literature cited there.

57 Ideas of this type are not original. One locus classicus is Richards's discussion of the effects of tragedy and of experiences whose unity is created through "inclusion" rather than "exclusion" (*Principles of Literary Criticism*, 245–50, esp. 249).

58 It is, actually, reminiscent of Aristotle's, as I, with the help of Belfiore and others, understand his analysis.

59 Aristotle, *Poetics* 1448b.

60 See, e.g., Young, *Nietzsche's Philosophy of Art*, 10–12, 14–15, 42–4 and the references to Schopenhauer and Nietzsche given there, or, more recently, Price, "Nietzsche and Tragedy," esp. 391–2.

61 Greenspan, *Emotions and Reasons*, 32–3.

62 See esp. Freud, "Creative Writers and Day-Dreaming," 14:141. The idea of forepleasure can already be found in Freud, *Jokes*, 168–9, 183, 187, et passim. Cf. Schönau, *Einführung in die psychoanalytische Literaturwissenschaft*, 24 and 49.

63 Hume, "Of Tragedy," 3:261.

64 A common attitude to literary form within the psychoanalytical tradition. See, e.g., Lesser, *Fiction and the Unconscious*, 128 and 134–6 and Holland, *Dynamics of Literary Response*, 101, 142, and 148; cf. Schönau, *Einführung in die psychoanalytische Literaturwissenschaft*, 24–7.

65 Winnicott, *Playing and Reality*, 52.

66 Ibid., esp. chap. 1. Quotations from 14.

67 Kristeller, "The Modern System of the Arts," 136–43, esp. 140–1; Gilbert and Kuhn, *A History of Aesthetics*, 274–81, esp. 275 (the relations between Aristotle and Dubos) and 279 (the relations between Dubos and Batteux).

68 Hegel, *Aesthetics*, 1:100–1. Cf., e.g., Karelis, "Hegel's Concept of Art," xxiv–xxviii.

69 Lotze, *Geschichte der Ästhetik in Deutschland*, 67.

70 Tolstoy, *What Is Art?*, 156.

71 Richards, *Principles of Literary Criticism*, 113 and 267 respectively.

72 Cf. Derek Matravers's remark that it is "generally agreed" that emotions concerning "something external to the work" are "not aesthetically relevant" (*Art and Emotion*, 148).

73 Eliot, *The Sacred Wood*, 100–1.

74 Eliot's example is slightly unsettling, since authors are normally said to "express" feelings only when they are expressing *their own* feelings.

75 The problems that pile up in connection with "objective correlative" do indeed cause serious trouble. In his book about Eliot's critical thinking, Richard Shusterman even refrains from analysing the concept, which he characterizes as "enigmatic" (*T.S. Eliot*, 26).

76 Beardsley and Wimsatt, "The Affective Fallacy," 21.

77 Ibid., 38.

78 Olsen, *Structure of Literary Understanding*, 39–41. I quote from 41.

79 Olsen, however, as one can see, avoids expressions with such implications.

80 Blocker, *Philosophy of Art*, chap. 3. The quotation comes from 109.

81 See, e.g., Margolis, *Art and Philosophy*, 21 (Margolis is speaking of art works in general, not specifically of literature). Concerning feelings and emotions, see ibid., 191–2.

82 Radford, "How Can We Be Moved by ... Anna Karenina?" 78.

83 There is even a book-length study of the paradox and the early discussion about it: Boruah, *Fiction and Emotion*.

84 In Swedish: "Dumma gorilla! Egoist och gorilla!"
   The relevant passage is on p. 12 in Lewis, *The Last Battle*; cf. Lewis, *Den sista striden*, 16. Earlier, Shift has manipulated Puzzle by implicitly accusing him of being egoistical (p. 10 in the English version). My daughter is now chastising Shift by letting him know that it is, indeed, he himself who is the egoist.

85 In a sense, my daughter's anger centres on Shift, but that does not prove that she is *angry with Shift*. A highly irritated person may kick a chair that stands in his way, but such an act hardly proves that he is in fact *angry at the chair*.

86 Cf. Nussbaum's discussion of her daughter's love for James Steerforth, one of the characters in Dickens's *David Copperfield* (*Love's Knowledge*, 335 and 354–5).

87 Cf. the perceptive remarks by Currie ("The Paradox of Caring," 69–70) and Dadlez (*What's Hecuba to Him?*, 9).

88 E.g., Morreall. See Morreall, "Fear without Belief," esp. 360–2.

89 Some theorists hold that there are specifically aesthetic emotions. The idea is advocated – with a different content and different arguments – by Olsen and by Peter Kivy (Olsen, *Structure of Literary Understanding*, 42–5; Kivy, "Auditor's Emotions"). In my opinion, there is room for

conceptions like Olsen's and Kivy's within the theoretical framework outlined in the next paragraphs.

90 See Collingwood, *The Principles of Art*, 115–17.

91 Paskins, "On Being Moved by Anna Karenina," 346.

92 Charlton, "Feeling for the Fictitious," 211–12.

93 In actual fact, Charlton's analysis is wider in scope and more interesting than I can account for here. It is based on unusually well thought out ideas about emotions and their motivational background.

94 Paskins and Charlton might reply that it is possible to give a weaker sense to "same" in "same bind" and to "like" in "like Karenin," "like Vronsky." Still it appears obvious to me that they have too simple and straightforward a conception of the relation between the elements of the fictional description and the emotionally operative factors in actual reality. (Incidentally, Paskins's analysis is explicitly confined to cases where the fictitious characters are relatively realistic, not "essentially fictional"; Paskins, "On Being Moved by Anna Karenina," 346.)

95 See Paskins, "On Being Moved by Anna Karenina," and Charlton, "Feeling for the Fictitious," 211.

96 Johnson, "Preface to Shakespeare," 7:78.

97 For a Swede, it is natural to think of Strindberg's words in the preface to *Miss Julie* (*Fröken Julie*, 1887): "The fact that the heroine arouses our pity depends only on our weakness in not being able to resist the sense of fear that the same fate could befall ourselves." Quoted from Brownstein and Daubert, *Analytical Sourcebook*, 217.

98 See, e.g., Jerrold Levinson, "Emotion," 23, and Dadlez, *What's Hecuba to Him?*, 75 and 132.

99 Currie, *The Nature of Fiction*, 188.

100 Jerrold Levinson has raised the same objection as Currie, with the same petitio principii: "despising a fictional character, for instance, is not simply reducible to despising people of that sort generally, or to despising some actual similar individual of one's acquaintance" ("Emotion," 23.)

101 Currie, *The Nature of Fiction*, 214.

102 Livingston and Mele, "Evaluating Emotional Responses," esp. 162–7 and 170–4.

103 Demetz, "Uwe Johnsons Blick," 196.

104 Discussion of how readers are "warranted in responding" (Feagin, *Reading with Feeling*, 216) emotionally to literature also plays a prominent role in Feagin's *Reading with Feeling*. In my opinion, one should avoid creating the impression that there is one, or only a few, correct or "warranted" emotional responses to a literary work.

105 See Walton, *Mimesis as Make-Believe*, 11–54.

106 Cf. esp. ibid., 368.

107 Ibid., 251. Walton's view of feelings for fictitious characters as fiction-ally existing feelings, quasi feelings within the frame of a game of make-believe, was first presented in his article "Fearing Fictions" in 1978.

108 Cf. the section "Fictional Utterances" in chap. 3 above and my article "On Walton's and Currie's Analyses," which contains a more detailed criticism of Walton's games-of-make-believe theory than I have been able to include here.

109 I am thinking, in the first place, of William Charlton, David Novitz, and Frank Palmer (Charlton, rev. of Walton, 370; Novitz, rev. of Walton, 122; Palmer, *Literature and Moral Understanding*, esp. 53). Cf. also Carroll's criticism of Walton (*The Philosophy of Horror*, 74–6).

110 Cf. Walton, *Mimesis as Make-Believe*, esp. 214.

111 Apart from Lamarque, this is also true at least for Berys Gaut (cf. Walton, "Spelunking, Simulation, and Slime," 49, note 16) and for Paisley Livingston and Alfred R. Mele (see Livingston and Mele, "Evalu-ating Emotional Responses," 160). Certainly we often have emotional experiences when reading fiction, and associate these with the charac-ters described in the fiction, but that does not necessarily mean that we feel for the fictitious characters; as Walton points out: "This is by no means intuitively obvious to everyone" ("Spelunking, Simulation, and Slime," 45).

112 Lamarque, "How Can We Fear and Pity Fictions?" 292–3. Lamarque's criticism of Walton concerns Walton's 1978 article.

113 Ibid., 293.

114 In Lamarque, *Fictional Points of View*, 113–24, the earlier essay is pre-sented in a slightly modified version. Also, a new appendix is added (ibid., 125–34). My two quotations from the 1981 article recur in 115–16 with insubstantial alterations ("interact with them" is changed to "interact with fictional characters" and "which I shall work out in detail" is replaced by "drawing on the theory developed in Chapters 2 and 3").

115 Lamarque, *Fictional Points of View*, 129; cf. also 132–4.

116 Lamarque would perhaps wish to deny that. He analyses fictional char-acters as abstractions; thus he could maintain, in the spirit of that analy-sis, that fictitious characters do in fact exist. See ibid., chaps. 2 and 3 (building on contributions from the early 1980s). I would not regard a defence along such lines as really relevant, but space does not permit me to discuss the matter further here.

117 See esp. Walton, *Mimesis as Make-Believe*, 203. Lamarque's latest rejoin-ders are found in his *Fictional Points of View*, 125–8.

118 In other words, Lamarque *presupposes* that emotions may be directed at non-existent objects, but he does not explain *in what sense of "directed"* they can be so, or *why that sense should be preferred* to, e.g., the sense

I sketched. These remarks are valid also where Lamarque's latest comments on the problem are concerned.

119 Scruton, *Art and Imagination*, 128–9; the quotation comes from 129. Cf. Scruton, "Fantasy, Imagination and Screen," 132–3.

120 Scruton thinks that the reader can, at most, be infected by, "drawn into sympathy with," the feelings which she imagines ("Fantasy, Imagination and Screen," 132–3). I would say that Scruton in reality focuses on the (certainly imagined) *feelings in the text* while he tends to perceive what I call *the reader's feelings* as unreal or of subordinate importance.

121 Ibid.

Chapter Eight

1 For the text, see Bly, ed., *Friends*, 135. The Swedish original reads: "Men på en annan ort har jag lärt / underjordens hemskhet: / Här är underjordens leende / Här finns minuter och sekunder / och den blanka randen mellan hav och himmel / Här finns den korta katastrofen och det korta utbrottet av glädje / Men du, var finns du, Sorg / som man kunde kasta sig i havet efter? / Natten kommer och månen går upp / Jag öppnar alla fönster / Jag vet att hon vid min sida älskar mig / men är det verkligen hon" (Ekelöf, *Strountes* 1955, 78–9).

"Strountes" is a practically meaningless word. It is the Swedish word "strung" – roughly: "nonsense – supplied with a pretentious French-looking spelling that makes it unrecognizable. In English, the title is usually rendered as *Strountes* or as *Nonsense*.

2 The poem lacks a proper title (cf. note 5 below). For practical reasons, however, I shall normally refer to it as "But Somewhere Else."

3 The only three exceptions are of a special character. Two of them are deliberately pedestrian, signed with the humorous pseudonym "A:lfr-d V:stl-nd" ("Ad memoriam" and "Epilog"; *Strountes* 1955, 23–4 and 120–1 respectively). The third is an older text by Ekelöf, a dramatized prose poem in French with the dating "(Paris 29)": "Légende du vieux Soupcacqa" (*Strountes* 1955, 102–6).

4 Ekelöf, *Dikter* 1965, 239–74 and the reprint in Ekelöf, *Dikter* 1983, 239–74.

In the table of contents of the first edition of *Strountes* (1955), our text is mentioned as "Men på en annan ort har jag lärt" ("But Somewhere Else I Have Learned"). In the 1965 omnibus edition and its 1983 reprint (p. 262 in both), the poem has been given the title "Men på en annan ort" ("But Somewhere Else"), a title it is also allowed to keep in Reidar Ekner's critical edition: Ekelöf, *Skrifter*, 2:34. In the second edition of *Strountes* (1966), the poems remained untitled, but a somewhat more space-saving typography was introduced.

5 As mentioned in the last note, the texts have also been given titles in Ekner's critical edition of Ekelöf's writings (the only one so far). The original lack of titles is not even commmented upon, something which I consider unfortunate. See Ekelöf, *Skrifter*, 2:13–48.

In fact, Ekner programmatically carries out a relatively far-reaching standardization of the typography of Ekelöf's poetry. He actually appears to regard the various kinds of typographical effects in the original editions as not being elements of the text proper. See Ekner, "Inledning" (Introduction) 15–16.

For my own part, I am definitely of the opinion that Ekelöf's *Strountes* poems, except the three mentioned in note 3 above, are to be seen as untitled (and that the absence of titles is not unimportant for the understanding of the poems). It appears obvious to me that Ekelöf deliberately, and for the sake of artistic impression, had the poems published without titles in *Strountes* 1955, and that he at least passively followed the same practice in *Strountes* 1966, the last edition during his lifetime. It is true that Ekelöf also, at least passively, approved of the use of titles in connection with originally untitled poems in the 1965 edition of selected poems, *Dikter*. In that edition, however, such titles are italicized, unlike the genuine titles in the earlier production and in "Epilog," the only one of the three *Strountes* poems with a title that was included in the 1965 edition. I find it natural to believe that when titles are used so consistently in *Dikter* in 1965, this is partly for economic reasons, partly in order to make *the edition in question* more uniform. Thus I do not think that Ekelöf in 1965 wanted to change the *Strountes* poems I am talking about by adding titles; I understand the titles, rather, as a practical measure and as intended for use in special contexts.

6 It is natural to say "he," since Ekelöf is male and the poem seems to contain no fictitious dramatic speaker (who would reasonably have to be conceived as male anyhow). According to my view of literary deixis, the "I" of a poem like this is, formally, the author. On the other hand, the reader is not meant to substitute "Ekelöf" for "I" in her mind: it is unimportant that it is *precisely Ekelöf* who utters the words. Cf. my *Theory of Literary Discourse*, 98–113.

7 In connection with a somewhat earlier poem by Ekelöf, Anders Olsson has maintained that "the underworld," as Ekelöf uses the expression, can be taken as "a metaphor of earthly existence in its entirety" and supported that contention with a statement by Ekelöf: "I hold *that it is in the underworld that we find ourselves* at present. But perhaps not at the very bottom" (Olsson, *Ekelöfs nej*, 211).

8 Charles Altieri has taken that fact as his starting point in his book *Act and Quality*, 174, where he speaks of literary utterance as "the self-conscious presentation of self in an act so that its qualities might be

assessed in relation to the situation and the laws or procedures appropriate to that situation." It is a very interesting description, though too generalized – as Altieri himself would probably think today. (Cf. my *Theory of Literary Discourse*, 140 and, for Altieri's later views, the section "How Does the Literary Form Come to Affect Us?" in chap. 9 below.)

9 I myself would, normally, see the sequence of signs as a sequence of graphemes. The question of how sequences of signs are to be defined in literary contexts is, however, too technical to be discussed here. I have dealt with it in my book *Verkbegreppet*, 46–53.

10 "Normally," for exceptions can certainly be found. See, e.g., my brief treatment of Rorty's view of interpretation in chap. 6 above, the section "Other Theories about the Validity of Thematizations."

11 See Hellström, *Livskänsla och självutplåning*, 213–15.

12 Ekelöf, *Strountes* 1955, 76–7. In describing the Positano apartment and connecting it with the poem about the coast of the sirens, I base myself on Sommar, *Gunnar Ekelöf*, 400–3. I refrain from discussing the not insignificant translational problems that the poem presents.

13 See, e.g., the entries "Sappho" and "Phaon" in Howatson, ed., *Oxford Companion to Classical Literature*. Ekelöf must certainly have been acquainted with this traditional story – cf. the next note.

14 Edmonds, ed., *Lyra Graeca*, 260–3; quotation from 263. In Sweden, this fragment is one of the best-known texts by Sappho, and there are several Swedish translations of it. (The fragment's attribution to Sappho is traditional but disputed; the latter fact is, however, of no significance in my context.)

Ekelöf, whose fascination with Sappho is well attested, must be assumed to have been familiar with the fragment at the time. He is known to have quoted it repeatedly in conversation in the years following the writing of the poem – in 1957: the English translation cited in the text; in 1960: the Greek original. Åström, *Gunnar Ekelöf och antiken*, 289–96, describes how Sappho's poetry is reflected in Ekelöf's work (as Bengt Landgren has kindly pointed out to me). For facts about Ekelöf's references to the poem, and about the Swedish translations, see Åström, *Gunnar Ekelöf och antiken*, 289–90.

15 Zilliacus, *Grekisk lyrik*, 187. Claes Lindskog's translation contains no such explicit reference to an appointment, but his accompanying text indicates that he, too, understands the lines in precisely that manner (Lindskog, *Grekiska kvinnogestalter*, 65).

16 Landgren, *Ensamheten, döden och drömmarna* is the pioneering, and to my mind still the best, account of the fundamental themes in Ekelöf's poetry. Its first chapter, concerned with loneliness and the feeling of community in Ekelöf, plays an especially important role for my general

understanding of Ekelöf and for my reasoning about "But Somewhere Else."

17 I am inclined to believe that (reasonably unconscious) associations with Sappho did in fact come into play – at least marginally – when Ekelöf was writing the poem. To argue more persuasively for my conviction I would, however, have to give a more detailed description of the contextual, intertextual, and biographical background.

18 Naturally, older literature causes special difficulties. The reader of such literature is normally faced with a text that is not adapted to her knowledge and experience (cf. chap. 6, note 45 and the brief discussion of the problem in *Theory of Literary Discourse*, 93–4). I see this as a complication of subordinate importance, however, not as a problem affecting the fundamental understanding of literary communication.

Chapter Nine

1 See, e.g., Beardsley, *Aesthetics*, 2nd ed. 165–6 or von Kutschera, *Ästhetik*, 177–8. René Wellek is probably the best-known critic of the indistinctness of the literary notion of form – see Wellek and Warren, *Theory of Literature* 140–1 and Wellek, "Concepts of Form," 54.

2 Lesser, *Fiction and the Unconscious*, 122; Rodway, "Form," 99.

3 See, e.g., Wellek and Warren, *Theory of Literature*, 140, von Kutschera, *Ästhetik*, 177, and Horn, *Grundlagen der Literaturästhetik*, 201.

4 See, e.g., Eldridge, "Form," 159 or Baldick, *Concise Oxford Dictionary of Literary Terms*, 86.

5 See figs. 4–5. (It is true that these two printings differ on the semantic level, too, since the poem has been provided with a title in the printing in fig. 5.)

6 When defining the linguistic sign-sequence one can follow somewhat different principles. Cf. chap. 8, note 9.

7 See, e.g., Ernst, "Die Entwicklung der optischen Poesie."

8 Jandl's poem is rendered after Jandl, *Gesammelte Werke*, 1:479. The poem is adduced by Ernst ("Die Entwicklung der optischen Poesie," 149).

9 In the special sense of "non-representational" used here. The visual pattern does not in itself represent any linguistic sign or sequence of such signs. It represents (depicts) a tower, but that is another matter.

10 See esp. the sections "The Reading of Literature: A Cognitive-Affective Processing Pattern" (chap. 2) and "A Cognitive-Emotive Model of Literature's Function" (chap. 7).

11 See, e.g., John Lyons, *Semantics*, 1:57–70, esp. 1:65.

12 See, above all, two well-known articles: Jakobson, "Closing Statement," and Jakobson and Lévi-Strauss, "Charles Baudelaire's 'Les Chats.'"

13 Richards, *Practical Criticism*, 229.

14 "Principally," for although I attach much importance to cognitive processing in this context, I find it natural to believe that a sort of reflex reaction (to the sound material, to thoughts introduced, etc.) also enters into the reader's post-communicative processing.

15 See Tsur, *Toward a Theory of Cognitive Poetics*, esp. 1–6. Quotation from 5–6.

16 Richards, *Practical Criticism*, 233.

17 Rose, *The Power of Form*, 139. Rose probably does not associate as precise a meaning with "sound," "sense," and "meaning" as I do with the terms "expressional form" and "communicative content." Therefore, it is not entirely clear what our disagreement consists in. Obviously, however, the spirit of Rose's analysis differs from mine.

Chapter Ten

1 See, e.g., Ingarden, "Das Form-Inhalt-Problem," esp. 55–63 and Garber, "Form."

2 Rudolf Arnheim has recently contended that only the abstract phenomena designated by such descriptive terms – the circle, the cube, etc. – are *forms* "in the strict sense of the concept" ("The Completeness of Physical and Artistic Form," 109). There is a plethora of such "peripheral" definitions of aesthetic form: of definitions singling out and making central an entity peripherally related to what is usually seen as aesthetic form. In the following I shall disregard definitions of that kind.

3 Cf. Franz von Kutschera's remark that form in the normal sense of the word is an object's "geometrically describable shape" (*Ästhetik*, 177). This meaning also appears to be central in the Latin "forma," the origin of the word "form."

4 It is true that we may also speak of form in connection with lines or visual patterns – "wave-like," "S-shaped," etc. – and such form is obviously a variety of physical form. For that reason, a physical form can sometimes be ascribed to a literary text: with respect to its visual pattern, e.g., Ernst Jandl's poem "easter week: a tower" is tower-shaped. (Cf. chap. 9, fig. 6.) But such instances are marginal exceptions. As a rule, a literary text, qua text, lacks a physical form (while each individual copy of the text possesses an artistically – but not aesthetically – irrelevant, optional form).

5 The metaphorical character of the concept of form used about literature and art has been pointed out in, e.g., Lubbock's *The Craft of Fiction*, 10–11 and in Pole's "The Excellence of Form," 82.

Someone might object that "form" is a well-established technical term in criticism with a fairly regularized use and that it is, therefore, *literally* true that Ekelöf's "But Somewhere Else" has formal properties like those of being non-stanzaic and unrhymed. But what I wish to underline is something different: the fact that, in the final analysis, the technical use of the term "form" in criticism rests on a metaphorical foundation.

6 Cf., e.g., Sweetser, "English Metaphors for Language." Speaking about, among other things, the metaphorical treatment of texts as physical objects, Sweetser refers to "the fact that physical experience and perception are both basic and shared between humans" (ibid., 719).

7 Greene, *The Arts and the Art of Criticism*, 31–2.

8 Ibid., chap. 6. This idea seems to be widely accepted. See, e.g., Wellek and Warren, *Theory of Literature*, 174 – "Language is quite literally the material of the literary artist" – and Sartwell, "Substance and Significance," 258: "Words are literally the *material* of poets, the *substance* in which and with which they pursue their craft. Words to the poet are like clay to the potter; language is to be *shaped, formed*, into a real object." (It is amusing and thought-provoking that both Wellek and Sartwell emphasize that they perceive this mode of expression as *literal*, not figurative.)

9 I do not maintain, of course, that Greene would have subscribed to the theory implicit in the system of metaphors in question. My contention is that he nevertheless clearly draws on the metaphors for his picture of the work of art.

10 To see that the poem is written in the first-person form, it is not enough to identify the sign-sequence. One has to understand its meaning.

11 I do not want to enter into a close examination of that distinction (which also concerns other elements). For a thorough account, see Schwinger, "Innere Form." One brief, modern presentation of the distinction is Best's "Form."

12 See, e.g., Hjelmslev, "Omkring Sprogteoriens Grundlæggelse," esp. 44–55. Cf., e.g., Chatman, *Story and Discourse*, 22–6.
   My conceptual apparatus, introduced in the last chapter, may appear similar to Hjelmslev's. Both in connection with expression and content, Hjelmslev distinguishes between the form and the substance. I myself separate formal and representational properties both where expression and communicated thought are concerned. In reality, however, my distinctions are rather unlike Hjelmslev's. For one thing, Hjelmslev is speaking of phenomena on the level of *language* – the form of expression of a certain language itself, etc. – while I am speaking of phenomena on the *utterance or text* level: the form of the expression (the form of the sign-sequence) in a particular text, etc. There are also several other important differences between Hjelmslev's perspective and my own.

13 Wellek, "Concepts of Form and Structure," 54.

14 See, e.g., Orsini, "The Ancient Roots." Cf., e.g., Garber, "Form," 420. (The closest Greek counterparts of the Latin "forma" are "morphē" and "eidos.")

15 See the literature cited in notes 11 and 14 above together with Orsini, "Form" and Davis, *The Act of Interpretation*, 1.

16 The aesthetically relevant meanings of "form" have been systematized in many different fashions. Three ambitious analyses of the concept (which I refrain from discussing in full detail) are Ingarden, "Das Form-Inhalt-Problem," Wellek, "Concepts of Form and Structure," and Tatarkiewicz, "Form."

17 See, e.g., Tatarkiewicz, "Form," 221 and Pole, "The Excellence of Form," 81.

18 Tatarkiewicz, "Form," 231.

19 Wellek and Warren, *Theory of Literature*, 140. According to the book's preface, Wellek carried the main responsibility for the passages at issue.

20 Ibid., 140–1.

21 Wellek is correct in saying that the pair of concepts "structure"– "materials" does not coincide with the pair "form"–"content." I find it evident, however, that it is the form/matter distinction that Wellek reintroduces by means of the terms "structure" and "materials." Wellek separates form and matter and thus avoids the Tatarkiewicz model's conflation of the two – while he, in turn, loses sight of the content category.

22 See, e.g., Tsur, *Toward a Theory of Cognitive Poetics*, 286.

23 Wellek, "Concepts of Form and Structure," 55. The Osborne quotation is taken from Osborne, *Aesthetics and Criticism*, 289.

24 Peck and Coyle, "Form and Content," 132.

25 Osborne, *Aesthetics and Criticism*, 289. Cf. Wellek, "Concepts of Form and Structure," 55.

26 Wellek's contributions are as much as thirty to forty years old. During the last few decades, however, literary theory has shown relatively little interest in the form/content problem; its energy has been spent elsewhere.

27 Greene, *The Arts and the Art of Criticism*, 33.

28 Brooks, "The Heresy of Paraphrase," 206.

29 Ibid., footnote.

30 If one makes aesthetical significance a necessary property of formal features (cf. the section "Literary Form: Two Complications" in chap. 9), expressional form not only *can* but *must* change the competent reader's impression.

31 The same is *in principle* true of non-literary texts. Each alteration of the newspaper notice about John Sykes (chap. 3, "Informational and Directive Discourse") could affect the reader's impression of the text. There is a pragmatic difference, however, in that minor variations in content are normally practically insignificant in informational discourse, where the reader is principally expected to assimilate the information, i.e., to register and evaluate the alleged state of affairs introduced. In presentational

discourse, where the stirring of mental associations is a crucial aspect, such things as the exact expressional and conceptional form do *in practice* play a much more important role.

32 For formalism in aesthetic contexts, see, e.g., Blocker, *Philosophy of Art*, chap. 4, or von Kutschera, *Ästhetik*, 176–85.

33 Tsur, *Toward a Theory of Cognitive Poetics*, 26. It is not altogether clear whether that description is also meant to apply to prose, but Tsur's generalizations often seem to have reference to all literature (see, above all, ibid., 1–2).

34 Shklovsky, "Art as Technique," 12, quoted from Tsur, *Toward a Theory of Cognitive Poetics*, 3–4.

35 Horn, *Grundlagen der Literaturästhetik*, 153–214, gives an extensive account – rich in examples and ideas – of different views of the aesthetic significance of form. About Šklovskij's position, see esp. ibid., 160 and 175–6.

36 Cf. note 33 above.

37 Eliot, *The Sacred Wood*, 54 ("Tradition and the Individual Talent").

38 Eldridge, "Form," 160.

39 I avoid Šklovskij's formula "as they are perceived and not as they are known," since it appears to build on the now discredited idea of the possibility of an "innocent eye," a seeing completely free from prior assumptions.

40 For ideas about form in psychoanalytical criticism see, e.g., Schönau, *Einführung in die psychoanalytische Literaturwissenschaft*, esp. 24–7 and 65–7.

41 Freud, "Creative Writers and Day-Dreaming," 141.

42 Lesser, *Fiction and the Unconscious*, 125.

43 Ibid., 128–31.

44 Rosebury, *Art and Desire*, 12.

45 For example: "Very loosely, then, we can say that form in a literary work corresponds to defense; content, to fantasy or impulse" (Holland, *Dynamics of Literary Response*, 131).

46 Ibid., 135.

47 Kofman, *The Childhood of Art*, 108.

48 Charles Altieri has attempted to show that this is a crucial element in the functioning of modernist American poetry: "it is now the forming activity itself that constitutes the fundamental content – not as an alternative to the world of experience, but as a new way to exemplify states and powers that can change our understanding of human needs and capacities" (*Painterly Abstraction*, esp. chap. 2; quotation from p. 57).

49 Rose, *The Power of Form*, 203.

Concluding Remarks

1 Above all, one can point to Göran Hermerén's analysis of different possible contents of the autonomy doctrine (*Aspects of Aesthetics*, chap. 4). Cf. also Casey, "The Autonomy of Art," esp. 66, and Altieri, "Autonomy, Poetic."

2 Altieri, e.g., in his historically arranged "Autonomy, Poetic" disregards the use of the *word* "autonomy" as a technical term in aesthetics.

3 The word "autonomy" occurs in Kant's *Critique of Judgement*, but in its general, non-aesthetical meaning: Kant speaks of the autonomy of nature etc. Kant, *Kritik der Urteilskraft*, e.g., 22 and 253; cf. Vorländer's index, 364.

4 I have given an account of my view of Jakobson's standpoint in *Theory of Literary Discourse*, 74–6.

5 In his *Russian Formalism*, 156, Victor Erlich documents the presence of this idea already in Jakobson's *Novejšaja russkaja poèzija* (1921) and points to a presumable influence from Jakobson in Boris Tomaševskij, who maintains, in his *Teorija literatury* (1925), that the communicative function is pushed into the background in literature, where linguistic structures acquire autonomous value.

6 Erlich, *Russian Formalism*, 170.

7 See chap. 5 above, "Traditional Analytical Theory of Literature and Truth: The Conventionalist View of Meaning."

8 Mukařovský, "L'Art comme fait sémiologique," 1067.

9 Ibid.

10 Ibid.

11 Ibid., 1068–9.

12 Ibid., 1067–8.

13 Cf. Bühler, *Theory of Language*, esp. 35.

14 See Mukařovský, "Two Studies," esp. 67–9.

15 Ibid., both 69 and 71.

16 Ibid., 73.

17 I translate from Mukařovský, "Ästhetische Funktion," 104–5.

18 Frye, *Anatomy of Criticism*, 74.

19 Esslin, Introduction, in Jan Kott, *Shakespeare Our Contemporary*, xi. I quote Esslin via Stecker, *Artworks*, 137.

20 Savile, *The Test of Time*, 42.

21 Horn, *Grundlagen der Literaturästhetik*, 88.

22 Markowitz, "Guilty Pleasures," 308.

23 Mukařovský obviously imagines that signs represent meanings by referring to them (which is to confuse meaning with reference). Somewhat absurdly, he further conceives of entire texts as being such referring

signs. Besides, he seems to overlook the fact that not only poems, novels, and the like but also things like newspaper articles and non-fiction books must be "autonomous signs" in the sense that their reference is not a distinctly determined object.

24 Which is not to say, of course, that I regard them as existing independently of human consciousness. My intuition is that, while the material objects used as signs (books, newspapers, etc.) would remain in existence even if the human race were wiped out, such things as linguistic expressions or meanings would no longer exist.

25 See the section "Form and Aesthetic Enjoyment" in chap. 10.

26 However, Robert Stecker has recently contended, using arguments similar to those put forward in the following, that "the chief value of artworks is a kind of instrumental value" but that the work of art is nevertheless "the unique, indispensable means" of realizing the valuable experience. See Stecker's *Artworks*, chap. 12, esp. 251–8 (quotations from 251 and 253 respectively).

27 It is natural to ask what literature's distinctive character as a means of orientation in the world could consist in. I find that problem both fascinating and crucial, and I have touched on it in several places in the book, especially in chaps. 2, 3, 6, 7, and 9. I have hopes of being able to revert to it in my future research. In the present context, however, a serious attempt to enter more deeply into the matter would unfortunately carry us much too far.

28 Horn, *Grundlagen der Literaturästhetik*, 86. In the rest of this section, references to Horn's book will be given in the text.

29 Lamarque and Olsen, *Truth, Fiction, and Literature*, viii.

30 The authors also explicitly say, in another context in the book, that they repudiate "arid aestheticism" and that "the idea of the special nature of literary value" (ibid., 22) is the core of their view of literature's autonomy.

In the rest of this section, references to Lamarque's and Olsen's book will be given in the text.

31 The agreement is explained, in part, by the fact that my theory on this point is influenced by Olsen's earlier formulations of the idea in, e.g., his *End of Literary Theory*. In Lamarque and Olsen's book, the conception of literature as a practice is worked out esp. in chap. 10.

32 It might be objected that that is too self-evident to need any explanation. I believe, however, that there is an important question that Lamarque and Olsen avoid. Is it an end in itself to understand how the theme of freedom is interpreted and developed in *Anna of the Five Towns*? Or is it a means of achieving something else that is valuable in our lives – and in that case, what? In the final analysis, Lamarque and Olsen seem to

waver concerning literature's anchorage in life. As I see it, there is a tension between their description of literature as "its own justification" (*Truth, Fiction, and Literature*, viii) and their characterization of it as "a special kind of cognition" (ibid., 452), a tension making the exact content of their plea for literature's autonomy somewhat unclear. Cf. also Stecker, *Artworks*, 289–91.

Some theorists have criticized Lamarque and Olsen for their unwillingness to perceive literature as offering truth (see Novitz, "The Trouble with Truth," Hagen, "På flukt fra sannhet," and Lamarque's reply to Hagen, "The High Price of Evading Boredom"). Though not wholly unrelated, the reservations I have just presented are different. I do not really dissent from Lamarque's and Olsen's ideas about literary truth, at least not from their precise formulations.

Bibliography

Aldrich, Virgil C. *Philosophy of Art*. Englewood Cliffs, NJ: Prentice-Hall, 1963.

Altieri, Charles. *Act and Quality: A Theory of Literary Meaning and Humanistic Understanding*. Amherst: University of Massachusetts Press, 1981.

– "Autonomy, Poetic." In Alex Preminger, T.V.F. Brogan, et al., eds, *The New Princeton Encyclopedia of Poetry and Poetics*. Princeton, NJ: Princeton University Press, 1993.

– *Painterly Abstraction in Modernist American Poetry: The Contemporaneity of Modernism*. Cambridge: Cambridge University Press, 1989.

Aristotle, *Poetics*. Ed. and trans. Stephen Halliwell. In Aristotle, *Poetics*, ed. and trans. Stephen Halliwell; Longinus, *On the Sublime*, trans. W.H. Fyfe, rev. by Donald Russell; Demetrius, *On Style*, ed. and trans. Doreen C. Innes based on W. Rhys Roberts. Cambridge, Mass. and London: Harvard University Press, 1995.

Armstrong, David F., William C. Stokoe, and Sherman E. Wilcox. *Gesture and the Nature of Language*. Cambridge, New York, and Melbourne: Cambridge University Press, 1995.

Armstrong, Paul B. *Conflicting Readings: Variety and Validity in Interpretation*. Chapel Hill and London: University of North Carolina Press, 1990.

Arnheim, Rudolf. "The Completeness of Physical and Artistic Form." *British Journal of Aesthetics* 34 (1994).

Åström, Paul. *Gunnar Ekelöf och antiken*. Jonsered: Paul Åströms förlag, 1992.

Austen, Jane. *Pride and Prejudice* (1813). Ed. Tony Tanner. Harmondsworth: Penguin Books, 1972.

Austin, John L. *How to Do Things with Words: The William James Lectures Delivered at Harvard University*, 2nd ed. Ed. J.O. Urmson and Marina Sbisà. London, Oxford, and New York: Oxford University Press, 1975.

Axelsson, Sun. "Ljusets frihet." In Ann Smith and Åke Hodell, eds, *Kärleks-Historier*. Höganäs: Bokförlaget Bra Böcker, 1984.

Bachrach, Jay E. "Type and Token and the Identification of the Work of Art." *Philosophy and Phenomenological Research* 31 (1971).

Baldick, Chris. *The Concise Oxford Dictionary of Literary Terms*. Oxford and New York: Oxford University Press, 1990.

Ball, Hugo. "Karawane." In Hugo Ball and Emmy Hennings, *Damals in Zürich: Briefe aus den Jahren 1915–1917*. Zurich: Im Verlag der Arche, 1978.

Barnes, Annette. *On Interpretation*. Oxford and New York: Basil Blackwell, 1988.

Barthes, Roland. "De l'œuvre au texte." *Revue d'esthétique* 24 (1971).

Bartsch, Renate. *Norms of Language: Theoretical and Practical Aspects* (1985). London and New York: Longman, 1987.

Baumgart, Reinhard. "Bibliothek – zum Lesen empfohlen. Uwe Johnson: Jahrestage 4." Norddeutscher Rundfunk, 7 October 1983. (Typescript in Uwe Johnson-Archiv, Frankfurt am Main.)

Beardsley, Monroe C. *Aesthetics: Problems in the Philosophy of Criticism*. New York: Harcourt, Brace and World, 1958.

– *Aesthetics: Problems in the Philosophy of Criticism* (1958), 2nd ed. Indianapolis and Cambridge: Hackett Publishing Co., 1981.

Beardsley, Monroe C., and W.K. Wimsatt, Jr. "The Affective Fallacy" (1949). In W.K. Wimsatt, *The Verbal Icon: Studies in the Meaning of Poetry*. London: Methuen and Co., 1970.

Becker, Rolf. "Eine Bitte für die Stunde des Sterbens: Über die Vollendung des Romanwerks 'Jahrestage' von Uwe Johnson" (1983). In Michael Bengel, ed., *Johnsons "Jahrestage."* Frankfurt am Main: Suhrkamp, 1985.

Belfiore, Elizabeth S. *Tragic Pleasures: Aristotle on Plot and Emotion*. Princeton, NJ: Princeton University Press, 1992.

Bengel, Michael. "Johnsons *Jahrestage* und einige ihrer Voraussetzungen." In Michael Bengel, ed., *Johnsons "Jahrestage."* Frankfurt am Main: Suhrkamp, 1985.

Bernstein, Richard J. *Beyond Objectivism and Relativism: Science, Hermeneutics, and Praxis*. Philadelphia: University of Pennsylvania Press, 1983.

Best, Otto F. "Form." In Otto F. Best, *Handbuch literarischer Fachbegriffe: Definitionen und Beispiele*, 2nd ed. Frankfurt am Main: Fischer Taschenbuch Verlag, 1982.

Bickerton, Derek. *Language and Species*. Chicago and London: University of Chicago Press, 1990.

Blocker, H. Gene. *Philosophy of Art*. New York: Charles Scribner's Sons, 1979.

Bly, Robert, ed. *Friends, You Drank Some Darkness: Three Swedish Poets –
Harry Martinson, Gunnar Ekelöf and Tomas Tranströmer.* Trans. Robert
Bly. Boston: Beacon Press, 1975.

Booth, Wayne C. *The Rhetoric of Fiction.* Chicago and London: University of
Chicago Press, 1961.

Boruah, Bijoy H. *Fiction and Emotion: A Study in Aesthetics and the Philosophy of Mind.* Oxford: Clarendon Press, 1988.

Bosanquet, Bernard. *Three Lectures on Aesthetic.* London: Macmillan and
Co., 1915.

Brenner, Charles. *An Elementary Textbook of Psychoanalysis* (1955), rev. ed.
New York: International Universities Press, 1973.

Brooks, Cleanth. "The Heresy of Paraphrase." In *The Well Wrought Urn:
Studies in the Structure of Poetry.* New York: Harcourt, Brace and World,
1947.

Brownstein, Oscar Lee, and Darlene M. Daubert. *Analytical Sourcebook of
Concepts in Dramatic Theory.* Westport, Conn. and London: Greenwood
Press, 1981.

Bühler, Karl. *Theory of Language: The Representational Function of Language*
(1934). Trans. Donald Fraser Goodwin. Amsterdam and Philadelphia: John
Benjamins Publishing Co., 1990.

Butchvarov, Panayot. "Thought." In Hans Burkhardt and Barry Smith, eds,
Handbook of Metaphysics and Ontology. Vol. 2. Munich: Philosophia Verlag, 1991.

Carroll, Noël. "Art, Narrative, and Emotion." In Mette Hjort and Sue Laver,
eds, *Emotion and the Arts.* New York and Oxford: Oxford University Press,
1997.

– *The Philosophy of Horror, or Paradoxes of the Heart.* New York and London: Routledge, 1990.

Casey, John. "The Autonomy of Art." In Julian Mitchell, ed., *Philosophy and the
Arts.* Royal Institute of Philosophy Lectures, vol. 6. London: Macmillan, 1973.

Cebik, L.B. *Fictional Narrative and Truth: An Epistemic Analysis.* Lanham,
NY, and London: University Press of America, 1984.

Chafe, Wallace L. *Meaning and the Structure of Language.* Chicago and London: University of Chicago Press, 1970.

Charlton, William. "Feeling for the Fictitious." *British Journal of Aesthetics*
24 (1984).

– Review of *Mimesis as Make-Believe*, by Kendall Walton. *British Journal of
Aesthetics* 31 (1991).

Chatman, Seymour. *Story and Discourse: Narrative Structure in Fiction and
Film.* Ithaca and London: Cornell University Press, 1978.

Churchland, Paul M. *Matter and Consciousness: A Contemporary Introduction to the Philosophy of Mind,* rev. ed. A Bradford Book. Cambridge,
Mass. and London: MIT Press, 1988.

Collingwood, Robin George. *The Principles of Art*. Oxford: At the Clarendon Press, 1938.

Crowther, Paul. *Art and Embodiment: From Aesthetics to Self-Consciousness*. Oxford: Clarendon Press, 1993.

Crystal, David. *A Dictionary of Linguistics and Phonetics*, 3rd ed. Oxford and Cambridge, Mass.: Basil Blackwell, 1991.

Culler, Jonathan. *Structuralist Poetics: Linguistics and the Study of Literature*. London: Routledge and Kegan Paul, 1975.

Currie, Gregory. *Image and Mind: Film, Philosophy, and Cognitive Science*. Cambridge, New York, and Melbourne: Cambridge University Press, 1995.

– *The Nature of Fiction*. Cambridge: Cambridge University Press, 1990.

– *An Ontology of Art*. Basingstoke and London: Macmillan Press, 1989.

– "The Paradox of Caring: Fiction and the Philosophy of Mind." In Mette Hjort and Sue Laver, eds, *Emotion and the Arts*. New York and Oxford: Oxford University Press, 1997.

– "What Is Fiction?" *Journal of Aesthetics and Art Criticism* 43 (1984/5).

Dadlez, E.M. *What's Hecuba to Him? Fictional Events and Actual Emotions*. University Park: Pennsylvania State University Press, 1997.

Davies, Steven. *Definitions of Art*. Ithaca and London: Cornell University Press, 1991.

Davis, Philip. *The Experience of Reading*. London and New York: Routledge, 1992.

Davis, Walter A. *The Act of Interpretation: A Critique of Literary Reason*. Chicago and London: University of Chicago Press, 1978.

Demetz, Peter. "Uwe Johnsons Blick in die Epoche: 'Aus dem Leben von Gesine Cresspahl' – der vierte Band der 'Jahrestage'" (1983). In Michael Bengel, ed., *Johnsons "Jahrestage."* Frankfurt: Suhrkamp, 1985.

Dennett, D.C. "Consciousness." In Richard L. Gregory and O.L. Zangwill, eds, *The Oxford Companion to the Mind*. Oxford and New York: Oxford University Press, 1987.

Dewey, Melvil. *Dewey Decimal Classification and Relative Index*, 19th ed. Ed. Benjamin A. Custer et al. Vol. 1. Albany, NY: Forest Press, 1979.

Dumas, Alexandre *fils*. *La Dame aux Camélias* (1848). Trans. David Coward. Oxford and New York: Oxford University Press, 1986.

Durzak, Manfred. *Gespräche über den Roman ... : Formbestimmungen und Analysen*. Frankfurt am Main: Suhrkamp, 1976.

Eco, Umberto. *A Theory of Semiotics*. Bloomington and London: Indiana University Press, 1976.

Edelman, Gerald M. *The Remembered Present: A Biological Theory of Consciousness*. New York: Basic Books, 1989.

Edmonds, J.M., ed. *Lyra Graeca: Being the Remains of All the Greek Lyric Poets from Eumelus to Timotheus excepting Pindar*. Trans. J.M. Edmonds. London: William Heinemann; New York: G.P. Putnam's Sons, 1922.

Ekelöf, Gunnar. *Dikter.* Stockholm: Albert Bonniers förlag, 1965.
- *Dikter.* Stockholm: MånPocket, 1983.
- *Skrifter.* Vol. 2. Ed. Reidar Ekner. Stockholm: Bonniers, 1991.
- *Strountes.* Stockholm: Albert Bonniers förlag, 1955.
- *Strountes* [2nd ed.]. Stockholm: Bokförlaget Aldus/Bonniers, 1966.
Ekner, Reidar, introduction to Gunnar Ekelöf, *Skrifter*, vol. 1, ed. Reidar Ekner. Stockholm: Bonniers, 1991.
Eldridge, Richard. "Form." In David E. Cooper, Joseph Margolis, and Crispin Sartwell, eds, *A Companion to Aesthetics.* Oxford: Blackwell, 1992.
"Election Choice." *Sunday Times,* 12 August 1990.
Elgin, Catherine Z. *With Reference to Reference.* Indianapolis and Cambridge: Hackett Publishing Co., 1983.
Eliot, T.S. *The Sacred Wood: Essays on Poetry and Criticism.* London: Methuen and Co., 1920.
Erlich, Victor. *Russian Formalism: History – Doctrine.* The Hague: Mouton en Co., 1955.
Ernst, Ulrich. "Die Entwicklung der optischen Poesie in Antike, Mittelalter und Neuzeit." In Ulrich Weisstein, ed., *Literatur und bildende Kunst: Ein Handbuch zur Theorie und Praxis eines komparatistischen Grenzgebietes.* Berlin: Erich Schmidt Verlag, 1992.
Escarpit, Robert. "La Définition du terme 'littérature.'" In Robert Escarpit et al., eds, *Le Littéraire et le social: Élements pour une sociologie de la littérature.* Paris: Flammarion, 1970.
Eysenck, Michael W., and Mark T. Keane. *Cognitive Psychology: A Student's Handbook.* Hove, London, and Hillsdale: Lawrence Erlbaum Associates, 1990.
Fahlke, Eberhard. "Heimat als geistige Landschaft: Uwe Johnson und Mecklenburg." *Börsenblatt,* 28 April 1992.
Feagin, Susan L. *Reading with Feeling: The Aesthetics of Appreciation.* Ithaca and London: Cornell University Press, 1996.
Fish, Stanley. *Is There a Text in This Class? The Authority of Interpretive Communities.* Cambridge, Mass. and London: Harvard University Press, 1980.
Forsyth, Frederick. *The Day of the Jackal.* London: Heinemann, 1971.
Frenzel, Elisabeth. *Stoffe der Weltliteratur: Ein Lexikon dichtungsgeschichtlicher Längsschnitte,* 6th improved ed., enlarged with an index. Stuttgart: Alfred Kröner Verlag, 1983.
Freud, Sigmund. "Creative Writers and Day-Dreaming" (1908). In *Art and Literature: Jensen's Gradiva, Leonardo da Vinci and Other Works.* Trans. James Strachey et al., ed. Albert Dickson. Pelican Freud Library, vol. 14. Harmondsworth: Penguin Books, 1985.
- *Jokes and Their Relation to the Unconscious* (1905). Ed. and trans. James Strachey, with a biographical introd. by Peter Gay. Standard Edition of the

Complete Psychological Works of Sigmund Freud, 24 vols. New York and London: W.W. Norton and Co., 1960.

– "Psychopathic Characters on the Stage" (1904, publ. 1942). Trans. James Strachey with modifications by Albert Dickson. In Art and Literature: Jensen's Gradiva, Leonardo da Vinci and Other Works. Trans. James Strachey et al., ed. Albert Dickson. Pelican Freud Library, vol. 14. Harmondsworth: Penguin Books, 1985.

Fries, Ulrich. Uwe Johnsons "Jahrestage": Erzählstruktur und politische Subjektivität. Göttingen: Vandenhoeck und Ruprecht, 1990.

Frijda, Nico H. The Emotions. Cambridge: Cambridge University Press; Paris: Editions de la Maison des Sciences de l'Homme, 1986.

– "The Laws of Emotion." American Psychologist 43 (1988).

Frye, Northrop. Anatomy of Criticism: Four Essays. Princeton, NJ: Princeton University Press, 1957.

Furberg, Mats. Saying and Meaning: A Main Theme in J.L. Austin's Philosophy. Oxford: Basil Blackwell, 1971.

Gadamer, Hans-Georg. Truth and Method (1960). Trans. William Glen-Doepel, 2nd ed. London: Sheed and Ward, 1979.

– Wahrheit und Methode: Grundzüge einer philosophischen Hermeneutik (1960), 4th ed. Tübingen: J.C.B. Mohr (Paul Siebeck), 1975.

Garber, Frederick. "Form." In Alex Preminger et al., eds, The New Princeton Encyclopedia of Poetry and Poetics. Princeton, NJ: Princeton University Press, 1993.

Garrod, Simon, and Anthony Sanford. "Referential Processes in Reading: Focusing on Roles and Individuals." In D.A. Balota, G.B. Flores d'Arcais, and K. Rayner, eds, Comprehension Processes in Reading. Hillsdale, NJ, Hove, and London: Lawrence Erlbaum Associates, 1990.

Gerlach, Ingeborg. "Aus der Sicht des vierten Bandes: Individuum und Gesellschaft in Uwe Johnsons Jahrestagen." In Michael Bengel, ed., Johnsons "Jahrestage." Frankfurt am Main: Suhrkamp, 1985.

Gerlach, Rainer, and Matthias Richter, eds. Uwe Johnson. Frankfurt am Main: Suhrkamp, 1984.

Gerrig, Richard J. Experiencing Narrative Worlds: On the Psychological Activities of Reading. New Haven and London: Yale University Press, 1993.

Gilbert, Katharine Everett, and Helmut Kuhn. A History of Aesthetics, rev. and extended ed. Westport, Conn.: Greenwood Press, 1954.

Goodman, Nelson. Languages of Art: An Approach to a Theory of Symbols. Indianapolis, New York, and Kansas City: Bobbs-Merrill Co., 1968.

– Languages of Art: An Approach to a Theory of Symbols (1968), 2nd ed. Indianapolis: Hackett Publishing Co., 1976.

Graesser, Arthur C., Murray Singer, and Tom Trabasso. "Constructing Inferences during Narrative Text Comprehension." Psychological Review 101 (1994).

Grambow, Jürgen. "Johnson, Uwe." In Walther Killy et al., eds, *Literatur Lexikon: Autoren und Werke deutscher Sprache.* Vol. 6. Gütersloh and Munich: Bertelsmann Lexikon Verlag, 1990.

Grady, Joe. "The 'Conduit Metaphor' Revisited." In Jean-Pierre Koenig, ed., *Discourse and Cognition: Bridging the Gap.* Stanford: Center for the Study of Language and Information, CSLI Publications, 1998.

Greene, Theodore Meyer. *The Arts and the Art of Criticism* (1940). New York: Gordian Press, 1973.

Greenspan, Patricia S. *Emotions and Reasons: An Inquiry into Emotional Justification.* New York and London: Routledge, 1988.

Grice, Paul. "Logic and Conversation." In Peter Cole and Jerry L. Morgan, eds, *Speech Acts.* Syntax and Semantics, vol. 3. New York, San Francisco, and London: Academic Press, 1975.

- *Studies in the Way of Words.* Cambridge, Mass. and London: Harvard University Press, 1989.

Gulz, Agneta. *The Planning of Action as a Cognitive and Biological Phenomenon.* Lund: Kognitionsforskning, 1991.

Haapala, Arto. *What Is a Work of Literature?* Helsinki: Societas Philosophica Fennica; Akateeminen Kirjakauppa distr., 1989.

Hagen, Erik Bjerck. "På flukt fra sannhet: Om Peter Lamarque og Stein Haugom Olsens *Truth, Fiction, and Literature*." *Nordisk estetisk tidskrift*, no. 17, 1998.

Hamilton, Ian. *Robert Lowell: A Biography.* New York: Random House, 1982.

Hansson, Gunnar. *Författaren dikten läsaren.* Stockholm: Läromedelsförlaget, 1969.

Harris, Roy. *The Language Myth.* London: Duckworth, 1981.

Harris, Wendell V. *Interpretive Acts: In Search of Meaning.* Oxford: Clarendon Press, 1988.

Heckhausen, Heinz. "Intervening Cognitions in Motivation." In D.E. Berlyne and K.B. Madsen, eds, *Pleasure, Reward, Preference: Their Nature, Determinants, and Role in Behavior.* New York and London: Academic Press, 1973.

Hegel, G.W.F. *Aesthetics: Lectures on Fine Art.* Trans. T.M. Knox. Vol. 1. Oxford: At the Clarendon Press, 1975.

Hellström, Pär. *Livskänsla och självutplåning: Studier kring framväxten av Gunnar Ekelöfs Strountesdiktning.* Uppsala: Skrifter utgivna av Lundequistska bokhandeln, 1976.

Hermerén, Göran. *Art, Reason, and Tradition: On the Role of Rationality in Interpretation and Explanation of Works of Art.* Stockholm: Almqvist och Wiksell International, 1991.

- *Aspects of Aesthetics.* Lund: CWK Gleerup, 1983.

Hirsch, E.D., Jr. *Validity in Interpretation.* New Haven and London: Yale University Press, 1967.

Hjelmslev, Louis. "Omkring Sprogteoriens Grundlæggelse." In *Festskrift udgivet af Københavns Universitet i Anledning af Universitetets Aarsfest November 1943*. Copenhagen: Københavns Universitet, 1943.

Holland, Norman. *The Critical I*. New York: Columbia University Press, 1992.

– *The Dynamics of Literary Response*. New York: Oxford University Press, 1968.

– *Five Readers Reading*. New Haven and London: Yale University Press, 1975.

Horn, András. *Grundlagen der Literaturästhetik*. Würzburg: Königshausen und Neumann, 1993.

Hospers, John. "Implied Truths in Literature" (1960). In Joseph Margolis, ed., *Philosophy Looks at the Arts: Contemporary Readings in Aesthetics*. New York: Charles Scribner's Sons, 1962.

– *Meaning and Truth in the Arts* (1946). Chapel Hill: University of North Carolina Press, 1967.

Howatson, M.C., ed. *The Oxford Companion to Classical Literature*, 2nd ed. Oxford and New York: Oxford University Press, 1989.

Hume, David. "Of Tragedy" (1757). In David Hume, *The Philosophical Works of David Hume*. Ed. T.H. Green and T.H. Grose, new impression. Vol. 3. London, New York, and Bombay: Longmans, Green, and Co., 1898.

Hutton, Christopher. *Abstraction and Instance: The Type-Token Relation in Linguistic Theory*. Oxford: Pergamon Press, 1990.

Hye, Roberta T. *Uwe Johnsons Jahrestage: Die Gegenwart als variierende Wiederholung der Vergangenheit*. Bern, Frankfurt am Main, and Las Vegas: Peter Lang, 1978.

Immroth, John Phillip. *Immroth's Guide to the Library of Congress Classification*, 3rd ed. Ed. Lois Mai Chan. Littleton, Colo.: Libraries Unlimited, 1980.

Ingarden, Roman. "Das Form-Inhalt-Problem im literarischen Kunstwerk." *Helicon* 1 (1938).

– *The Literary Work of Art: An Investigation on the Borderlines of Ontology, Logic, and Theory of Literature, with an Appendix on the Functions of Language in the Theater* (1930). Trans. George G. Grabowicz. Evanston: Northwestern University Press, 1973.

Iser, Wolfgang. *Der Akt des Lesens: Theorie ästhetischer Wirkung*, 2nd ed. Munich: Wilhelm Fink Verlag, 1984.

Jakobson, Roman. "Closing Statement: Linguistics and Poetics." In T.A. Sebeok, ed., *Style in Language*. Cambridge, Mass.: MIT Press, 1960.

Jakobson, Roman, and Claude Lévi-Strauss. "Charles Baudelaire's 'Les Chats.'" Trans. Katie Furness-Lane. In Michael Lane, ed., *Introduction to Structuralism*. New York: Basic Books, 1970.

Jandl, Ernst. "karwoche: ein turm (ostern 1957)." In Jandl's *Gesammelte Werke*. Vol. 1. Darmstadt and Neuwied: Luchterhand, 1985.

Johnson, Samuel. "Preface to Shakespeare" (1765). In *The Yale Edition of the Works of Samuel Johnson*. Vol. 7. Ed. Arthur Sherbo. New Haven and London: Yale University Press, 1968.

Johnson, Uwe. *Anniversaries: From the Life of Gesine Cresspahl*. 2 vols. Trans. Leila Vennewitz and Walter Arndt. San Diego, New York, and London: Harcourt Brace Jovanovich, 1975–87.

– *Begleitumstände: Frankfurter Vorlesungen*. Frankfurt am Main: Suhrkamp, 1980.

– "Einführung in die *Jahrestage*." In Michael Bengel, ed., *Johnsons "Jahrestage."* Frankfurt am Main: Suhrkamp, 1985.

– *Jahrestage: Aus dem Leben von Gesine Cresspahl*. 4 vols. Frankfurt am Main: Suhrkamp Verlag, 1970–83.

– "Vorschläge zur Prüfung eines Romans." In Eberhard Lämmert et al., eds, *Romantheorie: Dokumentation ihrer Geschichte in Deutschland seit 1880*. Köln: Kiepenheuer und Witsch, 1975.

Juhl, P.D. *Interpretation: An Essay in the Philosophy of Literary Criticism*. Princeton: Princeton University Press, 1980.

Just, Marcel Adam, and Patricia A. Carpenter. *The Psychology of Reading and Language Comprehension*. Boston: Allyn and Bacon, 1987.

Kafka, Franz. "Die Verwandlung" (1915). In *Erzählungen*. Ed. Max Brod. Frankfurt am Main: Fischer Taschenbuch Verlag, 1983.

Kant, Immanuel. *The Critique of Judgement* (1790). Trans. James Creed Meredith (1928). Oxford: At the Clarendon Press, 1952.

– *Kritik der Urteilskraft* (1790), 16th ed. Ed. Karl Vorländer, reprint. Hamburg: Verlag von Felix Meiner, 1974.

Karelis, Charles. "Hegel's Concept of Art: An Interpretative Essay." In G.W.F. Hegel, *Hegel's Introduction to Aesthetics, Being the Introduction to the Berlin Aesthetics Lectures of the 1820s*. Ed. Charles Karelis, trans. T.M. Knox. Oxford: Oxford University Press, 1979.

Katz, Jerold J. *Semantic Theory*. New York: Harper and Row, 1972.

Keane, Mark T. "Propositional Representations." In Michael W. Eysenck et al., eds, *The Blackwell Dictionary of Cognitive Psychology*. Oxford and Cambridge, Mass.: Blackwell Reference, 1990.

Kivy, Peter. "Auditor's Emotions: Contention, Concession and Compromise." *Journal of Aesthetics and Art Criticism* 51 (1993).

Knapp, Steven. *Literary Interest: The Limits of Anti-Formalism*. Cambridge, Mass. and London: Harvard University Press, 1993.

Kofman, Sarah. *The Childhood of Art: An Interpretation of Freud's Aesthetics* (1970). Trans. Winifred Woodhull. New York: Columbia University Press, 1988.

Kristeller, Paul Oskar. "The Modern System of the Arts" (1951). In Morris Weitz, ed., *Problems in Aesthetics: An Introductory Book of Readings*, 2nd ed. London: Macmillan Co., 1970.

Kuhns, Richard. *Tragedy: Contradiction and Repression*. Chicago and London: University of Chicago Press, 1991.

Lamarque, Peter. *Fictional Points of View*. Ithaca and London: Cornell University Press, 1996.

– "The High Price of Evading Boredom: A Reply to Erik Bjerck Hagen." *Nordisk estetisk tidskrift*, no. 18, 1999.

– "How Can We Fear and Pity Fictions?" *British Journal of Aesthetics* 21 (1981).

Lamarque, Peter, and Stein Haugom Olsen. *Truth, Fiction, and Literature: A Philosophical Perspective*. Oxford: Clarendon Press, 1994.

Landgren, Bengt. *Ensamheten, döden och drömmarna: Studier över ett motivkomplex i Gunnar Ekelöfs diktning*. Uppsala: Scandinavian University Books, 1971.

Larkin, Philip. *Collected Poems*. Ed. Anthony Thwaite. London and Boston: Marvell Press and Faber and Faber, 1988.

Lazarus, R.S. "Emotions and Adaptation: Conceptual and Empirical Relations." In W.J. Arnold, ed., *Nebraska Symposium on Motivation 1968*. Lincoln: University of Nebraska Press, 1968.

Leibowitz, Herbert. "Robert Lowell: Ancestral Voices." In Michael London and Robert Boyers, *Robert Lowell: A Portrait of the Artist in His Time*. New York: David Lewis, 1970.

Lesser, Simon O. *Fiction and the Unconscious*. Boston: Beacon Press, 1957.

"A Level Head Can Make Up for a Missing A-Level." *Guardian*, 18 August 1990.

Levinson, Jerrold. "Emotion in Respone to Art: A Survey of the Terrain." In Mette Hjort and Sue Laver, eds, *Emotion and the Arts*. New York and Oxford: Oxford University Press, 1997.

– "Intention and Interpretation in Literature." In *The Pleasures of Aesthetics: Philosophical Essays*. Ithaca and London: Cornell University Press, 1996.

– "The Work of Visual Art." In *The Pleasures of Aesthetics: Philosophical Essays*. Ithaca and London: Cornell University Press, 1996.

Levinson, Stephen C. *Pragmatics*. Cambridge: Cambridge University Press, 1983.

Lewis, C.S. *Den sista striden* (1956). Trans. Birgitta Hammar. Stockholm: Albert Bonniers förlag, 1976.

– *The Last Battle: A Story for Children*. London: Bodley Head, 1956.

Lewis, David K. *Convention: A Philosophical Study*. Cambridge, Mass.: Harvard University Press, 1969.

Lindskog, Claes. *Grekiska kvinnogestalter*. Stockholm: Hugo Gebers förlag, 1922.

Livingston, Paisley, and Alfred R. Mele. "Evaluating Emotional Responses to Fiction." In Mette Hjort and Sue Laver, eds, *Emotion and the Arts*. New York and Oxford: Oxford University Press, 1997.

Lotman, Jurij M. *Die Struktur literarischer Texte*. Trans. Rolf-Dietrich Keil. Munich: Wilhelm Fink Verlag, 1972.

Lotze, Hermann. *Geschichte der Ästhetik in Deutschland*. Munich: Literarisch-artistische Anstalt der J.G. Cotta'schen Buchhandlung, 1868.

Lowell, Robert. *Selected Poems*. London: Faber and Faber, 1965.

Lubbock, Percy. *The Craft of Fiction* (1921). London: Jonathan Cape, 1965.

Lyons, John. "Bedeutungstheorien." Trans. Arnim von Stechow. In Arnim von Stechow and Dieter Wunderlich, eds, *Semantik/Semantics: Ein internationales Handbuch der zeitgenössischen Forschung/An International Handbook of Contemporary Research*. Berlin and New York: Walter de Gruyter, 1991.

– *Semantics*. 2 vols. Cambridge: Cambridge University Press, 1977.

Lyons, William. *Emotion*. Cambridge: Cambridge University Press, 1980.

– "On Looking into Titian's Assumption." In Mette Hjort and Sue Laver, eds, *Emotion and the Arts*. New York and Oxford: Oxford University Press, 1997.

Macdonald, Margaret. "The Language of Fiction" (1954). In Joseph Margolis, ed., *Philosophy Looks at the Arts: Contemporary Readings in Aesthetics*. New York: Charles Scribner's Sons, 1962.

Mandler, George. *Mind and Body: Psychology of Emotion and Stress*. New York and London: W.W. Norton and Co., 1984.

Marc-Wogau, Konrad. *Filosofiska diskussioner*. Stockholm: Liber, 1955.

Margolis, Joseph. *Art and Philosophy*. Brighton, Sussex: Harvester Press, 1980.

– "The Identity of a Work of Art." *Mind* 68 (1959).

– "The Ontological Peculiarity of Works of Art." *Journal of Aesthetics and Art Criticism* 36 (1977).

– "The Ontology of Art." In Joseph Margolis, ed., *Philosophy Looks at the Arts: Contemporary Readings in Aesthetics*, 3rd ed. Philadelphia: Temple University Press, 1987.

Markiewicz, Henryk. "The Limits of Literature." In Ralph Cohen, ed., *New Directions of Literary History*. London: Routledge and Kegan Paul, 1974.

Markowitz, Sally. "Guilty Pleasures: Aesthetic Meta-Response and Fiction." *Journal of Aesthetics and Art Criticism* 50 (1992).

Maslow, A.H. *Motivation and Personality*, 3rd ed. Ed. Cynthia McReynolds. New York: HarperCollins, 1987.

Matravers, Derek. *Art and Emotion*. Oxford: Clarendon Press, 1998.

Mazzaro, Jerome. *The Poetic Themes of Robert Lowell*. Ann Arbor: University of Michigan Press, 1965.

McCormick, Peter J. *Fictions, Philosophies, and the Problems of Poetics*. Ithaca and London: Cornell University Press, 1988.

Mellor, D.H. "On Literary Truth." *Ratio* 10 (1968).

Michaelis, Rolf. *Kleines Adressbuch für Jerichow und New York: Ein Register zu Uwe Johnsons Roman "Jahrestage." Angelegt mit Namen, Orten, Zitaten und Verweisen.* Frankfurt am Main: Suhrkamp, 1983.

Moeller, Hans-Bernhard. "Uwe Johnson. Jahrestage IV: Aus dem Leben von Gesine Cresspahl ... " *World Literature Today*, Summer 1984.

Morgenstern, Christian. "Das grosse Lalula." In Christian Morgenstern, *Gesammelte Werke.* Ed. Margareta Morgenstern. Munich: R. Piper und Co., Verlag, 1965.

Morreall, John. "Fear without Belief." *Journal of Philosophy* 90 (1993).

Mukařovský, Jan. "L'Art comme fait sémiologique." In *Actes du huitième congrès international de philosophie à Prague 2–7 [s]eptembre 1934.* Prague: Comité d'organisation du congrès, 1936.

– "Ästhetische Funktion, Norm und ästhetischer Wert als soziale Fakten" (1936). In *Kapitel aus der Ästhetik*, trans. Walter Schamschula, ed. Günther Busch. Frankfurt am Main: Suhrkamp Verlag, 1970.

– "Two Studies of Poetic Designation: Poetic Designation and the Aesthetic Function of Language" (1936, 1938). In *The Word and Verbal Art: Selected Essays by Jan Mukarovsky*, trans. and ed. John Burbak and Peter Steiner. New Haven and London: Yale University Press, 1977.

Naylor, Gloria. *Mama Day.* London: Hutchinson, 1988.

Neill, Alex, essay review of *Reading with Feeling*, by Susan Feagin. *Journal of Aesthetics and Art Criticism* 57 (1999).

Neumann, Bernd. "'Heimweh ist eine schlimme Tugend': Über Uwe Johnsons Gedächtnis-Roman 'Jahrestage. Aus dem Leben von Gesine Cresspahl' von seinem vierten Band her gesehen." In Michael Bengel, ed., *Johnsons "Jahrestage."* Frankfurt am Main: Suhrkamp, 1985.

– *Utopie und Mimesis: Zum Verhältnis von Ästhetik, Gesellschaftsphilosophie und Politik in den Romanen Uwe Johnsons.* Kronberg/Ts.: Athenäum Verlag, 1978.

– *Uwe Johnson.* Hamburg: Europäische Verlagsanstalt, 1994.

Newell, Allen, Paul S. Rosenbloom, and John E. Laird. "Symbolic Architectures for Cognition." In Michael I. Posner, ed., *Foundations of Cognitive Science.* Cambridge, Mass. and London: MIT Press, 1989.

Novitz, David. *Knowledge, Fiction, and Imagination.* Philadelphia: Temple University Press, 1987.

– Review of *Mimesis as Make-Believe*, by Kendall Walton. *Philosophy and Literature* 15 (1991).

– "The Trouble with Truth." *Philosophy and Literature* 19 (1995).

Nussbaum, Martha C. *Love's Knowledge: Essays on Philosophy and Literature.* New York and Oxford: Oxford University Press, 1990.

Oatley, Keith. *Best Laid Schemes: The Psychology of Emotions.* Cambridge: Cambridge University Press; Paris: Editions de la Maison des Sciences de l'Homme, 1992.

- "Emotion." In Michael W. Eysenck et al., eds, *The Blackwell Dictionary of Cognitive Psychology*. Oxford and Cambridge, Mass.: Blackwell Reference, 1990.

Odenstedt, Bengt. "Further Reflections on the Meldorf Inscription." *Zeitschrift für deutsches Altertum und deutsche Literatur* 118 (1989).

Olsen, Stein Haugom. *The End of Literary Theory*. Cambridge: Cambridge University Press, 1987.

- *The Structure of Literary Understanding*. Cambridge: Cambridge University Press, 1978.

Olsson, Anders. *Ekelöfs nej*. Stockholm: Bonniers, 1983.

Orsini, G.N. "The Ancient Roots of a Modern Idea." In G.S. Rousseau, ed., *Organic Form: The Life of an Idea*. London and Boston: Routledge and Kegan Paul, 1972.

- "Form." In Alex Preminger et al., eds, *Princeton Encyclopedia of Poetry and Poetics*, enlarged ed. Princeton, NJ: Princeton University Press, 1974.

Orwell, George. *1984*. London: Secker & Warburg, 1949.

Osborne, Harold. *Aesthetics and Criticism*. London: Routledge and Kegan Paul, 1955.

Ovid. *Metamorphoses*. Trans. A.D. Melville, introd. and notes by E.J. Kenney. Oxford and New York: Oxford University Press, 1986.

Palmer, Frank. *Literature and Moral Understanding: A Philosophical Essay on Ethics, Aesthetics, Education, and Culture*. Oxford: Clarendon Press, 1992.

Parsons, Michael J. *How We Understand Art: A Cognitive Developmental Account of Aesthetic Experience*. Cambridge: Cambridge University Press, 1987.

Paskins, Barrie. "On Being Moved by Anna Karenina and *Anna Karenina*." *Philosophy* 52 (1977).

Peacocke, Christopher. *Sense and Content: Experience, Thought, and Their Relations*. Oxford: Clarendon Press, 1983.

- *Thoughts: An Essay on Content*. Oxford: Basil Blackwell, 1986.

Peck, John, and Martin Coyle. "Form and Content." In *Literary Terms and Criticism*. Basingstoke and London: Macmillan, 1984.

Pettersson, Anders. "On Walton's and Currie's Analyses of Literary Fiction." *Philosophy and Literature* 17 (1993).

- "The Ontology of Literary Works." *Theoria* 50 (1984).

- *A Theory of Literary Discourse*. Lund: Lund University Press; Bromley: Chartwell-Bratt, 1990.

- *Verkbegreppet: En litteraturteoretisk undersökning*. Oslo: Novus forlag, 1981.

Pettersson, Torsten. *Literary Interpretation: Current Models and a New Departure*. Åbo: Åbo Academy Press, 1988.

Ploog, Detlev W. "The Evolution of Vocal Communication." In Hanus Papousek, Uwe Jürgens, and Mechthild Papousek, *Nonverbal Vocal Communication: Comparative and Developmental Approaches*. Cambridge:

Cambridge University Press; Paris. Éditions de la Maison des Sciences de l'Homme, 1992.

Poe, Edgar Allan. "The Philosophy of Composition" (1846). In *The Complete Poems and Stories of Edgar Allan Poe: With Selections from His Critical Writings*. Ed. A. Hobson Quinn and E.H. O'Neill. New York: Alfred A. Knopf, 1946.

Pole, David. "The Excellence of Form in Works of Art." In *Aesthetics, Form and Emotion*. Ed. George Roberts. London: Duckworth, 1983.

Pollard, D.E.B. "Literature and Representation: A Note." *British Journal of Aesthetics* 32 (1992).

Prado, Carlos Gonzales. *Making Believe: Philosophical Reflections on Fiction*. Westport, Conn. and London: Greenwood Press, 1984.

Price, Amy. "Nietzsche and the Paradox of Tragedy." *British Journal of Aesthetics* 38 (1998).

Procopiow, Norma. *Robert Lowell: The Poet and His Critics*. Chicago: American Library Association, 1984.

Quine, W.V.O. "Ontological Relativity." *Journal of Philosophy* 65 (1968).

Quirk, Randolph, et al. *A Comprehensive Grammar of the English Language*. London and New York: Longman, 1985.

Radford, Colin. "How Can We Be Moved by the Fate of Anna Karenina?" In *The Aristotelian Society: Supplementary Volume 49, The Symposia Read ... 18–20 July 1975*. London: Methuen & Co. in association with the Aristotelian Society, 1975.

Reddy, Michael. "The Conduit Metaphor – A Case of Frame Conflict in Our Language about Language." In Andrew Ortony, ed., *Metaphor and Thought*. Cambridge: Cambridge University Press, 1986.

Richards, I.A. *Practical Criticism*. London: Routledge and Kegan Paul, 1929.
– *Principles of Literary Criticism*. London: Routledge and Kegan Paul, 1924.

Ricœur, Paul. *Interpretation Theory: Discourse and the Surplus of Meaning*. Fort Worth: Texas Christian University Press, 1976.

Riordan, Colin. *The Ethics of Narration: Uwe Johnson's Novels from Ingrid Babendererde to Jahrestage*. London: Modern Humanities Research Association and Institute of Germanic Studies, University of London, 1989.

Rodway, Allan. "Form." In Roger Fowler, ed., *A Dictionary of Modern Critical Terms*, rev. and enlarged ed. London and New York: Routledge and Kegan Paul, 1987.

Roediger, Henry L. III, et al. *Psychology*, 2nd ed. Boston and Toronto: Little, Brown and Co., 1987.

Rorty, Richard. *Philosophy and the Mirror of Nature*. Oxford: Basil Blackwell, 1980.
– "The Pragmatist's Progress." In Umberto Eco et al., *Interpretation and Overinterpretation*, ed. Stefan Collini. Cambridge: Cambridge University Press, 1992.

Rose, Gilbert. *The Power of Form: A Psychoanalytic Approach to Aesthetic Form*. New York: International Universities Press, 1980.

Rosebury, Brian. *Art and Desire: A Study in the Aesthetics of Fiction*. Houndmills, Basingstoke, and London: Macmillan Press, 1988.

Rudner, Richard. "The Ontological Status of the Esthetic Object." *Philosophy and Phenomenological Research* 10 (1950).

Santayana, George. *The Sense of Beauty: Being the Outline of Aesthetic Theory* (1896). New York: Dover Publications, 1955.

Sartwell, Crispin. "Substance and Significance: A Theory of Poetry." *Philosophy and Literature* 15 (1991).

Saussure, Ferdinand de. *Course in General Linguistics*. Ed. Charles Bally, Albert Sechehaye, and Albert Riedlinger, trans. Wade Baskin. New York: McGraw-Hill Book Co., McGraw-Hill Paperbacks, 1966.

Savile, Anthony. *The Test of Time: An Essay in Philosophical Aesthetics*. Oxford: Clarendon Press, 1982.

Schiffer, Stephen R. *Meaning*. Oxford: At the Clarendon Press, 1972.

Schloz, Günther, review of *Jahrestage 4*, by Uwe Johnson. In Südfunk (Süddeutscher Rundfunk), 18 January 1984. (Typescript in Uwe Johnson-Archiv, Frankfurt am Main.)

Scholz, Hans. "Mutmassungen über Uwe: Uwe Johnson hat seine 'Jahrestage' mit dem vierten Band abgeschlossen." *Der Tagesspiegel* (Berlin), 20 November 1983.

Schönau, Walter. *Einführung in die psychoanalytische Literaturwissenschaft*. Stuttgart: J.B. Metzlersche Verlagsbuchhandlung, 1991.

Schumach, Murray. "New York City." In *The New Encyclopaedia Britannica*, 15th ed. Vol. 24. Chicago: Encyclopaedia Britannica, 1988.

Schwinger, Reinhold. "Innere Form: Ein Beitrag zur Definition des Begriffes auf Grund seiner Geschichte von Shaftesbury bis W. v. Humboldt." In Reinhold Schwinger and Heinz Nicolai, *Innere Form und dichterische Phantasie: Zwei Vorstudien zu einer neuen deutschen Poetik*. München: C.H. Beck'sche Verlagsbuchhandlung, 1935.

Sclafani, Richard J. "The Logical Primitiveness of the Concept of a Work of Art." *British Journal of Aesthetics* 15 (1975).

Scruton, Roger. *Art and Imagination: A Study in the Philosophy of Mind*. London: Methuen and Co., 1974.

– "Fantasy, Imagination and the Screen." In *The Aesthetic Understanding: Essays in the Philosophy of Art and Culture*. London and New York: Methuen, 1983.

Searle, John R. *Expression and Meaning: Studies in the Theory of Speech Acts*. Cambridge: Cambridge University Press, 1979.

– *Intentionality: An Essay in the Philosophy of Mind*. Cambridge: Cambridge University Press, 1983.

– *Speech Acts: An Essay in the Philosophy of Language*. Cambridge: Cambridge University Press, 1969.

Searle, John R., and Daniel Vanderveken. *Foundations of Illocutionary Logic*. Cambridge: Cambridge University Press, 1985.

Shaw, Bernard. *Pygmalion: A Romance in Five Acts* (1912). London: Longmans, Green and Co., 1957.

Sheppard, Anne. *Aesthetics: An Introduction to the Philosophy of Art*. Oxford and New York: Oxford University Press, 1987.

Shukman, Ann. *Literature and Semiotics: A Study of the Writings of Yu. M. Lotman*. Amsterdam, New York, and Oxford: North-Holland Publishing Company, 1977.

Shusterman, Richard. *The Object of Literary Criticism*. Amsterdam: Rodopi; Würzburg: Königshausen und Neumann, 1984.

– *Pragmatist Aesthetics: Living Beauty, Rethinking Art*. Oxford and Cambridge, Mass.: Blackwell, 1992.

– *T.S. Eliot and the Philosophy of Criticism*. London: Duckworth, 1988.

Skilleås, Ole Martin. "Anachronistic Themes and Literary Value: *The Tempest*." *British Journal of Aesthetics* 31 (1991).

Smith, Ann, and Åke Hodell, preface to *KärleksHistorier*. Höganäs: Bokförlaget Bra Böcker, 1984.

Smith, N.V. "On Generics." *Transactions of the Philological Society* (1975).

Sommar, Carl Olov. *Gunnar Ekelöf: En biografi*. Stockholm: Bonniers, 1989.

Sperber, Dan, and Deirdre Wilson. *Relevance: Communication and Cognition*. Oxford: Basil Blackwell, 1986.

Stecker, Robert. "Art Interpretation." *Journal of Aesthetics and Art Criticism* 52 (1994).

– *Artworks: Definition, Meaning, Value*. University Park: Pennsylvania State University Press, 1997.

– "Incompatible Interpretations." *Journal of Aesthetics and Art Criticism* 50 (1992).

Stevenson, Charles L. "On 'What Is a Poem.'" *Philosophical Review* 66 (1957).

Stillings, Neil A., et al. *Cognitive Science: An Introduction*. A Bradford Book. Cambridge, Mass. and London: MIT Press, 1995.

Stolnitz, Jerome. "On the Cognitive Triviality of Art." *British Journal of Aesthetics* 32 (1992).

Strawson, P.F. *Logico-Linguistic Papers*. London: Methuen and Co., 1971.

Sweetser, Eve E. "English Metaphors for Language: Motivations, Conventions, and Creativity." *Poetics Today* 13 (1992).

Tatarkiewicz, Wladyslaw. "Form: History of One Term and Five Concepts." In *A History of Six Ideas: A Study in Aesthetics*. The Hague: Martinus Nijhoff; Warsaw: PNN/Polish Scientific Publishers, 1980.

"Thought." In J.A. Simpson and E.S.C. Weiner, eds, *Oxford English Dictionary*, 2nd ed. Vol. 17. Oxford: Clarendon Press, 1989.

Tilghman, Benjamin R. "The Literary Work of Art." In Benjamin R. Tilghman, ed., *Language and Aesthetics: Contributions to the Philosophy of Art*. Lawrence, Manhattan, and Wichita: University Press of Kansas, 1973.

Timofeev, L.I. *Osnovy teorii literatury* (1940), 4th ed. Moskva: Izdatel'stvo Prosveščenie, 1971.

Tolhurst, William E. "On What a Text Is and How It Means." *British Journal of Aesthetics* 19 (1979).

Tolkien, J.R.R. *The Lord of the Rings*. 3 vols. London: Allen and Unwin, 1954–5.

Tolstoy, Leo [N.]. *Anna Karenina*. Trans. David Magarshack. A Signet Classic. Harmondsworth: Penguin Books, 1961.

– *What Is Art?* (1898). Trans. Richard Pevear and Larissa Volokhonsky. Harmondsworth: Penguin Books, 1995.

Tormey, Alan. *The Concept of Expression: A Study in Philosophical Psychology and Aesthetics*. Princeton, NJ: Princeton University Press, 1971.

Träger, Claus, ed., *Wörterbuch der Literaturwissenschaft*. Leipzig: Bibliographisches Institut, 1986.

Tsur, Reuven. *Toward a Theory of Cognitive Poetics*. Amsterdam: North-Holland, 1992.

Tye, Michael. *The Imagery Debate*. Cambridge, Mass. and London: MIT Press, 1991.

Updike, John. "Pygmalion." In *Trust Me: Stories*. London: André Deutsch, 1987.

van den Broek, Paul. "The Causal Inference Maker: Towards a Process Model of Inference Generation in Text Comprehension." In D.A. Balota, G.B. Flores d'Arcais, and K. Rayner, eds, *Comprehension Processes in Reading*. Hillsdale, NJ, Hove, and London: Lawrence Erlbaum Associates, 1990.

van Dijk, Teun A., and Walter Kintsch. *Strategies of Discourse Comprehension*. New York and London: Academic Press, 1983.

von Kutschera, Franz. *Ästhetik*. Berlin and New York: Walter de Gruyter, 1988.

Walton, Kendall L. "Fearing Fictions." *Journal of Philosophy* 75 (1978).

– *Mimesis as Make-Believe: On the Foundations of the Representational Arts*. Cambridge, Mass. and London: Harvard University Press, 1990.

– "Spelunking, Simulation, and Slime: On Being Moved by Fiction." In Mette Hjort and Sue Laver, eds, *Emotion and the Arts*. New York and Oxford: Oxford University Press, 1997.

Wellek, René. "Concepts of Form and Structure in Twentieth-Century Criticism." In *Concepts of Criticism*, ed. Stephen G. Nichols, Jr. New Haven and London: Yale University Press, 1963.

– "What Is Literature?" In Paul Hernadi, ed., *What Is Literature?* Bloomington and London: Indiana University Press, 1978.

Wellek, René, and Austin Warren. *Theory of Literature* (1949), 3rd rev. ed. London: Jonathan Cape, 1966.

Williamson, Alan. *Pity the Monsters: The Political Vision of Robert Lowell.* New Haven and London: Yale University Press, 1974.

Wimsatt, W.K., Jr. "The Concrete Universal" (1947). In *The Verbal Icon: Studies in the Meaning of Poetry.* London: Methuen and Co, 1954.

Winnicott, D.W. *Playing and Reality.* London: Tavistock Publications, 1971.

Wittgenstein, Ludwig. *Philosophical Investigations.* Trans. G.E.M. Anscombe, 2nd ed. Oxford: Basil Blackwell, 1958.

Wollheim, Richard. *Art and Its Objects: An Introduction to Aesthetics.* New York: Harper and Row, 1968.

Wolman, Benjamin B. *Dictionary of Behavioral Science,* 2nd ed. San Diego: Academic Press, 1989.

Wolterstorff, Nicholas. "Are Texts Autonomous? An Interaction with the Hermeneutic of Paul Ricœur." In Rudolf Haller, ed., *International Wittgenstein Symposium 8 1983 Kirchberg am Wechsel/Akten des 8. Internationalen Wittgenstein Symposiums.* Vol. 1. Wien: Hölder-Pichl, 1984.

– "Toward an Ontology of Art Works." *Noûs* 9 (1975).

– *Works and Worlds of Art.* Oxford: At the Clarendon Press, 1980.

Young, Julian. *Nietzsche's Philosophy of Art.* Cambridge: Cambridge University Press, 1992.

Zilliacus, Emil. *Grekisk lyrik,* 2nd ed. Stockholm: Hugo Gebers förlag, 1928.

Zwaan, Rolf A. *Aspects of Literary Comprehension: A Cognitive Approach.* Amsterdam and Philadelphia: John Benjamins Publishing Co., 1993.

Index